Lecture Notes in Computer Science 12818

More information about this subseries at http://www.springer.com/series/7408

Hossein Hojjat · Mieke Massink (Eds.)

Fundamentals of
Software Engineering

9th International Conference, FSEN 2021
Virtual Event, May 19–21, 2021
Revised Selected Papers

 Springer

Editors
Hossein Hojjat (iD)
Tehran Institute for Advanced Studies
Tehran, Iran

Mieke Massink (iD)
CNR - ISTI
Pisa, Italy

ISSN 0302-9743 ISSN 1611-3349 (electronic)
Lecture Notes in Computer Science
ISBN 978-3-030-89246-3 ISBN 978-3-030-89247-0 (eBook)
https://doi.org/10.1007/978-3-030-89247-0

LNCS Sublibrary: SL2 – Programming and Software Engineering

This Springer imprint is published by the registered company Springer Nature Switzerland AG
The registered company address is: Gewerbestrasse 11, 6330 Cham, Switzerland

Preface

The increasing complexity of software and hardware systems and their ever more central role in society poses many challenges concerning their reliability, safety, correctness, and robustness. Based on a variety of fundamental concepts from theoretical computer science, formal methods techniques aim at making a significant contribution to better quality systems. The development and use of formal methods aspire to mathematically sound methods and tools for system analysis and verification.

This volume contains the selected and revised papers of the 9th IPM International Conference on Fundamentals of Software Engineering (FSEN 2021). Due to the continuing effects of the COVID-19 pandemic, this event was held as a virtual event and run from Tehran, Iran, during May 19–21, 2021. This biennial event is organized by the School of Computer Science at the Institute for Research in Fundamental Sciences (IPM) in Iran in cooperation with ACM SIGSOFT and IFIP Working Group 2.2. The topics of interest in FSEN span over all aspects of formal methods, especially those related to advancing the application of formal methods in the software industry and promoting their integration with practical engineering techniques.

The Program Committee of FSEN 2021 consisted of 42 top researchers from 16 countries. This edition of FSEN received 38 submissions from 18 countries. Each submission was reviewed by at least three independent referees, for its quality, originality, contribution, clarity of presentation, and its relevance to the conference topics. After thorough discussions on each individual paper, the Programme Committee has accepted 12 regular full papers and 4 short papers for inclusion in the present proceedings.

Many people contributed to make FSEN 2021 a success. We would like to thank the two distinguished keynote speakers that gave their excellent and stimulating presentations at FSEN 2021: Marta Kwiatkowska and Mira Mezini. We also would like to thank the many authors that submitted high-quality papers. Special thanks also go to the Institute for Research in Fundamental Sciences (IPM) in Tehran, Iran, for their financial support and to the local organization team of FSEN 2021 that ran this virtual edition of the conference in an excellent way, including the exceptional virtual guided tours through some of the most magnificent places of Iran. Many thanks also go to: the General Chairs Farhad Arbab and Pejman Lotfi-Kamran and the Steering Committee of FSEN, especially its Chair Marjan Sirjani, for their valuable support and feedback during all phases of the organization; the members of the Program Committee for their time, effort, and excellent and timely contributions to ensure that FSEN remains a high-quality international conference; and to the Publicity Chair Maurice ter Beek for his excellent job in advertising the conference. We are also grateful to IFIP, the IFIP Working Group 2.2, and ACM for their continuing support of the FSEN conference series. Furthermore, we thank the providers of the EasyChair conference management system, whose tool greatly helped us run the review process and facilitate the preparation of these proceedings. Finally, we are indebted to all conference attendees for their active and lively participation in the FSEN research community, ultimately contributing to the success of this special conference series.

August 2021   Hossein Hojjat
                                                                 Mieke Massink

Organization

Conference Chairs

Hossein Hojjat   Tehran Institute for Advanced Studies, Iran
Mieke Massink   CNR-ISTI, Italy

Publicity Chair

Maurice H. ter Beek   CNR-ISTI, Italy

Program Committee

Erika Abraham	RWTH Aachen University, Germany
Gul Agha	University of Illinois at Urbana-Champaign, USA
Ebru Aydin Gol	Middle East Technical University, Turkey
Christel Baier	Technical University of Dresden, Germany
Ezio Bartocci	Vienna University of Technology, Austria
Marcello Bonsangue	University of Leiden, The Netherlands
Mario Bravetti	University of Bologna, Italy
Michael Butler	University of Southampton, UK
Rocco De Nicola	IMT School for Advanced Studies Lucca, Italy
Erik De Vink	Eindhoven University of Technology, The Netherlands
Giovanna Di Marzo Serugendo	University of Geneva, Switzerland
Alessandra Di Pierro	University of Verona, Italy
Ali Ebnenasir	Michigan Technological University, USA
Fathiyeh Faghih	McMaster University, Canada
Wan Fokkink	Free University of Amsterdam, The Netherlands
Adrian Francalanza	University of Malta, Malta
Fatemeh Ghassemi	University of Tehran, Iran
Jan Friso Groote	Eindhoven University of Technology, The Netherlands
Hassan Haghighi	Shahid Beheshti University, Iran
Osman Hasan	National University of Sciences and Technology (NUST), Pakistan
Hossein Hojjat	Tehran Institute for Advanced Studies, Iran
Mohammad Izadi	Sharif University of Technology, Iran
Narges Khakpour	Linnaeus University, Sweden
Ehsan Khamespanah	University of Tehran, Iran
Ramtin Khosravi	University of Tehran, Iran
Eva Kühn	Vienna University of Technology, Austria
Zhiming Liu	Southwest University, China
Mieke Massink	CNR-ISTI, Italy

Emanuela Merelli	University of Camerino, Italy
Hassan Mirian-Hosseinabadi	Sharif University of Technology, Iran
Mohammadreza Mousavi	King's College London, UK
Ali Movaghar	Sharif University of Technology, Iran
Jose Proenca	CISTER-ISEP and HASLab-INESC TEC, Portugal
Wolfgang Reisig	Humboldt-Universität zu Berlin, Germany
Philipp Ruemmer	Uppsala University, Sweden
Gwen Salaün	University of Grenoble Alpes, France
Cristina Seceleanu	Mälardalen University, Sweden
Marjan Sirjani	Mälardalen University, Sweden
Marielle Stoelinga	University of Twente, The Netherlands
Meng Sun	Peking University, China
Carolyn Talcott	SRI International, USA
Martin Wirsing	Ludwig Maximilian University of Munich, Germany
Lijun Zhang	Institute of Software, Chinese Academy of Sciences, China
Peter Ölveczky	University of Oslo, Norway

Steering Committee

Farhad Arbab	CWI and Leiden University, The Netherlands
Christel Baier	Technical University of Dresden, Germany
Frank de Boer	CWI and Leiden University, The Netherlands
Ali Movaghar	Sharif University of Technology, Iran
Hamid Sarbazi-azad	IPM and Sharif University of Technology, Iran
Marjan Sirjani (Chair)	Mälardalen University, Sweden
Carolyn Talcott	SRI International, USA
Martin Wirsing	Ludwig Maximilians University Munich, Germany

Additional Reviewers

Abbaspour Asadollah, Sara	Galletta, Letterio
Afsharchi, Mohsen	Habibi, Elahe
Aghamohammadi, Alireza	Jansen, David N.
Bacchiani, Lorenzo	Latella, Diego
Backeman, Peter	Laveaux, Maurice
Bagheri, Maryam	Lu, Yuteng
Bella, Giampaolo	Mahmoudzadeh, Elham
Bruni, Roberto	Malm, Jean
Carra, Damiano	Martens, Jan
Cledou, Guillermina	Moradi, Fereidoun
Crass, Stefan	Mukherjee, Dipayan
De Masellis, Riccardo	Salehi Fathabadi, Asieh
Esen, Zafer	Sengstschmid, Martina

Snook, Colin
Strüber, Daniel
Timmers, Ferry
Tini, Simone
Turrini, Andrea

van Spaendonck, Flip
Yang, Yilong
Zameni, Tannaz
Zhang, Xiyue

Contents

Coordination

Protocol Scheduling

Kasper Dokter[(✉)] and Farhad Arbab

Centrum Wiskunde & Informatica, Amsterdam, The Netherlands
`K.P.C.Dokter@cwi.nl`

Abstract. Interactions amongst different processes in concurrent software are governed by a protocol. The blocking I/O operations involved in a protocol may temporarily suspend the execution of some processes in an application. Scheduling consists of the allocation of available processors to the appropriate non-suspended processes in an application, such that some specified criteria (e.g., shortest execution time or highest throughput) are met. We use a generic, game-theoretic scheduling framework to find optimal non-preemptive schedules for an application. We then show how such schedules themselves can be encoded as protocols, which in our framework, can be composed with the original application protocol. The resulting composed protocol restricts the number of ready processes to the number of available processors, which enables standard preemptive schedulers of modern operating-systems to closely approximate the behavior and the performance of the optimal non-preemptive scheduler of the application. We evaluate our work by comparing the throughput of two versions of a cyclo-static dataflow network: one version with the usual protocol, and the other version with a restricted protocol.

1 Introduction

Context. Reliable concurrent software is notoriously complex to develop. The main factor that contributes to this complexity is the vastness of the number of possible sequences of interactions amongst concurrent processes. Many such sequences of interactions lead to bad states. The protocol in a concurrent software aims to prevent occurrences of such sequences.

In most programming languages, a protocol manifests implicitly as relatively few operations performed on locks and buffers, intermixed with a manifold larger number of computational operations. Consequently, it is practically impossible to directly analyze the protocol and verify its correctness. Exogenous coordination languages (such as Reo [2–4]) define a protocol explicitly as the medium through which all application processes interact. As such, concurrency protocols expressed in these languages can be developed and analyzed in isolation.

Problem. By construction, the protocol introduces dependencies amongst the different processes in an application. For example, the rate at which a producer process can fill a buffer of bounded capacity depends on the rate at which a

© IFIP International Federation for Information Processing 2021
Published by Springer Nature Switzerland AG 2021
H. Hojjat and M. Massink (Eds.): FSEN 2021, LNCS 12818, pp. 3–17, 2021.
https://doi.org/10.1007/978-3-030-89247-0_1

consumer process drains it. For optimal performance of a concurrent software, the scheduler must take these dependencies into account.

However, operating systems schedulers are application-independent and remain oblivious to the dependency information inherent in a protocol, even if such information is available. At best, these schedulers detect consequential effects of a protocol, such as blocking on an I/O-operation or waiting for a lock.

Contribution. In our current work, we refine the protocol of a concurrent application such that it enforces a custom schedule and derives an improved performance from the operating system scheduler. Our work demonstrates a close connection between a protocol and a schedule. Our protocol refinement uses the fact that the operating system scheduler executes only processes that are not blocked or waiting. We enforce a custom schedule by blocking all application processes, except for those that should run according to the application's desired schedule. We block a process by prolonging existing blocking operations like I/O operations or waiting for a lock. Therefore, our approach assumes that the application's desired custom schedule is non-preemptive.

Outline. We represent (Sect. 2) a concurrent application as a work automaton [9], which is a finite-state machine together with a finite set of real-valued variables, called jobs, each of which measures the progress of a single process.

We synthesize non-preemptive schedules for concurrent applications using algorithms for games on graphs (Sect. 3). A graph game is a two-player zero-sum game played by moving a token on a directed graph, wherein each vertex is owned by one of the players. Typically, the ownership of the nodes along a path through the graph alternates between the two players. If the token is at a vertex owned by a player, this player moves the token along one of the outgoing edges to the next vertex, after which the process repeats. The winning condition determines the player that wins based on the resulting path of the token.

Following our earlier results [10], we represent the scheduling problem as a graph game between the scheduler and the application (Sect. 4). The scheduler selects the processes that can execute, and the application resolves possible non-determinism within the processes of the concurrent program. Game-theoretic machinery computes a strategy for the scheduler that optimizes the execution of the concurrent program (according to an objective function that embodies some desired performance measure). Here, we consider only the objective of maximizing throughput, but similar techniques can also optimize for other scheduling performance measures, like fairness, context-switches, or energy consumption.

We view the resulting non-preemptive scheduling strategy itself as a scheduling protocol, and we compose the original protocol with this scheduling protocol to obtain a composite, scheduled protocol (Sect. 5). To evaluate the effect of the restricted protocol on a practical situation, we implement a reference version and a scheduled version of a simple cyclo-static dataflow network. This network consists of four processes, called actors, that interact asynchronously via five buffers (Fig. 1). A buffer can handle overflows by dropping items to match its capacity. We measure the throughput (i.e., the time between consecutive productions) of both versions of the program. The throughput of the reference version varies significantly, and is on average worse than the throughput of the scheduled version, which, moreover, shows only a small variation.

Finally, we conclude and point to future work in Sect. 6.

Related Work. There is a wealth of literature on different models for concurrent software, ranging from the well-known Petri nets [15], to the lesser-known higher-dimensional automata [12,16]. The syntax of work automata equals that of timed automata [1], but their semantics differ significantly, as jobs in work automata may progress independently at differing rates.

Our implementation of the scheduler as a composition is very similar to the definition of a scheduler defined by Goubault [13]. In his work, Goubault specifies the application as a higher dimensional automaton and views the scheduler as a subautomaton. While our scheduling framework builds on graph games, his work depends on the solution of a particular problem on huge sparse matrices.

2   Work Automata

The foundation of our scheduling framework consists of work automata [9], which provide a precise, formal specification of a concurrent application. A work automaton records the state and the progress of a finite set of processes. The state is recorded as an element, q, from a finite set of states, Q. The progress is recorded as an assignment $p : J \to \mathbb{R}$ of real-number values to a finite set J of jobs. A tuple (q, p) defines the complete configuration of the concurrent program.

A work automaton restricts the progress of its jobs by means of boolean expressions, which are conjunctions and disjunctions of atomic expressions of the form $j \sim n$, with $j \in J$ a job, $n \in \mathbb{N}$ an integer, and $\sim \in \{\leq, =, \geq\}$ a relation. The precise shape of the boolean expressions is irrelevant for our work; we just assume the existence of a set $\mathcal{B}_J$ of boolean expressions over J, together with a satisfaction relation $p \models \phi$ that relates assignments $p : J \to \mathbb{R}$ and expressions $\phi \in \mathcal{B}_J$.

Definition 1. *A work automaton is a tuple $(Q, \Sigma, J, T, I, c_0)$, where Q is a finite set of states, Σ is a finite set of signals, J is a finite set of jobs, $T \subseteq Q \times \Sigma \times \mathcal{B}_J \times 2^J \times Q$ is a (finite) transition relation, $I : Q \to \mathcal{B}_J$ an invariant, and $c_0 \in Q \times \mathbb{N}_0^J$ is an initial configuration.*

Although a work automaton consists of finitely many elements, it defines a continuously evolving system, due to the real-valued progress of jobs.

The semantics of work automata requires some auxiliary notation of job assignments. For every subset $X \subseteq J$ of jobs, the job assignment $[X] : J \to \mathbb{R}$ maps every $j \in J$ to 0 or 1, such that $[X](j) = 1$ if $j \in X$, and $[X](j) = 0$, otherwise. Furthermore, we allow composition of job assignments via componentwise addition, multiplication, and scalar multiplication: for any two job assignments $p, p' : J \to \mathbb{R}$ and any scalar $t \in \mathbb{R}$, we have $(p + p')(j) = p(j) + p'(j)$, $(p \cdot p')(j) = p(j) \cdot p'(j)$, and $(t \cdot p)(j) = t \cdot p(j)$, for all $j \in J$.

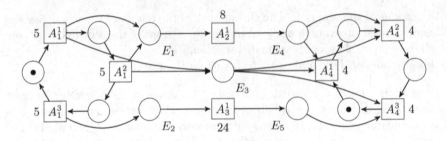

Fig. 1. Petri net representation of a small cyclo-static dataflow graph.

Definition 2. *The semantics $[\![A]\!]$ of a work automaton $A = (Q, \Sigma, J, T, I, c_0)$ is a labeled graph, with vertices $C = Q \times \mathbb{R}^J$, labels $L = \Sigma \cup \mathbb{R}_+^J$, initial vertex $c_0 \in C$, and edges $\rightarrow \subseteq C \times L \times C$ defined by the following two rules:*

$$\frac{d : J \rightarrow \mathbb{R}_+, \quad \forall t \in [0,1] \ (p + t \cdot d \models I(q))}{(q, p) \xrightarrow{d} (q, p + d)}$$

and

$$\frac{(q, \sigma, g, R, q') \in T, \quad p \models g, \quad p \cdot [J \setminus R] \models I(q')}{(q, p) \xrightarrow{\sigma} (q', p \cdot [J \setminus R])}$$

We demonstrate the utility of work automata by formalizing a simple cyclo-static dataflow network, which serves as our running example.

Example 1. Figure 1 shows the Petri net representation [15] of a small cyclo-static dataflow (CSDF) graph from [5, p. 29]. Recall that a Petri net consists of places (depicted as circles) that contain zero or more tokens, and transitions (depicted as rectangles). A transition firing consumes a single token from each of its input places and produces a token in each of its output places.

The system in Figure 1 consists of 4 actors (A_1 to A_4), which are connected via 5 buffers (E_1 to E_5). The original example in [5] does not make any assumptions on the nature of the buffers: they can be FIFO, LIFO, lossy, or priority buffers. For our purpose, we assume that writing to a full buffer loses the written data. For simplicity, Fig. 1 represents each buffer as a place in the Petri net. The losing behaviour is made precise in the work automaton in Fig. 2(e).

Each actor A_i, for $1 \leq i \leq 4$, cycles through a number of phases (hence the name cyclo-static). Figure 1 represents each phase as a transition A_i^j, for some index j, in the Petri net. Each phase of an actor requires time to execute. Although the actual times may vary, we consider only the worst-case execution times (WCET). We assume that all phases of a given actor have the same WCET. The integer value next to each transition in Fig. 1 specifies its WCET.   ◇

Although the functional behavior (as a Petri net) of the dataflow network in Fig. 1 is very precise, its non-functional behavior (the timing of transitions) is still unclear. The following example makes this precise by providing a work automaton for each actor and buffer in Fig. 1:

Example 2. Figure 2 shows the work automata that encode the informal description of the behavior of the CSDF graph in Example 1. The work automaton for A_i, with $1 \leq i \leq 4$, has a real-valued job variable j_i that measures the progress of its respective actor. The initial condition $j_1 = 0$ in Fig. 2(a) shows that actor A_1 must first perform 5 units of work on j_1 before it can produce on E_1 and E_3. In contrast, the initial condition $j_4 = 4$ in Fig. 2(b) shows that actor A_4 can immediately consume tokens from E_3 and E_4. The work automata for A_2 and A_3 in Figs. 2(c) and 2(d) are very similar. Each first consumes a datum from its input buffer, then executes for a given amount of time, and finally produces a datum in its output buffer. Figure 2(e) shows the work automaton for a buffer of capacity 4 (buffers of other capacity are defined similarly). The self-loop transition on state s_4 loses the data, if the buffer is full.   ◇

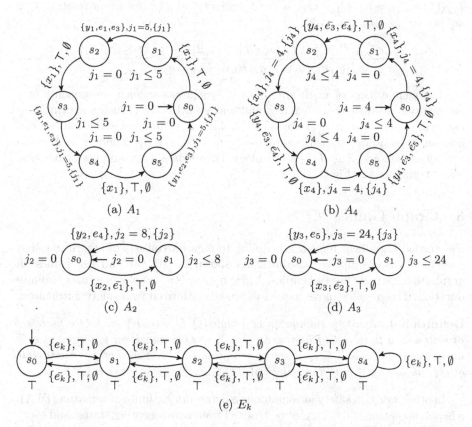

(a) A_1

(b) A_4

(c) A_2

(d) A_3

(e) E_k

Fig. 2. Work automata for the dataflow graph in Fig. 1, without the idling transitions $(s_i, \emptyset, \top, \emptyset, s_i)$, for all states i. The self-loop transition in (e) loses the data, if the buffer is full.

One of the important features of work automata (which we use repeatedly in our work) is that they can be composed to obtain the specification of a larger system. The composition operator combines two work automata by synchronizing on their respective signals [9]. The original definition of work automata synchronizes signals in a specific way, but this is again not important for the purpose of our work. Therefore, we simply assume the existence of a composition operator, $\bowtie$, on sets of signals. For any two sets of (local) signals Σ_1 and Σ_2, we obtain a set of (global) signals $\Sigma_1 \bowtie \Sigma_2$, and a injective function $\pi : \Sigma_1 \bowtie \Sigma_2 \to \Sigma_1 \times \Sigma_2$ that decomposes any global signal $\sigma \in \Sigma_1 \bowtie \Sigma_2$ into two local signals $\pi(\sigma) = (\sigma_1, \sigma_2) \in \Sigma_1 \times \Sigma_2$. Injectivity of π ensures that the global signal, σ, is completely determined by its local components σ_1 and σ_2.

Definition 3. *Let $A_i = (Q_i, \Sigma_i, J_i, T_i, I_i, q_{0i}, \phi_{0i})$, for $i \in \{1, 2\}$, be two work automata. Their composition is the work automaton $A_1 \bowtie A_2 = (Q_1 \times Q_2, \Sigma_1 \bowtie \Sigma_2, J_1 \cup J_2, T, I, (q_{01}, q_{02}), \phi_{01} \wedge \phi_{02})$, where $\wedge$ is conjunction; $I(q_1, q_2) = I(q_1) \wedge I(q_2)$, for $(q_1, q_2) \in Q_1 \times Q_1$, is the invariant; and the transition relation T is defined by the following rule:*

$$\frac{(q_i, \sigma_i, g_i, R_i, q_i') \in T_i \text{ for all } i \in \{1, 2\} \qquad \pi(\sigma) = (\sigma_1, \sigma_2)}{((q_1, q_2), \sigma, g_1 \wedge g_2, R_1 \cup R_2, (q_1', q_2')) \in T}$$

The composition of work automata is synchronous: both components in a composition produce their signals simultaneously. However, such a synchronous execution is not always desirable. To simulate asynchronous execution, we can add auxiliary idling transitions of the form $(q, \varepsilon, \top, \emptyset, q)$, where $\varepsilon \in \Sigma$ is an 'empty signal', and $\top \in \mathcal{B}_J$ is a tautology. For readability, we do not show these idling transitions in Fig. 2.

3   Graph Games

The second ingredient for our scheduling framework consists of algorithms that construct non-preemptive schedules. As shown in [10], we can use games on graphs to construct these schedules. A graph game is a two-player game of infinite duration. The possible move sequences are characterized by a safety automaton:

Definition 4. *A safety automaton is a tuple $(Q, \Sigma, \delta, q_0, F)$, with Q a finite set of states, Σ a finite set of moves, $\delta : Q \times \Sigma \to Q$ a transition function, $q_0 \in Q$ an initial state, and $F \subseteq Q$ a set of accepting states, such that for every state $q \in Q$, we have $q \in F$ if and only if $\delta(q, \sigma) \in F$, for some move $\sigma \in \Sigma$.*

In other words, a safety automaton is a deterministic finite automaton (DFA), wherein accepting states cannot be reached from non-accepting states, and every accepting state has an accepting successor.

As usual, we extend the transition function δ to finite move sequences by defining $\delta(q, \lambda) = q$ and $\delta(q, s\sigma) = \delta(\delta(q, s), \sigma)$, for every state $q \in Q$, finite move sequence $s \in \Sigma^*$, move $\sigma \in \Sigma$, and empty sequence $\lambda \in \Sigma^*$.

Since we are interested in infinite games only, we define the accepted language of a safety automaton as follows:

Definition 5. *The accepted language $L(A)$ of a safety automaton A is the set of infinite words $\sigma_1\sigma_2\cdots \in \Sigma^\omega$, such that $\delta(q_0, \sigma_1 \cdots \sigma_n) \in F$, for all $n \geq 0$.*

Instantiating Definition 5 for $n = 0$, we see that $\delta(q_0, \sigma_1 \cdots \sigma_n) = \delta(q_0, \lambda) = q_0 \in F$, which means that the accepted language is non-empty if and only if the initial state q_0 is accepting.

Consider a state $q \in Q$ of a safety automaton. While all moves are possible in q (the transition function is defined for all pairs of states and moves), not every move is enabled in the sense that it leads to an accepted word. In view of Definition 5, we consider the set $\Sigma_q = \{\sigma \mid \delta(q, \sigma) \in F\}$ of enabled moves at q. By Definition 4, Σ_q is non-empty, for accepting states $q \in F$.

Based on safety automata, we construct a graph game as follows:

Definition 6. *A graph game is a tuple (A, C, W), with $A = (Q, \Sigma, \delta, q_0, F)$ a safety automaton, $C \subseteq Q$ a set of controlled states, and $W \subseteq \Sigma^\omega$ a winning condition.*

A graph game (A, C, W) is played by two players (say Player 1 and Player 2) who take turns to move a token from state to state. We consider Player 1 a protagonist and Player 2 an antagonist. To simplify notation, we write $C_1 = C$ for the states controlled by Player 1, and we write $C_2 = Q \setminus C$ for the states controlled by Player 2. Initially, the token is in state $q_0 \in Q$. If the token is in state $q \in C_k$, with $k \in \{1, 2\}$, then Player k selects an enabled move $\sigma \in \Sigma_q$ and moves the token to state $\delta(q, \sigma)$. As a result, the token moves along a path

$$q_0 \xrightarrow{\sigma_1} q_1 \xrightarrow{\sigma_2} q_2 \xrightarrow{\sigma_3} \cdots$$

through the safety automaton. Player 1 wins if the sequence $\sigma_1\sigma_2\sigma_3\cdots \in \Sigma^\omega$ of moves is contained in the winning condition W. Otherwise, Player 2 wins.

A joint strategy (for both players) is a function $\zeta : \Sigma^* \to \Sigma$ that selects a move, for every finite move sequence. A strategy for Player $k \in \{1, 2\}$ is a function $\zeta_k : P_k \to \Sigma$, with $P_k = \{\sigma_1 \cdots \sigma_n \in \Sigma^* \mid \delta(q_0, \sigma_1 \cdots \sigma_n) \in C_k\}$, that selects a move, for every finite move sequence that leads to a state controlled by Player k. If Player k follows a strategy ζ_k, then the resulting move sequence is contained in the set

$$L(\zeta_k) = \{\sigma_1\sigma_2\sigma_3 \cdots \in L(A) \mid \zeta_k(\sigma_1 \cdots \sigma_n) = \sigma_{n+1} \text{ whenever defined}\}$$

of outcomes of the game that are ensured by following strategy s_k. A strategy ζ_1 for Player 1 is winning if $L(\zeta_1) \subseteq W$. That is, strategy ζ_1 ensures that the resulting move sequence is contained in W, irrespective of the moves of Player 2. Winning strategies for Player 2 are defined similarly. A strategy ζ_k for Player k is optimal, if it is winning or if no winning strategy for Player k exists.

Of course, for a given game, it is impossible that both players have a winning strategy. However, for general winning conditions, it is possible that neither player has a winning strategy. In this case, the game is not determined. Nevertheless, Martin proved [14] that graph games are determined if the winning condition is a Borel set[1]. Unfortunately, the results by Martin are descriptive and do not suggest a practical algorithm to find a winning strategy.

For simpler winning conditions, such as the ratio objective, we do have algorithms that compute a winning strategy:

Definition 7. *A ratio game is a graph game with a winning condition*

$$W_{s/t \geq v} = \left\{ \sigma_1 \sigma_2 \sigma_3 \cdots \in \Sigma^\omega \ \Big| \ \liminf_{n \to \infty} \frac{\sum_{i=1}^{n} s(\sigma_i)}{\sum_{i=1}^{n} t(\sigma_i)} \geq v \ and \ t(\sigma_1) \neq 0 \right\}$$

for some functions $s : \Sigma \to \mathbb{Z}$ *and* $t : \Sigma \to \mathbb{N}_0$, *and value* $v \in \mathbb{Q}$.

To the best of our knowledge, ratio games are introduced by Bloem et al. for the synthesis of robust systems [6]. The winning condition $W_{s/t \geq v}$ stipulates that, for every $\epsilon \geq 0$ there exists some time $N \geq 0$, such that for all $n \geq N$ after this time, the fraction $(\sum_{i=1}^{n} s(\sigma_i))/(\sum_{i=1}^{n} t(\sigma_i))$ is at most ϵ less than v.

If $t(\sigma) = 1$, for all moves $\sigma \in \Sigma$, then we obtain a mean-payoff game. Much research has been devoted to finding efficient algorithms that solve mean-payoff games. One of the best known algorithms for mean-payoff games is due to Brim et al. [7]. Their solution for mean-payoff games generalize easily to ratio games. We provide a brief explanation of this algorithm, and refer to [7] for full details.

A classical result by Ehrenfeucht and Mycielsky [11], called memoryless determinacy, states that there exists a positional optimal joint strategy for mean-payoff games (and ratio games).

Definition 8. *A joint strategy* $\zeta : \Sigma^* \to \Sigma$ *is positional, if* $\delta(q_0, s_1) = \delta(q_0, s_2)$ *implies* $\zeta(s_1) = \zeta(s_2)$, *for all move sequences* $s_1, s_2 \in \Sigma^*$.

A positional strategy depends only on the current state $\delta(q_0, s)$, instead of the full history $s \in \Sigma^*$. If both players follow some positional strategy, the outcome of the game is a path

$$q_0 \xrightarrow{\sigma_1} \cdots \to q_k \xrightarrow{\sigma_k} \cdots \to q_n \xrightarrow{\sigma_n} q_k \xrightarrow{\sigma_k} \cdots \tag{1}$$

in the safety automaton that ends with a cycle in the distinct states $q_k, \ldots, q_n$. The outcome of a ratio game is winning for a value $v = a/b \in \mathbb{Q}$ if and only if $(\sum_{i=k}^{n} s(\sigma_i))/(\sum_{i=k}^{n} t(\sigma_i)) \geq v = a/b$, which is equivalent to $\sum_{i=k}^{n} w(\sigma_i) \geq 0$, with $w(\sigma) = b \cdot s(\sigma) - a \cdot t(\sigma)$, for all moves $\sigma \in \Sigma$.

Brim et al. observed that positional winning strategies for Player 1 in a ratio game correspond with consistent valuations:

Definition 9. *A valuation* $f : Q \to \mathbb{N}_0 \cup \{\infty\}$ *is consistent in state* $q \in Q$ *iff*

1. $q \in C_1$ *implies* $f(q) + w(\sigma) \geq f(\delta(q, \sigma))$, *for some move* $\sigma \in \Sigma_q$, *or*
2. $q \in C_2$ *implies* $f(q) + w(\sigma) \geq f(\delta(q, \sigma))$, *for every move* $\sigma \in \Sigma_q$,

A valuation is consistent if it is consistent in every state.

---

[1] A Borel set is a subset of Σ^ω obtained from languages of safety automata by repeated complements and countable intersections.

Algorithm 1: Synthesis problem for ratio games.

Input : A ratio game $(A, C, W_{s/t \geq v})$, with $A = (Q, \Sigma, \delta, q_0, F)$, functions $s : \Sigma \to \mathbb{Z}$ and $t : \Sigma \to \mathbb{N}_0$, and a value $v = \frac{a}{b} \in \mathbb{Q}$.

Output: A the largest quasi-strategy $\zeta : Q \to 2^{\Sigma}$ that is winning.

1 **foreach** $\sigma \in \Sigma$ **do** $w(\sigma) \leftarrow b \cdot s(\sigma) - a \cdot t(\sigma)$;

2 **foreach** $q \in Q$ **do** $f(q) \leftarrow 0$;

3 **foreach** $q \in C$ **do** $c(q) \leftarrow |\{\sigma \in \Sigma_q \mid f(q) + w(\sigma) < f(\delta(q, \sigma))\}|$;

4 $B \leftarrow \sum_{q \in Q} \max(\{0\} \cup \{-w(q, \sigma) \mid \sigma \in \Sigma_q\})$;

5 $L \leftarrow \{q \in Q \mid f \text{ inconsistent in } q\}$;

6 **while** $L \neq \emptyset \neq \{q \in Q \mid f(q) = 0\}$ *and* $f(q_0) < \infty$ **do**

7   Pick $q \in L$, with $f(q)$ minimal;

8     $f_q \leftarrow f(q)$;

9     $f(q) \leftarrow \min\{n \in \{1, \ldots, B, \infty\} \mid f[q \mapsto n] \text{ consistent in } q\}$;

10     $L \leftarrow L \setminus \{q\}$;

11   **if** $q \in C$ **then** $c(q) \leftarrow |\{\sigma \in \Sigma_q \mid f(q) + w(\sigma) < f(\delta(q, \sigma))\}|$;

12   **foreach** (p, σ) *with* $\delta(p, \sigma) = q \neq p$ *and* $f(p) + w(\sigma) < f(q)$ **do**

13   **if** $p \in C$ **then**

14   **if** $f(p) + w(\sigma) \geq f_q$ **then** $c(p) \leftarrow c(p) - 1$;

15   **if** $c(p) = 0$ **then** $L \leftarrow L \cup \{p\}$;

16   **if** $p \in Q_0$ **then** $L \leftarrow L \cup \{p\}$;

17 **foreach** $q \in Q$ **do** $\zeta(q) \leftarrow \{\sigma \in \Sigma_q \mid f(q) + w(\sigma) \geq f(\delta(q, \sigma)), \text{ and } f(q) < \infty\}$;

Suppose that there exists a consistent valuation $f : Q \to \mathbb{N}_0 \cup \{\infty\}$. Repeated application of Definition 9 to the path in Eq. (1) yields $f(q_k) + \sum_{i=1k}^{n} w(\sigma_i) \geq f(\delta(q_k, \sigma_1 \cdots \sigma_n)) = f(q_k)$. If $f(q_k) < \infty$ is finite, then the outcome is winning for Player 1.

Brim et al. suggest a value iteration method to find the smallest possible valuation (we compare valuations pointwise: $f \leq f'$ iff $f(q) \leq f'(q)$, for all states $q \in Q$). Our Algorithm 1 shows a variation of their algorithm with only a few minor, but novel, adjustments.

The first modification is on Lines 6 and 7. Let $a = \min_{q \in Q} f_*(q)$ be the smallest value of the smallest valuation f_*. If $a < \infty$, then the valuation $f' : Q \to \mathbb{N}_0$ defined as $f'(q) = f_*(q) - a$, for all $q \in Q$, is less than or equal to f_*. Minimality of f_* shows that $a = 0$, which means that there exists a state $q \in Q$ with $f_*(q) = 0$. We refer to $q \in Q$ with $f_*(q) = 0$ as a pivot state. If there are no more pivot states, we can terminate the value iteration.

The second (minor) modification is on Line 9, which becomes appearent for states $q \in Q$ with a negative self loop transition (i.e., some $\sigma \in \Sigma$ with $\delta(q, \sigma) = q$ and $w(\sigma) < 0$). While the original algorithm by Brim et al. repeatedly adds $-w(\sigma)$ to the valuation $f(q)$ at state q, Algorithm 1 immediately jumps to the smallest valuation that resolves the inconsistency at q.

Value Problem. For given functions s and t, we have a family $\{W_{s/t \geq v} \mid v \in \mathbb{Q}\}$ of winning conditions. Since Player 1 wishes to maximize the ratio between the cumulatives of s and t, it is natural to look for the largest value $v \in \mathbb{Q}$ for which

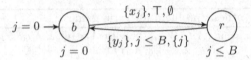

Fig. 3. Work automaton specifying cooperative behavior of a job j. Signal x_j executes job j, and signal y_j yields job j. The bound $B \in \mathbb{N}_0$ ensures job j eventually yields.

there exists a winning strategy. This problem is known as the value-problem. The set of values that are winning for Player 1 is a half-open interval $(-\infty, v_*]$, with v_* the optimal value. Using Algorithm 1, we can test the query $v \geq v_*$ for any value $v \in \mathbb{Q}$. Hence, the value problem can be solved by a binary search. Comin and Rizzi [8] improved this idea by reusing results from earlier queries.

4   Scheduling Game

We now apply the results in Sects. 2 and 3 to define a game-theoretic framework for the synthesis of non-preemptive schedules. We assume that a concurrent program is given in the form of a work automaton $(Q, \Sigma, J, T, I, c_0)$. Of course, we assume that the work automaton accurately models the real application. It may be nontrivial to verify whether or not the work automaton in fact models the application sufficiently accurately, but this concern is beyond the scope of our work on scheduling. In the worst case, one can ensure the application's compliance with the work automaton model by means of runtime verification.

By definition, non-preemptive scheduling relies on the cooperation of the application for managing its execution. We therefore, assume that the work automaton is cooperative:

Definition 10. *A work automaton A is cooperative if and only if for every job $j \in J$ of A, we have that $A \bowtie A_j$ and A are identical up to renaming of states, where A_j is the work automaton in Fig. 3.*

To obtain a scheduling game from a given cooperative work automaton A, we compose A with the auxiliary work automaton G_A in Fig. 4 that allows us to determine which player is to move and what moves are allowed by each player. In the composition $A \bowtie G_A$, every state is either controlled (if G_A is in state 0) or uncontrolled (if G_A is in state 1).

In the sequel, we assume without loss of generality that the work automaton G_A is already integrated in the specification of the cooperative work automaton:

Definition 11. *A cooperative work automaton is playable iff $A \bowtie G_A$ and A are identical up to state renaming.*

The semantics of a playable cooperative work automaton A from Definition 2 cannot be used directly in a graph game, because there are infinitely many ways to make progress via the d-transitions. Of course, not all progressions are equally

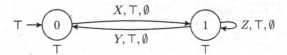

Fig. 4. Work automaton G_A specifying the rules of the scheduling game for a work automaton A. The scheduler selects any signal $X \subseteq N$ that intersects $X_J = \{x_j \mid j \in J\}$. The application selects a signal $Y \subseteq N \setminus X_J$ that intersects $Y_J = \{y_j \mid j \in J\}$ or a signal $Z \subseteq N \setminus X_J$ that does not intersect Y_J.

likely to happen. In fact, if sufficiently many processors are available, we expect that all running processes make an equal amount of progress. We assume that these processes run uninterruptedly and at equal speeds. We denote the expected transition in the semantics with a double arrow:

Definition 12. *The expected semantics $[\![A]\!]_e$ of a work automaton A is the subgraph of $[\![A]\!]$ with the $\Rightarrow$ edges defined by the rules*

$$\frac{c \xrightarrow{[S]} c' \qquad if\ c \xrightarrow{[S']} c' \ and\ S' \neq S \ then\ S \not\subseteq S'}{c \xRightarrow{[S]} c'} \qquad and \qquad \frac{c \xrightarrow{\sigma} c'}{c \xRightarrow{\sigma} c'}$$

The expected transition relation is just a subrelation of the real transition relation of the semantics of a work automaton. Note that there is no guarantee that the real execution follows the expected one. However, we show in Sect. 5 that deviations of real execution from expected execution do not cause deadlocks.

Lemma 1. *The expected semantics of a cooperative work automaton is finite.*

Proof. Since A is cooperative, the progress of every job is bounded by $B \in \mathbb{N}_0$ in every state (Fig. 3). By a simple induction, it follows that the configurations of the expected semantics are contained in the finite set $Q \times \{0, \dots, B\}^J$. □

The final ingredient for a scheduling game is an objective. The only restriction that we impose on a scheduling objective is that it must be expressible as a ratio objective $W_{s/t \geq v}$, in terms of some functions $s : M \to \mathbb{Z}$ and $t : M \to \mathbb{N}_0$.

Example 3. The composition of the work automata in Figs. 2 and 4 yields a game graph. We maximize the throughput, which we define as the ratio between the number of productions and the number of time steps (ticks). We can count the productions by counting how often e_5 fires. Hence, we define

$$s(a_1 \cdots a_n) = |\{i \mid e_5 \in a_i \in \Sigma\}| \quad and \quad t(a_1 \cdots a_n) = |\{i \mid a_i \in \mathbb{R}_+^J\}|.$$

Algorithm 1 finds a subgame for which every play is of optimal throughput.

As the CSDF graph is a deterministic program, all non-determinism is controlled by the scheduler. Since all options ensure optimal throughput, we can resolve the non-determinism arbitrarily. We resolve non-determinism by preferring idling. The deterministic scheduling strategy for this example can be presented as a Gantt chart, shown in Fig. 5.   ◊

Fig. 5. Generated schedule. The vertical dashed line indicates the start of the period.

5   Protocol Restriction

Consider a playable cooperative work automaton A from Sect. 2 and a non-preemptive scheduling strategy $\zeta : C \to \Sigma$ from Sect. 4, with C the set of configurations of the expected semantics $[\![A]\!]_e$ of A. Now we intend to implement the schedule ζ as a protocol $A(\zeta)$ that blocks precisely those jobs that are not supposed to make progress, such that the operating system scheduler has to closely follow the desired scheduling strategy.

The solution to ratio games in Algorithm 1 returns a subgraph of the original game graph. For a scheduling game, vertices are configurations of A, and the edge come from the expected transition relation. Hence, the resulting scheduling strategy can be easily transformed back into a work automaton.

Definition 13. *The scheduling work automaton $A(\zeta)$ of a scheduling strategy ζ is defined as the tuple $(C, \Sigma, \emptyset, \to, I, c_0)$ with states $C = Q \times \mathbb{N}_0^J$, trivial invariant $I(c) = \top$ for all states $c \in C$, and transition relation defined by the rule*

$$\frac{c \in C \text{ controlled} \quad c \xrightarrow{a} c' \quad \zeta(c) \text{ defined implies } a = \zeta(c)}{c \xrightarrow{a, \top, \emptyset} c'}$$

We enforce the scheduling strategy by considering the composition $A \bowtie A(\zeta)$. The composition $A \bowtie A(\zeta)$ does not introduce any new, undesired executions, but merely restricts the composition to a subset of desired executions of A. By construction, A and $A(\zeta)$ synchronize only on signals, which agrees with the fact that the schedule ζ is non-preemptive.

For the construction of the scheduling game in Sect. 4, we assume that scheduled jobs run as expected, i.e., they run continuously and at constant speed. However, it is actually very likely that the actual execution deviates from the expected execution. A natural question is whether such deviations may confuse the scheduler enough to introduce deadlocks.

Theorem 1. *If A is a composition of simple work automata, then $A \bowtie A(\zeta)$ is deadlock free.*

A simple work automaton is a work automaton with at most one job and no silent transitions that in every configuration can either make progress or fire a transition, but cannot do both. The work automata in Fig. 2 are examples of simple work automata.

Proof (of Theorem 1). The state-space of $A \bowtie A(\zeta)$ is defined by tuples consisting of a state $q \in Q$ and a configuration (q', p') of $A(\zeta)$. Let $c = ((q, (q', p')), p) \in$

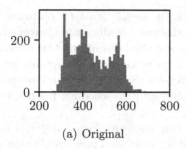
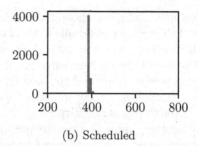

(a) Original   (b) Scheduled

Fig. 6. Throughput of original program (a) and scheduled program (b). The horizontal axis is the time in milliseconds between successive firings of A_4^3 (grouped in bins of 10 milliseconds), and the vertical axis is the frequency of each bin.

$(Q \times (Q \times \mathbb{N}_0^J)) \times \mathbb{R}^J$ be a reachable configuration of $A \bowtie A(\zeta)$. The absence of silent transitions ensures that the scheduler $A(\zeta)$ knows the state of A (i.e., we have $q = q'$). The progress $p : J \to \mathbb{R}$ of the jobs may still be unknown (i.e., $p \neq p'$ is possible). By construction, there exists some expected execution of $A \bowtie A(\zeta)$ that passes through the same state q (although the progress may be different from p) and enables a transition $t = (q, \sigma, g, R, q')$. Since the work automaton for each job is simple, the guard g of transition t states that the progress of a subset of jobs is maximal (while the progress of other jobs is irrelevant). Hence, from c we can make sufficient progress to enable transition t, which implies that c is not a deadlock.   □

Example 4. To evaluate the schedule in Fig. 5, we implement the CSDF graph in Fig. 1 in Python. We performed the experiment on a 64-bit Windows 10 Home Edition with a Intel® Core™ i7-7700HQ CPU at 2.80 GHz and 16 GB RAM. We executed the source code with a 64-bit Python 3.9.0 interpreter.

The source code of the scheduled application is a manual, but mechanical, transformation of the original source code. The transformation adds barrier synchronizations between the actors and a scheduler process. This scheduler process implements the non-preemptive schedule in Fig. 5.

Figure 6 shows the histogram (with a bin-size of 10 ms) of the output of both versions of the program. We measure the throughput (i.e., the time between successive productions) of each version. Both the expected value and the standard deviation of the two versions differ. The original version has an expected throughput of 441 ms with a standard deviation of 95 ms. The scheduled version has an expected throughput of 386 ms and a standard deviation of 6 ms.

The quality of the schedule alone does not explain the improvement of the expected throughput; the characteristics of the original protocol are the most important factor in this example. Recall that we use overflow buffers, which means that an actor loses its datum, if its respective buffer is full. If a datum is lost, all effort invested in its production is also lost. The general-purpose scheduler of the operating system is unaware of these losses.   ◊

Although the game-theoretic framework in Sect. 3 aims to optimize the expected throughput, Example 4 shows that the most significant improvement in the scheduled protocol is in its impact on the standard deviation of the throughput. The time between successive productions is much more predictable for the scheduled version compared to the original version. Since we force the operating system scheduler to closely follow a fixed, deterministic schedule, predictability of the throughtput is not surprising.

Predictable timing is a requirement for many systems. For example, a pacemaker must assist a patient's heart to beat at a regular and predictable rate, and a self-driving car must sense and analyze its environment at a predictable rate to avoid collisions. The results of Example 4 show that the unpredictable behavior of the scheduler of the operating systems can be made tightly predictable by restricting the protocol through composition with a scheduling protocol.

6   Conclusion

Protocols contain valuable information indispensable for construction of optimal (non-preemptive) schedules for allocation of resources to execute a concurrent application. Exogenous languages like Reo express a protocol as an explicit software construct, which makes this scheduling information accessible. We express protocols together with their scheduling information in terms of the work automaton semantics of Reo. We construct a generic scheduling framework based on ratio games to find optimal non-preemptive schedules for an application defined as a work automaton. By composing such a scheduling protocol with the original protocol of an application, we obtain a composite scheduled protocol that forces generic operating system preemptive schedulers to closely follow the desired optimal schedule. The exogenous nature of Reo guarantees that the application code remains oblivious to the substitution of the composite scheduled protocol for its original protocol. An experiment shows that a scheduled version of a cyclo-static dataflow network (with the composite protocol) has higher and more predictable throughput compared to its original version.

Future Work. The algorithm by Brim et al. to solve ratio games requires the full state-space of an application. In view of the state-space explosion problem, we can use other schemes (like Monte-Carlo tree search) to find good schedules.

Although the work presented in our current paper focuses on maximizing throughput, the ratio objective can express many other scheduling performance measures, like fairness, context-switches, or energy consumption. We intend to express these performance measures in terms of ratio objectives.

Acknowledgements. We thank Benjamin Lion for his suggestion to use the overflow semantics for the buffers in the CSDF graph and the anonymous reviewers of FSEN 2021 for their constructive comments.

References

1. Alur, R., Dill, D.: Automata for modeling real-time systems. In: Paterson, M.S. (ed.) ICALP 1990. LNCS, vol. 443, pp. 322–335. Springer, Heidelberg (1990). https://doi.org/10.1007/BFb0032042

2. Arbab, F.: Reo: a channel-based coordination model for component composition. Math. Struct. Comput. Sci. **14**(3), 329–366 (2004). https://doi.org/10.1017/S0960129504004153

3. Arbab, F.: Abstract behavior types: a foundation model for components and their composition. Sci. Comput. Program. **55**(1–3), 3–52 (2005). https://doi.org/10.1016/j.scico.2004.05.010

4. Arbab, F.: Proper protocol. In: Ábrahám, E., Bonsangue, M., Johnsen, E.B. (eds.) Theory and Practice of Formal Methods. LNCS, vol. 9660, pp. 65–87. Springer, Cham (2016). https://doi.org/10.1007/978-3-319-30734-3_7

5. Bamakhrama, M.A.M.: On hard real-time scheduling of cyclo-static dataflow and its application in system-level design. Ph.D. thesis, Leiden University (2014)

6. Bloem, R., Greimel, K., Henzinger, T.A., Jobstmann, B.: Synthesizing robust systems. In: Proceedings of FMCAD, pp. 85–92. IEEE (2009). https://doi.org/10.1109/FMCAD.2009.5351139

7. Brim, L., Chaloupka, J., Doyen, L., Gentilini, R., Raskin, J.: Faster algorithms for mean-payoff games. Formal Methods Syst. Des. **38**(2), 97–118 (2011). https://doi.org/10.1007/s10703-010-0105-x

8. Comin, C., Rizzi, R.: Improved pseudo-polynomial bound for the value problem and optimal strategy synthesis in mean payoff games. Algorithmica **77**(4), 995–1021 (2017). https://doi.org/10.1007/s00453-016-0123-1

9. Dokter, K., Arbab, F.: Exposing latent mutual exclusion by work automata. In: Mousavi, M.R., Sgall, J. (eds.) TTCS 2017. LNCS, vol. 10608, pp. 59–73. Springer, Cham (2017). https://doi.org/10.1007/978-3-319-68953-1_6

10. Dokter, K., Jongmans, S.-S., Arbab, F.: Scheduling games for concurrent systems. In: Lluch Lafuente, A., Proença, J. (eds.) COORDINATION 2016. LNCS, vol. 9686, pp. 84–100. Springer, Cham (2016). https://doi.org/10.1007/978-3-319-39519-7_6

11. Ehrenfeucht, A., Mycielski, J.: Positional strategies for mean payoff games. Int. J. Game Theory **8**(2), 109–113 (1979)

12. van Glabbeek, R.J.: On the expressiveness of higher dimensional automata. Theor. Comput. Sci. **356**(3), 265–290 (2006). https://doi.org/10.1016/j.tcs.2006.02.012

13. Goubault, E.: Schedulers as abstract interpretations of higher-dimensional automata. In: Proceedings of the of PEPM, pp. 134–145. ACM (1995)

14. Martin, D.A.: Borel determinacy. Ann. Math. 363–371 (1975)

15. Murata, T.: Petri nets: properties, analysis and applications. Proc. IEEE **77**(4), 541–580 (1989)

16. Pratt, V.R.: Modeling concurrency with geometry. In: Wise, D.S. (ed.) Proceedings of POPL, pp. 311–322. ACM Press (1991). https://doi.org/10.1145/99583.99625

Automated Replication of Tuple Spaces
via Static Analysis

Aline Uwimbabazi[2(✉)], Omar Inverso[2], and Rocco De Nicola[1]

[1] IMT School for Advanced Studies, Piazza S. Francesco, 19, 55100 Lucca, Italy
`rocco.denicola@imtlucca.it`
[2] Gran Sasso Science Institute, Viale F. Crispi, 7, 67100 L'Aquila, Italy
`{aline.uwimbabazi,omar.inverso}@gssi.it`

Abstract. Coordination languages for tuple spaces can offer significant advantages in the specification and implementation of distributed systems, but often do require manual programming effort to ensure consistency. We propose an experimental technique for automated replication of tuple spaces in distributed systems. The system of interest is modelled as a concurrent Go program where different threads represent the behaviour of the separate components, each owning its own local tuple repository. We automatically transform the initial program by combining program transformation and static analysis, so that tuples are replicated depending on the components' read-write access patterns. In this way, we turn the initial system into a replicated one where the replication of tuples is automatically achieved, while avoiding unnecessary replication overhead. Custom static analyses may be plugged in easily in our prototype implementation. We see this as a first step towards developing a fully-fledged framework to support designers to quickly evaluate many classes of replication-based systems under different consistency levels.

1 Introduction

When designing a distributed system, adopting a suitable coordination model can be of fundamental importance. To facilitate the specification of inter-process communication patterns, some coordination languages provide explicit data-access primitives. In Linda [13], processes can concurrently access an associative data store referred to as *tuple space*, where *tuples*, i.e., sequences of typed data atoms, can be stored to or fetched from. Processes synchronise and communicate in this way. Klaim [8] extends this approach to multiple tuple spaces with explicit localities for greater flexibility.

On large, data-intensive distributed systems, techniques to optimise data distribution and locality may significantly improve efficiency. One such technique, *replication*, fits very well within the coordination languages framework. The idea is quite simple: on a store operation, tuples are deployed to a set of target spaces rather than just to a single one. This increases locality and thus reduces latency, but brings along the problem of consistency: once a specific copy of a given tuple is modified, how are the remaining copies to be affected?

© IFIP International Federation for Information Processing 2021
Published by Springer Nature Switzerland AG 2021
H. Hojjat and M. Massink (Eds.): FSEN 2021, LNCS 12818, pp. 18–34, 2021.
https://doi.org/10.1007/978-3-030-89247-0_2

RepliKlaim [1] addresses such tension between performance and consistency by extending Klaim's operational semantics with replica-aware data manipulation primitives. The programmer can use these primitives to control the distribution of the data as well as the consistency level. Yet, doing so requires programming ingenuity to specify and coordinate the replicas. Such manual reasoning can be particularly cumbersome because of process interleaving, and hardly feasible in the presence of a large number of complex processes. For the same reasons, evaluating different replication strategies with respect to the intended performance-reliability trade-off can be rather tricky.

In this paper, we address the above shortcomings by proposing an experimental approach to support the design of replication policies in distributed systems that use tuple spaces for process coordination and data storage. More concretely, we present an automated technique to transform the specifications of any such given system into an equivalent version where the tuples are replicated. The overall approach is sketched in the following diagram.

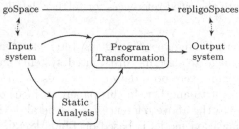

The system of interest is modelled as a concurrent Go [22] program. The behaviour of each system component of the system is defined by a separate thread of the program. Coordination takes place via goSpace [15], a recent Go implementation of Klaim.

To attain automated replication, we first work at the programming interface level, by implementing extended primitives for replica-aware manipulation of tuples. Taking inspiration from the way Klaim's operational semantics was extended in RepliKlaim, we extend goSpace's programming interface to obtain what we call RepligoSpaces. The extended primitives make it possible to target multiple tuple spaces for a single store operation. In addition, an embedded tracking mechanism allows to consistently remove the replicated data at need.

At this point one could immediately obtain full consistency by naively using the extended primitives to replicate every tuple to every shared space in the system. This could be automatically obtained via program transformation, by replacing the tuple manipulation operations with their replica-aware versions, but would likely result in unnecessary overhead. For this reason, between the replica-aware data-handling layer and the program transformation part, we introduce a static analysis pass to refine the target spaces for each store operation.

This simple workflow is easily extensible, given the modularity between the data-handling layer, the program transformation schema, and the static analysis procedure. Different static analysis techniques may be plugged in effortlessly. At the same time, alternative consistency models can be quickly prototyped by altering the existing replica-aware primitives. We see this as a first step towards developing an integrated framework to experiment with data replication in distributed systems with tuple spaces.

The rest of the paper is organised as follows. Section 2 provides a preliminary introduction to Klaim, RepliKlaim, and pSpaces. Section 3 presents our RepligoSpaces prototype that implements the replica-aware tuple manipulation routines. Section 4 presents our automated replication schema based on static analysis and program transformation. Section 5 provides some details of our prototype implementation and an experimental evaluation of our approach. Sections 6 and 7 discuss related work, conclusion, and future work.

2   Preliminaries

In this section, we introduce the main languages representing the starting points of our work. Due to space limits, we limit our description to the minimum necessary. We refer to the cited references for further details.

Klaim. Klaim (Kernel Language for Agents Interaction and Mobility) [8] is a coordination language to describe distributed systems and that supports a programming paradigm where both data and processes can be moved from one computing environment to another. In this paper, we focus on the data aspects and refer the reader to the above reference for a general description of Klaim.

Klaim's communication model is based on Linda [8,13], that enables asynchronous communication via a set of operations that allow to exchange information through a shared environment referred to as *tuple space*. A *tuple space* is a collection of tuples. A *tuple* is a finite sequence of *actual* fields (e.g., expressions, values, processes) or *formal* fields (i.e., variables). Tuples that contain variables are also called *templates*. ("Journalist", "Sport", 2018) is an example of a tuple, while ("Journalist", category, year) is a template with two variables category and year. In Linda and its variants, tuples are retrieved by *pattern matching*. Two tuples match if they have the same number of fields, and all the pairs of fields at the same position *match*: two actual fields match if their values are equal; an actual field and a variable match if they are of the same *type*.

Klaim extends Linda by allowing multiple tuple spaces and offering communication primitives with explicit *localities*. Processes and tuple spaces can be located on different *nodes*, and localities represent unique identifiers for such nodes. Explicit localities allow to distribute and to retrieve data to and from the localities, and to structure the tuple space. In fact, the data manipulation operations of Klaim are based on the standard Linda primitives for tuple spaces but, in addition, they explicitly require the target tuple space as a reference ($@\ell$) to the intended locality.

The non-blocking output operation $\mathtt{out}(t)@\ell$ places a tuple t in the tuple space at location ℓ. The $\mathtt{read}(T)@\ell$ operation selects via pattern matching one of the tuples at locality ℓ that matches template T; this operation blocks until a tuple matching T is found at ℓ. The $\mathtt{in}(T)@\ell$ input operation is similar to $\mathtt{read}$ but it also removes the matched tuple from the tuple space.

In both Linda and Klaim it is also possible to spawn new processes respectively via $\mathtt{eval(-)}$ and $\mathtt{eval(-)}@\ell$. We do not consider process spawning here as it is not currently implemented in RepliKlaim nor pSpaces, and it is not relevant for our analysis.

RepliKlaim. RepliKlaim [1] adds to Klaim extended tuple manipulation primitives for replica-aware programming. Similarly to Klaim, RepliKlaim provides a set of blocking and non-blocking operations that add, search and remove tuples from or to tuple spaces. Tuples in RepliKlaim, i.e., *replicated tuples*, have the same format as Klaim's tuples.

The non-blocking output operation $\mathtt{outRK}(t, \ell_1 \ldots \ell_n)$ permits to add the shared tuple t to the data repositories located at all localities $\ell \epsilon L$ (L$= \ell_1 \ldots \ell_n$) atomically (when strong consistency is required) or asynchronously (in case of weak consistency). Thus, the shared tuple is replicated to every locality in L.

The input operation $\mathtt{readRK}(T, \ell)$ reads a tuple space. It uses a pattern T to retrieve a matching tuple (if any) from locality ℓ, but it does not remove the matching tuple. In case no matching tuple is found, the operation blocks until a matching tuple becomes available. The operation $\mathtt{readRK}_{nb}(T, \ell)$ is similar to $\mathtt{readRK}(T, \ell)$ except that it is non-blocking, and returns an empty tuple when no matching tuple is found.

The input operation $\mathtt{inRK}(T, \ell)$ retrieves a tuple matching the pattern T at ℓ and atomically removes all replicas of that tuple, thus preserving strong consistency. Operation $\mathtt{inRK}_{nb}(T, \ell)$ can also be performed on tuple spaces asynchronously in order to remove all replicas of a tuple that match T. This operation only preserves weak consistency. In the rest of the paper, we focus on replication under strong consistency.

PSpaces. pSpaces[1] is a family of implementations based on Klaim's formal semantics and targeted at different modern development platforms, such as Go, Java, and Swift. In this paper we focus on the Go implementation, goSpace.

In pSpaces, a *space* is a collection of tuples. Spaces can be either local or remote, in the sense that they can be possibly located on another device. A remote space supports the same operations as for local spaces, but it needs slightly different operations to be created and connected with. Every space is associated with a unique uniform resource identifier (URI) encoded as a string, i.e., the *space identifier*. In the rest of the paper, we make no explicit distinction between local and remote spaces: each component manipulating the tuple spaces is also associated its own URI, which makes it possible to figure out whether a space is local or not.

The implementation of pSpaces relies on communication primitives similar to those of Klaim, essentially a set of blocking and non-blocking actions to

---

[1] https://github.com/pSpaces/.

add, search, and remove tuples to or from a space. A new tuple t is added to a space s by invoking the non-blocking operation $s.\texttt{Put}(t)$. The operation $s.\texttt{Query}(T)$ scans a tuple space using pattern matching, blocking until a tuple is found. The non-blocking version $s.\texttt{QueryP}(T)$ instead looks for a tuple in the space and returns the tuple, if any, and a boolean value indicating whether the operation was successful. The non-blocking operation $s.\texttt{GetP}(T)$ is similar to $s.\texttt{QueryP}(T)$, but it also removes the matching tuple, if any, from the space.

3   Programming Interface Extension for Replication

We now present RepligoSpaces, our replica-aware extension of goSpace [15]. Both pSpaces and goSpace (Sect. 2) allow to manipulate tuples within a single space. With RepligoSpaces, we instead allow to manipulate tuples across multiple spaces. Our extension follows a similar approach to RepliKlaim with Klaim (Sect. 2). As with RepliKlaim, a store operation takes as an argument the set of targeted spaces. A tuple t is added to spaces $s_1 \ldots s_n$ via an $\texttt{MPut}(t, s_1 \ldots s_n)$ operation. The operation $\texttt{MQueryP}(s, T)$ queries a specific space s for tuples matching pattern T. It returns the found tuple, if any, or an empty tuple. The operation $\texttt{MQuery}(s, T)$ is similar, but blocks until a matching tuple is found. The operation $\texttt{MGetP}(s, T)$ returns a tuple matching T and removes it from space s and from any other space where it was previously replicated. In the rest of the section, we provide further details about $\texttt{MPut}(t, s_1 \ldots s_n)$, $\texttt{MQueryP}(s, T)$ and $\texttt{MGetP}(s, T)$. We omit the details for $\texttt{MQuery}(s, T)$ due to space limits. Note that we are currently only considering strong consistency, i.e., atomic operations on tuples; Also note that in this paper, we are concerned with efficiency (and thus data locality) rather than robustness (redundancy).

Extended Operations. The MPut operation in Listing 1 adds a tuple to a set of spaces. It takes as input a tuple t and a set S of space identifiers, in the form of strings that encode their URIs.

```
 1  func MPut(t Tuple, Sp Replispace, S []string) Tuple {
 2      Sp.mux.Lock()
 3
 4      // create tuple t' = {t,S}
 5      var data []interface{}
 6      data = append(data, t.Fields...)
 7      data = append(data, S)
 8      var t1 Tuple = CreateTuple(data...)
 9
10      // add t' to each space in S
11      for i := 0; i < len(S); i++ {
12          Sp.Sp[S[i]].Put(t1.Fields...)
13      }
14
15      Sp.mux.Unlock()
16      return CreateTuple(t1)
17  }
```

Listing 1. The MPut operation replicates a tuple over a set of spaces

The idea is then to simply perform a normal goSpace Put operation for every space in S (lines 10–13). To do so, we need a reference to the space object identified by the URI at any given position of the set S. For this, we use a global map Sp from URIs to references to space objects. Note that this is not a limiting factor as our source transformation procedure will automatically populate Sp for us (Sect. 4). Note that the actual tuple being stored is not exactly t, but an extended tuple obtained by appending S to t (lines 4–7). This avoids centralized tracking of the storage locations [1] and simplifies the implementation. We are interested in strong consistency, thus the sequence of Put operations is enclosed in a critical section (lines 2 and 15) to enforce atomicity.

```
1  ,func MQueryP(p Tuple, Sp Replispace, s Space) Tuple {
2      Sp.mux.Lock()
3
4      // create template p' = {t,S}
5      var y []string // <--- extra field to match the space list S
6      var data []interface{}
7      data = append(data, p.Fields...)
8      data = append(data, &y)
9      var p1 Tuple = CreateTuple(data...)
10
11     // query a tuple via a pattern matching from a specific space
12     t1, e := s.QueryP(p1.Fields...)
13
14     if e == nil {
15         // no error: return the matching tuple without the last field
16         var u = CreateTuple(t1.Fields[:len(t1.Fields)-1]...)
17         Sp.mux.Unlock()
18         return u
19     }
20
21     Sp.mux.Unlock()
22     return CreateTuple()    // returns an empty tuple when no tuple is available
23 }
```

Listing 2. The MQueryP operation to search for a replicated tuple

The MQueryP operation illustrated in Listing 2 searches the given space for tuples matching the given pattern. It takes as input a tuple p (i.e., a pattern) and a space identifier s, and returns as output a tuple, if any. As the result of the previous MPut operation as described above, every stored tuple is extended with an extra field that contains the set of target spaces. Therefore, our search pattern p will need to be adapted accordingly by appending to p an extra field to be used as a placeholder to match the set of targeted spaces in the last field of any stored tuple (line 5 and lines 6–9). The modified pattern p1 so obtained is used instead of p to retrieve matching tuples at space s (line 12). On a successful search (lines 14–19), the last field of the returned tuple is removed as no longer relevant (line 16), and the tuple originally stored is returned. Otherwise, an empty tuple is returned (line 22). Note that the operation MQuery is similar to MQueryP, except that it blocks until a tuple is found.

The MGetP operation illustrated in Listing 3 uses a pattern p to search and remove a matching tuple from space s and any other space where it was replicated. It returns as output the tuple, if any. As for the other operations, the pattern p needs to be adapted with an extra placeholder to match the set of target spaces appended to the stored tuples by an MPut operation. We can then use the modified pattern p1 to scan space s for matching tuples (line 12). On a successful search (lines 14–35), we extract from the matched tuple, the set S of spaces holding a replica of the tuple (line 16). To perform a standard goSpace GetP operation on every space in S, we use the map Sp to retrieve a reference to the relevant space object identified by the URI in S, similarly to the procedure used to implement the MPut operation. Thus, upon searching for the matching tuples from space s (line 12), the list S of all spaces containing a replica of the matching tuple is extracted and transformed in the form of strings of spaces identifiers (lines 16–19). The loop (lines 22–34) performs a GetP operation for every space in the set S of space identifiers (line 24) using the map Sp and the modified pattern p1. On a successful search (lines 26–34), at the last iteration, the tuple is stripped from the extra field containing the target URIs and returned. Note that, since we are assuming only strong operations, it should not be possible for the search to be unsuccessful after passing the first check (line 14). Eventually the operation returns an empty tuple in case none is found (line 38).

```
 1 func MGetP(p Tuple, Sp Replispace, s Space) Tuple {
 2     Sp.mux.Lock()
 3
 4     // create template p' = {t,S}
 5     var y []string // <--- extra field to match the space list S
 6     var data []interface{}
 7     data = append(data, p.Fields...)
 8     data = append(data, &y)
 9     var p1 Tuple = CreateTuple(data...)
10
11     // search the tuple from space s
12     t1, e := s.QueryP(p1.Fields...)
13
14     if e == nil {
15         // extract the list of all spaces
16         var S = (t1.Fields[len(t1.Fields)-1])
17         // transform the interface type of spaces into the string type
18         var v []string
19         v = S.([]string)
20
21         // for each space in the set S of space identifiers
22         for s := range v {
23             // remove the tuple from the relevant spaces
24             u, e1 := Sp.Sp[v[s]].GetP(p1.Fields...)
25
26             if e1 == nil {
27                 if s == len(v)-1 {
28                     // no error: tuple successfully removed from the space
29                     u = CreateTuple(u.Fields[:len(u.Fields)-1]...)
30                     Sp.mux.Unlock()
31                     return u
32                 }
33             }
34         }
35     }
36
37     Sp.mux.Unlock()
38     return CreateTuple()    // returns an empty tuple when no tuple is available
39 }
```

Listing 3. The MGetP operation for removing a replicated tuple

4 Static Analysis and Program Transformation

We now discuss our approach to automatically transform an initial Go program that uses goSpace for data manipulation into an equivalent program that uses RepligoSpaces (Sect. 3). Intuitively, a fully-consistent but inefficient replicated system may be easily obtained by atomically re-applying every output operation to every shared space (regardless of the originally intended target) using the extended programming interface of Sect. 3. We aim at reducing unnecessary overhead by automatically inspecting the program to refine the set of target spaces. To that end, we rely on static analysis to extract from the initial program the data access patterns, and then use this information during a program transformation phase.

Input Structure. Our initial program (Listing 4) is composed of a set P of n parallel processes performing concurrent computations over a set S of n shared tuple spaces. It is worth to observe that the input program may represent an *abstract model* of a more complex system whose computations that do not directly involve tuples are simply abstracted away.

We assume that each process is defined by a separate and unique *process definition function*, and that all such functions are collected into the input program. We denote the process definition functions with $P = p_1, \ldots, p_n$. We also assume that the input program additionally contains a main section where all the shared tuple spaces are created beforehand and associated to unique space identifiers, and all the processes are spawned as separate threads. Finally, we denote with $S = s_1, \ldots, s_n$ the set of spaces shared among the processes, and associate to each process p_i a local tuple space s_i; we consider every tuple manipulation operation performed within a process to be a *local* operation if it refers to that space, and a *remote* operation otherwise.

Output Structure. The output program (Listing 5) retains the same structure as the input program. The global section of the initial program is extended with auxiliary data structures, such as the map sp from space identifiers to concrete references to space objects (line 12) and the map uri from space objects to space identifiers (line 13) (used for example in Listing 5). An additional package with the definitions of the extended tuple manipulation routines (Listings 1, 2, etc.), is added to the import section at the beginning of the output program (line 3). In the process definition functions $p_1, \ldots, p_n$ every call to a goSpace routine is transformed into a call to the corresponding extended primitive (Sect. 3) to achieve replication accordingly. For MPut operations, the set of target spaces for replication is added as an argument (e.g., cf. line 21 of Listing 4 and Listing 5). Each such set is over-approximated by the procedure described in the following section. Any other access operation, such as GetP, Query or QueryP (lines 31 and 40) is instead changed to always refer to the local space.

Overapproximating the Sets of Target Spaces. It is worth noticing that the extended tuple manipulation routines (Sect. 3) are independent from the specific technique used for reducing the set of target spaces for data replication. In the following, we simply describe a lightweight static analysis technique for overapproximating such sets of target spaces. The goal of our static analysis procedure is to work out a refined set of target spaces, i.e., the *data-access tables*, for replicating the tuples while preserving strong consistency.

Let us consider a tuple t and a process p_i performing an output operation of t into a specific space s_j. The key idea of our approach consists in determining the set of processes $P' \subseteq P$ that can potentially perform a subsequent read operation on that tuple. We identify such processes by looking at the patterns used in the input operations within the corresponding definition functions, approximating the actual pattern matching mechanism of the normal tuple manipulation routines. In practice, given on the one hand an output operation and on the other hand an input operation, we check for a potential match between the tuple being stored and the given search tuple or template. We repeat this for every process except p_i and for every input operation in the corresponding process definition function, obtaining P' by progressively excluding from P any process that is *definitely* not involved in an input operation matching the tuple t. Eventually, the data-access table for replicating t will be the set $S' \subseteq S$ induced by P' on S.

For simplicity, let us assume that a field of a tuple t given as input to an MPut operation can be either a constant or a variable identifier, while a field of a pattern p taken by MGetP or MQueryP can be either a constant value or a formal field, namely a typed variable reference. Due to space limitations, we only give an informal description.

The matching mechanism initially compares the number of fields of t and p: if they are different, then certainly there is no match; otherwise, there is still the possibility for t and p to match. The matching is then refined based on the actual fields of the tuple and the pattern, ignoring any formal fields or placeholders. A difference of any actual field at the same position of t and p indicates a mismatch. The matching is eventually refined again by taking into account the type of the formal fields of p. A type mismatch between an actual field of t (either a constant or a variable) and the corresponding formal field of p means no match.

It is worth to notice that combining the matching mechanism described above with the replica-aware routines from Sect. 3 preserves consistency, because

1. the matching algorithm only avoids replication for those spaces where a tuple is definitely never going to be accessed (i.e., no matching input operations for that tuple exist in the whole process definition function corresponding to that space), and therefore safely over-approximates the set of target spaces for replication, and
2. the tracking mechanism embedded within the replica-aware tuple manipulation routines guarantees that, when one copy of a tuple is removed, all its replicas are atomically removed as well.

Program Transformation. We can now transform the initial program to automatically achieve replication, by converting all the operations to goSpace into calls to the new RepligoSpaces routines introduced in Sect. 3, and using as target locations for write operations the sets computed by the matching technique above.

The program transformation procedure takes as input the initial program and the data-access tables built via the static analysis pass described above, and generates a program where each tuple is replicated as indicated by the corresponding access lists. This can be done by parsing the input program into an abstract syntax tree, and then performing a series of pattern-based transformations on (parts of) this tree.

To see how pattern-based syntax tree transformations work, let us now consider the function call at line 21 of Listing 4, where process1 performs a Put operation of the tuple ("A", 10) into the local tuple space s1. This fragment of code will trigger transformation because the referenced object (s1) is a tuple space (which is detected via a symbol table lookup) and the Put method is among the relevant ones. In the syntax tree, the corresponding subtree for the whole expression is therefore changed into a call to MPut (see Listing 1 from Sect. 3); new child nodes are appended to the function call node in the syntax tree for the extra parameters as shown in Listing 5. Un-parsing the syntax tree modified in this way will produce the transformed program.

Example. We now show how the procedure described above leads from the program of Listing 4 to the one in Listing 5.

```
 1 import (
 2   . "github.com/pspaces/gospace"
 3   ...
 4 )
 5
 6
 7
 8
 9
10 func main() {
11   s1 := NewSpace("tcp://host:123/s1")
12   go Process1(&s1)
13   ...
14 }
15
16
17
18 func process1() {
19   var choice bool
20   ...
21   s1.Put("A",10)
22   ...
23   s1.Put(choice,10)
24   ...
25 }
26
27 func process2() {
28   ...
29   if check {
30     var key int
31     s1.GetP("A",&key)
32   }
33   ...
34 }
35
36 func process3() {
37   ...
38   var choice bool
39   var desc string
40   s1.GetP(&desc,&choice)
41   ...
42 }
43
44 ...
```

```
 1 import (
 2   . "github.com/pspaces/gospace"
 3   . "repligospaces"
 4   ...
 5 )
 6
 7 var uri = make(map[space]string)
 8 var sp = make(map[string]*Space)
 9
10 func main() {
11   s1 := NewSpace("tcp://host:123/s1")
12   sp["tcp://localhost:123/s1"] = &s1
13   uri[s1] = "tcp://host:123/s1"
14   go Process1()
15   ...
16 }
17
18 func process1() {
19   var choice bool
20   ...
21   MPut("A",10,targets0)
22   ...
23   MPut(choice,10,targets1)
24   ...
25 }
26
27 func process2() {
28   ...
29   if check {
30     var key int
31     MGetP("A",&key,uri[s2])
32   }
33   ...
34 }
35
36 func process3() {
37   ...
38   var choice bool
39   var desc string
40   MGetP(&desc,&choice,uri[s3])
41   ...
42 }
43
44 ...
```

Listing 4. Initial program   **Listing 5.** Transformed program

The graphs that represent the data distribution for the initial program (see Listing 4) and the transformed program (see Listing 5) are shown in Figs. 1a and 1c, respectively. Figure 1b represents universal replication and is included for comparison. In the figures, arrows from left to right indicate write operations; arrows from right to left read operations.

Let us consider the tuple ("A", 10) stored by process1 at line 21. The GetP operation at line 31 process2 uses as the pattern a string constant and a formal field of integer type. Therefore the local tuple space s2 is included in the set of spaces for replication of ("A", 10). Note that the analysis is control-flow insensitive, as the branch condition at line 29 is ignored.

Now let us consider process3. The size of the pattern given at line 40 and of the tuple ("A", 10) under consideration match. The types of the last fields respectively of the tuple and of the pattern do not match (bool vs integer). Therefore, the tuple is not replicated to s3.

Let us now focus on the tuple (choice,10) stored by process1 at line 23. The type of the first field of the tuple is known, but its value depends on previous computations. The pattern used in the input operation in process2 at line 31 does not match this type. The tuple is thus not replicated at s2 or at s3.

Indeed in the transformed program (Fig. 1c) the only replicated tuple is ("A", 10), which is replicated to s2 as it can potentially be accessed by process2. Note that there is no need to store this tuple to s1, as no subsequent matching read operation within process1 occurs. It is worth to observe that in general this program transformation does not depend on the specific static analysis technique to work out the set of target locations (i.e., shown as targets0 and targets1 in Fig. 1c).

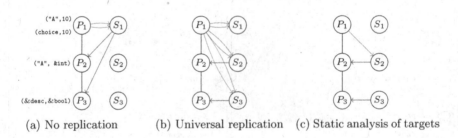

(a) No replication   (b) Universal replication   (c) Static analysis of targets

Fig. 1. Example replication strategies

5   Implementation and Experimental Evaluation

In this section, we describe the implementation of our prototype and provide an experimental evaluation on our technique.

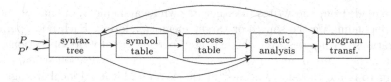

Fig. 2. Static analysis and source transformation for automated replication

Overall Workflow and Technical Details. Having defined the structure of the input program P and of the output program P' (Sect. 4), we can now describe more precisely the overall workflow of our approach (Fig. 2).

The program P is initially parsed to generate an *abstract syntax tree*. The syntax tree is traversed to generate the *symbol table*. During this process we start visiting the body of the process definition functions, and then of the nested blocks recursively. As we go along, we assign blocks unique identifiers, so that as soon a new variable declaration occurs in the syntax tree, that variable is added to the set of symbols for the current block; the *type* of the variable is also extracted from the syntax tree and stored in the symbol table.

The next step consists in building the *access table* by extracting information from the syntax tree and the symbol table. In particular, we visit the syntax tree again to detect all the operations on tuples. At the same time, we search the symbol table to figure out the type of fields for each tuple occurring as an argument for any of such operations. Eventually, we obtain for each tuple operation the actual tuple along with the type of each field of the tuple.

We can now perform *static analysis* by visiting the syntax tree a third time and combining information from the symbol table and the access table in order to overapproximate the set of target spaces for replication.

A program transformation module alters the syntax tree to replace the tuple manipulation operations occurring in the initial program with their replica-aware counterparts, where the set of target spaces for each Put operation has been determined by the static analyser. We finally obtain the modified program P' by un-parsing the modified syntax tree. The code of our open-source prototype is available at https://github.com/Uwimbabazi/Replication/releases/tag/v1.

Experimental Evaluation. Let us now consider a distributed system composed of n computational nodes, each executing a separate program, and interacting through a decentralised data store of capacity m elements. Following a similar schema to those used in distributed lookup protocols (e.g., Chord [26]), memory entries are represented as key-value pairs, with a partitioned address space among the nodes. Each node is responsible for storing m/n memory entries.

A node reads from and writes to either its own local memory, or that of another node, depending on the source or target memory address. Each node performs o operations, with p denoting the expected percentage of write operations.

For such a system, one might consider adopting a replication schema in the attempt to reduce non-local access (at the cost of additional local storage, plus some overhead for replication to non-local storage). To experiment with this idea, we model the nodes as separate processes, and the local memory of a node as the local tuple space of the corresponding process, with tuples (*address, value*) representing values held at different memory addresses. The structure of the program follows that of Listing 4. For simplicity, we assume that all read operations are QueryP. Write operations are of course Put.

To evaluate the effect of replication on the system, we conduct the following experiments. We initially considered a system with $\{n = 4, m = 32\}$, then one with twice as much memory $\{n = 4, m = 64\}$, then a larger system $\{n = 32, m = 256\}$, and eventually a larger system with twice as much memory $\{n = 32, m = 512\}$. For all these systems, we set $o = 16$, while varying p in $\{10, 20, \ldots, 90\}$. For each combination of the chosen values for n, m, and p, we generate 10 test cases (i.e., programs) with random data access patterns. We run each test case 10 times, leading to rounds of 100 runs each. We repeat each such round twice: once on the initial program, and once on the replicated program obtained with our tool (Sect. 4), for an overall number of 1800 runs for each of the four considered systems. We eventually compare the average number of local and remote read and write operations. The experiments were conducted on a standard laptop. The experiments are summarised in Figs. 3a, 3b, 3c and 3d where we compare the average count of non-local memory accesses with and without replication, for each configuration.

Without replication, both read and write access can be non-local, depending on the address being accessed. With replication, read operations are always local, because tuples are always replicated where they can be potentially accessed. However, this comes at the cost of extra non-local write access to replicate the data. If the system tends to read from the shared memory more often than writing to it, our approach can be beneficial. In Figs. 3a–3d, the number of non-local accesses with replication is maximised when the read and write operations occur with the same probability. Replication seems to be more beneficial with larger memory size (from 32 to 64, or from 256 to 512).

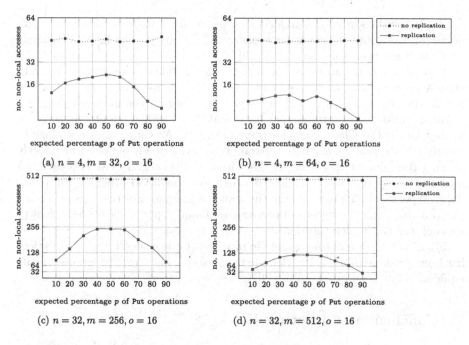

Fig. 3. Non-local read or write operations with and without replication

6   Related Work

In addition to the pSpaces family of implementations, tuple space systems have been proposed in different programming languages. Java implementations include Klava [4] for Klaim, and jRESP[2] for SCEL [9]. jSpace, the implementation of pSpaces in Java, was initially based on a fork of jRESP. We chose to work on top of pSpaces because it is actively maintained.

Besides RepliKlaim [1], tuple replication has also been implemented in X10 [2], a general-purpose language for large-scale distributed systems [25]. An extension of Lime, a distributed tuple space for mobile ad-hoc networks, relies on replication to increase availability [21]. In all these approaches, the responsibility to control replication is left to the programmer.

In the attempt to increase scalability, a hierarchical tuple space model with partial replication has been proposed in [6]. Spatial distribution of tuples is a rather different approach to ours where tuples contain both content and replication rules [20]; in this model the propagation of the tuples is asynchronous and thus strong consistency has to be explicitly programmed. Alternative distribution mechanisms for tuple spaces based on the concept of ghost tuples have been proposed in [10], where it is the system that may decide not to eliminate tuples for using them later.

---

[2] http://jresp.sourceforge.net/.

Tuple-based coordination models focusing on fault tolerance have been proposed [3]. Consistency models for replicated data are covered in [12]. Dynamic replication has been considered in [5,24].

Several program transformation frameworks for different languages are available. A popular framework for C and C++ is ROSE [23], where the syntax tree can be directly modified and then un-parsed to obtain the modified program. Another transformation framework for C and C++, widely adopted in software verification, is the Clang compiler framework [19]. As Clang does not allow to modify the abstract syntax tree, program transformation is obtained by directly altering the relevant fragments of the initial source code. In our approach the model of the system to be replicated is expressed as a Go program, and standard Go packages support either of the above techniques. For this reason, among the available implementations of pSpaces, we found it particularly convenient to focus on the Go implementation.

Static verification of concurrent Go programs for bounded liveness and safety has been considered in [17,18]. Bounded analysis of concurrent programs for safe replication has been proposed in [14].

7   Conclusion and Future Work

We have presented RepligoSpaces, a replica-aware extension of goSpace, an implementation of Klaim (pSpaces) in Go. We have also discussed how RepligoSpaces fits within a fully-mechanisable procedure for automated replication of programs over tuple spaces that relies on combining static analysis and program transformation. A lightweight static analysis pass on the initial program computes the sets of target spaces for replication, so that the standard tuple manipulation routines can be replaced by equivalent replica-aware versions. The combined approach preserves strong consistency, thanks to a tracking mechanism embedded in the tuple manipulation routines and to the fact that the set of target spaces is safely over-approximated.

In the near future, we plan to consider further scenarios where replication has successfully been applied to other contexts, such as database systems [11], and cloud computing [16], as well as other consistency models [12,27]. We also plan further work on the static analysis procedure to improve the accuracy of the over-approximation in the presence of formal fields, i.e., placeholders in the pattern or variables in the tuple to be stored. We plan to initially focus on simple and efficient techniques to complement the existing analysis with limited effort. To name a few, constant propagation [28] can reduce the overall number of formal fields or restrict the possible values of a given formal field collecting them over different branching paths; abstract interpretation [7] can overapproximate the interval ranges of the integer variables used as formal fields.

We consider our contribution to be a first step towards developing an integrated framework to experiment with data replication in distributed systems with tuple spaces. We aim at providing different analyses and consistency models to choose from, in order to appreciate the effect of different consistency levels on many interesting classes of more or less complex distributed systems where data replication is heavily used. This would allow, for instance, to evaluate under different consistency levels many interesting classes of systems, such as models of hardware cache or complex interaction models, where replication is heavily used and performance is particularly sensitive to variations in the data distribution.

Acknowledgements. Work partially funded by MIUR project PRIN 2017FTXR7S IT MATTERS (Methods and Tools for Trustworthy Smart Systems).

References

1. Andrić, M., De Nicola, R., Lafuente, A.L.: Replica-based high-performance tuple space computing. In: Holvoet, T., Viroli, M. (eds.) COORDINATION 2015. LNCS, vol. 9037, pp. 3–18. Springer, Cham (2015). https://doi.org/10.1007/978-3-319-19282-6_1
2. Andrić, M., De Nicola, R., Lluch Lafuente, A.: Replicating data for better performances in X10. In: Probst, C.W., Hankin, C., Hansen, R.R. (eds.) Semantics, Logics, and Calculi. LNCS, vol. 9560, pp. 236–251. Springer, Cham (2016). https://doi.org/10.1007/978-3-319-27810-0_12
3. Bessani, A.N., Alchieri, E.A.P., Correia, M., da Silva Fraga, J.: DepSpace: a Byzantine fault-tolerant coordination service. In: EuroSys, pp. 163–176. ACM (2008)
4. Bettini, L., De Nicola, R., Pugliese, R.: KLAVA: a Java package for distributed and mobile applications. Softw. Pract. Exp. **32**(14), 1365–1394 (2002)
5. Casadei, M., Viroli, M., Gardelli, L.: On the collective sort problem for distributed tuple spaces. Sci. Comput. Program. **74**(9), 702–722 (2009)
6. Corradi, A., Leonardi, L., Zambonelli, F.: Distributed tuple spaces in highly parallel systems. Technical report, DEISLIA-96-005, UNIBO (Italy) (1996)
7. Cousot, P., Halbwachs, N.: Automatic discovery of linear restraints among variables of a program. In: POPL, pp. 84–96. ACM Press (1978)
8. De Nicola, R., Ferrari, G.L., Pugliese, R.: KLAIM: a kernel language for agents interaction and mobility. IEEE Trans. Softw. Eng. **24**(5), 315–330 (1998)
9. De Nicola, R., et al.: The SCEL language: design, implementation, verification. In: Wirsing, M., Hölzl, M., Koch, N., Mayer, P. (eds.) Software Engineering for Collective Autonomic Systems. LNCS, vol. 8998, pp. 3–71. Springer, Cham (2015). https://doi.org/10.1007/978-3-319-16310-9_1
10. De Nicola, R., Pugliese, R., Rowstron, A.: Proving the correctness of optimising destructive and non-destructive reads over tuple spaces. In: Porto, A., Roman, G.-C. (eds.) COORDINATION 2000. LNCS, vol. 1906, pp. 66–80. Springer, Heidelberg (2000). https://doi.org/10.1007/3-540-45263-X_5
11. Elnikety, S., Dropsho, S.G., Zwaenepoel, W.: Tashkent+: memory-aware load balancing and update filtering in replicated databases. In: EuroSys, pp. 399–412. ACM (2007)
12. Fekete, A.D., Ramamritham, K.: Consistency models for replicated data. In: Charron-Bost, B., Pedone, F., Schiper, A. (eds.) Replication. LNCS, vol. 5959, pp. 1–17. Springer, Heidelberg (2010). https://doi.org/10.1007/978-3-642-11294-2_1
13. Gelernter, D.: Generative communication in Linda. ACM (TOPLAS) **7**(1), 80–112 (1985)

14. Kaki, G., Earanky, K., Sivaramakrishnan, K.C., Jagannathan, S.: Safe replication through bounded concurrency verification. Proc. ACM Program. Lang. **2**(OOPSLA), 164:1–164:27 (2018)

15. Kaminskas, L., Lluch, L.A.: Aggregation policies for tuple spaces. In: Di Marzo Serugendo, G., Loreti, M. (eds.) COORDINATION 2018. LNCS, vol. 10852, pp. 181–199. Springer, Cham (2018). https://doi.org/10.1007/978-3-319-92408-3_8

16. Karandikar, R.R., Gudadhe, M.B.: Comparative analysis of dynamic replication strategies in cloud. IJCA **TACIT2016**(1), 26–32 (2016)

17. Lange, J., Ng, N., Toninho, B., Yoshida, N.: Fencing off go: liveness and safety for channel-based programming. In: POPL, pp. 748–761. ACM (2017)

18. Lange, J., Ng, N., Toninho, B., Yoshida, N.: A static verification framework for message passing in Go using behavioural types. In: ICSE, pp. 1137–1148. ACM (2018)

19. Lattner, C.: LLVM and Clang: next generation compiler technology. In: The BSD Conference (2008)

20. Mamei, M., Zambonelli, F., Leonardi, L.: Tuples on the air: a middleware for context-aware multi-agent systems. In: WOA, pp. 108–116. PEB (2002)

21. Murphy, A.L., Picco, G.P.: Using LIME to support replication for availability in mobile ad hoc networks. In: Ciancarini, P., Wiklicky, H. (eds.) COORDINATION 2006. LNCS, vol. 4038, pp. 194–211. Springer, Heidelberg (2006). https://doi.org/10.1007/11767954_13

22. Pike, R.: Go at Google. In: SPLASH, pp. 5–6. ACM (2012)

23. Quinlan, D., Liao, C.: The ROSE source-to-source compiler infrastructure. In: Cetus Users and Compiler Infrastructure Workshop, in conj. with PACT (2011)

24. Russello, G., Chaudron, M., van Steen, M.: Dynamically adapting tuple replication for managing availability in a shared data space. In: Jacquet, J.-M., Picco, G.P. (eds.) COORDINATION 2005. LNCS, vol. 3454, pp. 109–124. Springer, Heidelberg (2005). https://doi.org/10.1007/11417019_8

25. Saraswat, V., Jagadeesan, R.: Concurrent clustered programming. In: Abadi, M., de Alfaro, L. (eds.) CONCUR 2005. LNCS, vol. 3653, pp. 353–367. Springer, Heidelberg (2005). https://doi.org/10.1007/11539452_28

26. Stoica, I., Morris, R.T., Karger, D.R., Kaashoek, M.F., Balakrishnan, H.: Chord: a scalable peer-to-peer lookup service for internet applications. In: SIGCOMM, pp. 149–160. ACM (2001)

27. Terry, D.: Replicated data consistency explained through baseball. Commun. ACM **56**(12), 82–89 (2013)

28. Wegman, M.N., Zadeck, F.K.: Constant propagation with conditional branches. ACM Trans. Program. Lang. Syst. **13**(2), 181–210 (1991)

Incremental Refinement of Goal Models with Contracts

Piergiuseppe Mallozzi[1(✉)], Pierluigi Nuzzo[2], and Patrizio Pelliccione[1,3]

[1] Chalmers University of Technology, University of Gothenburg, Gothenburg, Sweden
`mallozzi@chalmers.se`
[2] University of Southern California, Los Angeles, USA
`nuzzo@usc.edu`
[3] Gran Sasso Science Institute (GSSI), L'Aquila, Italy
`patrizio.pelliccione@gssi.it`

Abstract. Goal models and contracts offer complementary approaches to requirement analysis. Goal modeling has been effectively used to capture designer's intents and their hierarchical structure. Contracts emphasize modularity and formal representations of the interactions between system components. In this paper, we present CoGoMo (Contract-based Goal Modeling), a framework for systematic requirement analysis, which leverages a new formal model, termed *contract-based goal tree*, to represent goal models in terms of hierarchies of contracts. Based on this model, we propose algorithms that use contract operations and relations to check goal consistency and completeness, and support incremental and hierarchical refinement of goals from a library of goals. Model and algorithms are implemented in a tool which enables incremental formalization and refinement of goals from a web interface. We show the effectiveness of our approach on an illustrative example motivated by vehicle platooning.

1 Introduction

Missing or erroneously formulated requirements can have a negative impact on the quality of a design. Designers are often faced with the challenge of ensuring the correctness of an implementation despite the growing complexity of the requirement corpora [29]. Existing requirement-management tools are mostly based on natural-language constructs that leave space for ambiguities, redundancies, and conflicts [13,23]. Furthermore, the requirement elicitation process is itself challenging, as it revolves around human-related considerations that are intrinsically difficult to capture.

Goal modeling (e.g., as in KAOS [9,31]) has been used over the years as an intuitive and effective means to capture the designer's intents and their hierarchical structure. The refinement process, however, mostly follows informal procedures, e.g., by posing *how* questions about existing high-level goals (top-down process) or *why* questions about low-level goals for the system under consideration (bottom-up process) [29,32]. The main modeling challenges are framed

© IFIP International Federation for Information Processing 2021
Published by Springer Nature Switzerland AG 2021
H. Hojjat and M. Massink (Eds.): FSEN 2021, LNCS 12818, pp. 35–50, 2021.
https://doi.org/10.1007/978-3-030-89247-0_3

in terms of ensuring *completeness* and *consistency* of a specification. A set of hierarchically organised goals is *incomplete* when the high-level goal remains unsatisfied even if the low-level goals, which are expected to capture its decomposition, are satisfied, meaning that the designer could not anticipate all the possible operating scenarios for the design. There is, instead, a *conflict* when the satisfaction of a goal prevents the satisfaction of another goal [30]. The process of completely refining a goal into sub-goals is not straightforward [11]. On the other hand, independently-developed goals can include overlapping and conflicting behaviors [12]. Systematic methods to detect conflicts and incomplete requirements remain an active research area [4, 14, 21].

This paper presents a framework, CoGoMo (Contract-based Goal Modeling), which addresses these challenges by representing goals via contract models. Contract-based modeling has shown to enable formal requirement analysis in a modular way, rooted in sound representations of the system semantics and decomposition architecture [2, 8, 22–25, 27]. A *contract* specifies the behavior of a component by distinguishing the responsibilities of the component (*guarantees*) from those of its environment (*assumptions*). Contract operations and relations provide formal support for notions such as stepwise *refinement* of high-level contracts into lower-level contracts, *compositional reasoning* about contract aggregations, and *reuse* of pre-designed components satisfying a contract. CoGoMo addresses correctness and completeness of goal models by formulating and solving contract consistency and refinement checking problems. Specifically, the contributions of the paper can be summarised as follows:

- A novel formal model, namely, *contract-based goal tree (CGT)*, which represents a goal model as a hierarchy of assume-guarantee (A/G) contracts.
- Algorithms that exploit the CGT as well as contract-based operations to detect conflicts and perform complete hierarchical refinements of goals. Specifically, we introduce mechanisms that help resolve inconsistencies between goals during refinement and a *goal extension* algorithm to automatically refine the CGT using new goals from a library.
- A tool, which implements the proposed model and algorithms to incrementally formalize and refine goals via an easy-to-use web-interface.

We illustrate the applicability of CoGoMo on a case study motivated by vehicle platooning.

2   Background

Goals. A goal is a prescriptive statement of intent that the system should satisfy, formulated in a declarative way. Goals can be decomposed, progressing from high-level objectives to fine-grained system prescriptions [31]. For example, an AND-refinement link relates a goal to a set of sub-goals. The parent can be satisfied if all the sub-goals in the refinement are also satisfied. Establishing *correctness* of the refinement amounts to ensuring that the sub-goals are *consistent*, i.e., there are no *conflicts* among them, and *complete*, i.e., there are no behaviours left unspecified that could result in a violation of the high-level goal even if the lower-level goals are satisfied. We only refer to *internal completeness*, i.e., we are not concerned with investigating whether all the information required to define a design problem is in the specification [34]. Formally, we say that the refinement of goal $\mathcal{G}$ into sub-goals $\mathcal{G}_1, \mathcal{G}_2, \ldots, \mathcal{G}_n$ is correct if and only if

$$\underbrace{\{\mathcal{G}_1, \mathcal{G}_2, \ldots, \mathcal{G}_n\} \not\models \textbf{false}}_{\text{consistency}} \quad \wedge \quad \underbrace{\{\mathcal{G}_1, \mathcal{G}_2, \ldots, \mathcal{G}_n\} \models \mathcal{G},}_{\text{completeness}}$$

where we denote by $\models$ the entailment operator between goals and say that $\{\mathcal{G}_1, \ldots, \mathcal{G}_n\}$ entails $\mathcal{G}$ to mean that, if all $\mathcal{G}_1, \ldots, \mathcal{G}_n$ are satisfied then $\mathcal{G}$ is satisfied. Similarly, we write $\{\mathcal{G}_1, \mathcal{G}_2, \ldots, \mathcal{G}_n\} \not\models \textbf{false}$ to indicate that the logical conjunction of $\{\mathcal{G}_1, \mathcal{G}_2, \ldots, \mathcal{G}_n\}$ does not lead to false.

Contracts. A *contract* $\mathcal{C}$ is a triple (V, A, G) where V is a set of *variables*, and A and G are sets of behaviors over V. Behaviors are generic. For example, they can be traces generated by the execution of a finite state machine, i.e., infinite sequences of assignments to the variables in V, consisting of the input, output, and state variables of the state machine. For simplicity, whenever possible, we drop V from the definition and refer to contracts as pairs of assumptions and guarantees, i.e., $\mathcal{C} = (A, G)$. A expresses the behaviors that a system expects from its environment, while G expresses the behaviors that a system implementation promises under the environment assumptions. An environment E satisfies a contract $\mathcal{C}$ whenever E and $\mathcal{C}$ are defined over the same set of variables and all the behaviors of E are included in the assumptions of $\mathcal{C}$, i.e., when $|E| \subseteq A$, where $|E|$ is the set of behaviors of E. An implementation M satisfies a contract $\mathcal{C}$ whenever M and $\mathcal{C}$ are defined over the same set of variables and all the behaviors of M are included in the guarantees of $\mathcal{C}$ when considered in the context of the assumptions A, i.e., when $|M| \cap A \subseteq G$. A contract $\mathcal{C} = (A, G)$ can be placed in saturated form by re-defining its guarantees as $G_{sat} = G \cup \overline{A}$, where $\overline{A}$ denotes the complement of A. A contract and its saturated forms are semantically equivalent, i.e., they have the same set of environments and implementations. Therefore, in the rest of the paper, we assume that all the contracts are expressed in saturated form [2].

We say that a contract is *well-formed* if and only if it is *compatible*, i.e., $A \neq \emptyset$ and *consistent*, i.e., $G \neq \emptyset$, that is, if and only if there exists at least an environment and an implementation that satisfy the contract. Contract *refinement* formalizes a notion of substitutability among contracts. Let $\mathcal{C} = (A, G)$ and $\mathcal{C}' = (A', G')$ be two contracts. $\mathcal{C}$ refines $\mathcal{C}'$ if and only if all the assumptions of $\mathcal{C}'$ are contained in the assumptions of $\mathcal{C}$ and all the guarantees of $\mathcal{C}$ are included in the guarantees of $\mathcal{C}'$, that is, $\mathcal{C} \preceq \mathcal{C}'$ if and only if $A \supseteq A'$ and $G \subseteq G'$. Refinement entails relaxing the assumptions and strengthening the guarantees. If $\mathcal{C} \preceq \mathcal{C}'$, we also say that $\mathcal{C}'$ is an *abstraction* of $\mathcal{C}$ and can be replaced by $\mathcal{C}$.

Contracts can be combined through the operations of *composition* and *conjunction*. Let $\mathcal{C}_1 = (A_1, G_1)$ and $\mathcal{C}_2 = (A_2, G_2)$ be two contracts. The composition $\mathcal{C}_\| = (A, G) = \mathcal{C}_1 \parallel \mathcal{C}_2$ can be computed using the following expressions:

$A = (A_1 \cap A_2) \cup \overline{(G_1 \cap G_2)}$ and $G = G_1 \cap G_2$. The conjunction $\mathcal{C}_\wedge = \mathcal{C}_1 \wedge \mathcal{C}_2$ can instead be computed by taking the intersection of the guarantees and the union of the assumptions, that is, $\mathcal{C}_\wedge = (A_1 \cup A_2, G_1 \cap G_2)$. Intuitively, an implementation satisfying $\mathcal{C}_\parallel$ or $\mathcal{C}_\wedge$ must satisfy the guarantees of both $\mathcal{C}_1$ and $\mathcal{C}_2$, hence the operation of intersection. The situation is different for the environments. Composition requires that an environment satisfy the assumptions of both contracts, motivating the conjunction of A_1 and A_2. On the other hand, contract conjunction requires that an implementation operate under all the environments of $\mathcal{C}_1$ and $\mathcal{C}_2$, motivating the disjunction of A_1 and A_2.

In the following, we denote by $\mathcal{C}_i = (\psi_i, \phi_i)$ the contract formalizing a goal $\mathcal{G}_i$, where ψ_i and ϕ_i are logic formulas used to represent the assumptions and the guarantees, respectively. Finally, we perform operations among goals by translating them into operations on the corresponding contracts.

3   Running Example: Vehicle Platooning

We consider a case study inspired by vehicle platooning as an illustrative example throughout the paper. We define goals for a vehicle participating in a platoon in the *following mode*, which adjusts speed and steering angle based on what is communicated by the leading vehicle. We assume that all the vehicles in the platoon communicate via Vehicle Ad hoc Networks (VANETs), established with the IEEE 802.11p standard, a specially designed protocol for intelligent transportation systems (ITS) [33], offering at most 27 Mbps of data transmission rate. The propagation delay is the difference between the time-stamps for message reception, t_{Rx}, and message transmission, t_{Tx}, i.e., $d = t_{Rx} - t_{Tx}$. The necessary time interval $d_{(i,j)}$ for a successful end-to-end transmission of a message of L bits between a pair of vehicles (i, j) is:

$$d_{(i,j)} = \frac{L}{f_{(i,j)}}, \tag{1}$$

where $f_{(i,j)}$ is the *transmission rate* between the i-th and the j-th vehicle. We consider a platoon consisting of N vehicles, where the first one is the leader and the remaining $N - 1$ are the followers. To reach all followers, a message generated by the leader propagates for at most $N - 1$ hops. We assume the same transmission rate $f = 3$ Mbps between adjacent vehicles and a fixed message length size $L = 400$ bytes.

4   The CoGoMo Approach

CoGoMo revolves around a new formal model, termed *contract-based goal tree* (CGT), and a set of operations on it. A CGT is a tree $T = (\varUpsilon, \varSigma)$, where each node $v \in \varUpsilon = \varGamma \cup \varDelta$ is either a *goal node* $\gamma \in \varGamma$ or an *operator node* $\delta \in \varDelta$, with $\varGamma \cap \varDelta = \emptyset$. Each goal node contains the formalization of a goal in terms of a contract. Each operator node assumes a value in the set $\{\parallel, \wedge, \curlywedge\}$ of available

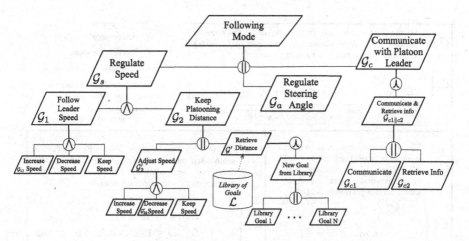

Fig. 1. Portion of the CGT for the vehicle platooning example.

operators, namely, composition, conjunction, and refinement, respectively. Each edge $\sigma \in \Sigma$ connects a goal node in Γ to an operator node in Δ or *vice versa*. Figure 1 shows a portion of a CGT for the vehicle platooning example, where each goal node includes a textual description of a goal. A *library* $\mathcal{L}$ of goals, at the bottom of the figure, is used to automatically extend the CGT. A library of goals is a set of pre-defined goals, e.g., specification patterns, that can be labelled by a *cost*, capturing the overhead incurred when employing a certain goal to extend the CGT, as further illustrated below.

A CGT can be built interactively using a web interface and with the support of a proof-of-concept tool, which is released open-source [18]. A designer can insert (new) goals by typing or uploading a structured text file, while the contracts are specified by formulas expressed in the language of an SMT solver [10]. The specification formalization process then iterates between two activities: (i) goal identification and formalization with A/G contracts, and (ii) goal manipulation, incrementally linking goals via composition, conjunction, and refinement. The outcome is a formal specification in terms of a CGT.

4.1 Goal Formalization

CoGoMo enables requirement formalization by representing goals in terms of contracts. It then solves contract verification problems to detect conflicts and incompleteness among goals. Specifically, completeness and consistency checking problems translate into checking the satisfiability and validity of logic formulas via an SMT solver [10]. In this paper, we express contract assumptions and guarantees as formulas in propositional logic, where atomic propositions include Boolean variables or arithmetic predicates on real variables.

Detecting Conflicts. CoGoMo detects conflicts by checking the compatibility, consistency, and feasibility of each contract formalizing a goal in the CGT.

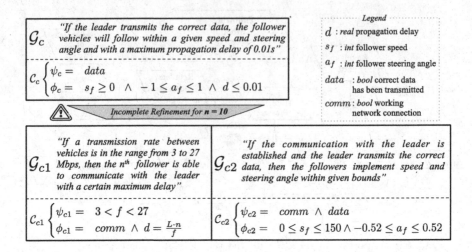

Fig. 2. Examples of three goals formalized by contracts. After linking the goals via composition and refinement, CoGoMo detects that the refinement is incomplete.

Feasibility checking aims to verify that there exists at least an implementation which does not violate the assumptions, that is, for contract $C = (A, G)$, $A \cap G \neq \emptyset$ holds. CoGoMo verifies compatibility, consistency, and feasibility of a contract (ψ, ϕ) by checking whether ψ, ϕ, and $\psi \wedge \phi$ are satisfiable, respectively. In case of conflict, the SMT solver provides an explanation of infeasibility in terms of an *unsat core*, i.e., a subset of clauses that are mutually unsatisfiable [10]. CoGoMo then links the conflicting clauses to the goals that generated them and presents these goals to the designer.

Checking Completeness. CoGoMo checks completeness by verifying that all the refinement links of the CGT are correct. Given two contracts, $C = (\psi, \phi)$ and $C' = (\psi', \phi')$, $C \preceq C'$ holds if and only if $\psi' \rightarrow \psi$ and $\phi \rightarrow \phi'$ are *valid* formulas, i.e., they are tautologies for the language, where $\rightarrow$ denotes the implication. Validity checking can be translated into checking the satisfiability of $\overline{\psi' \rightarrow \psi}$ or $\overline{\phi \rightarrow \phi'}$. If no solution is found, then the refinement is correct; otherwise, the returned solution serves as a certificate of incompleteness, and is exhibited to the designer.

4.2   Goal Manipulation via Composition and Refinement

CoGoMo uses composition to capture with a single goal the composite behaviors resulting from the composition of modules (implementations) that are separately specified by different goals. For example, goal $\mathcal{G}_c$ in Fig. 1 can be refined by the composition of $\mathcal{G}_{c1}$ with $\mathcal{G}_{c2}$. Figure 2 proposes an initial formalization of $\mathcal{G}_c$ as a contract C_c and its further decomposition into two goals, $\mathcal{G}_{c1}$ and $\mathcal{G}_{c2}$, establishing requirements on the network connection and the follower's speed and angle ranges, respectively. $\mathcal{G}_{c1}$ specifies the propagation delay d according to the transmission rate f (in Mbps), the message length L, and the position n of the follower participating in the platoon. Assuming a working network connection, $\mathcal{G}_{c2}$ guarantees that the speed of the follower is at most 150 km/h and its steering angle at most $30°$ (0.52 rad). We would like to show that $\mathcal{G}_{c1} \parallel \mathcal{G}_{c2} = \mathcal{G}_{c1\parallel c2}$ can be connected to the top goal $\mathcal{G}_c$ via refinement, i.e., $\mathcal{G}_{c1\parallel c2} \preceq \mathcal{G}_c$. To do so, CoGoMo first checks for conflicts between $\mathcal{G}_{c1}$ and $\mathcal{G}_{c2}$ by verifying that the contract associated with $\mathcal{G}_{c1\parallel c2}$ is compatible, consistent, and feasible, which is the case in our example. However, CoGoMo detects that $\mathcal{G}_{c1\parallel c2}$ is not a refinement of $\mathcal{G}_c$ and provides a certificate showing that, for the 10th follower in the platoon, the propagation delay is slightly larger than $d = 0.01$, which violates the guarantees of $\mathcal{C}_c$. It is, however, still possible to circumvent the incompleteness of the refinement by strengthening the assumptions of $\mathcal{G}_{c1\parallel c2}$ to limit the size of the platoon to less than 10 vehicles, and by "propagating" this restriction to $\mathcal{G}_c$ via a mechanism of *assumption propagation*, as detailed below.

Assumptions Propagation. When eliciting the top-level goals of a specification in a hierarchical way, we may discover additional assumptions, associated with lower-level goals in the hierarchy, which were not known *a priori*. This inconsistency between assumptions at different levels of the hierarchy may be a reason for incompleteness in the refinement. Let $\mathcal{G}_a$ and $\mathcal{G}_r$ be two goals, and $\mathcal{C}_a = (\psi_a, \phi_a)$ and $\mathcal{C}_r = (\psi_r, \phi_r)$ their respective contracts. Assumption propagation ensures that $\psi_a \rightarrow \psi_r$ is valid, by propagating the assumption formula from the lower-level contract to the upper-level contract and conjoining it with the assumptions of the higher-level contract so that behaviors that are not in ψ_r are removed from ψ_a and ψ_a is redefined as $(\psi_a \wedge \psi_r)$. After assumption propagation, the top-level guarantees will also be updated by bringing $\mathcal{C}_a$ again in saturated form, i.e., by setting the guarantees to $\phi_a \vee \overline{(\psi_a \wedge \psi_r)}$. In our example, the new assumptions for $\mathcal{C}_c$ after propagation become

$$\psi_c = \quad 3 < f < 27 \quad \wedge \quad data \quad \wedge \quad n < 10,$$

which makes refinement complete and allows creating a refinement node in the CGT as in Fig. 1.

4.3   Goal Manipulation via Conjunction

CoGoMo uses conjunction to generate a goal that refines multiple goals or *scenarios*, which are active under different assumptions, and may not be simultaneously satisfiable. In our example, the goal $\mathcal{G}_s$, 'Regulate Speed,' in Fig. 1 can be decomposed into two sub-goals, $\mathcal{G}_1$ and $\mathcal{G}_2$, specifying how the speed of a vehicle s should be regulated according to the leader's speed s_l or according to the distance d_{front} to the front vehicle, respectively. Because $\mathcal{G}_1$ and $\mathcal{G}_2$ should both be satisfied, albeit in different situations, we can define a single goal $\mathcal{G}_s = \mathcal{G}_1 \wedge \mathcal{G}_2$ for the system. The same procedure applies to the decomposition of $\mathcal{G}_1$ and $\mathcal{G}_2$. For example, the goal 'Adjust Speed' in Fig. 1 can be achieved by satisfying 'Increase Speed' or 'Decrease Speed' or 'Keep Speed,' which are not simultaneously satisfiable but are active under different assumptions.

If the assumptions of $\mathcal{G}_1$ and $\mathcal{G}_2$ are not mutually exclusive, the conjunction may require that potentially conflicting guarantees be satisfied simultaneously. For example, one of the contracts contributing to $\mathcal{G}_1$ may prescribe an *increase* of the follower's speed when there is an increase in the leader's speed, i.e., $\mathcal{C}_{11} = (s_t < s_l,\ s_{t+1} > s_t)$ where s_l, s_t and s_{t+1} represent the current speed of the leader and the speed of follower vehicle at times t and $t+1$, respectively. On the other hand, one of the contracts contributing to $\mathcal{G}_2$ may prescribe a *decrease* in the follower's speed when the distance to the vehicle in front is detected and it is less than a certain threshold, i.e., $\mathcal{C}'_{22} = (dist \wedge d_{\text{front}} < D_p,\ s_{t+1} < s_t)$, where *dist* evaluates to true if and only if the distance from the vehicle in front was detected correctly and $d_{\text{front}} < D_p$ indicates that the distance should be less than a constant (i.e., "the platooning distance"). The assumptions of $\mathcal{C}_{11}$ and $\mathcal{C}'_{22}$ can be satisfied simultaneously, possibly causing conflicts in the guarantees of the joint contract $(\psi_{11} \rightarrow (s_{t+1} > s_t)) \wedge (\psi'_{22} \rightarrow (s_{t+1} < s_t))$. CoGoMo prevents such conflicts via a *goal priority* mechanism.

Goal Priority. A *goal priority* mechanism $\mathcal{P}(\mathcal{G}_1, \mathcal{G}_2)$ avoids such potential conflicts by making the assumptions mutually exclusive so that only one goal is effective under any environment. For instance, a priority mechanism may set $\mathcal{C}_2 = (\psi_2 \wedge \overline{\psi_1}, \phi_2)$, assuming that $\psi_2 \wedge \overline{\psi_1}$ is satisfiable, so that $\mathcal{C}_1$ is granted higher priority and dominates whenever both ψ_2 and ψ_1 hold. Because the assumptions of $\mathcal{C}_2$ become stronger, an assumption propagation step may also be needed to keep the refinement relations correct across the CGT. In our example, prioritizing $\mathcal{G}_1$ versus $\mathcal{G}_2$ solves the potential conflict. $\mathcal{G}_s$ can then be satisfied if the vehicle adjusts its speed according to the information provided by the distance sensor. When d_{front} is not available, as denoted by *dist*, the vehicle regulates its speed according to the speed of the leader of the platoon.

When composing a goal that was previously obtained by conjunction, e.g., when composing $\mathcal{G}_2$ with $\mathcal{G}_c$ in Fig. 1, it may be useful to separately reason about the different scenarios involved in the composition. To do so, we use the fact that, given three contracts $\mathcal{C}_1$, $\mathcal{C}_2$, and $\mathcal{C}_c$, $[(\mathcal{C}_1 \wedge \mathcal{C}_2) \parallel \mathcal{C}_c] = [(\mathcal{C}_1 \parallel \mathcal{C}_c) \wedge (\mathcal{C}_2 \parallel \mathcal{C}_c)]$ holds, and we can separately identify the scenarios associated with $(\mathcal{C}_1 \parallel \mathcal{C}_c)$ and $(\mathcal{C}_2 \parallel \mathcal{C}_c)$ in the composition. In words, while composition is not distributive over conjunction in general [2], the distributive property holds in the special case of three contracts as above. A proof of this result is in the appendix.

5   CGT Extension

Given a leaf node $\mathcal{G}'$ in a CGT and a library of goals $\mathcal{L}$, the extension problem consists in finding a set of goals $\mathcal{G}_1, \mathcal{G}_2, \ldots, \mathcal{G}_n$ in $\mathcal{L}$, that, once composed, refine $\mathcal{G}'$. The CGT is then extended by linking $\mathcal{G}'$ to a node $\mathcal{G}_s$ via refinement, and $\mathcal{G}_s$ to $\mathcal{G}_1, \mathcal{G}_2, \ldots, \mathcal{G}_n$ via composition. Formally, we require:

Algorithm 1: Goals Selection

Input: Library of goals $\mathcal{L} = \{\mathcal{G}_1, \mathcal{G}_2, ..., \mathcal{G}_n\}$ with contracts $\{\mathcal{C}_1, \mathcal{C}_2, ..., \mathcal{C}_n\}$ respectively, input-goal $\mathcal{G}'$ with contract $\mathcal{C}' = (\psi', \phi')$

Output: Set of goals $\mathcal{L}_c \subseteq \mathcal{L}$ that composed would result in a goal $\mathcal{G}_l$ and contract $\mathcal{C}_l = (\psi_l, \phi_l)$ such that $\psi_l \wedge \psi'$ is satisfiable and $\phi_l \rightarrow \phi'$ is valid.

1 $\mathcal{L}_c = \emptyset$ is the set of goals to be returned

2 $R = \{(\mathcal{G}_1, \mathcal{G}_2, \mathcal{G}_4), (\mathcal{G}_1, \mathcal{G}_5), (\mathcal{G}_2, \mathcal{G}_3), ...\}$ is a set of *candidate compositions*, where each element $R_i \subseteq \mathcal{L}$ and the composition of the goals contained in R_i results in a goal with a contract $\mathcal{C}_p = (\psi_p, \phi_p)$, such that
  - $\psi_p \wedge \psi'$ is a satisfiable formula
  - $\phi_p \rightarrow \phi'$ is a valid formula

3 $K = \{\mathcal{G}_i, \mathcal{G}_j, .., \mathcal{G}_m\} = \mathbf{optimal\_selection}(R)$

4 $\mathcal{L}_c \leftarrow K$ adds the selected goals to $\mathcal{L}_c$

5 $\mathcal{S} \leftarrow K$ where $\mathcal{S}$ is the set of goals whose assumptions need to be searched in the library

6 while $\mathcal{S} \neq \emptyset$ **do**

7   **for** *goal* $\mathcal{G}_s$ *in* $\mathcal{S}$ *where* $\mathcal{C}_s = (\psi_s, \phi_s)$ **do**

7.1 $Q = \{(\mathcal{G}_1, \mathcal{G}_2, \mathcal{G}_3), (\mathcal{G}_2, \mathcal{G}_5), (\mathcal{G}_1, \mathcal{G}_3), ...\}$ is a set of *candidate compositions*, where each element $Q_i \subseteq \mathcal{L}$ and the composition of the goals in Q_i has a contract $\mathcal{C}_q = (\psi_q, \phi_q)$ such that:
  - $\psi_q \wedge \psi' \wedge \psi_s$ is a satisfiable formula
  - $\phi_q \rightarrow \psi_s$ is a valid formula

7.2 $H = \{\mathcal{G}_i, \mathcal{G}_j, .., \mathcal{G}_m\} = \mathbf{optimal\_selection}(Q)$

7.3 $\mathcal{L}_c \leftarrow \mathcal{L}_c \cup H, \quad \mathcal{S} \leftarrow \mathcal{S} \cup H$

7.4 $\mathcal{S} \leftarrow \mathcal{S} - \{\mathcal{G}_s\}$ removes the $\mathcal{G}_s$ from $\mathcal{S}$

8 return $\mathcal{L}_c$

$$\mathcal{C}_s = \mathcal{C}_1 \parallel \mathcal{C}_2 \parallel .... \parallel \mathcal{C}_n = (\psi_s, \phi_s),$$

where $\psi_s \wedge \psi'$ is satisfiable   and $\phi_s \rightarrow \phi'$ is valid.

When connecting $\mathcal{G}_s$ to $\mathcal{G}'$ via a refinement edge, CoGoMo also uses assumption propagation, as described in Sect. 4.2, to ensure that $\psi' \rightarrow \psi_s$ is valid.

Algorithm 1 proposes a procedure to automatically extend a CGT leaf node. The algorithm takes as inputs a goal node $\mathcal{G}'$ and a library of goals $\mathcal{L}$, and returns the set of goals to be composed as output. We assume that each goal in the library is labeled by a *cost* that is proportional to the number of clauses in the assumptions. The cost of a solution is the sum of the costs of all the selected goals. We first choose the lowest-cost selection of goals from $\mathcal{L}$ whose guarantees, once composed, imply the guarantees of $\mathcal{C}'$. Then, we choose the lowest-cost selection of goals from $\mathcal{L}$ whose guarantees, once composed, imply the assumptions of the goals selected in the previous iteration, and repeat this step until there are no more goals in the library or there are no assumptions that can be relaxed, i.e., discharged by the guarantees of another contract from

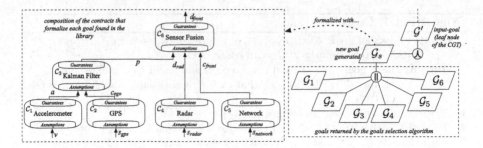

Fig. 3. Example of CGT extension via a library of goals. The left-hand side shows the composition of contracts used to formalize $\mathcal{G}_s$ and extend the CGT on the right-hand side.

the library. Concretely, given a input-goal $\mathcal{G}'$, where $\mathcal{C}' = (\psi', \phi')$, we look for all the combinations of goals in $\mathcal{L}$ such that their composition $\mathcal{C}_l = (\psi_l, \phi_l)$, has guarantees ϕ_l that imply either the guarantees of the input goal ϕ' (line 2) or its assumptions ψ' (line 7.1). We evaluate the cost of all the candidate compositions and select the candidate with the lowest cost (lines 3, 7.2). If multiple candidates have the same cost, we compose all the goals in each candidate set and select the composition that has the weakest assumptions.

Our cost metric favors the selection of goals with weaker assumptions (shorter assumption formulas), as they pose less constraints to the environment and support a larger number of contexts. On the other hand, a goal with a longer assumption formula tends to accept a smaller set of environments and require a more complex aggregation of goals from the library to discharge the assumptions. However, other cost functions are also possible. Searching for a composition of goals in the library that minimizes a cost function can be exponential in the size of the library. We circumvent the worst-case complexity by adopting a greedy strategy, which select the lowest-cost goal at each iteration, even if this does not necessarily lead to a globally optimal solution. As new goals are selected, they are aggregated via composition. Therefore, at each iteration, Algorithm 1 searches for the weakest-assumption contract whose guarantees discharge the assumptions of the composite contract obtained in the previous iteration.

As an example, we extend $\mathcal{G}'$ in Fig. 1, which specifies the precision with which the distance from the vehicle in front is retrieved, when this information is available. The associated contract $\mathcal{C}' = (--, \, dist \, \wedge \, d_{\text{front}} > 0 \, \wedge \, |d_{\text{front}} - d_{\text{real}}| < \delta)$ guarantees that the information on the distance $dist$ is available and that the perceived distance with the vehicle in front d_{front} is positive and has a precision δ in all contexts, where δ is a constant. We then use a library of goals specifying GPS modules, accelerometers, several kinds of radars with different levels of accuracy, and communication components. The extension algorithm returns 6 goals whose composition $\mathcal{G}_s$ is linked via refinement to $\mathcal{G}'$ in Fig. 3.

The left-hand side of Fig. 3 shows the contracts formalizing the new goal $\mathcal{G}_s$ and their interconnection structure. Each edge between contracts is labeled with a proposition that represents the logic predicate forming the assumptions

Table 1. Average execution times (sec) of 100 runs for different configurations of library size (number of goals in the columns) and contract complexity (rows).

	100	200	300	400	500	600	700	800	900	1000
4	0.49	0.94	1.32	1.78	2.14	2.53	2.99	3.45	3.82	4.09
8	1.42	2.71	3.89	5.20	6.49	7.73	9.09	10.41	11.82	13.10
16	4.84	10.74	16.04	18.97	23.27	29.05	35.16	36.85	41.30	46.61
20	6.33	12.62	18.40	24.58	32.70	39.83	45.45	56.09	63.83	70.33
24	8.79	17.14	25.59	34.07	49.45	54.98	64.34	71.91	84.10	94.13

or the guarantees of a contract (or both in case the guarantees of one contract imply some of the propositions in the assumptions of another contract). For example, the contract $\mathcal{C}_3$ in Fig. 3, which specifies a Kalman Filter component, has assumptions $a \wedge c_{ego}$ and guarantees p. The composition of $\mathcal{C}_3$ with $\mathcal{C}_1 = (v, a)$ and $\mathcal{C}_2 = (s_{gps}, c_{ego})$ results in a contract, where a and c_{ego} are no longer present in the assumptions, since they are already supported by the guarantees. The net result is a simpler assumption formula. By composing all the goals retrieved from the library we obtain a new goal $\mathcal{G}_s$ and associated contract $\mathcal{C}_s = (\psi_s, \phi_s)$, where

$$\psi_s = v \wedge s_{gps} \wedge s_{radar} \wedge s_{network} \wedge a \wedge c_{ego} \wedge p \wedge d_{rad} \wedge c_{front}$$
$$\vee \overline{(a \wedge c_{ego} \wedge p \wedge d_{rad} \wedge c_{front} \wedge d_{front})}$$
$$\phi_s = a \wedge c_{ego} \wedge p \wedge d_{rad} \wedge c_{front} \wedge d_{front}.$$

As in the previous example, the assumption formula reduces to $\psi_s = (v \wedge s_{gps} \wedge s_{radar} \wedge s_{network} \vee \overline{d_{front}})$. We observe that ϕ_s refines the guarantees of $\mathcal{C}'$ because $d_{front} = dist \wedge d_{\text{front}} > 0 \wedge |d_{\text{front}} - d_{\text{real}}| < \epsilon$ where ϵ is a constant and $\epsilon \leq \delta$. Finally, to preserve the completeness of the refinement, CoGoMo propagates the assumptions ψ_s to $\mathcal{C}'$ and then to the parent nodes of $\mathcal{G}'$ recursively, by following the edges of the CGT up to the root.

Numerical Validation. Algorithm 1 is sound and complete. The soundness is provided by the SMT solver, which checks the validity and satisfiability of the formulas. The completeness is given by the fact that the algorithm searches over the entire goal library. Because of the greedy procedure, the computation time scales linearly with the number of goals in the library. We performed numerical evaluation of synthetically generated libraries of different sizes populated by randomly generated goals. Goals are captured by simple propositional logic contracts, whose assumptions and guarantees are conjunctions of Boolean propositions. We use the length of these formulas, i.e., to quantify the complexity of each contract. A configuration is defined by the number of goals in the library and the complexity of the contracts. We evaluated the algorithm on up to 1000 library goals and up to 24 logical propositions in each contract for a total of 50 different configurations. For each configuration, we ran Algorithm 1 with 100 different input goals. Table 1 shows the average execution time for each configuration normalized by the number of goals returned by the algorithm. Figure 4

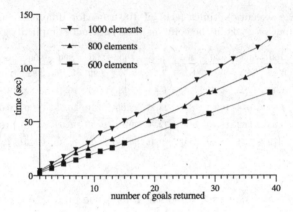

Fig. 4. Execution times as a function of the number of returned goals for 3 simulation configurations, with libraries of 600, 800, and 1000 elements, respectively, and contract complexity equal to 4.

shows the execution times for 3 configurations, which scale linearly with the number of returned goals and the size of the library.[1]

6   Related Work

In the context of contract-based verification, tools like OCRA [5] and AGREE [7] use contracts to model system components and their aggregations and formally prove the correctness of contract refinements [6] by using model checkers [3]. Related to system engineering, CONDEnSe [28] propose a methodology and a tool that leverages the algebra of contracts to integrate artifacts developed in mechatronic systems. More oriented toward requirement engineering, the CHASE [23] framework combines a front-end formal specification language based on patterns with rigorous, contract-based verification and synthesis. It uses a declarative style to define the top-level requirements that are then translated into temporal logic, verified for consistency and, when possible, synthesized into a reactive model. CoGoMo's hierarchical and incremental approach to refinement of goal models is complementary and can be naturally incorporated into CHASE.

In the context of goal-oriented requirement engineering, significant work has addressed completeness and conflict detection using formal methods for goal models based on KAOS [1,11,12]. While these approaches mostly focus on algorithms that operate on a fixed set of requirements and environment expectations, CoGoMo proposes a step-wise approach where refinement checking and conflict analysis are performed contextually in an incremental way as the goal tree is built. Frameworks like COVER [20] use TROPOS as a goal modeling framework, Modal Transition Systems (MTS) to model the system design, and Fluent

---

[1] Complete results: http://bit.ly/3s5XD0L.

Linear Temporal Logic (FLTL) as a specification language for functional requirements. COVER checks the satisfaction of all the requirements by verifying the properties on the system model. Requirement verification using formal methods is common to the goal-oriented approaches above; however, to the best of our knowledge, CoGoMo is the first effort toward formalizing goal models using contracts, thus enhancing modularity and reuse in goal models.

Compositional synthesis of reactive systems, i.e., finding generic aggregations of reactive components such that their composition realizes a given specification, is an undecidable problem [17,26]. The problem becomes decidable by imposing a bound on the total number of component instances that can be used, but remains difficult due to its combinatorial nature [16]. Our approach relates to the one by Iannopollo et al. [15,16], proposing scalable algorithms for compositional synthesis and refinement checking of temporal logic specifications out of contract libraries. Our goal selection algorithm is, however, different, as it uses a cost function based on the complexity of a specification, and a greedy procedure that favors more compact and generic specifications (i.e., contracts with weakest assumptions) to refine the goal tree, while keeping the problem tractable.

7 Conclusions

We presented CoGoMo, a framework that guides the designer in building goal models by leveraging a contract-based formalism. CoGoMo leverages contract operations and relations to check goal consistency, completeness, and support the incremental and hierarchical refinement of goals from a library of goals. An example motivated by vehicle platooning shows its effectiveness for incrementally constructing contract-based goal trees in a modular way, with formal guarantees of correctness. Numerical results also illustrate the scalability of the proposed greedy heuristic to further extend a goal tree out of a library of goals. As future work, we plan to extend the expressiveness of CoGoMo by i) supporting contracts expressed in temporal logic and ii) supporting OR-refinements between goals by allowing optional refinement relations between multiple candidate contracts. Furthermore, we plan to improve the tool and incorporate its features into CROME [19], our recent framework for formalizing, analyzing, and synthesizing robotic missions.

Acknowledgments. The authors wish to acknowledge Alberto Sangiovanni-Vincentelli, Antonio Iannopollo, and Íñigo Íncer Romeo for helpful discussions. This work was supported in part by the Wallenberg AI Autonomous Systems and Software Program (WASP), funded by the Knut and Alice Wallenberg Foundation. In addition, the authors gratefully acknowledge the support by the US National Science Foundation (NSF) under Awards 1846524 and 1839842, the US Defense Advanced Projects Agency (DARPA) under Award HR00112010003, the US Office of Naval Research (ONR) under Award N00014-20-1-2258, and Raytheon Technologies Corporation. The views, opinions, or findings contained in this article should not be interpreted as representing the official views or policies, either expressed or implied, by the US Government. This content is approved for public release; distribution is unlimited.

A   Distribution of Composition over Conjunction

Given contracts $\mathcal{C}_1 = (\psi_1, \phi_1)$, $\mathcal{C}_2 = (\psi_2, \phi_2)$, and $\mathcal{C}_3 = (\psi_3, \phi_3)$, we show that

$$(\mathcal{C}_1 \wedge \mathcal{C}_2) \parallel \mathcal{C}_3 = (\mathcal{C}_1 \parallel \mathcal{C}_3) \wedge (\mathcal{C}_2 \parallel \mathcal{C}_3). \tag{2}$$

Proof. Let (L_A, L_G) and (R_A, R_G) be the contracts on the left and right side of (2), respectively. We prove that $L_A = R_A$ and $L_G = R_G$. Both the composition and conjunction operations requires the conjunction of the guarantees, hence we obtain $L_G = R_G = \phi_1 \wedge \phi_2 \wedge \phi_3$. The assumptions of the contract on the left side can be computed as

$$L_A = (\psi_1 \vee \psi_2) \wedge \psi_3 \vee \overline{(\phi_1 \wedge \phi_2 \wedge \phi_3)} = (\psi_1 \wedge \psi_3) \vee (\psi_2 \wedge \psi_3) \vee \overline{\phi}_1 \vee \overline{\phi}_2 \vee \overline{\phi}_3.$$

On the right side, we obtain

$$\mathcal{C}_1 \parallel \mathcal{C}_3 = \left((\psi_1 \wedge \psi_3) \vee \overline{(\phi_1 \wedge \phi_3)}, \phi_1 \wedge \phi_3 \right) \text{ and}$$

$$\mathcal{C}_2 \parallel \mathcal{C}_3 = \left((\psi_2 \wedge \psi_3) \vee \overline{(\phi_2 \wedge \phi_3)}, \phi_2 \wedge \phi_3 \right),$$

which leads to

$$R_A = (\psi_1 \wedge \psi_3) \vee \overline{(\phi_1 \wedge \phi_3)} \vee (\psi_2 \wedge \psi_3) \vee \overline{(\phi_2 \wedge \phi_3)}$$
$$= (\psi_1 \wedge \psi_3) \vee (\psi_2 \wedge \psi_3) \vee \overline{\phi}_1 \vee \overline{\phi}_2 \vee \overline{\phi}_3.$$

Finally, we also obtain $L_A = R_A$, which concludes our proof (2).

References

1. Alrajeh, D., Kramer, J., Van Lamsweerde, A., Russo, A., Uchitel, S.: Generating obstacle conditions for requirements completeness. In: 2012 34th International Conference on Software Engineering (ICSE), pp. 705–715. IEEE (2012)
2. Benveniste, A., Caillaud, B., Nickovic, D., Passerone, R., et al.: Contracts for system design. Found. Trends Electron. Des. Autom. **12**(2–3), 124–400 (2018)
3. Cavada, R., et al.: The NUXMV symbolic model checker. In: Biere, A., Bloem, R. (eds.) CAV 2014. LNCS, vol. 8559, pp. 334–342. Springer, Cham (2014). https://doi.org/10.1007/978-3-319-08867-9_22
4. Cheng, B.H., Atlee, J.M.: Research directions in requirements engineering. In: 2007 Future of Software Engineering, pp. 285–303. IEEE Computer Society (2007)
5. Cimatti, A., Dorigatti, M., Tonetta, S.: OCRA: a tool for checking the refinement of temporal contracts. In: ASE 2013, pp. 702–705. IEEE (2013)
6. Cimatti, A., Tonetta, S.: Contracts-refinement proof system for component-based embedded systems. Sci. Comput. Program. **97**, 333–348 (2015)
7. Cofer, D., Gacek, A., Miller, S., Whalen, M.W., LaValley, B., Sha, L.: Compositional verification of architectural models. In: Goodloe, A.E., Person, S. (eds.) NFM 2012. LNCS, vol. 7226, pp. 126–140. Springer, Heidelberg (2012). https://doi.org/10.1007/978-3-642-28891-3_13

8. Damm, W., Hungar, H., Josko, B., Peikenkamp, T., Stierand, I.: Using contract-based component specifications for virtual integration testing and architecture design. In: 2011 Design, Automation & Test in Europe, pp. 1–6. IEEE (2011)
9. Darimont, R., Van Lamsweerde, A.: Formal refinement patterns for goal-driven requirements elaboration. ACM SIGSOFT Softw. Eng. Not. **21**(6), 179–190 (1996)
10. de Moura, L., Bjørner, N.: Z3: an efficient SMT solver. In: Ramakrishnan, C.R., Rehof, J. (eds.) TACAS 2008. LNCS, vol. 4963, pp. 337–340. Springer, Heidelberg (2008). https://doi.org/10.1007/978-3-540-78800-3_24
11. DeVries, B., Cheng, B.H.: Automatic detection of incomplete requirements via symbolic analysis. In: MODELS (2016)
12. DeVries, B., Cheng, B.H.: Automatic detection of feature interactions using symbolic analysis and evolutionary computation. In: 2018 IEEE International Conference on Software Quality, Reliability and Security (QRS), pp. 257–268. IEEE (2018)
13. Feldman, Y.A., Broodney, H.: A cognitive journey for requirements engineering. In: INCOSE International Symposium, vol. 26, pp. 430–444. Wiley Online Library (2016)
14. Ferrari, A., dell'Orletta, F., Spagnolo, G.O., Gnesi, S.: Measuring and improving the completeness of natural language requirements. In: Salinesi, C., van de Weerd, I. (eds.) REFSQ 2014. LNCS, vol. 8396, pp. 23–38. Springer, Cham (2014). https://doi.org/10.1007/978-3-319-05843-6_3
15. Iannopollo, A., Nuzzo, P., Tripakis, S., Sangiovanni-Vincentelli, A.: Library-based scalable refinement checking for contract-based design. In: 2014 Design, Automation & Test in Europe Conference & Exhibition (DATE), pp. 1–6. IEEE (2014)
16. Iannopollo, A., Tripakis, S., Sangiovanni-Vincentelli, A.: Constrained synthesis from component libraries. Sci. Comput. Program. **171**, 21–41 (2019)
17. Lustig, Y., Vardi, M.Y.: Synthesis from component libraries. Int. J. Softw. Tools Technol. Transfer **15**(5–6), 603–618 (2013)
18. Mallozzi, P.: CoGoMo tool - Web Interface and source code (2020). http://cogomo.duckdns.org/. https://github.com/pierg/cogomo
19. Mallozzi, P., Nuzzo, P., Pelliccione, P., Schneider, G.: Crome: contract-based robotic mission specification. In: 2020 18th ACM-IEEE International Conference on Formal Methods and Models for System Design (MEMOCODE). IEEE (2020)
20. Menghi, C., Spoletini, P., Ghezzi, C.: Integrating goal model analysis with iterative design. In: Grünbacher, P., Perini, A. (eds.) REFSQ 2017. LNCS, vol. 10153, pp. 112–128. Springer, Cham (2017). https://doi.org/10.1007/978-3-319-54045-0_9
21. Moitra, A., et al.: Towards development of complete and conflict-free requirements. In: 2018 IEEE 26th International Requirements Engineering Conference (RE), pp. 286–296. IEEE (2018)
22. Nuzzo, P., Finn, J., Iannopollo, A., Sangiovanni-Vincentelli, A.L.: Contract-based design of control protocols for safety-critical cyber-physical systems. In: Proceedings of the Design, Automation & Test in Europe Conference (DATE), pp. 1–4, March 2014
23. Nuzzo, P., Lora, M., Feldman, Y.A., Sangiovanni-Vincentelli, A.L.: CHASE: contract-based requirement engineering for cyber-physical system design. In: Proceedings of DATE 2018. IEEE (2018)
24. Nuzzo, P., Sangiovanni-Vincentelli, A., Bresolin, D., Geretti, L., Villa, T.: A platform-based design methodology with contracts and related tools for the design of cyber-physical systems. Proc. IEEE **103**(11) (2015)

25. Nuzzo, P., et al.: A contract-based methodology for aircraft electric power system design. IEEE Access **2**, 1–25 (2014). https://doi.org/10.1109/ACCESS.2013.2295764

26. Pneuli, A., Rosner, R.: Distributed reactive systems are hard to synthesize. In: 31st Annual Symposium on Foundation of Computer Science. IEEE (1990)

27. Sangiovanni-Vincentelli, A., Damm, W., Passerone, R.: Taming Dr. Frankenstein: contract-based design for cyber-physical systems. Eur. J. Control **18**(3) (2012)

28. Ribeiro dos Santos, C.A., Saleh, A., Schrijvers, T., Nicolai, M.: Condense: contract-based design synthesis. In: Proceedings of Models 2019 (2019)

29. Van Lamsweerde, A.: Requirements engineering in the year 00: a research perspective. In: Proceedings of the 22nd International conference on Software Engineering (2000)

30. Van Lamsweerde, A.: Goal-oriented requirements engineering: a guided tour. In: International Symposium on Requirements Engineering (2001)

31. Van Lamsweerde, A.: Requirements Engineering: From System Goals to UML Models to Software, vol. 10. Wiley, Chichester (2009)

32. Van Lamsweerde, A., Darimont, R., Massonet, P.: Goal-directed elaboration of requirements for a meeting scheduler: problems and lessons learnt. In: RE 1995 (1995)

33. Wang, Y., Duan, X., Tian, D., Lu, G., Yu, H.: Throughput and delay limits of 802.11p and its influence on highway capacity. Procedia Soc. Behav. Sci. **96**(Cictp), 2096–2104 (2013)

34. Zowghi, D., Gervasi, V.: On the interplay between consistency, completeness, and correctness in requirements evolution. Inf. Softw. Technol. **45**(14), 993–1009 (2003). https://doi.org/10.1016/S0950-5849(03)00100-9

Logic

Adding Proof Calculi to Epistemic Logics with Structured Knowledge

Mario Benevides[1], Alexandre Madeira[2(✉)], and Manuel A. Martins[2]

[1] Universidade Federal Fulminence, Niterói, Brazil
[2] CIDMA and Dep. Mathematics of Universidade de Aveiro, Aveiro, Portugal
madeira@ua.pt

Abstract. Dynamic Epistemic Logic (DEL) is used in the analysis of a wide class of application scenarios involving multi-agents systems with local perceptions of information and knowledge. In its classical form, the knowledge of epistemic states is represented by sets of propositions. However, the complexity of the current systems, requires other richer structures, than sets of propositions, to represent knowledge on their epistemic states. Algebras, graphs or distributions are examples of useful structures for this end. Based on this observation, we introduced a parametric method to build dynamic epistemic logics on-demand, taking as parameter the specific knowledge representation framework (e.g., propositional, equational or even a modal logic) that better fits the problems in hand. In order to use the built logics in practices, tools support is needed. Based on this, we extended our previous method with a parametric construction of complete proof calculi. The complexity of the model checking and satisfiability problems for the achieved logics are provided.

1 Introduction

Multi-agent (dynamic) epistemic logics [5,8,14] play an important role in a number of applied areas of Computer Science, including the analysis of secure protocols, knowledge acquisition systems, or cooperative multi-agents platforms (see [25]). Dyamic epistemic logic was introduced to represent and reason about agents, or groups of agents, knowledge and beliefs. Models for these logics are Epistemic Kripke Structures - multi-modal Kripke structures, whose states formalize information as set of propositions, and, for each agent, an equivalence relation between edges, relating indistinguishable states from the point of view of each agent.

In order to deal with scenarios that involve information and knowledge better represented using richer structures than simple sets of propositions, we proposed in our previous paper [19] a method to construct more expressive epistemic logics. From this method, called 'epistemisation', we derived a number of epistemic logics able to represent the knowledge of states as the usual structures of computer science, including propositions, graphs or abstract data types. The parameter

H. Hojjat and M. Massink (Eds.): FSEN 2021, LNCS 12818, pp. 53–68, 2021.
https://doi.org/10.1007/978-3-030-89247-0_4

used in this method, called knowledge representation framework, is defined by a set of formulas, a set of models, and a satisfaction relation. The formulas of the lower level play the role of the (atomic) propositions of the epistemic logic in the upper level; and these structures are used to represent the knowledge in each epistemic state on the models of the achieved logic.

The instantiations of the method discussed in the paper [19], some of them recalled below, provide an interesting starting point for their application to real scale case studies. However, as usual, the effective handling of real cases needs some level of tools support. This paper, extends the work presented in [19] in two different directions: firstly, we study the complexity of the model checking and the SAT problems on generic epistemisations; secondly, we introduce a parametric construction of Hilbert style calculus and we establish its completeness and decidability. The structure of knowledge representation, as introduced in the reference [19], was further endowed with an entailment system adequate for the respective satisfaction relation. The parametric principle of the constructions of logic calculus and the respective characterisations are inspired in the approach we followed for parametrised hybrid logics in the reference [22].

There are works that use epistemic models, in which states have a structure (e.g. [1,13]). In the work reported in [1], a multi-agent epistemic logic is introduced in which states are positions in $\mathbb{R}^n$ and the accessibility relations represent the possible states (positions) compatible with the current one. Also in the works reported in [13,15,16], (dynamic) epistemic logics based on the notion of visibility or observability of propositional variables are presented, i.e., some propositional variable are observable and others are not. Other works deal with values in an epistemic setting (e.g. [6,7,26]). Here, states are equipped with register that can store values (as in the paper [6]) or with constants that can have their values updated (as done in references [7,26]). In the case of the epistemisation of equational logic it reminds first order modal logic (see [10]), where epistemic states are relational structures.

Outline. The remaining of the paper is organized as follows: Sect. 2 overviews the epistemisation method introduced in [19] and a set of interesting instantiations is recalled. On view of the current paper aims, an enrichment of the notion of knowledge representation framework, the Boolean knowledge framework, was introduced. Then, in Sect. 3, we introduced a method to endow epistemisations with proof support. The method derive (complete) logical calculus for any epistemisation built on a (complete) calculus for the base knowledge representation framework. The complexity of the model checking and SAT problem for epistemisation is discussed in Sect. 4. Some final remarks are provided in Sect. 5.

2   Overview on Parametric Construction of Epistemic Logics with Structured States

This section overviews and extends the parametric construction of Epistemic Logics with structured states that we introduced in [19].

2.1 The Parameter

In order to represent knowledge of structured states, a generic notion of logic is needed. In our previous work [19], we introduced the *knowledge representation framework*. Basically, this framework will used to express properties about the (local) knowledge in states (e.g. if with propositions, equations or modal formulas), and to support its structure (if by valuations, algebras or graphs). Now, we enrich this notion with an inference relation satisfying the necessary conditions for the developments of the paper. This (local) inference relation will be used as the base of the (global) built logic.

Definition 1 ((Boolean) Knowledge Representation Framework). *A Knowledge Representation Framework is a tuple*

$$\mathcal{L} = (\mathrm{Fm}_{\mathcal{L}}, \mathrm{Mod}_{\mathcal{L}}, \models_{\mathcal{L}}, \vdash_{\mathcal{L}})$$

where

- $\mathrm{Fm}_{\mathcal{L}}$ *is a countable set of formulas,*
- $\mathrm{Mod}_{\mathcal{L}}$ *is a set of models for* $\mathcal{L}$,
- *relation* $\models_{\mathcal{L}} \subseteq \mathrm{Mod}_{\mathcal{L}} \times \mathrm{Fm}_{\mathcal{L}}$ *is a relation called* satisfaction relation *of* $\mathcal{L}$. *We write* $\Gamma \models_{\mathcal{L}} \varphi$ *whenever for any model* $M \in \mathrm{Mod}_{\mathcal{L}}$ *such that* $M \models_{\mathcal{L}} \gamma$, *for all* $\gamma \in \Gamma$, *it holds that* $M \models_{\mathcal{L}} \varphi$;
- $\vdash_{\mathcal{L}} \subseteq \mathcal{P}(\mathrm{Fm}_{\mathcal{L}}) \times \mathrm{Fm}_{\mathcal{L}}$ *is a relation called* entailment *of* $\mathcal{L}$.

A knowledge representation framework $\mathcal{L}$ *is a* Boolean knowledge representation framework, knowledge framework *for short, if:*

- *it has* semantic negation *i.e. for any formula* $\varphi \in \mathrm{Fm}_{\mathcal{L}}$ *there is a formula* $\neg\varphi \in \mathrm{Fm}_{\mathcal{L}}$ *such that, for any model* $M \in \mathrm{Mod}_{\mathcal{L}}$:

$$M \models_{\mathcal{L}} \neg\varphi \text{ iff it is false that } M \models_{\mathcal{L}} \varphi \tag{1}$$

- *is has* semantic conjunction, *i.e. for any finite set of formulas* $\Gamma \subseteq \mathrm{Fm}_{\mathcal{L}}$ *there is a formula* $\bigwedge \Gamma \in \mathrm{Fm}_{\mathcal{L}}$ *such that, for any model* $M \in \mathrm{Mod}_{\mathcal{L}}$,

$$\text{for any } \gamma \in \Gamma, M \models \gamma, \text{ iff } M \models \bigwedge \Gamma \tag{2}$$

(if Γ *has exactly two formulas* φ *and* φ' *we denote* $\bigwedge \Gamma$ *by* $\varphi \wedge \varphi'$).
- *is has* semantic implication, *i.e. for any two formulas* $\varphi, \varphi' \in \mathrm{Fm}_{\mathcal{L}}$ *there is a formula* $\varphi \to \varphi'$ *such that, for any model* $M \in \mathrm{Mod}_{\mathcal{L}}$,

$$M \models \varphi \to \varphi' \text{ iff } M \models \varphi \text{ implies that } M \models \varphi' \tag{3}$$

We say that a knowledge framework $\mathcal{L}$ is *sound* if for any $\varphi \in \mathrm{Fm}_{\mathcal{L}}$,

$$\text{if } \Gamma \vdash_{\mathcal{L}} \varphi \text{ then } \Gamma \models_{\mathcal{L}} \varphi \tag{4}$$

and we say that it is *complete* if for any $\varphi \in \mathrm{Fm}_{\mathcal{L}}$,

$$\text{if } \Gamma \models_{\mathcal{L}} \varphi \text{ then } \Gamma \vdash_{\mathcal{L}} \varphi \tag{5}$$

Now we proved two lemmas that will be used for the proof of the completeness of the logics built from the epistemisation method.

Lemma 1. *Let $\mathcal{L}$ be a knowledge framework and $\Gamma \subseteq \mathrm{Fm}_{\mathcal{L}}$ be finite set of formulas. Then, the following properties hold:*

1. *$\Gamma \models_{\mathcal{L}} \bigwedge \Gamma$*
2. *$\Gamma \models_{\mathcal{L}} \varphi$ iff $\models_{\mathcal{L}} \bigwedge \Gamma \to \varphi$*
3. *$\Gamma \models_{\mathcal{L}} \varphi$ and $\Gamma \subseteq \Delta$, then $\Delta \models_{\mathcal{L}} \varphi$*

A set of formulas $\Gamma \subseteq \mathrm{Fm}_{\mathcal{L}}$ is said $\mathcal{L}$-*consistent* iff does not exists a formula $\varphi \in \mathrm{Fm}_{\mathcal{L}}$ such that $\Gamma \vdash_{\mathcal{L}} \varphi$ and $\Gamma \vdash_{\mathcal{L}} \neg\varphi$. Moreover, $\Gamma \subseteq \mathrm{Fm}_{\mathcal{L}}$ is said $\mathcal{L}$-*maximal consistent* if it is $\mathcal{L}$-consistent and there is no $\mathcal{L}$-consistent set that properly contains it.

Lemma 2. *Let $\mathcal{L}$ be a sound and complete knowledge framework. For any finite consistent set of formulas $\Gamma \subseteq \mathrm{Fm}_{\mathcal{L}}$, there is a model $M_{\Gamma} \in \mathrm{Mod}_{\mathcal{L}}$ such that*

$$M_{\Gamma} \models_{\mathcal{L}} \bigwedge \Gamma \tag{6}$$

Proof. By 1. of Lemma 1, we know that $\Gamma \models_{\mathcal{L}} \bigwedge \Gamma$ and by (4) and (5) that by $\Gamma \vdash_{\mathcal{L}} \bigwedge \Gamma$. Since Γ is $\mathcal{L}$-consistent, we have also that $\Gamma \nvdash_{\mathcal{L}} \neg \bigwedge \Gamma$. By (4) and (5), $\Gamma \nvDash_{\mathcal{L}} \neg \bigwedge \Gamma$ and hence, there is a model $M_{\Gamma} \in \mathrm{Mod}_{\mathcal{L}}$ such that $M_{\Gamma} \models_{\mathcal{L}} \bigwedge \Gamma$ and $M_{\Gamma} \nvDash_{\mathcal{L}} \neg \bigwedge \Gamma$. Therefore, $M_{\Gamma} \models_{\mathcal{L}} \bigwedge \Gamma$.

2.2   The Method

As examples of Knowledge representation frameworks we can enumerate all the logics with a complete calculus. Classic Propositional, Equational Logic or the Hybrid Logic with Binders [3] can be useful in a number of application scenarios (see [19]).

Then, for a fixed knowledge representation $\mathcal{L}$ we define *the epistemisation of* $\mathcal{L}$ denoted by $\mathcal{E}(\mathcal{L})$. The set of formulas for the $\mathcal{L}$-epistemic logic for a finite set of agents Ag, in symbols $\mathrm{Fm}_{\mathcal{E}(\mathcal{L})}$, is defined by the following grammar:

$$\varphi ::= \varphi_0 \mid \neg\varphi \mid \varphi \wedge \varphi \mid K_a\varphi \mid E_G \mid C_G\varphi$$

where $\varphi_0 \in \mathrm{Fm}_{\mathcal{L}}$, $a \in \mathrm{Ag}$ and $G \subseteq \mathrm{Ag}$. If Γ is a finite set of formulas, the expression $\bigwedge \Gamma$ denote the conjunction of all the formulas in Γ.

The standard connectives can be presented as abbreviations, namely $\varphi \vee \varphi' \equiv \neg(\neg\varphi \wedge \neg\varphi')$, $\varphi \to \varphi' \equiv \neg(\varphi \wedge \neg\varphi')$, $B_a\varphi \equiv \neg K_a\neg\varphi$ and $E_G\varphi \equiv \bigwedge_{a \in G} K_a\varphi$. Here we are assuming that the Boolean connectives and the agent modalities symbols do not occur in the formulas $\mathrm{Fm}_{\mathcal{L}}$. If this is not the case we make the renaming of symbols.

The intuitive meaning of the modal formulas are:

- φ_0 - is an assertion about the (structured) epistemic states, expressed in the knowledge representation framework $\mathcal{L}$;
- $K_a\varphi$ - agent a knows φ;
- $E_G\varphi$ - every agent $a \in G$ knows φ;
- $C_G\varphi$ - it is common knowledge among all members of group G that it is the case that φ.

An $\mathcal{L}$-*epistemic model* for a finite set of agents Ag, Ag-model for short, is a tuple $\mathcal{M} = (W, \sim, M)$ where

- W is a non-empty set of states;
- $\sim$ is an Ag-family of equivalence relations $(\sim_a \subseteq W \times W)_{a \in Ag}$; and
- $M : W \to \text{Mod}_{\mathcal{L}}$ is a function, that assigns the knowledge structure of each state.

We also consider the relations $\sim_G = \bigcup_{a \in G} \sim_a$ and $\sim_G^* = (\sim_G)^*$, where $(\sim_G)^*$ is the reflexive, transitive closure of $\sim_G$. The set of $\mathcal{L}$-epistemic models for a set of agents Ag is denoted by $\text{Mod}_{\mathcal{E}(\mathcal{L})}$.

For any Ag-model $\mathcal{M} = (W, \sim, M)$, for any $w \in W$, and $\varphi \in \text{Fm}_{\mathcal{E}(\mathcal{L})}$, the satisfaction relation

$$\models \, \subseteq \, \text{Mod}_{\mathcal{E}(\mathcal{L})} \times \text{Fm}_{\mathcal{E}(\mathcal{L})}$$

is recursively defined as follows:

- $\mathcal{M}, w \models \varphi_0$ iff $M(w) \models_{\mathcal{L}} \varphi_0$, for any $\varphi_0 \in \text{Fm}_{\mathcal{L}}$
- $\mathcal{M}, w \models \neg\varphi$ iff $\mathcal{M}, w \not\models \varphi$
- $\mathcal{M}, w \models \varphi \wedge \psi$ iff $\mathcal{M}, w \models \varphi$ and $\mathcal{M}, w \models \psi$
- $\mathcal{M}, w \models K_a\varphi$ iff for all $w' \in W : w \sim_a w' \Rightarrow \mathcal{M}, w' \models \varphi$
- $\mathcal{M}, w \models E_G\varphi$ iff for all $w' \in W$ we have $w \sim_G w' \Rightarrow \mathcal{M}, w' \models \varphi$
- $\mathcal{M}, w \models C_G\varphi$ iff for all $w' \in W : w \sim_G^* w' \Rightarrow \mathcal{M}, w' \models \varphi$

We write $\mathcal{M} \models \varphi$ whenever, for any $w \in W$, $\mathcal{M}, w \models \varphi$.

It is easy to see that

- $\mathcal{M}, w \models B_a\varphi$ iff there is a $w' \in W$ such that $w \sim_a w'$ and $\mathcal{M}, w' \models \varphi$.

Note that the semantic interpretation of the Boolean connectives in $\mathcal{E}(\mathcal{L})$ coincides with the corresponding ones of the base logic $\mathcal{L}$.

Beyond of the Epistemisation of Propositional Logic $\mathcal{E}(\mathcal{PL})$, that captures the standard Epistemic Logic, we recall here a non standard epistemic logic obtained with this method:

Example 1. Let us present the 'epistemisation' of equational logic, the logic $\mathcal{E}(\mathcal{EQ})$. For that we consider a similar game of the classic envelops example from [5] (see also [19]) . From the four algebras (in a signature with a binary symbol $\odot$, an unary operation symbol *inv* and a constant symbol e) depicted in the model $\mathcal{N}$ represented below, one algebra is chosen. There are three players, Ana, Bob and Clara represented by the symbols a, b and c, that have some information about the chosen algebra. The epistemic representation of the scenario is depicted in the following diagram:

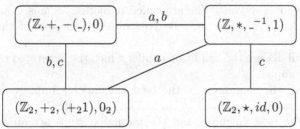

The operations of the algebras of the top line are the usual integers sum and product and the respective inverses. The operations of the bottom left algebra are the standard sum and inverse on the cyclic field $\mathbb{Z}_2$. The binary operation $\star$ of the bottom right algebra is defined by

$$\star(x,y) = \begin{cases} 1 & \text{if } x = 0, y = 1 \\ 0 & \text{otherwise} \end{cases}.$$

The following properties are valid in this model: *Ana knows that $\odot$ is associative*, expressed by the sentence $K_a\big((x \odot y) \odot z = x \odot (y \odot z)\big)$; *Bob knows that e is a neutral element* expressed by $K_b\big(x \odot e = x \wedge e \odot x = x\big)$; and finally, *Clara knows that every element has an inverse*, expressed by the sentence $K_c\big(x \odot x^{-1} = e \wedge x^{-1} \odot x = e\big)$.

3   Proof Calculus

In order to axiomatize the logic $\mathcal{E}(\mathcal{L})$, it is only necessary to add the epistemic axioms to the axioms of $\mathcal{L}$. This is exactly what the Definition 2 does.

Definition 2. *Hilbert style axioms and rules for $\mathcal{E}(\mathcal{L})$*

Axioms: *(Epistemic)*

1. *All instantiations of propositional tautologies replacing formulas for propositional symbols,*
2. $\vdash K_a(\varphi \to \psi) \to (K_a\varphi \to K_a\psi)$,
3. $\vdash K_a\varphi \to \varphi$,
4. $\vdash K_a\varphi \to K_a K_a\varphi$ *(+ introspection)*,
5. $\vdash \neg K_a\varphi \to K_a \neg K_a\varphi$ *(− introspection)*,
6. $\vdash C_G\varphi \leftrightarrow E_G C_G\varphi$
7. $\vdash C_G(\varphi \to E_G\varphi) \to (\varphi \to C_G\varphi)$

(Local) $\vdash \varphi$, *for all* $\phi \in \mathrm{Fm}_\mathcal{L}$ *s.t.* $\vdash_\mathcal{L} \varphi$
Rules:

(MP)   If $\vdash \varphi \to \psi$ and $\vdash \varphi$ then $\vdash \psi$
(Gen)   If $\vdash \varphi$ then $\vdash K_a\varphi$

The consequence relation $\Gamma \vdash \varphi$ is defined as usual (cf. [11]).

Axioms 2, 3, 4 and 5 are the standard S5 axioms. Axioms 6 and 7 are the well-known Segeberg axioms. The are called induction axioms. They define the common knowledge operator as reflexive transitive closure of the everybody knowledge.

Next, we will discuss the conditions under which the generated calculus $\vdash^{\mathcal{E}(\mathcal{L})}$ is sound and complete.

As expected, the soundness of the base calculus $\vdash_\mathcal{L}$ implies the soundness of $\vdash^{\mathcal{E}(\mathcal{L})}$. The proof is achieved by induction. The atomic case is exactly the soundness of the base calculus, and the induction steps are analogous to the ones of $\mathcal{E}$. Hence, whenever $\mathcal{L}$ is sound, we have:

Theorem 1. *Let $\mathcal{L}$ be a sound knowledge framework. Then, for any formula $\varphi \in Fm_{\mathcal{E}(\mathcal{L})}$,*

$$\vdash^{\mathcal{E}(\mathcal{L})} \varphi \text{ implies } \models^{\mathcal{E}(\mathcal{L})} \varphi$$

3.1 Completeness

We are going to prove completeness using Fisher and Ladner constructions ([9]), because we are interested in studying the model checking problem of our resulting logics.

In this section, we use the abbreviations $D_G\varphi \equiv \neg C_G\neg\varphi$ and $F_G\varphi \equiv \neg E_G\neg\varphi$. They are the duals of the common knowledge operator, C_G, and the everybody in the group G know operator E_G respectively.

The canonical model construction for $\mathcal{E}(\mathcal{L})$ follows the same steps of the construction of the canonical model for Propositional Dynamic Logic [4,11,18]. Next, we define the Fischer and Ladner Closure, which is a set of (sub-)formulae that are used to build the canonical model.

Definition 3. *(Fischer and Ladner Closure): Let Γ be a set of formulas, $G = \{a_1, \cdots, a_n\}$ be a finite set of agents. The **closure** of Γ, notation $C_{FL}(\Gamma)$, is the smallest set of formulas satisfying the following conditions:*

1. $C_{FL}(\Gamma)$ is closed under subformulas,
2. if $D_G\varphi \in C_{FL}(\Gamma)$, then $F_G D_G\varphi \in C_{FL}(\Gamma)$,
3. if $F_G\varphi \in C_{FL}(\Gamma)$, then $B_{a_1}\varphi \vee ... \vee B_{a_n}\varphi \in C_{FL}(\Gamma)$,
4. if $\varphi \in C_{FL}(\Gamma)$ and φ is not of the form $\neg\psi$, then $\neg\varphi \in C_{FL}(\Gamma)$.

The proof that if Γ is a finite set of formulas, then the closure $C_{FL}(\Gamma)$ of Γ is also finite, is rather standard and it can be found in the reference [9].

Next definition, introduces the notion of atoms, which are the correspondent of maximal consistent sets in standard canonical model proofs.

Definition 4. *Let Γ be a set of formulas. A set of formulas $\mathcal{A}$ is said to be an **atom of** Γ if it is a maximal consistent subset of $C_{FL}(\Gamma)$. The set of all atoms of Γ is denoted by $At(\Gamma)$.*

We need to guarantee that for every consistent set formulas, we can build an atom which contains it.

Lemma 3. *Let Γ be a finite set of formulas. If $\psi \in C_{FL}(\Gamma)$ and ψ is consistent then there exists an atom $\mathcal{A} \in At(\Gamma)$ such that $\psi \in \mathcal{A}$.*

Proof. We can construct the atom $\mathcal{A}$ as follows. First, we enumerate the elements of $C_{FL}(\Gamma)$ as $\varphi_1, \ldots, \varphi_n$. We start the construction making $\mathcal{A}_1 = \{\psi\}$, then for $1 < i < n$, we know that $\vdash \bigwedge \mathcal{A}_i \leftrightarrow (\bigwedge \mathcal{A}_i \wedge \varphi_{i+1}) \vee (\bigwedge \mathcal{A}_i \wedge \neg\varphi_{i+1})$ is a tautology and therefore either $\mathcal{A}_i \cup \{\varphi_{i+1}\}$ or $\mathcal{A}_i \cup \{\neg\varphi_{i+1}\}$ is consistent. We take $\mathcal{A}_{i+1}$ as the union of $\mathcal{A}_i$ with the consistent member of the previous disjunction. At the end, we make $\mathcal{A} = \mathcal{A}_n$.

For a given set of agents Ag, we defined $Ag^* = \{G | G \subseteq Ag\} \cup \{G^* | G \subseteq Ag\}$. The definition of the canonical relation have to consider the three modalities patterns:

Definition 5. *Let $\Gamma \subseteq Fm_{\mathcal{E}(\mathcal{L})}$ be finite. The* **canonical relation over** Γ, S^{Γ}, *is an Ag-family of relations* $(S_{\alpha}^{\Gamma} \subseteq At(\Gamma) \times At(\Gamma))_{\alpha \in Ag^*}$ *defined, for each* $\alpha \in Ag^*$, *as follows:*
If $\alpha = a \in Ag$

$$\mathcal{A} S_a^{\Gamma} \mathcal{B} \text{ iff } \bigwedge \mathcal{A} \wedge B_a \bigwedge \mathcal{B} \text{ is consistent.} \tag{7}$$

If $\alpha = G \subseteq Ag$

$$\mathcal{A} S_a^{\Gamma} \mathcal{B} \text{ iff } \bigwedge \mathcal{A} \wedge E_G \bigwedge \mathcal{B} \text{ is consistent.} \tag{8}$$

If $\alpha = G^*$ *for some* $G \subseteq Ag$

$$\mathcal{A} S_a^{\Gamma} \mathcal{B} \text{ iff } \bigwedge \mathcal{A} \wedge C_G \bigwedge \mathcal{B} \text{ is consistent.} \tag{9}$$

In order to introduce a notion of canonical model for $\mathcal{E}(\mathcal{L})$, next lemma states that for any $\mathcal{E}(\mathcal{L})$-consistent set of formulas $\Gamma \subseteq Fm_{\mathcal{E}(\mathcal{L})}$, the subset $\Gamma_{\mathcal{L}} \subseteq \Gamma$ of the $\mathcal{L}$-formulas of Γ is $\mathcal{L}$-consistent. Hence, Lemma 2 assures the existence of a $\mathcal{L}$-model that satisfy it.

Lemma 4. *Let $\Gamma \subseteq Fm_{\mathcal{E}(\mathcal{L})}$ be finite and $\Gamma_{\mathcal{L}} = \{\varphi | \varphi \in \Gamma \text{ and } \varphi \in Fm_{\mathcal{L}}\}$. Then, if Γ is $\mathcal{E}(\mathcal{L})$-consistent, $\Gamma_{\mathcal{L}}$ is $\mathcal{L}$-consistent.*

Proof. Suppose that $\Gamma_{\mathcal{L}}$ is not $\mathcal{E}(\mathcal{L})$-consistent. Hence, there is a $\varphi_{\mathcal{L}} \in \Gamma_{\mathcal{L}}$ such that $\Gamma_{\mathcal{L}} \vdash_{\mathcal{L}} \varphi_{\mathcal{L}}$ and $\Gamma_{\mathcal{L}} \vdash_{\mathcal{L}} \neg\varphi_{\mathcal{L}}$. Hence, we have

$$
\begin{array}{llll}
\Gamma_{\mathcal{L}} \vdash_{\mathcal{L}} \varphi_{\mathcal{L}} \Leftrightarrow & \Gamma_{\mathcal{L}} \models_{\mathcal{L}} \varphi_{\mathcal{L}} & \text{by (4) and (5)} \\
\Leftrightarrow & \models_{\mathcal{L}} \bigwedge \Gamma_{\mathcal{L}} \rightarrow \varphi_{\mathcal{L}} & \text{by 1. of Lemma 1} \\
\Leftrightarrow & \vdash_{\mathcal{L}} \bigwedge \Gamma_{\mathcal{L}} \rightarrow \varphi_{\mathcal{L}} & \text{by (4) and (5)} \\
\Rightarrow & \vdash \bigwedge \Gamma_{\mathcal{L}} \rightarrow \varphi_{\mathcal{L}} & \text{by defn of } \vdash \\
\Rightarrow & \Gamma \vdash \varphi_{\mathcal{L}} &
\end{array}
$$

Analogously, from $\Gamma_{\mathcal{L}} \vdash_{\mathcal{L}} \neg\varphi_{\mathcal{L}}$ we obtain $\Gamma \vdash \neg\varphi_{\mathcal{L}}$, contradicting the assumption about the $\mathcal{E}(\mathcal{L})$-consistency of Γ. Therefore $\Gamma_{\mathcal{L}}$ is $\mathcal{L}$-consistent.

Remark 1. Note that as happens for $\mathcal{L}$, $\mathcal{E}(\mathcal{L})$ have semantic conjunction, negation and implication. Hence, Lemma 1 can be enunciated for $\mathcal{E}(\mathcal{L})$. Moreover, due its unicity, these connectives coincide.

Once we have defined atoms and canonical relations, we are ready to define our notion of model.

Definition 6. *Let Γ be a set of formulas, $At(\Gamma) = \{\mathcal{A}_1, \ldots, \mathcal{A}_n\}$. For each $1 \leq i \leq n$, $\mathcal{A}_i^{\mathcal{L}} = \{\varphi_1^i, \ldots, \varphi_{n_i}^i\} \subseteq \mathrm{Fm}_{\mathcal{L}}$ denotes the set of all $\mathcal{L}$-formulas in $\mathcal{A}_i$ and $M_{\mathcal{A}_i^{\mathcal{L}}}$ a $\mathcal{L}$-model that satisfies $\mathcal{A}_i^{\mathcal{L}}$ (cf. Lemma 2). A* **canonical model over** *Γ is a tuple*

$$\mathcal{M}^{\Gamma} = (At(\Gamma), S^{\Gamma}, M^{\Gamma})$$

such that $M^{\Gamma}(\mathcal{A}_i) = M_{\mathcal{A}_i^{\mathcal{L}}}$.

Next lemma, ensures that our knowledge modalities are working as expected over canonical models.

Lemma 5. *Let $\mathcal{A} \in At(\Gamma)$ and $B_a\varphi \in C_{FL}(\Gamma)$. Then:*

$$B_a\varphi \in \mathcal{A} \text{ iff there exists } \mathcal{B} \in At(\Gamma) \text{ such that } \mathcal{A}S_a^{\Gamma}\mathcal{B} \text{ and } \varphi \in \mathcal{B}. \tag{10}$$

Proof. $\Rightarrow$: Suppose $B_a\varphi \in \mathcal{A}$. By Definition 4, we have that $\bigwedge \mathcal{A} \wedge B_a\varphi$ is consistent. Using the tautology $\vdash \varphi \leftrightarrow ((\varphi \wedge \phi) \vee (\varphi \wedge \neg\phi))$, we have that either $\bigwedge \mathcal{A} \wedge B_a(\varphi \wedge \phi)$ is consistent or $\bigwedge \mathcal{A} \wedge B_a(\varphi \wedge \neg\phi)$ is consistent. So, by the appropriate choice of ϕ, for all formulas $\phi \in C_{FL}$, we can construct an atom $\mathcal{B}$ such that $\varphi \in \mathcal{B}$ and $\bigwedge \mathcal{A} \wedge B_a(\varphi \wedge \bigwedge \mathcal{B})$ is consistent and, by Definition 5, $\mathcal{A}S_a^{\Gamma}\mathcal{B}$.

$\Leftarrow$: Suppose there is $\mathcal{B}$ such that $\varphi \in \mathcal{B}$ and $\mathcal{A}S_a^{\Gamma}\mathcal{B}$. Then $\bigwedge \mathcal{A} \wedge B_a\bigwedge\mathcal{B}$ is consistent and also $\bigwedge \mathcal{A} \wedge B_a\varphi$ is consistent. But $B_a\varphi \in C_{FL}$ and by maximality $\langle a\rangle\varphi \in \mathcal{A}$.

Next lemma establishes that the canonical relation of a group of agents $G = \{a_1, \ldots, a_n\}$ is the union of the canonical relation for each agent a_i in the group in G.

Lemma 6. *Let $\Gamma \subseteq \mathrm{Fm}_{\mathcal{E}}(\mathcal{L})$ be a finite and $\mathcal{M}^{\Gamma} = (At(\Gamma), S^{\Gamma}, M^{\Gamma})$ a canonical model over Γ. Then, $S_G^{\Gamma} = S_{a_1}^{\Gamma} \cup \cdots \cup S_{a_n}^{\Gamma}$, for $G = \{a_1, \ldots, a_n\}$.*

Proof. $\Rightarrow$: Suppose $\mathcal{A}S^{\Gamma}{}_G\mathcal{B}$. This is iff $\bigwedge \mathcal{A} \wedge E_G\bigwedge \mathcal{B}$ is consistent. By definition $E_G\varphi \equiv B_{a_1}\varphi \vee \cdots \vee B_{a_n}\varphi$ and so $\bigwedge \mathcal{A} \wedge B_{a_1}\bigwedge\mathcal{B} \vee \cdots \vee B_{a_n}\bigwedge\mathcal{B}$ is consistent.

But for at least one a_i, $\bigwedge \mathcal{A} \wedge B_{a_i}\bigwedge\mathcal{B}$ is consistent. And then, $\mathcal{A}S_{a_i}^{\Gamma}\mathcal{B}$ and thus $\mathcal{A}(S_{a_1}^{\Gamma} \cup \cdots \cup S_{a_n}^{\Gamma})\mathcal{B}$.

$\Leftarrow$: Suppose $\mathcal{A}(S_{a_1} \cup \cdots \cup S_{a_n})\mathcal{B}$, so for at least one a_i, $\mathcal{A}S_{a_i}\mathcal{B}$. This is iff $\bigwedge \mathcal{A} \wedge B_{a_i}\bigwedge\mathcal{B}$ is consistent. But $\bigwedge \mathcal{A} \wedge B_{a_1}\bigwedge\mathcal{B} \vee \cdots \vee B_{a_n}\bigwedge\mathcal{B}$ is also consistent. By definition, $E_G\varphi \equiv B_{a_1}\varphi \cup \cdots \cup B_{a_n}\varphi$ and so $\bigwedge \mathcal{A} \wedge E_G\bigwedge\mathcal{B}$ is consistent. Thus, $\mathcal{A}S_G\mathcal{B}$.

Next lemma, ensures that our group modalities are working as expected over canonical models.

Lemma 7. *Let $\mathcal{A} \in At(\Gamma)$ and $E_G\varphi \in C_{FL}(\Gamma)$. Then,*

$$E_G\varphi \in \mathcal{A} \text{ iff there exists } \mathcal{B} \in At(\Gamma) \text{ such that } \mathcal{A}S_G\mathcal{B} \text{ and } \varphi \in \mathcal{B}. \tag{11}$$

Proof. ⇐: Suppose there exists $\mathcal{B} \in At(\Gamma)$ such that $\mathcal{AS}_G\mathcal{B}$ and $\varphi \in \mathcal{B}$. By Lemma 6, there exists $\mathcal{B} \in At(\Gamma)$ such that $(S_{a_1}^{\Gamma} \cup \cdots \cup S_{a_n}^{\Gamma})$ and $\varphi \in \mathcal{B}$. So for at least one a_i, there exists $\mathcal{B} \in At(\Gamma)$ such that $\mathcal{AS}_{a_i}^{\Gamma}\mathcal{B}$ and $\varphi \in \mathcal{B}$. By Lemma 5, $B_{a_i}\varphi \in \mathcal{A}$ and also $B_{a_1}\varphi \vee \cdots \vee B_{a_i}\varphi \vee \cdots \vee B_{a_n}\varphi \in \mathcal{A}$. By definition, $E_G\varphi \equiv B_{a_1}\varphi \vee \cdots \vee B_{a_n}\varphi$. Thus, $E_G\varphi \in \mathcal{A}$.

⇒: Suppose $E_G\varphi \in \mathcal{A}$. Then, By definition $E_G\varphi \equiv B_{a_1}\varphi \vee \cdots \vee B_{a_n}\varphi$, and so, by the definition of the closure, $B_{a_1}\varphi \vee \cdots \vee B_{a_n}\varphi \in \mathcal{A}$. But for at least one a_i, $B_{a_i}\varphi \in \mathcal{A}$. By Lemma 5, there exists $\mathcal{B} \in At(\Gamma)$ such that $\mathcal{AS}_{a_i}^{\Gamma}\mathcal{B}$ and $\varphi \in \mathcal{B}$. And also, there exists $\mathcal{B} \in At(\Gamma)$ such that $\mathcal{A}(S_{a_1}^{\Gamma} \cup \cdots \cup S_{a_n}^{\Gamma})\mathcal{B}$ and $\varphi \in \mathcal{B}$. By Lemma 6, there exists $\mathcal{B} \in At(\Gamma)$ such that $\mathcal{AS}_G^{\Gamma}\mathcal{B}$ and $\varphi \in \mathcal{B}$. ∎

This lemma, ensures that our common knowledge modalities are working as expected over canonical models.

Lemma 8. *Let $\mathcal{A}, \mathcal{B} \in At(\Gamma)$ and $G \subseteq$ Ag. Then,*

$$\text{if } \mathcal{AS}_{G*}^{\Gamma}\mathcal{B}, \text{ then } \mathcal{AS}_G^{\Gamma^*}\mathcal{B}. \tag{12}$$

Proof. Suppose $\mathcal{AS}_{G*}^{\Gamma}\mathcal{B}$. Let $\mathbf{C} = \{\mathcal{C} \in At(\Gamma) \mid \mathcal{AS}_{G*}^{\Gamma}\mathcal{C}\}$. We want to show that $\mathcal{B} \in \mathbf{C}$. Let $\mathbf{C}_{\vee}^{\wedge} = (\bigwedge \mathcal{C}_1 \vee \cdots \vee \bigwedge \mathcal{C}_n)$, where $\mathcal{C}_i \in \mathbf{C}$ for $1 \leq i \leq n$, be the disjunction of the conjunctions of the atoms in $\mathbf{C}$.

It is true that $\mathbf{C}_{\vee}^{\wedge} \wedge E_G\neg\mathbf{C}_{\vee}^{\wedge}$ is inconsistent, otherwise for some $\mathcal{D}$ not reachable from $\mathcal{A}$, $\mathbf{C}_{\vee}^{\wedge} \wedge E_G \bigwedge \mathcal{D}$ would be consistent, and for some $\mathcal{C}_i \in \mathbf{C}$, $\bigwedge \mathcal{C}_i \wedge E_G \bigwedge \mathcal{D}$ was also consistent, which would mean that $\mathcal{D} \in \mathbf{C}$, which is not the case. From a similar reasoning we know that $\bigwedge \mathcal{A} \wedge E_G\neg\mathbf{C}_{\vee}^{\wedge}$ is also inconsistent and hence $\vdash \bigwedge \mathcal{A} \rightarrow F_G\mathbf{C}_{\vee}^{\wedge}$ is a theorem.

As $\mathbf{C}_{\vee}^{\wedge} \wedge E_G\neg\mathbf{C}_{\vee}^{\wedge}$ is inconsistent, so its negation is a theorem $\vdash \neg(\mathbf{C}_{\vee}^{\wedge} \wedge E_G\neg\mathbf{C}_{\vee}^{\wedge})$ and also $\vdash (\mathbf{C}_{\vee}^{\wedge} \rightarrow F_G\mathbf{C}_{\vee}^{\wedge})$ (1), applying generalization $\vdash D_G(\mathbf{C}_{\vee}^{\wedge} \rightarrow F_G\mathbf{C}_{\vee}^{\wedge})$. Using Segerberg axiom (axiom 6), we have $\vdash (F_G\mathbf{C}_{\vee}^{\wedge} \rightarrow D_G\mathbf{C}_{\vee}^{\wedge})$ and by (1) we obtain $\vdash (\mathbf{C}_{\vee}^{\wedge} \rightarrow D_G\mathbf{C}_{\vee}^{\wedge})$. As $\vdash \bigwedge \mathcal{A} \rightarrow F_G\mathbf{C}_{\vee}^{\wedge}$ is a theorem, then $\vdash \bigwedge \mathcal{A} \rightarrow D_G\mathbf{C}_{\vee}^{\wedge}$. By supposition, $\bigwedge \mathcal{A} \wedge C_G \bigwedge \mathcal{B}$ is consistent and so is $\bigwedge \mathcal{B} \wedge \mathbf{C}_{\vee}^{\wedge}$. Therefore, for at least one $\mathcal{C} \in \mathbf{C}$, we know that $\bigwedge \mathcal{B} \wedge \bigwedge \mathcal{C}$ is consistent. By maximality, we have that $\mathcal{B} = \mathcal{C}$. And by the definition of $\mathbf{C}_{\vee}^{\wedge}$, we have $\mathcal{AS}_G^{*}\mathcal{B}$. ∎

Below, we define our notion of standard models, which are the expected desired models.

Definition 7. *Let $\Gamma \subseteq Fm_{\mathcal{E}}(\mathcal{L})$ be finite. A* **standard model over** Γ *is the tuple*
$$\mathcal{M}^{\Gamma} = (At(\Gamma), R, M^{\Gamma}), \text{ where}$$

- $R = (R_{\alpha} \subseteq W \times W)_{\alpha \in Ag^*}$ *defined as follows:*
    $R_a = S_a^{\Gamma}$;
    $R_G = R_{a_1} \cup \cdots \cup R_{a_n}$, *for* $G = \{a_1, \ldots, a_n\}$;
    $R_{G^*} = R_G^*$.
- $M^{\Gamma}(\mathcal{A}) = M_{\mathcal{A}^c}$

This lemma establishes the canonical model constructed is almost a standard model. But this result is enough to guarantee the construction of the standard canonical model need for the completeness proof.

Lemma 9. $S_G^\Gamma = R_G$ and $S_{G^*}^\Gamma \subseteq R_{G^*}$

Proof. This proof is straigthforward from Definition 7 and Lemma 6 and Lemma 8.

This lemma, ensures that our modalities also are working as expected over standard canonical models.

Lemma 10 (Existence Lemma). *Let* $\mathcal{A} \in At(\Gamma)$, $G \subseteq \mathrm{Ag}$. *Then,*

$$E_G\varphi \in \mathcal{A} \text{ iff there exists } \mathcal{B} \in At(\Gamma) \text{such that } \mathcal{A}R_{\overline{G}}\mathcal{B} \text{ and } \varphi \in \mathcal{B}$$

and

$$C_G\varphi \in \mathcal{A} \text{ iff there exists } \mathcal{B} \in At(\Gamma) \text{ such that } \mathcal{A}R_{G^*}\mathcal{B} \text{ and } \varphi \in \mathcal{B}.$$

Proof. $\Rightarrow$: it is analogous to the one presented for basic programs in Lemma 5 and the previous Lemma 9 that states that $S_\alpha \subseteq R_\alpha$.
$\Leftarrow$: By induction on the structure of α. This proof is rather standard in PDL literature (c.f. [11]).

Now we are in conditions to prove the Truth Lemma for $\mathcal{E}(\mathcal{L})$, a crucial piece to achieve the completeness. It states that for every formula in the closure, it belongs to an atom if and only if it is true at the correspondent state in the standard canonical model.

Lemma 11 (Truth Lemma).
Let $\psi \in Fm_{\mathcal{E}(\mathcal{L})}$ *and* M^ψ *the standard model over* $\{\psi\}$. *Then, for any* $\mathcal{A} \in At(\{\psi\})$, *and for all* $\varphi \in C_{FL}(\psi)$,

$$\mathcal{M}, \mathcal{A} \models^{\mathcal{E}(\mathcal{L})} \varphi \text{ iff } \varphi \in \mathcal{A}.$$

Proof. : The proof is by induction on the construction of φ.

- For $\mathcal{L}$-formulas the proof is straightforward from the definition of satisfaction and the definition of **M**.
- For Boolean operators: the proof is straightforward from the definition of satisfaction and the induction hypothesis.

Modality C_G:

$\Rightarrow$ Suppose $\mathcal{M}, \mathcal{A} \models^{\mathcal{E}(\mathcal{L})} C_G\varphi$, then there exists $\mathcal{A}'$ such that $\mathcal{A}R_G\mathcal{A}'$ and $\mathcal{M}, \mathcal{A}' \models^{\mathcal{E}(\mathcal{L})} \varphi$. By the induction hypothesis we know that $\varphi \in \mathcal{A}'$, and by Lemma 10 we have $C_G\varphi \in \mathcal{A}$.

$\Leftarrow$ Suppose $\mathcal{M}, \mathcal{A} \not\models^{\mathcal{E}(\mathcal{L})} C_G\varphi$, by the definition of satisfaction we have $\mathcal{M}, \mathcal{A} \models^{\mathcal{E}(\mathcal{L})} \neg C_G\varphi$.

Then for all $\mathcal{A}'$, $\mathcal{A}R_G\mathcal{A}'$ implies $\mathcal{M}, \mathcal{A}' \not\models^{\mathcal{E}(\mathcal{L})} \varphi$. By the induction hypothesis we know that $\varphi \notin \mathcal{A}'$, and by Lemma 10 we have $C_G\varphi \notin \mathcal{A}$.

The proof for the remaining modalities is analogous.

Now, we are ready to prove completeness showing that for every consistent formula we can build a standard canonical model which satisfies it.

Next, we state and prove the completeness theorem.

Theorem 2 (Completeness). $\mathcal{E}(\mathcal{L})$ *is complete.*

Proof. For every consistent formula φ we can build a model over $\{\varphi\}$, $\mathcal{M}^{\{\varphi\}}$. By Lemma 3, there exists an atom $\mathcal{A} \in At(\{\varphi\})$ such that $\varphi \in \mathcal{A}$, and by the Truth Lemma 11 $\mathcal{M}^{\{\varphi\}}, \mathcal{A} \models^{\mathcal{E}(\mathcal{L})} \varphi$.

4 Model Checking and Satisfiability Problem

In this section we are assuming that the model checking problem in $\mathcal{L}$ is decidable and its complexity is $\mathcal{MC}(\mathcal{L})$. We show that the model checking problem for $\mathcal{E}(\mathcal{L})$ is in PTime $\times \mathcal{MC}(\mathcal{L})$. It means that if $\mathcal{L}$ is a logic which the model checking problem is in PTime, then, this problem is also in PTime for $\mathcal{E}(\mathcal{L})$.

Definition 8. *The model checking problem consist of, given a formula φ and a finite $\mathcal{E}(\mathcal{L})$-model $\mathcal{M} = (W, \sim, M)$, determining the set $\mathcal{S}(\varphi) = \{v \in W \mid \mathcal{M}, v \models \varphi\}$.*

Next, we present the model checking algorithms for our epistemic logic for structured knowledge $\mathcal{E}(\mathcal{L})$ (Algorithm 1). Lets $label(v)$ denote the set of sub-formulas of ϕ that hold at state v, for all $v \in W$.

For the implementation of the algorithm CheckDIAM, we will use the notation $\langle x \rangle \varphi_1$, with $x = a, G, G^*$ as follows:

- $B_a\varphi$ is represented by $\langle a \rangle \varphi \equiv \langle \{a\} \rangle \varphi$;
- $F_G\varphi$, with $G = \{a_1, \ldots, a_n\}$ is represented by $\langle G \rangle \varphi \equiv \langle a_1 \cup \cdots \cup a_n \rangle \varphi$; and
- $C_G\varphi$ is represented by $\langle G^* \rangle \varphi$.

Theorem 3. *The model-checking problem for $\mathcal{E}(\mathcal{L})$ is linear in the product of the size of the model, the length of the formula and the $\mathcal{MC}(\mathcal{L})$ (the computational complexity of model checking a $\mathcal{L}$ formula).*

Proof. The algorithm Check_E(L)(ϕ) is called once for each sub-formula of ϕ which is $O(|\phi|)$ and each time it activates the algorithms Check_L, CheckNOT, CheckAND and CheckDIAM. The later, in worse case, has to search the whole model, this is $O(|W| + | \sim_x |)$ (for $x = a, G, G^*$), i.e., the order of the size of the model. So, the complexity of Check_E(L)(ϕ) is $O(|\phi| \times (|W| + | \sim_x |)) \times \mathcal{MC}(\mathcal{L})$. The algorithms CheckNOT and CheckAND take constant time.

Thus, the complexity of Check_E(L)(ϕ) is $O(|\phi| \times (|W| + |R_x|) \times \mathcal{MC}(\mathcal{L}))$.

In order to o build the set $S(\phi)$ we only need to search $label(v)$ for all $v \in W$ and check if $\phi \in label(v)$.

Algorithm 1. procedure Check_E(L)(ϕ)

---

if $\phi \in \mathcal{L}$ then
   $Check\_\mathcal{L}(\phi)$
end if
while $|\phi| \geq 1$ do
  if $\phi = (\neg\phi_1)$ then
    Check_E(L)(ϕ_1); $CheckNOT(\phi_1)$
  else if $\phi = (\phi_1 \wedge \phi_2)$ then
    Check_E(L)(ϕ_1); Check_E(L)(ϕ_2); $CheckAND(\phi_1, \phi_2)$
  else if $\phi = \langle x \rangle \phi_1$, for $x = a, G, G^*$ then
    Check_E(L)(ϕ_1)
    $CheckDIAM(\phi_1, x)$
  end if
end while

Algorithm 2. procedure CheckNOT(ϕ)

---

for all $v \in W$ do
  if $\phi \notin label(v)$ then
    $label(v) := label(v) \cup \{(\neg\phi)\}$
  end if
end for

Algorithm 3. procedure CheckAND(($\phi_1 \wedge \phi_2$))

---

for all $v \in W$ do
  if $\phi_1 \in label(v)$ and $\phi_2 \in label(s)$ then
    $label(v) := label(v) \cup \{(\phi_1 \wedge \phi_2)\}$
  end if
end for

Algorithm 4. procedure CheckDIAM(ϕ_1, x)

---

if $x = G$ then
  $\sim_x = \sim_G = \bigcup_{a \in G} \sim_a$
end if
if $x = G^*$ then
  $\sim_x = (\sim_G)^* = (\bigcup_{a \in G} \sim_a)^*$, {where $(\sim_G)^*$ is the reflexive, transitive closure of $\sim_G$.}
end if
$T := \{v \mid \phi_1 \in label(v)\}$ {T is the set of states to be visited.}
while $T \neq \emptyset$ do
  choose $v \in T$ { v is a state in W where ϕ_1 holds.}
  $T := T \setminus \{v\}$
  for all t such that $\langle t, v \rangle \in \sim_x$, do
    if $\langle x \rangle \phi_1 \notin label(t)$ then
      $label(t) := label(t) \cup \{\langle x \rangle \phi_1\}$
    end if
  end for
end while

---

5   Conclusion

This work aimed to endow the epistemic logics with structured states, build on the epistemisations method introduced in [19], as tool support. Firstly, a parametric way to define a logic calculus is introduced, on top of a calculus of the base knowledge representation framework. Moreover, we show that the method preserves the completeness of the base calculus under the natural conditions. This result paves the way for the implementation of dedicated theorem provers for specific epistemisations, but also for a parametric proof system, taking as parameter a base calculus. On the other hand, it studied the complexity of the Model Checking and of the SAT problem for generic epistemisations.

This is just part of a research agenda that we intends to pursue, for instance, by extending the calculus generation to other versions of epistemisation, including the variant with public announcement also introduced in the paper [19]. Moreover, as noted in the work [19], this method provide a significant potential on applications to be explored. For instance, its role in the modelling of an autonomous hybrid system, by understanding sensors as agents that partially know the state of the system (e.g. some of them known the vertical acceleration, some other the current position etc.), using as knowledge representation framework the differential dynamic logic ([24]), is a line in our research agenda. There are other interesting extensions. For instance, to derive the 'epistemisation' for probabilistic logic presented in [23] or of fuzzy logics (e.g. [12]) and to analyse their relation with the probabilistic and multi-valued epistemic logics of the references [2,17].

Finally, it is worth noting that this work is framed in our long term research on demand driven generation of specification logics, parametric to the specificities of some classes of complex systems (e.g. [2,20,21]).

Acknowledgement. The first author is also partially supported by the Brazilian research agencies CNPq, CAPES and FAPERJ. Second and third authors are partially supported by the ERDF—European Regional Development Fund through the Operational Programme for Competitiveness and Internationalisation - COMPETE 2020 Programme and by National Funds through the Portuguese funding agency, FCT - Fundação para a Ciência e a Tecnologia, within project POCI-01-0145-FEDER-030947 and by UID/MAT/04106/2019 at CIDMA.

References

1. Balbiani, P., Gasquet, O., Schwarzentruber, F.: Agents that look at one another. Logic J. IGPL **21**(3), 438–467 (2013). https://doi.org/10.1093/jigpal/jzs052
2. Benevides, M.R.F., Madeira, A., Martins, M.A.: A family of graded epistemic logics. In: Alves, S., Wasserman, R. (eds.) 12th Workshop on Logical and Semantic Frameworks, with Applications, LSFA 2017, Brasília, Brazil, 23–24 September 2017. Electronic Notes in Theoretical Computer Science, vol. 338, pp. 45–59. Elsevier (2017). https://doi.org/10.1016/j.entcs.2018.10.004

3. Blackburn, P., ten Cate, B.: Pure Extensions, Proof Rules and Hybrid Axiomatics. In: Schmidt, R., Pratt-Hartmann, I., Reynolds, M., Wansing, H. (eds.) Proceedings of the Advances in Modal Logic 2004 (AiML 2004) (2004)
4. Blackburn, P., de Rijke, M., Venema, Y.: Modal Logic. Cambridge University Press, Cambridge (2001)
5. van Ditmarsch, H., van der Hoek, W., Kooi, B.: Dynamic Epistemic Logic. Synthese Library, vol. 337. Springer, Dordrecht (2008). https://doi.org/10.1007/978-1-4020-5839-4
6. van Eijck, J., Gattinger, M.: Elements of epistemic crypto logic. In: Proceedings of the 2015 International Conference on Autonomous Agents and Multiagent Systems. AAMAS '15, pp. 1795–1796. International Foundation for Autonomous Agents and Multiagent Systems, Richland, SC (2015). http://dl.acm.org/citation.cfm?id=2772879.2773441
7. van Eijck, J., Gattinger, M., Wang, Y.: Knowing values and public inspection. In: Ghosh, S., Prasad, S. (eds.) ICLA 2017. LNCS, vol. 10119, pp. 77–90. Springer, Heidelberg (2017). https://doi.org/10.1007/978-3-662-54069-5_7
8. Fagin, R., Halpern, J., Moses, Y., Vardi, M.: Reasoning About Knowledge. MIT Press, Cambridge (1995)
9. Fisher, M.J., Ladner, R.F.: Propositional dynamic logic of regular programs. J. Comput. Syst. Sci. **18**, 194–211 (1979)
10. Fitting, M., Mendelsohn, R.: First-Order Modal Logic. Synthese Library Studies in Epistemology Logic, Methodology, and Philosophy of Science, vol. 277. Springer, Dordrecht (1998). https://doi.org/10.1007/978-94-011-5292-1 https://books.google.com.br/books?id=JMV9ZOg3KkUC
11. Goldblatt, R.: Logics of Time and Computation. CSLI Lecture Notes 7, CSLI, Stanford (1992)
12. Hájek, P.: Basic fuzzy logic and BL-algebras. Soft Comput. **2**(3), 124–128 (1998). https://doi.org/10.1007/s005000050043
13. Herzig, A., Lorini, E., Maffre, F.: A poor man's epistemic logic based on propositional assignment and higher-order observation. In: van der Hoek, W., Holliday, W.H., Wang, W. (eds.) LORI 2015. LNCS, vol. 9394, pp. 156–168. Springer, Heidelberg (2015). https://doi.org/10.1007/978-3-662-48561-3_13
14. Hintikka, J.: Knowledge and Belief. Cornell University Press, Ithaca (1962)
15. van der Hoek, W., Iliev, P., Wooldridge, M.: A logic of revelation and concealment. In: International Conference on Autonomous Agents and Multiagent Systems, AAMAS 2012, Valencia, Spain, 4–8 June 2012 (3 Volumes), pp. 1115–1122 (2012). http://dl.acm.org/citation.cfm?id=2343856
16. van der Hoek, W., Troquard, N., Wooldridge, M.: Knowledge and control. In: 10th International Conference on Autonomous Agents and Multiagent Systems (AAMAS 2011), Taipei, Taiwan, 2–6 May 2011, vol. 1–3, pp. 719–726 (2011). http://portal.acm.org/citation.cfm?id=2031720&CFID=54178199&CFTOKEN=61392764
17. Kooi, B.P.: Probabilistic dynamic epistemic logic. J. Logic Lang. Inf. **12**(4), 381–408 (2003). https://doi.org/10.1023/A:1025050800836
18. Kozen, D., Parikh, R.: An elementary proof of the completeness of PDL. Theoret. Comput. Sci. **14**, 113–118 (1981)
19. Madeira, A., Martins, M.A., Benevides, M.R.F.: Epistemic logics with structured knowledge. In: Accattoli, B., Olarte, C. (eds.) Proceedings of the 13th Workshop on Logical and Semantic Frameworks with Applications, LSFA 2018, Fortaleza, Brazil, 26–28 September 2018. Electronic Notes in Theoretical Computer Science, vol. 344, pp. 137–149. Elsevier (2018). https://doi.org/10.1016/j.entcs.2019.07.009

20. Madeira, A., Neves, R., Barbosa, L.S., Martins, M.A.: A method for rigorous design of reconfigurable systems. Sci. Comput. Program. **132**, 50–76 (2016). https://doi.org/10.1016/j.scico.2016.05.001

21. Madeira, A., Neves, R., Martins, M.A.: An exercise on the generation of many-valued dynamic logics. J. Log. Algebr. Meth. Program. **85**(5), 1011–1037 (2016). https://doi.org/10.1016/j.jlamp.2016.03.004

22. Neves, R., Madeira, A., Martins, M.A., Barbosa, L.S.: Proof theory for hybrid(ISED) logics. Sci. Comput. Program. **126**, 73–93 (2016). https://doi.org/10.1016/j.scico.2016.03.001

23. Nilsson, N.J.: Probabilistic logic. Artif. Intell. **28**(1), 71–88 (1986). https://doi.org/10.1016/0004-3702(86)90031-7

24. Platzer, A.: Logical Foundations of Cyber-Physical Systems. Springer, Cham (2018). https://doi.org/10.1007/978-3-319-63588-0 http://www.springer.com/978-3-319-63587-3

25. van Ditmarsch, H., van der Hoek, W., Halpern, J., Kooi, B. (eds.): Handbook of Epistemic Logic. College Publications (2015)

26. Wang, Y.: Beyond knowing that: a new generation of epistemic logics. In: van Ditmarsch, H., Sandu, G. (eds.) Jaakko Hintikka on Knowledge and Game-Theoretical Semantics. OCL, vol. 12, pp. 499–533. Springer, Cham (2018). https://doi.org/10.1007/978-3-319-62864-6_21

Introducing Interval Differential Dynamic Logic

Daniel Figueiredo$^{(\boxtimes)}$

CIDMA – University of Aveiro, Aveiro, Portugal
daniel.figueiredo@ua.pt

Abstract. Differential dynamic logic ($d\mathcal{L}$) is a dynamic logic with first-order features which allows us to describe and reason about hybrid systems. We have already used this logic to reason about biological models. Here we explore some variants of its semantics in order to obtain a simplified and more intuitive way of describing errors/perturbations, unavoidable in real-case scenarios. More specifically, we introduce interval differential dynamic logic which takes $d\mathcal{L}$ as its base and adapts its semantics for the interval setting.

Keywords: Interval differential dynamic logic · Differential dynamic logic · Interval arithmetics

1 Introduction

Differential dynamic logic ($d\mathcal{L}$) is a very expressive language which is able to describe properties of systems involving complex dynamics. Due to its specification of atomic programs, it is specially designed for *hybrid systems*, *i.e.*, those which admit continuous evolutions along with discrete events (also called *discrete jump sets*). A classic example of this is the bouncing ball (Example 1.2 from [1]) where the continuous evolution of the ball position and velocity is interrupted by a discrete event that is the bounce in the ground. $d\mathcal{L}$ was introduced by Platzer in [1], where a proof calculus was also proposed. The proof calculus is sound but not complete, which means that not all valid formulas admit a proof (a weaker version of completeness is proved in [1]); moreover the first-order structure embedded in this logic turns it undecidable. It has been applied in diverse contexts from railway, plane and automotive traffic [2–6] to autonomous robotics [7] and even surgical robots [8]. In all these works, the $d\mathcal{L}$ proof calculus has shown to be a powerful tool for the verification of hybrid systems correctness.

While $d\mathcal{L}$ is a really useful logic, we also look at some complementary ones. Gao has developed a verification tool for hybrid systems – dReach [9] – based on dReal [10], which evaluates δ-satisfiability for SMT formulas, *i.e.* checks satisfiability of a formula under a bounded error δ. dReach embeds the capacity

© IFIP International Federation for Information Processing 2021
Published by Springer Nature Switzerland AG 2021
H. Hojjat and M. Massink (Eds.): FSEN 2021, LNCS 12818, pp. 69–75, 2021.
https://doi.org/10.1007/978-3-030-89247-0_5

of handling a bounded error and is used for reachability problems. The typical question that dReach can answer is: "Is it possible to move from an initial region to an unsafe region under a bounded error δ?". When compared to $d\mathcal{L}$ proof calculus, dReach has the advantage of being able to generally handle complex differential equations described by SMT formulas (including polynomials, trigonometric functions, exponential functions, Lipschitz-continuous ODEs, etc.). This is because dReach admits a bounded perturbation δ and it can handle numerical solutions for differential equations. However, this is also a drawback because dReach needs to compute all combinations between continuous evolutions and discrete reconfigurations, not being able to work symbolically. Since this is impossible in practice, differential dynamic logic is more suited for safety while dReach is preferred for reachability. This symbiosis has already been proposed in [11].

In this paper we introduce the basic notions for an interval version of differential dynamic logic – interval differential dynamic logic ($\mathcal{I}d\mathcal{L}$). The syntax and semantics of differential dynamic logic are adapted to interval paradigma and used in problems where variables are associated to uncertainty. Moreover, in previous works [11,12], some examples of application of $d\mathcal{L}$ to microbiological contexts were presented. Due to the small scale of the components involved there is always some uncertainty involved and, therefore, the development of an interval version of $d\mathcal{L}$ logic is welcome. Although it was conceptually different, some related work can be found in [13,14], where the interval paradigm was applied to dynamic logic. We assume that the reader is familiarized with $d\mathcal{L}$ notation and its basic properties.

Outline. Section 2 recalls interval arithmetics and introduces the interval paradigm. In Sect. 3 we introduce $\mathcal{I}d\mathcal{L}$ and illustrate the utility of this logic. Finally, we discuss some future work.

2   Interval Paradigm

In this section we present the basis for interval paradigm and motivate its integration in differential dynamic logic. During the 60's, in his PhD thesis [15], Ramon Moore introduced and studied arithmetic for intervals. For a general function $f : \mathbb{R}^n \to \mathbb{R}^m$ where $f(a_1, ..., a_n) = (f_1(a_1, ..., a_n), ..., f_m(a_1, ..., a_n))$, we can obtain the function $f^{\mathcal{I}(\mathbb{R})} : \mathcal{I}(\mathbb{R})^n \to \mathcal{I}(\mathbb{R})^m$ as the function that, for closed intervals $A_1, ..., A_n$ with $A_1 \times ... \times A_n$ being contained in the domain of f,

$$f^{\mathcal{I}(\mathbb{R})}(A_1, ..., A_n) = (f_1^{\mathcal{I}(\mathbb{R})}(A_1, ..., A_n), ..., f_m^{\mathcal{I}(\mathbb{R})}(A_1, ..., A_n)) \text{ and, } \forall i \in 1, ...m$$

$$f_i^{\mathcal{I}(\mathbb{R})}(A_1, ..., A_n) =$$
$$([\min_{a_1 \in A_1, ..., a_n \in A_n} f_i(a_1, ..., a_n), \max_{a_1 \in A_1, ..., a_n \in A_n} f_i(a_1, ..., a_n)]$$

Note. In this context, we still consider a real number x as a degenerated closed interval $[x, x]$. Indeed, this notation was introduced by Moore in [15] and allows usual arithmetics to be embedded in interval arithmetics.

Example 1. We present the generalization of some basic operations.

- $[a,b] + [c,d] = [a+c, b+d]$
- $-[a,b] = [-b,-a]$
- $[a,b] \cdot [c,d] = [\min(P), \max(P)]$ where $P = \{a \cdot c, a \cdot d, b \cdot c, b \cdot d\}$
- $[a,b]^{-1} = [\frac{1}{b}, \frac{1}{a}]$ provided that $0 \in]a,b[$

The development of interval arithmetics generates some questions about how to act on intervals. Hickey, Ju & Emden, in [16], propose some properties that interval arithmetic implementations should verify. We are interested in two:

- *Correctness*: $a_1 \in A_1, ..., a_n \in A_n \implies f(a_1, ..., a_n) \in f^{\mathcal{I}(\mathbb{R})}(A_1, ..., A_n)$;
- *Optimality*: $a \in f^{\mathcal{I}(\mathbb{R})}(A_1, ..., A_n) \implies \exists\, a_1 \in A_1, ..., a_n \in A_n, f(a_1, ..., a_n) = a$.

Correctness guarantees that an interval $f^{\mathcal{I}(\mathbb{R})}(A_1, ..., A_n)$ contains all results of pointwise evaluations of f based on point values that are elements of the argument intervals and optimality assures that $f^{\mathcal{I}(\mathbb{R})}(A_1, ..., A_n)$ generates an interval which is not wider than necessary.

Proposition 1. *If f is continuous, than the interval generalization $f^{\mathcal{I}(\mathbb{R})}$ is correct and optimal.*

Proof. Since f is continuous, correctness and optimality can be trivially obtained from the Weierstrass and Bolzano theorems, respectively. □

Example 2. Consider a function $f : \mathbb{R}^3 \to \mathbb{R}^2$ defined as $f(x,y,z) = (x+y, -xz)$. Considering $I = \{2\} \times [0,1] \times [1,2]$, we can compute $f^{\mathcal{I}(\mathbb{R})}(2, [0,1], [1,2])$ as:

$$([\min_{(x,y,z) \in I} x+y, \max_{(x,y,z) \in I} x+y], [\min_{(x,y,z) \in I} -xz, \max_{(x,y,z) \in I} -xz]) = ([2,3], [-4,-2])$$

In a similar way, given an n-ary propositions P over reals, we define $P^{\mathcal{I}(\mathbb{R})}$, a proposition over $\mathcal{I}(\mathbb{R})$ such that $P^{\mathcal{I}(\mathbb{R})}(A_1, ..., A_n) = true \Leftrightarrow \forall a_1 \in A_1, ..., a_n \in A_n, P(a_1, ..., a_n) = true$

Example 3. $A \leq^{\mathcal{I}(\mathbb{R})} B \Leftrightarrow \forall a \in A, \forall b \in B, a \leq b$.

3   Interval Functions for $d\mathcal{L}$

Although $d\mathcal{L}$ is able to reason about hybrid systems, in general, when one works with differential equations, it is known that small changes in initial conditions can lead to great changes in a continuous evolution. For instance, consider the following differential equation and its analytic solution:

$$\begin{cases} x' = y^2 - x \\ y' = y \end{cases} \qquad \| \qquad \begin{cases} x(t) = \frac{y_0^2}{3}(e^{2t} - e^{-t}) + x_0.e^{-t} \\ y(t) = y_0.e^t \end{cases} \tag{1}$$

For $x = 0$ and y close to 0, a small change of y makes a great difference in the exact value of y because $x = y = 0$ is an unstable steady state and, for $\neq 0$, the value of y will evolve either to large positive or large negative values.

This turns to be a great issue in real life systems since it is virtually impossible to measure exact values for variables like distance and velocity. Consider that a state variable x belonging to an interval ($x \in [a, b]$) is, sometimes, more useful than defining a exact value for x. For instance, piecewise-linear models in biological regulatory networks consider the behavior of a variable for certain intervals rather than the exact values of those variables [12]. To accommodate this, we propose an interval version of $d\mathcal{L}$. In our version, the variables are not evaluated as real values, but as closed intervals, leading to a methodological representation of uncertainty and experimental error. At this point, it is important to mention that $d\mathcal{L}$ syntax is also able to specify the evaluation of variables as intervals, namely $x = [a, b]$ is equivalent to $x \geq a \wedge x \leq b$.

Interval Differential Dynamic Logic. $d\mathcal{L}$ is a dynamic logic with a first-order structure. The set of atomic programs is composed of two kinds of programs: discrete jump sets (discrete assignments) and continuous evolutions (directed by differential equations). We can obtain hybrid behavior by combining both kinds of atomic programs. The syntax of $d\mathcal{L}$ admits a set X of logical variables (which can be quantified) and a signature containing function and relation symbols as well as the set Σ_{fl} of state variables, which are variables whose interpretation is not fixed (contrary to the other symbols in Σ).

The syntax of $\mathcal{I}d\mathcal{L}$ are those of $d\mathcal{L}$ and the semantics are adapted. Real numbers are considered as degenerated intervals of the form $[a, a]$ for $a \in \mathbb{R}$. The semantics of $\mathcal{I}d\mathcal{L}$ consider a "strict" interpretation over closed intervals, i.e. a symbol like $+ \in \Sigma$ is interpreted as "interval sum", for instance. Also, logical and state variables are evaluated over $\mathcal{I}(\mathbb{R})$. Three functions are used to interpret formulas: an interpretation I – for rigid symbols in $\Sigma \backslash \Sigma_{fl}$; an assignment η – for logical variables in X; and a state v – for state variables in Σ_{fl}. A formula is said to be valid if it is true for every triple (I, η, v). The semantics of $d\mathcal{L}$ can be seen as a particular case of the one of $\mathcal{I}d\mathcal{L}$ since the interpretation of its formulas is done over the reals (the set of degenerated intervals). The semantics of $d\mathcal{L}$ (see [1]) is straightforwardly adapted to the interval version. However, the main difference is observed in continuous evolutions (differential equations constrained by a first-order formula χ). Given an initial state u, a system of differential equations $\overrightarrow{x}' = (f_1(\overrightarrow{x}), ..., f_n(\overrightarrow{x}))$ and a first-order formula χ, the set of reachable states is obtained by computing the solution $F(t) = (F_1(t), ..., F_n(t))$ of the differential equation f whose initial conditions are set by the state u. For each $\bar{t} \in \mathbb{R}_0^+$ we can define a reachable state v according to $F^{\mathcal{I}(\mathbb{R})}(\bar{t})$ and χ in such a way that $b \in \mathbb{R}^n \in F^{\mathcal{I}(\mathbb{R})}(\bar{t})$ if there is an initial state $a \in \mathbb{R}^n$ such that $F(\bar{t}) = b$ and $F(t)$ satisfies χ for every $t \in [0, \bar{t}]$. This definition verifies correctness and optimality because of the continuity of F.

We present two examples. One illustrating how continuous evolutions are evaluated and another one evaluating a formula of $\mathcal{I}d\mathcal{L}$.

Example 4. Let us consider a system whose dynamics is described by the system of differential equations previously presented in Sect. 3. Also, for the purpose of this example, we consider a first-order condition stating the positivity of state variables $\chi \equiv x \geq 0 \wedge y \geq 0$. We obtain the following hybrid program to describe the dynamics of this system: $\alpha \equiv (x' = y^2 - x, y' = y \ \& \ x \geq 0 \wedge y \geq 0)$.

In this example, we desire to obtain the set $\rho_{I,\eta}(\alpha)$ – set of reachable states from α (see [1]). Note that I and η are not relevant because only state variables occur in α. Let us consider a state u such that $u(x) = [0,1]$ and $u(y) = [0,1]$. We describe the process to obtain the set of pairs (u, v) which are contained in $\rho_{I,\eta}(\alpha)$. Firstly, we need to obtain the analytical solution of the system of differential equations, which is shown in 1 with $x_0 = x(0)$ and $y_0 = y(0)$.

Let us denote $\min\limits_{(x_0,y_0)\in[0,1]^2} x(\bar{t})$ by $\underline{x(\bar{t})}$, $\max\limits_{(x_0,y_0)\in[0,1]^2} x(\bar{t})$ $\overline{x(\bar{t})}$, $\min\limits_{(x_0,y_0)\in[0,1]^2} y(\bar{t})$ by $\underline{y(\bar{t})}$ and $\max\limits_{(x_0,y_0)\in[0,1]^2} y(\bar{t})$ by $\overline{y(\bar{t})}$. For each non-negative value of $\bar{t}$, we obtain an attainable reachable state $v_{\bar{t}} = u[x \to [\underline{x(\bar{t})}, \overline{x(\bar{t})}]][y \to [\underline{y(\bar{t})}, \overline{y(\bar{t})}]]$ for every $\bar{t}$ satisfying $val_{I,\eta}(v_t, \chi) = true$, for every $0 \leq t \leq \bar{t}$. For instance, if $v = u[x \to [0, \frac{5}{3}]][y \to [0, 2]]$, then $(u, v) \in \rho_{I,\eta}$, and $R = \ln(2)$ is the witness.

We end this section with an academic example of the evaluation of a formula of $\mathcal{I}d\mathcal{L}$.

Example 5. In this example, we will simply write a instead of $[a, a]$. Let us consider a system like the one from Example 4 but where the initial value of x and y is $[0, 1]$ and the value of y resets to 0 whenever it reaches the value of 5.

This is described by the following hybrid program:

$$\beta \equiv \Big((?(y \leq 5); (x' = y^2 - x, y' = y \ \& \ x \geq 0 \wedge 0 \leq y \leq 5)) \cup (?y = 5; y := 0) \Big)^*$$

Note that the hybrid program checks $y \leq 5$ before to proceed with the continuous evolution which never allows y to go above 5. When $y = 5$, the program can check again if $y = 5$ (because of the $*$ and $\cup$ operators) and proceed with the discrete jump set $y := 0$, setting y to $[0, 0]$. Then, the continuous evolution can resume (again, due to the $*$ operator). Note that, since we are considering the interval paradigm, when we check $y \leq 5$, we are checking if the upper limit of the interval is less or equal to 5. Finally, we evaluate the formula: $\varphi \equiv (x \leq [0,1] \wedge y \leq [0,1]) \to [\beta]x < 6$. Note that the choice of I, η is not important, since only state variables occur in this formula: $val_{I,\eta}(u, \varphi) = true \Leftrightarrow val_{I,\eta}(u, x \leq [0,1]) = false$ or $val_{I,\eta}(u, y \leq [0,1]) = false$ or $val_{I,\eta}(u, [\beta]x < 6) = true$.

If $u(x)(\leq)^{\mathcal{I}(\mathbb{R})}[0, 1]$ is false or $u(y)(\leq)^{\mathcal{I}(\mathbb{R})}[0, 1]$ is false, then the formula is *true*. Otherwise, we are in the same conditions as in Example 4. From Example 4, we know that is possible to reach a state $v_{\bar{R}}$ with $v_{\bar{R}}(y) = [0, 5]$ when $R = \ln(5)$ and, at the same state $v_{\bar{R}}(x) = \frac{77}{15}$. Furthermore, this is the maximum value it takes for $R \in [0, \ln(5)]$ because the analytical solution for $x(r)$ is monotonically increasing. After the discrete jump set which sets y to $[0, 0]$, the continuous evolution can be run again. From the state $v_{\bar{R}}$, the continuous evolution will permanently set y to $[0, 0]$ while $v_R(X) = [0, \frac{77}{15}.e^{-R}]$, for $R \geq \ln(5)$. Considering that $\frac{77}{15}.e^{-R}$ is a monotonically decreasing function, x will never take a value above 6. Because of this, we can conclude that $val_{I,\eta}(u, \varphi)$ is *true* for every I, η and u and thus it is valid.

4   Conclusions and Future Work

In this work we present an interval version of $d\mathcal{L}$ in order to make it more user-friendly in contexts where the use of intervals is more appropriated. The proof calculus of $d\mathcal{L}$ is compared to dReach, which is used to approach reachability problems in hybrid systems and that already admits a notion of δ-perturbation. Since $d\mathcal{L}$ is particularly designed for safety properties, we believe that $\mathcal{I}d\mathcal{L}$ can be an interesting complement to dReach, which is designed for reachability properties.

Although we highlight the connection between $d\mathcal{L}$ and $\mathcal{I}d\mathcal{L}$, we are interested in proving some properties relating both languages. Moreover, in the future, we intend to adapt the proof calculus of $d\mathcal{L}$ to $\mathcal{I}d\mathcal{L}$. Furthermore, in order to make $\mathcal{I}d\mathcal{L}$ more appealing, an interval version of KeYmaera (a semi-automatic prover for the $d\mathcal{L}$ proof calculus) could be developed to assist in the process of proving a $\mathcal{I}d\mathcal{L}$ formula.

Other interesting developments would be the inclusion of new interval operators and relations such as $\cap$ and $\subseteq$; the development of a fuzzy and interval logic; and study how the notion of differential equation in this paper relates with the one in [17].

Acknowledgements. This work was supported by ERDF - The European Regional Development Fund through the Operational Programme for Competitiveness and Internationalisation - COMPETE 2020 Programme and by National Funds through the Portuguese funding agency, FCT - Fundação para a Ciência e a Tecnologia, within project POCI-01-0145-FEDER-030947 and project with reference UIDB/04106/2020 at CIDMA.

References

1. Platzer, A.: Logical Analysis of Hybrid Systems: Proving Theorems for Complex Dynamics. Springer, Heidelberg (2010). https://doi.org/10.1007/978-3-642-14509-4
2. Platzer, A., Quesel, J.-D.: European train control system: a case study in formal verification. In: Breitman, K., Cavalcanti, A. (eds.) ICFEM 2009. LNCS, vol. 5885, pp. 246–265. Springer, Heidelberg (2009). https://doi.org/10.1007/978-3-642-10373-5_13
3. Mitsch, S., Loos, S.M., Platzer, A.: Towards formal verification of freeway traffic control. In: Lu, C. (ed.) ICCPS, pp. 171–180. IEEE (2012)
4. Loos, S.M., Platzer, A., Nistor, L.: Adaptive cruise control: hybrid, distributed, and now formally verified. In: Butler, M., Schulte, W. (eds.) FM 2011. LNCS, vol. 6664, pp. 42–56. Springer, Heidelberg (2011). https://doi.org/10.1007/978-3-642-21437-0_6
5. Platzer, A., Clarke, E.M.: Formal verification of curved flight collision avoidance maneuvers: a case study. In: Cavalcanti, A., Dams, D.R. (eds.) FM 2009. LNCS, vol. 5850, pp. 547–562. Springer, Heidelberg (2009). https://doi.org/10.1007/978-3-642-05089-3_35

6. Jeannin, J.-B., et al.: A formally verified hybrid system for the next-generation airborne collision avoidance system. In: Baier, C., Tinelli, C. (eds.) TACAS 2015. LNCS, vol. 9035, pp. 21–36. Springer, Heidelberg (2015). https://doi.org/10.1007/978-3-662-46681-0_2

7. Mitsch, S., Ghorbal, K., Platzer, A.: On provably safe obstacle avoidance for autonomous robotic ground vehicles. In: Newman, P., Fox, D., Hsu, D. (eds.) Robotics: Science and Systems (2013)

8. Kouskoulas, Y., Renshaw, D., Platzer, A., Kazanzides, P.: Certifying the safe design of a virtual fixture control algorithm for a surgical robot. In: Proceedings of the 16th International Conference on Hybrid Systems: Computation and Control, pp. 263–272. ACM (2013)

9. Kong, S., Gao, S., Chen, W., Clarke, E.: dReach: δ-reachability analysis for hybrid systems. In: Baier, C., Tinelli, C. (eds.) TACAS 2015. LNCS, vol. 9035, pp. 200–205. Springer, Heidelberg (2015). https://doi.org/10.1007/978-3-662-46681-0_15

10. Gao, S., Kong, S., Clarke, E.M.: dReal: an SMT solver for nonlinear theories over the reals. In: Bonacina, M.P. (ed.) CADE 2013. LNCS (LNAI), vol. 7898, pp. 208–214. Springer, Heidelberg (2013). https://doi.org/10.1007/978-3-642-38574-2_14

11. Figueiredo, D.: Logic foundations and computational tools for synthetic biology. Ph.D. thesis, Universities of Minho, Aveiro and Porto (joint doctoral program) (2020)

12. Figueiredo, D., Martins, M.A., Chaves, M.: Applying differential dynamic logic to reconfigurable biological networks. Math. Biosci. **291**, 10–20 (2017)

13. Santiago, R., Bedregal, B., Madeira, A., Martins, M.A.: On interval dynamic logic: introducing quasi-action lattices. Sci. Comput. Program. **175**, 1–16 (2019)

14. Santiago, R.H.N., Bedregal, B., Madeira, A., Martins, M.A.: On interval dynamic logic. In: Ribeiro, L., Lecomte, T. (eds.) SBMF 2016. LNCS, vol. 10090, pp. 129–144. Springer, Cham (2016). https://doi.org/10.1007/978-3-319-49815-7_8

15. Moore, R.E.: Interval arithmetic and automatic error analysis in digital computing. Ph.D. thesis, Stanford University (1962)

16. Hickey, T., Ju, Q., Van Emden, M.H.: Interval arithmetic: from principles to implementation. J. ACM (JACM) **48**(5), 1038–1068 (2001)

17. Ramezanadeh, M., Heidari, M., Fard, O.S., Borzabadi, A.H.: On the interval differential equation: novel solution methodology. Adv. Differ. Eqn. **2015**(1), 338 (2015)

A Program Logic for Fresh Name Generation

Harold Pancho Eliott[1]([⊠]) and Martin Berger[1,2]

[1] Department of Informatics, University of Sussex, Brighton, UK
panchoeliott@gmail.com, contact@martinfriedrichberger.net
[2] Turing Core, Huawei 2012 Labs, London, UK

Abstract. We present a program logic for Pitts and Stark's ν-calculus, an extension of the call-by-value simply-typed λ-calculus with a mechanism for the generation of fresh names. Names can be compared for equality and inequality, producing programs with subtle observable properties. Hidden names produced by interactions between generation and abstraction are captured logically with a second-order quantifier over type contexts. We illustrate usage of the logic through reasoning about well-known difficult cases from the literature.

1 Introduction

Naming is a long-standing problem in computer science. Most programming languages can define naming constructs, which, when called, yield a fresh name. The π-calculus [11] made naming and the ν-operator, a constructor for name creation, a first-class construct, leading to a flurry of research, e.g. [6–8,14,15,18]. Initially it was unclear if the π-calculus approach had purchase beyond process calculi. Pitts and Stark [16] as well as Odersky [12] added the ν-operator to the simply-typed λ-calculus (STLC from now on), and showed that the subtleties of naming are already present in the interplay between higher-order functions and fresh name generation. This raises the question of how compositionally to reason about programs that can generate fresh names? There are program logics for ML-like languages that can generate fresh references, such as [4,19], but, to the best of our knowledge, always in the context of languages with other expressive features such as aliasing, mutable higher-order state or pointer arithmetic, leading to complex logics, where the contribution of fresh name generation to the difficulties of reasoning is not apparent. This is problematic because, while the type Nm carries the same information as Ref(Unit) in ML, we are often interested in reasoning about languages that combine fresh name generation with other features, such as meta-programming [3]. Can we study reasoning about fresh names in as simple a programming language as possible?

Research Question. Is there a Hoare-style program logic for the ν-calculus, conservatively extending program logics for the STLC in a natural manner, that allows for compositional reasoning about fresh name generation?

H. Hojjat and M. Massink (Eds.): FSEN 2021, LNCS 12818, pp. 76–91, 2021.
https://doi.org/10.1007/978-3-030-89247-0_6

The present paper gives an affirmative answer to the research question, and presents the first program logic for the ν-calculus.

Informal Explanation. By the ν-calculus we mean the STLC with a type Nm of names, a constructor gensym of type Unit $\rightarrow$ Nm and a destructor, in form of equality and inequality on names (gensym and ν are essentially identical, but the former is more widely used). Immediately we realise that the ν-calculus loses extensionality, as gensym() = gensym() evaluates to false. While the loss of extensionality is expected in a stateful language, the ν-calculus does not have state, at least not in a conventional sense.

A first difficulty is expressing freshness in logic. What does it mean for a name x to be fresh? A first idea might be to say that x is guaranteed to be distinct from all existing names. We cannot simply say

$$\{T\}\ \text{gensym}()\ :_u\ \{\forall x.u \neq x\}$$

since we must prevent $\forall x.u \neq x$ being instantiated to $u \neq u$. We want to say something like:

$$\forall x.\{T\}\ \text{gensym}()\ :_u\ \{u \neq x\} \tag{1}$$

Unfortunately we cannot quantify over Hoare triples. A second problem is that (1) is not strong enough, in the sense that gensym does not just create names that are fresh w.r.t. existing names, but also w.r.t. all future calls to gensym. We introduce a new quantifier to deal with both problems at the same time. A third difficulty is that fresh names can be exported or remain hidden, with observable consequences. Consider:

$$\text{let } x = \text{gensym}() \text{ in } \lambda y.x = y \tag{2}$$

of type Nm $\rightarrow$ Bool. It receives a name y as argument and compares it with fresh name x. Since x is never exported to the outside, no context can ever supply this fresh x to $\lambda y.x = y$. Hence (2) must be contextually indistinguishable from $\lambda y.\text{false}$. Operationally, this is straightforward. But how can we prove this compositionally? Note that this is not a property of $\lambda y.x = y$, but it is also not a consequence of x's being freshly generated, for x is also fresh in this program:

$$\text{let } x = \text{gensym}() \text{ in } \langle x, \lambda y.x = y \rangle \tag{3}$$

But in (3), $\lambda y.x = y$ can return true, for example if we use (3) in this context:

$$\text{let } p = [\cdot] \text{ in } (\pi_2\ p)(\pi_1\ p)$$

In program logics like [9], the specification of any abstraction $\lambda y.M$ will be a universally quantified formula $\forall y.A$. With fresh names, instantiation of quantification is a core difficulty. Recall that in first-order logic, $\forall y.A$ always implies $A[e/y]$, for all ambient expressions e. Clearly, in the case of (2) we cannot conclude to $A[x/y]$ from $\forall y.A$, because x is, in some sense, not available for instantiation. In contrast, in the case of (3) we can infer $A[x/y]$. Hence we need to answer the question how to express logically the inability to instantiate a universal quantifier with a fresh and hidden name like x in (2). We introduce a novel restricted quantifier, limiting the values based on a type context, and a new quantifier over type contexts to extend the reach of restricted quantifiers.

2   Programming Language

Our programming language is essentially the ν-calculus of [16], with small additions in particular pairs, included for the sake of convenience. We assume a countably infinite set of variables, ranged over by $x, y, \ldots$ and a countably infinite set, disjoint from variables, of names, ranged over by $r, \ldots$. Constants ranged over by c are Booleans true, false, and Unit (). For simplicity we also call our language ν-calculus. It is given by the following grammar, where α ranges over types, Γ over *standard type contexts* (STC), V over values and M over programs. (Key additions over the STLC highlighted.)

$$\alpha ::= \mathsf{Unit} \mid \mathsf{Bool} \mid \mathsf{Nm} \mid \alpha \to \alpha \mid \alpha \times \alpha \quad \Gamma ::= \emptyset \mid \Gamma, x : \alpha$$

$$V ::= r \mid \mathsf{gensym} \mid x \mid c \mid \lambda x.M \mid \langle V, V \rangle$$
$$M ::= V \mid MM \mid \mathsf{let}\ x = M\ \mathsf{in}\ M \mid M = M$$
$$\mid\ \mathsf{if}\ M\ \mathsf{then}\ M\ \mathsf{else}\ M \mid \langle M, M \rangle \mid \pi_i(M)$$

Free variables in M, written $\mathsf{fv}(M)$ are defined as usual. M is *closed* if $\mathsf{fv}(M) = \emptyset$. There are no binders for names so the set $\mathring{a}(M)$ of *all names* in M, is given by the obvious rules, including $\mathring{a}(r) = \{r\}$ and $\mathring{a}(MN) = \mathring{a}(M) \cup \mathring{a}(N)$. If $\mathring{a}(M) = \emptyset$ then M is *compile-time* syntax. The $\nu n.M$ constructor from the ν-calculus [16] is equivalent to let $n = \mathsf{gensym}()$ in M as $\mathsf{gensym}()$ generates fresh names. The typing judgements is $\Gamma \vdash M : \alpha$, with the STC Γ being an unordered mapping from variables to types. Typing rules are standard [13] with the following extensions: $\Gamma \vdash \mathsf{gensym} : \mathsf{Unit} \to \mathsf{Nm}$ and $\Gamma \vdash r : \mathsf{Nm}$.

The operational semantics of our ν-calculus is straightforward and the same as [16]. A *configuration of type* α is a pair (G, M) where M is a closed term of type α, and G a finite set of previously <u>G</u>enerated names such that $\mathring{a}(M) \subseteq G$. The standard call-by-value reduction relation, $\to$, has the following key rules.

$$
\begin{aligned}
(G,\ (\lambda x.M)V) &\ \to\ (G,\ M[V/x]) \\
(G,\ \mathsf{gensym}()) &\ \to\ (G \cup \{n\},\ n) &&(n \notin G) \\
(G \cup \{n\},\ n = n) &\ \to\ (G \cup \{n\},\ \mathsf{true}) \\
(G \cup \{n_1, n_2\},\ n_1 = n_2) &\ \to\ (G \cup \{n_1, n_2\},\ \mathsf{false}) &&(n_1 \neq n_2)
\end{aligned}
$$

$$(G,\ M) \to (G',\ N) \quad \text{implies} \quad (G,\ \mathcal{E}[M]) \to (G',\ \mathcal{E}[N])$$

Here $M[V/x]$ is the usual capture-avoiding substitution, and $\mathcal{E}[\cdot]$ ranges over the usual reduction contexts of the STLC. Finally, $\Downarrow$ is short for $\to^*$.

3   Logical Language

This section defines the syntax of the logic. As is customary for program logics, ours is an extension of first order logic with equality. *Expressions*, ranged over by $e, e', ...$, *formulae*, ranged over by $A, B, C, ...$ and *Logical Type Contexts* (LTCs), ranged over by $\mathit{\Gamma}, \mathit{\Gamma}', \mathit{\Gamma}_i, ...$, are given by the grammar below. (Adaptations over [9] highlighted.)

$$e \quad ::= x^\alpha \mid c \mid \langle e, e \rangle \mid \pi_i(e)$$

$$\mathit{\Gamma} \quad ::= \quad \emptyset \mid \mathit{\Gamma} + x : \alpha \mid \mathit{\Gamma} + \delta : \mathbb{TC}$$

$$A \quad ::= \quad e = e \mid \neg A \mid A \wedge A \mid e \bullet e = x^\alpha\{A\} \mid \forall x^\alpha \in (\mathit{\Gamma}).A \mid \forall \delta.A$$

Expressions, e, are standard, where constants, c, range over Booleans and (), but do *not* include names or gensym as constants. Equality, negation and conjunction are standard. Evaluation formulae $e \bullet e' = m\{A\}$ internalise triples [9] and express that if the program denoted by e is executed with argument denoted by e', then the result, denoted by m, satisfies A. Since the ν-calculus has no recursion, all applications terminate and we do not distinguish partial from total correctness. We write $e_1 \bullet e_2 = e_3$ as shorthand for $e_1 \bullet e_2 = m\{m = e_3\}$.

Given variables represent values, ensuring hidden names cannot be revealed in an unsafe manner requires the idea that a value is *derived* from an LTC if a name free term uses the variables in the LTC to evaluate to said value. Specifically define a name as reachable from said LTC if it can be derived from it, and hidden otherwise.

Freshness is not an absolute notion. Instead, a name is fresh with respect to something, in this case names generated in the past, and future of the computation. Formulae refer to names by variables, and variables are tracked in the STC. Freshness is now defined in two steps: (1) First we characterise freshness of a name w.r.t. the current STC, meaning the name cannot be derived from the variables in the STC. Then, (2) we define freshness w.r.t. all future extension of the current STC, details in Sect. 4. The modal operator is used in [19] in order to express "for all future extensions", but we found modalities inconvenient, since they don't allow us to name extensions. We introduce a new quantifier $\forall x^\alpha \in (\mathit{\Gamma}).A$ instead, where $\mathit{\Gamma}$ ranges over LTCs from which x can be derived. To make this precise, we need LTCs (explained next), a generalisation of STCs.

LTCs. Like STCs, LTCs map variables to types, and are needed for typing expressions, formulae and triples (introduced in Sect. 6), LTCs generalise STCs in two ways: they are *ordered*, and they don't just contain program variables, but also *type context variables* (TCVs), ranged over by δ. TCVs are always mapped to the new type $\mathbb{TC}$, short for *type context*. The ordering in LTCs is essential because $\mathit{\Gamma} + \delta : \mathbb{TC}$ implies δ represents an *extension* of the LTC $\mathit{\Gamma}$.

Restricted Universal Quantification. The meaning of $\forall x^\alpha \in (\mathit{\Gamma}).A$ is intuitively simple: A must be true for all x that range only over values of type α, derived from $\mathit{\Gamma}$ that do *not* reveal hidden names. For example if the model contained the name r but only as $\lambda y.y = r$, then r was hidden and whatever x in

$\forall x^\alpha \in (I\!\!\Gamma).A$ ranged over, it must not reveal r. Formalising this requirement is subtle.

Quantification over LTCs. Below we formalise the axiomatic semantics of gensym by saying that the result of each call to this function is fresh w.r.t. all future extensions of the present state (with the present state being included). The purpose of $\forall \delta.A$ is to allow us to do so: $\forall \delta.A$ implies for all future states derived from the current state (included), when the LTC for that state is assigned to the TCV δ, then A holds.

A Convenient Shorthand, the Freshness Predicate. We express freshness of the name e relative to the LTC $I\!\!\Gamma$ as $\forall z \in (I\!\!\Gamma).e \neq z$. and, as this predicate is used pervasively, abbreviate it to $e \# I\!\!\Gamma$. Intuitively, $e \# I\!\!\Gamma$, a variant of a similar predicate in [19], states that the name denoted by e is not derivable, directly or indirectly, from the LTC $I\!\!\Gamma$.

Typing of Expressions, Formulae and Triples. We continue with setting up definitions that allow us to type expressions, formulae and triples. The ordered union of $I\!\!\Gamma$ and $I\!\!\Gamma'$ with $\mathsf{dom}(I\!\!\Gamma) \cap \mathsf{dom}(I\!\!\Gamma') = \emptyset$ is written $I\!\!\Gamma + I\!\!\Gamma'$, and should be understood as: every variable from $\mathsf{dom}(I\!\!\Gamma)$ comes before every variable from $\mathsf{dom}(I\!\!\Gamma')$. Other abbreviations include $\exists x^\alpha \in (I\!\!\Gamma).A \stackrel{def}{=} \neg \forall x^\alpha \in (I\!\!\Gamma).\neg A$, and where types are obvious then $I\!\!\Gamma + y \stackrel{def}{=} I\!\!\Gamma + y : \alpha$ and $I\!\!\Gamma + \delta \stackrel{def}{=} I\!\!\Gamma + \delta : \mathbb{TC}$. For simplicity, where not explicitly required, $I\!\!\Gamma + \delta$ is written δ. Functions on LTCs are defined as expected including mapping variables, $I\!\!\Gamma(x)$, and TCVs, $I\!\!\Gamma(\delta)$; obtaining the domain, $\mathsf{dom}(I\!\!\Gamma)$; ordered removal of a variable, $I\!\!\Gamma \backslash x$; ordered removal of all TCV, $I\!\!\Gamma \backslash_{-TCV}$; and removal of TCV to produce a STC, $I\!\!\Gamma \downarrow_{-TC}$. We define free variables of LTC, $\mathsf{fv}(I\!\!\Gamma) \stackrel{def}{=} \mathsf{dom}(I\!\!\Gamma \downarrow_{-TC}) \stackrel{def}{=} \mathsf{dom}(I\!\!\Gamma \backslash_{-TCV})$, then free variables of formulae defined as expected, with the addition of $\mathsf{fv}(e \# I\!\!\Gamma) \stackrel{def}{=}$ $\mathsf{fv}(I\!\!\Gamma) \cup \mathsf{fv}(e)$, $\mathsf{fv}(\forall x \in (I\!\!\Gamma).A) \stackrel{def}{=} (\mathsf{fv}(A) \backslash \{x\}) \cup \mathsf{fv}(I\!\!\Gamma)$, and $\mathsf{fv}(\forall \delta.A) \stackrel{def}{=} \mathsf{fv}(A)$. Similarly $\mathsf{ftcv}(I\!\!\Gamma)$ and $\mathsf{ftcv}(A)$ define all TCV occurring in $I\!\!\Gamma$ and unbound by $\forall \delta.$ in A respectively, calling $I\!\!\Gamma$ *TCV-free* if $\mathsf{ftcv}(I\!\!\Gamma) \stackrel{def}{=} \emptyset$. The typing judgement for LTCs, written $I\!\!\Gamma \Vdash I\!\!\Gamma'$, checks that $I\!\!\Gamma'$ is an 'ordered subset' of $I\!\!\Gamma$. Type checks on expressions, formulae and triples use LTC as the base, written $I\!\!\Gamma \Vdash e : \alpha$, $I\!\!\Gamma \Vdash A$ and $I\!\!\Gamma \Vdash \{A\} M :_u \{B\}$ respectively. Figure 1 gives the rules defining the typing judgements. From now on we adhere to the following convention: *All expressions, formulae and triples are typed*, and we will mostly omit being explicit about typing.

Advanced Substitutions. Reasoning with quantifiers requires quantifier instantiation. This is subtle with $\forall \delta.A$, and we need to define two substitutions, $A[e/x]_{I\!\!\Gamma}$ (substitutes expressions for variables) and $A[I\!\!\Gamma_0/\delta]_{I\!\!\Gamma}$ (substitutes LTCs for TCVs). First extend the definition e *is free for* x^α *in* A in [10], to ensure if e contains destructors i.e. $\pi_i(\ )$ or $=$, then all free occurrences of x in any LTC $I\!\!\Gamma_0$ in A must imply $I\!\!\Gamma_0 \Vdash e : \alpha$. Below, we assume the standard substitution $e[e'/x]$ of expressions for variables in expressions, simple details omitted.

We define $A[e/x]_{\Gamma}$, *logical substitution of e for x in A in the context of Γ*, if e is free for x in A with e and A typed by Γ, by the following clauses (simple cases omitted) and the auxiliary operation on LTCs below. We often write $A[e/x]$ for $A[e/x]_{\Gamma}$.

$$\frac{b \in \{\text{true}, \text{false}\}}{\Gamma \Vdash b : \text{Bool}} \qquad \frac{-}{\Gamma \Vdash () : \text{Unit}} \qquad \frac{\Gamma(x) = \alpha}{\Gamma \Vdash x : \alpha} \qquad \frac{\Gamma \Vdash e : \alpha \quad \Gamma \Vdash e' : \alpha'}{\Gamma \Vdash \langle e, e' \rangle : \alpha \times \alpha'} \qquad \frac{\Gamma \Vdash e : \alpha_1 \times \alpha_2}{\Gamma \Vdash \pi_i(e) : \alpha_i}$$

$$\frac{-}{\Gamma \Vdash \emptyset} \qquad \frac{\Gamma \Vdash \Gamma_0}{\Gamma + x : \alpha \Vdash \Gamma_0 + x : \alpha} \qquad \frac{\Gamma \Vdash \Gamma_0}{\Gamma + \delta \Vdash \Gamma_0 + \delta} \qquad \frac{\Gamma \Vdash \Gamma_0}{\Gamma + \Gamma' \Vdash \Gamma_0}$$

$$\frac{\Gamma \Vdash e_1 : \alpha \quad \Gamma \Vdash e_2 : \alpha}{\Gamma \Vdash e_1 = e_2} \qquad \frac{\Gamma \Vdash A_1 \quad \Gamma \Vdash A_2}{\Gamma \Vdash A_1 \wedge A_2} \qquad \frac{\Gamma \Vdash A}{\Gamma \Vdash \neg A} \qquad \frac{\Gamma + \delta : \text{TC} \Vdash A}{\Gamma \Vdash \forall \delta. A}$$

$$\frac{\Gamma \Vdash e : \alpha \to \beta \quad \Gamma \Vdash e' : \alpha \quad \Gamma + x : \beta \Vdash A}{\Gamma \Vdash e \bullet e' = x^{\beta}\{A\}} \qquad \frac{\Gamma \Vdash e : \text{Nm} \quad \Gamma \Vdash \Gamma'}{\Gamma \Vdash e \# \Gamma'}$$

$$\frac{\Gamma \Vdash \Gamma' \quad \Gamma + x : \alpha \Vdash A}{\Gamma \Vdash \forall x^{\alpha} \in (\Gamma'). A} \qquad \frac{\Gamma \Vdash A \quad \Gamma \downarrow_{-TC} \vdash M : \alpha \quad \Gamma + m : \alpha \Vdash B}{\Gamma \Vdash \{A\} M :_m \{B\}}$$

Fig. 1. Typing rules for LTCs, expressions, formulae and triples (see Sect. 6). Simple cases omitted. M in the last rule is compile-time syntax.

$$(e' \bullet e'' = m\{A\})[e/x]_{\Gamma} \overset{def}{=} e'[e/x] \bullet e''[e/x] = m\{A[e/x]_{\Gamma+m}\} \quad (x \neq m, \ m \notin \text{fv}(\Gamma))$$
$$(e_1 \# \Gamma')[e/x]_{\Gamma} \overset{def}{=} e_1[e/x] \# (\Gamma'[e/x]_{\Gamma})$$
$$(\forall m \in (\Gamma'). A)[e/x]_{\Gamma} \overset{def}{=} \forall m \in (\Gamma'[e/x]_{\Gamma}).(A[e/x]_{\Gamma+m}) \quad (x \neq m, \ m \notin \text{fv}(\Gamma))$$
$$(\forall \delta. A)[e/x]_{\Gamma} \overset{def}{=} \forall \delta.(A[e/x]_{\Gamma+\delta})$$
$$\Gamma'[e/x]_{\Gamma} \overset{def}{=} \begin{cases} \Gamma'_e \text{ s.t. } \text{dom}(\Gamma'_e) = \text{fv}(e) \cup \text{dom}(\Gamma' \backslash x), \ \Gamma \Vdash \Gamma'_e & x \in \text{dom}(\Gamma') \\ \Gamma' & x \notin \text{dom}(\Gamma') \end{cases}$$

Type Context Substitution. $A[\Gamma_0/\delta]_{\Gamma}$ instantiates δ with Γ_0 in A, similar to classical substitution. We often write $[\Gamma_0/\delta]$ for $[\Gamma_0/\delta]_{\Gamma}$ as Γ is used for ordering and is obvious. As above, the omitted cases are straightforward and the auxiliary operation on LTCs is included.

$$(x \# \Gamma')[\Gamma_0/\delta]_{\Gamma} \overset{def}{=} x \# (\Gamma'[\Gamma_0/\delta]_{\Gamma})$$
$$(e_1 \bullet e_2 = m\{A\})[\Gamma_0/\delta]_{\Gamma} \overset{def}{=} e_1 \bullet e_2 = m\{A[\Gamma_0/\delta]_{\Gamma+m}\} \quad (m \notin \text{dom}(\Gamma_0))$$
$$(\forall x \in (\Gamma'). A)[\Gamma_0/\delta]_{\Gamma} \overset{def}{=} \forall x \in (\Gamma'[\Gamma_0/\delta]_{\Gamma}).(A[\Gamma_0/\delta]_{\Gamma+x}) \quad (x \notin \text{dom}(\Gamma_0))$$
$$(\forall \delta'. A)[\Gamma_0/\delta]_{\Gamma} \overset{def}{=} \begin{cases} (\forall \delta'. A[\Gamma_0/\delta]_{\Gamma+\delta'}) & \delta \neq \delta' \quad (\delta' \notin \text{dom}(\Gamma_0)) \\ \forall \delta. A & \text{otherwise} \end{cases}$$
$$\Gamma'[\Gamma_0/\delta]_{\Gamma} \overset{def}{=} \begin{cases} \Gamma_1 \text{ s.t. } \text{dom}(\Gamma_1) = \text{dom}(\Gamma_0, \Gamma'), \ \Gamma \Vdash \Gamma_1 & \delta \in \text{dom}(\Gamma') \\ \Gamma' & \delta \notin \text{dom}(\Gamma') \end{cases}$$

4   Model

We define a *model* ξ as a finite (possibly empty) map from variables and TCV to closed values and TCV-free LTCs respectively.

$$\xi ::= \emptyset \mid \xi \cdot x : V \mid \xi \cdot \delta : \mathit{\Gamma}'$$

Standard actions on models ξ are defined as expected and include: variable mappings to values, $\xi(x)$, or TCV mapping to LTC, $\xi(\delta)$; removal of variable x as $\xi \backslash x$ (with $(\xi \cdot \delta : \mathit{\Gamma}_1)\backslash x = (\xi\backslash x) \cdot \delta : (\mathit{\Gamma}_1\backslash x)$); removal of TCV δ as $\xi\backslash\delta$; removal of all TCVs as $\xi\backslash_{-TCV}$; and defining all names in ξ as $\mathring{a}(\xi)$ noting that $\mathring{a}(\mathit{\Gamma}) = \emptyset$.

A model ξ is typed by a LTC $\mathit{\Gamma}$ written $\xi^{\mathit{\Gamma}}$, if $\mathit{\Gamma} \Vdash \xi$ as defined below, were $\mathit{\Gamma}_d = \mathit{\Gamma}_d\backslash_{-TCV}$ formalises that $\mathit{\Gamma}_d$ is TCV-free.

$$\frac{-}{\emptyset \Vdash \emptyset} \qquad \frac{\mathit{\Gamma} \Vdash \xi \quad \emptyset \vdash V : \alpha}{\mathit{\Gamma}+x : \alpha \Vdash \xi \cdot x : V} \qquad \frac{\mathit{\Gamma} \Vdash \xi \quad \mathit{\Gamma} \Vdash \mathit{\Gamma}_d \quad \mathit{\Gamma}_d = \mathit{\Gamma}_d\backslash_{-TCV}}{\mathit{\Gamma}+\delta \Vdash \xi \cdot \delta : \mathit{\Gamma}_d}$$

The *closure* of a term M by a model ξ, written $M\xi$ is defined as standard with the additions, $\mathsf{gensym}\xi \overset{def}{=} \mathsf{gensym}$ and $r\xi \overset{def}{=} r$. Noting that $M\xi\backslash_{-TCV} = M\xi = M\xi \cdot \delta : \mathit{\Gamma}'$ holds for all δ and $\mathit{\Gamma}'$ as $\mathit{\Gamma} \downarrow_{-TC}\vdash M : \alpha$.

The *interpretation of expression* e in a model $\xi^{\mathit{\Gamma}}$, written $[\![e]\!]_\xi$, is standard, e.g. $[\![c]\!]_\xi \overset{def}{=} c$, $[\![x]\!]_\xi \overset{def}{=} \xi(x)$, $[\![\langle e, e'\rangle]\!]_\xi \overset{def}{=} \langle[\![e]\!]_\xi, [\![e']\!]_\xi\rangle$, etc.

The *interpretation of LTCs* $\mathit{\Gamma}_0$ in a model $\xi^{\mathit{\Gamma}}$, written $[\![\mathit{\Gamma}_0]\!]_\xi$, outputs a STC. It is assumed $\mathit{\Gamma}$ types the LTC in the following definition:

$$[\![\emptyset]\!]_\xi \overset{def}{=} \emptyset \qquad [\![\mathit{\Gamma}_0+x : \alpha]\!]_\xi \overset{def}{=} [\![\mathit{\Gamma}_0]\!]_\xi, x : \alpha \qquad [\![\mathit{\Gamma}_0+\delta : \mathbb{TC}]\!]_\xi \overset{def}{=} [\![\mathit{\Gamma}_0]\!]_\xi \cup [\![\xi(\delta)]\!]_\xi$$

Write $M \overset{[\mathit{\Gamma}, \xi]}{\leadsto} V$ as the *derivation of a value* V from term M which is typed by the LTC $\mathit{\Gamma}$ and closed and evaluated in a model ξ. This ensures names are derived from actual reachable values in ξ as if they were programs closed by the model, hence not revealing hidden names from ξ. $M \overset{[\mathit{\Gamma}, \xi]}{\leadsto} V$ holds exactly when:

- $\mathring{a}(M) = \emptyset$
- $[\![\mathit{\Gamma}]\!]_\xi \vdash M : \alpha$
- $(\mathring{a}(\xi), M\xi) \Downarrow (\mathring{a}(\xi) \cup G', V)$

Model extensions aim to capture the fact that models represent real states of execution, by stating a model is only constructed by evaluating terms derivable from the model.

A model ξ' is a *single step model extension* to another model $\xi^{\mathit{\Gamma}}$, written $\xi \preccurlyeq \xi'$, if the single new value in ξ' is derived from ξ or the mapped LTC is $\mathit{\Gamma}$ with TCVs removed. Formally $\xi^{\mathit{\Gamma}} \preccurlyeq \xi'$ holds if either of the following hold:

- There is M_y^α such that $M_y \overset{[\mathit{\Gamma}, \xi]}{\leadsto} V_y$ and $\xi'^{\mathit{\Gamma}+y:\alpha} = \xi \cdot y : V_y$.
- $\xi'^{\mathit{\Gamma}+\delta} = \xi \cdot \delta : \mathit{\Gamma}\backslash_{-TCV}$ for some δ.

We write $\preccurlyeq^\star$ for the transitive, reflexive closure of $\preccurlyeq$. If $\xi \preccurlyeq^\star \xi'$ we say ξ' is an *extension* of ξ and ξ is a *contraction* of ξ'.

A model ξ is *constructed by* $\mathit{\Gamma}$, written $\mathit{\Gamma} \triangleright \xi$, if any TCV represents a model extension. Formally we define $\mathit{\Gamma} \triangleright \xi$ by the following rules:

$$\frac{-}{\emptyset \triangleright \emptyset} \qquad \frac{\mathit{\Gamma} \triangleright \xi \quad \text{exists } M^\alpha. M \overset{[\mathit{\Gamma}, \xi]}{\leadsto} V}{\mathit{\Gamma}+x:\alpha \triangleright \xi \cdot x:V} \qquad \frac{\mathit{\Gamma} \triangleright \xi_0 \quad \xi_0 \preccurlyeq^\star \xi^{\mathit{\Gamma}_2} \quad \mathit{\Gamma}_1 = \mathit{\Gamma}_2 \backslash_{-TCV}}{\mathit{\Gamma}+\delta \triangleright \xi \cdot \delta : \mathit{\Gamma}_1}$$

A model $\xi^{\mathit{\Gamma}}$ is *well constructed* if there exists an LTC, $\mathit{\Gamma}'$, such that $\mathit{\Gamma}' \triangleright \xi$, noting that $\mathit{\Gamma} \Vdash \mathit{\Gamma}'$.

Model extensions and well constructed models represent models derivable by ν-calculus programs, ensuring names cannot be revealed by later programs. Consider the basic model: $y : \lambda a.\text{if } a = r_1 \text{ then } r_2 \text{ else } r_3$, if r_1 could be added to the model, this clearly reveals access to r_2 otherwise r_2 is hidden. Hence the assumption that all models are well constructed from here onwards.

Contextual equivalence of two terms requires them to be contextually indistinguishable in all variable-closing single holed contexts of Boolean type in any valid configuration, as is standard [1,17]. When M_1 and M_2 are closed terms of type α and $\mathring{a}(M_1) \cup \mathring{a}(M_2) \subseteq G$, we write $M_1 \cong_\alpha^G M_2$ to be equivalent to $G, \emptyset \vdash M_1 \equiv M_2 : \alpha$ from [1].

4.1   Semantics

The *satisfaction relation* for formula A in a well constructed model $\xi^{\mathit{\Gamma}}$, written $\xi \models A$, assumes $\mathit{\Gamma} \Vdash A$, and is defined as follows:

- $\xi \models e = e'$ if $[\![e]\!]_\xi \cong_\alpha^{\mathring{a}(\xi)} [\![e']\!]_\xi$.
- $\xi \models \neg A$ if $\xi \not\models A$.
- $\xi \models A \wedge B$ if $\xi \models A$ and $\xi \models B$.
- $\xi \models e \bullet e' = m\{A\}$ if $ee' \overset{[\emptyset, \xi]}{\leadsto} V$ and $\xi \cdot m : V \models A$
- $\xi \models \forall x^\alpha \in (\mathit{\Gamma}').A$ if for all M. $M \overset{[\mathit{\Gamma}', \xi]}{\leadsto} V$ implies $\xi \cdot x : V \models A$
- $\xi \models \forall \delta.A$ if forall $\xi'^{\mathit{\Gamma}'}.\xi \preccurlyeq^\star \xi'$ implies $\xi' \cdot \delta : (\mathit{\Gamma}'\backslash_{-TCV}) \models A$
- $\xi \models e \# \mathit{\Gamma}_0$ if there is no M such that $M \overset{[\mathit{\Gamma}_0, \xi]}{\leadsto} [\![e]\!]_\xi$

In first-order logic, if a formula is satisfied by a model, then it is also satisfied by extensions of that model, and vice-versa (as long as all free variables of the formula remain in the model). This can no longer be taken for granted in our logic. Consider the formula $\forall \delta.\exists z \in (\delta).(z \# \mathit{\Gamma} \wedge \neg z \# \delta)$ Validity of this formula depends on how many names exist in the ambient model: it may become invalid under contracting the model. Fortunately, such formulae are rarely needed when reasoning about programs. In order to simplify our soundness proofs we will therefore restrict some of our axioms and rules to formulae that are stable under model extension and contractions. Sometimes we need a weaker property, where formulae preserve their validity when a variable is removed from a model. Both concepts are defined semantically next.

We define formula A as *model extensions independent*, short Ext-Ind, if for all $I\!\!\Gamma, \xi^{I\!\!\Gamma}, \xi'$ such that $I\!\!\Gamma \Vdash A$ and $\xi \preccurlyeq^* \xi'$ we have: $\xi \models A$ iff $\xi' \models A$.

We define formula A as *thin* w.r.t. x, written A thin w.r.t x^α, if for all $I\!\!\Gamma$ such that $I\!\!\Gamma \backslash x \Vdash A$ and $x^\alpha \in \text{dom}(I\!\!\Gamma)$ we have for all well constructed models $\xi^{I\!\!\Gamma}$ and $\xi \backslash x$ that: $\xi \models A$ implies $\xi \backslash x \models A$.

5   Axioms

Axioms and axiom schemas are similar in intention to those of the logic for the STLC, but expressed within the constraints of our logic. Axiom schemas are indexed by the LTC that types them and the explicit types where noted. We introduce the interesting axioms (schemas) and those used in Sect. 7.

Equality axioms are standard where $(eq1)$ allows for substitution. Most axioms for universal quantification over LTCs $(u1)$-$(u5)$ are inspired by those of first order logic. The exceptions are $(u2)$ which allows for the reduction of LTCs and $(u5)$ which holds only on Nm-free types. Axioms for existential quantification over LTCs $(ex1)$-$(ex3)$ are new aside from $(ex1)$ which is the dual of $(u1)$. Axiom $(ex2)$ introduces existential quantification from evaluation formulae that produce a fixed result. Reducing $I\!\!\Gamma$ in $\exists x \in (I\!\!\Gamma).A$ is possible via $(ex3)$ for a specific structure. We use base types $\alpha_b ::= \text{Unit} \mid \text{Bool} \mid \alpha_b \times \alpha_b$ as core lambda calculus types excluding functions. Freshness axioms $(f1)$-$(f2)$ show instances LTCs can be extended, whereas $(f3)$-$(f4)$ reduce the LTC. Axiom $(f1)$ holds due to f being derived from $I\!\!\Gamma + x$, and the rest are trivial.

$(eq1)$ $I\!\!\Gamma \Vdash A(x) \wedge x = e \leftrightarrow A(x)[e/x]_{I\!\!\Gamma}$

$(u1)$ $I\!\!\Gamma \Vdash \forall x^\alpha \in (I\!\!\Gamma_0).A \rightarrow A[e/x]_{I\!\!\Gamma}$ $\qquad\qquad\qquad I\!\!\Gamma_0 \vdash e : \alpha$

$(u2)$ $\forall x \in (I\!\!\Gamma_0 + I\!\!\Gamma_1).A \rightarrow (\forall x \in (I\!\!\Gamma_0).A) \wedge (\forall x \in (I\!\!\Gamma_1).A)$

$(u3)$ $A^{-x} \leftrightarrow \forall x \in (I\!\!\Gamma_0).A^{-x}$ $\qquad\qquad\qquad A - \text{Ext-Ind}$

$(u4)$ $\forall x \in (I\!\!\Gamma_0).(A \wedge B) \leftrightarrow (\forall x \in (I\!\!\Gamma_0).A) \wedge (\forall x \in (I\!\!\Gamma_0).B)$

$(u5)$ $\forall x^\alpha \in (I\!\!\Gamma_0).A \leftrightarrow \forall x^\alpha \in (\emptyset).A$ $\qquad\qquad \alpha$ is Nm-free

$(ex1)$ $I\!\!\Gamma \Vdash A[e/x]_{I\!\!\Gamma} \rightarrow \exists x' \in (I\!\!\Gamma_0).A$ $\quad I\!\!\Gamma \Vdash I\!\!\Gamma_0$ and $I\!\!\Gamma_0 \vdash e : \alpha$

$(ex2)$ $I\!\!\Gamma + x + I\!\!\Gamma_0 \Vdash a \bullet b = c\{c = x\} \rightarrow \exists x' \in (I\!\!\Gamma_0).x = x'$ $\quad \{a, b\} \subseteq \text{dom}(I\!\!\Gamma_0)$

$(ex3)$ $I\!\!\Gamma + x \Vdash \forall y \in (\emptyset).\exists z^{\text{Nm}} \in (I\!\!\Gamma_0 + y).x = z \quad \rightarrow \quad \exists z \in (I\!\!\Gamma_0).x = z$

$(f1)$ $I\!\!\Gamma + x + f : \alpha \rightarrow \alpha_b \Vdash x \# I\!\!\Gamma \rightarrow x \# I\!\!\Gamma + f : \alpha \rightarrow \alpha_b$

$(f2)$ $I\!\!\Gamma \Vdash x \# I\!\!\Gamma_0 \wedge \forall y^\alpha \in (I\!\!\Gamma_0).A \leftrightarrow \forall y^\alpha \in (I\!\!\Gamma_0).(x \# (I\!\!\Gamma_0 + y) \wedge A)$

$(f3)$ $x \# I\!\!\Gamma_0 \rightarrow x \neq e$ $\qquad\qquad\qquad\qquad I\!\!\Gamma_0 \vdash e : \text{Nm}$

$(f4)$ $x \# (I\!\!\Gamma_0 + I\!\!\Gamma_1) \rightarrow x \# I\!\!\Gamma_0 \wedge x \# I\!\!\Gamma_1$

Axioms for quantification over LTCs are also similar to those for the classical universal quantifier except (utc2) which extends the restricted quantifier to any future LTC which can only mean adding fresh names.

$(utc1)$ $I\!\!\Gamma \Vdash \forall \delta.A \rightarrow A[I\!\!\Gamma/\delta]_{I\!\!\Gamma}$

$(utc2)$ $I\!\!\Gamma \Vdash \forall x^{\text{Nm}} \in (I\!\!\Gamma).A^{-\delta} \leftrightarrow \forall \delta.\forall x^{\text{Nm}} \in (I\!\!\Gamma + \delta).A$ $\quad A - \text{Ext-Ind}$

$(utc3)$ $A^{-\delta} \leftrightarrow \forall \delta.A^{-\delta}$ $\qquad\qquad\qquad\qquad A - \text{Ext-Ind}$

$(utc4)$ $\forall \delta.(A \wedge B) \leftrightarrow (\forall \delta.A) \wedge (\forall \delta.B)$

Axioms for the evaluation formulae are similar to those of [2]. The interaction between evaluation formulae and the new constructors are shown. All STLC values are included in the variables of Nm-free type, and if we let $\mathsf{Ext}(e_2, e_2)$ stand for $\forall x \in (\emptyset).e_1 \bullet x = m_1\{e_2 \bullet x = m_2\{m_1 = m_2\}\}$ then (ext) maintains extensionality in this logic for the STLC terms. Typing restrictions require $m \notin \mathsf{fv}(A)$ in (e1) and $\mathsf{fv}(e_1, e_2, m) \cap \mathsf{dom}(\mathbf{\Gamma}+x) = \emptyset$ in (e2).

$$
\begin{array}{lll}
(e1) & e_1 \bullet e_2 = m\{A \wedge B\} \leftrightarrow (A \wedge e_1 \bullet e_2 = m\{B\}) & A - \text{Ext-Ind} \\
(e2) & e_1 \bullet e_2 = m\{\forall x \in (\mathbf{\Gamma}).A\} \leftrightarrow \forall x \in (\mathbf{\Gamma}).e_1 \bullet e_2 = m\{A\}) & \\
(e3) & e_1 \bullet e_2 = m^{\alpha_{\flat}}\{\forall \delta.A\} \leftrightarrow \forall \delta.e_1 \bullet e_2 = m^{\alpha_{\flat}}\{A\} & A - \text{Ext-Ind} \\
(ext) & \mathsf{Ext}(e_1, e_2) \leftrightarrow e_1 =^{\alpha_1 \to \alpha_2} e_2 & \alpha_1 \to \alpha_2 \text{ is Nm-free}
\end{array}
$$

6 Rules

Our logic uses standard *triples* $\{A\}\ M :_m \{B\}$ where in this logic, the program M is restricted to compile-time syntax. Triples are typed by the rule in Fig. 1. Semantics of triples is standard: if the *pre-condition* A holds and the value derived from M is assigned to the *anchor* m then the *post-condition* B holds. In detail: let $\xi^{\mathbf{\Gamma}}$ be a model.

$$
\xi^{\mathbf{\Gamma}} \models \{A\}\ M :_m \{B\} \qquad \text{if} \qquad \xi \models A \text{ implies } (M \overset{[\mathbf{\Gamma}, \xi]}{\rightsquigarrow} V \text{ and } \xi \cdot m : V \models B)
$$

The triple is *valid*, written $\models \{A\}\ M :_m \{B\}$, if for all $\mathbf{\Gamma}$ and $\xi_0^{\mathbf{\Gamma}_0}$ we have

$$
\mathbf{\Gamma} \Vdash \{A\}\ M :_m \{B\} \text{ and } \mathbf{\Gamma} \triangleright \xi_0 \text{ together imply: } \xi_0 \models \{A\}\ M :_m \{B\}
$$

From here on we will assume all models are well constructed, noting that the construction of models is the essence of $\forall \delta$. as it allows for all possible future names generated. Variables occurring in $\mathsf{dom}(\xi_0) - \mathsf{dom}(\mathbf{\Gamma})$ may never occur directly in the triple, but their mapped values will have an effect.

The rules of inference can be found in Fig. 2 and Fig. 3. We write $\vdash \{A\}\ M :_m$ $\{B\}$ to indicate that $\{A\}\ M :_m \{B\}$ can be derived from these rules. Our rules are similar to those of [9] for vanilla λ-calculi, but suitably adapted to the effectful nature of the ν-calculus. All rules are typed. The typing of rules follows the corresponding typing of the programs occurring in the triples, but with additions to account for auxiliary variables. We have two substantially new rules: [GENSYM] and [LET]. The former lets us reason about fresh name creation by gensym, the latter about the let $x = M$ in N. Operationally, let $x = M$ in N is often just an abbreviation for $(\lambda x.N)M$, but we have been unable to derive [LET] using the remaining rules and axioms. Any syntactic proof of [LET] requires [LAM] and [APP], which requires the postcondition: C thin w.r.t p for p the anchor of the [LAM] rule. We have not been able to prove this thinness for all models of the relevant type.

In comparison with [9,19], the primary difference with our rules is our substitution. Our changes to substitution only affects [EQ] and [PROJ(i)] which are reduced in strength by the new definition of substitution as more constraints are placed on the formulae to ensure correct substitution occurs. All other rules remain equally strong. The other difference from [9] is the need for thinness to replace the standard 'free from', which is discussed above. Removal of variables via thinness is required in the proof of soundness, for example [APP], which produces u from m and n, hence Ext-Ind is insufficient given the order of $\mathit{\Gamma} + m + n + u \Vdash C$, i.e. u introduced after m and n. We explain the novelty in the rules in more detail below.

$$\frac{\overline{}}{\{A[x/m]\}\ x :_m \{A\}}\ {\scriptstyle[\text{VAR}]} \qquad \frac{\overline{}}{\{\mathsf{T}\}\ \mathsf{gensym} :_u \{\forall \delta. u \bullet () = m\{m\#\delta\}\}}\ {\scriptstyle[\text{GENSYM}]}$$

$$\frac{\overline{}}{\{A[c/m]\}\ \mathsf{c} :_m \{A\}}\ {\scriptstyle[\text{CONST}]} \qquad \frac{\{A\}\ M :_m \{B\} \quad \{B\}\ N :_n \{C[m = n/u]\}}{\{A\}\ M = N :_u \{C\}}\ {\scriptstyle[\text{EQ}]}$$

$$\frac{A - \mathsf{Ext\text{-}Ind} \quad \mathit{\Gamma} + \delta + x : \alpha \vdash \{A^{\neg x} \wedge B\}\ M :_m \{C\}}{\mathit{\Gamma} \vdash \{A\}\ \lambda x^\alpha . M :_u \{\forall \delta. \forall x^\alpha \in (\delta).(B \to u \bullet x = m\{C\})\}}\ {\scriptstyle[\text{LAM}]}$$

$$\frac{\{A\}\ M :_m \{B\} \quad \{B\}\ N :_n \{m \bullet n = u\{C\}\}}{\{A\}\ MN :_u \{C\}}\ {\scriptstyle[\text{APP}]}$$

$$\frac{\{A\}\ M :_m \{B\} \quad \{B[b_i/m]\}\ N_i :_u \{C\} \quad b_1 = \mathsf{true} \quad b_2 = \mathsf{false} \quad i = 1,2}{\{A\}\ \mathsf{if}\ M\ \mathsf{then}\ N_1\ \mathsf{else}\ N_2 :_u \{C\}}\ {\scriptstyle[\text{IF}]}$$

$$\frac{\{A\}\ M :_m \{B\} \quad \{B\}\ N :_n \{C[\langle m,n\rangle/u]\}}{\{A\}\ \langle M,N\rangle :_u \{C\}}\ {\scriptstyle[\text{PAIR}]} \qquad \frac{\{A\}\ M :_m \{C[\pi_i(m)/u]\}}{\{A\}\ \pi_i(M) :_u \{C\}}\ {\scriptstyle[\text{PROJ}(i)]}$$

$$\frac{\{A\}\ M :_m \{B\} \quad \{B\}\ N :_u \{C\}}{\{A\}\ \mathsf{let}\ m^\alpha = M\ \mathsf{in}\ N :_u \{C\}}\ {\scriptstyle[\text{LET}]} .$$

Fig. 2. Rules for the core language, cf. [2,9,19]. We require C thin w.r.t m in [PROJ(i), LET] and C thin w.r.t m, n in [EQ, APP, PAIR]. We omit LTCs where not essential.

In [GENSYM], $u \bullet () = m\{m\#\delta\}$ indicates the name produced by $u()$ and stored at m is not derivable from the LTC δ. If there were no quantification over LTCs prior to the evaluation we could only say m is fresh from the current typing context, however we want to say that even if there is a future typing context with new names and we evaluate $u()$, this will still produce a fresh name. Hence we introduce the $\forall \delta.$ to quantify over all future LTCs (and hence all future names). Elsewhere in reasoning it is key that the post-condition of [GENSYM] is Ext-Ind and hence holds in all extending and contracting models (assuming the anchor for gensym is present), reinforcing the re-applicability of gensym in any context.

Rules for λ-abstraction in previous logics for lambda-calculi [9,19] universally quantify over all possible arguments. Our corresponding [LAM] rule refines this and quantifies over current or future values that do not reveal hidden names. Comparing the two LTCs typing the assumption and conclusion implies $\mathmf{\Gamma}+\delta+x$ extends $\mathmf{\Gamma}$ to any possible extension assigned to δ, and extends to x a value derived from $\mathmf{\Gamma}+\delta$. Hence the typing implies precisely what is conveyed in the post-condition of the conclusion: '$\forall\delta.\forall x \in (\delta).$'. Constraints on δ and x are introduced by B, and $A -$ Ext-Ind implies A still holds in all extensions of $\mathmf{\Gamma}$ including $\mathmf{\Gamma}+\delta+x$. The rest is trivial when we consider $((\lambda x.M)x)\xi \cong_{\alpha}^{\mathring{a}(\xi)} M\xi$.

The STLC's [LET] rule introduces x in the post-condition by means of an '$\exists x.C$'. This fails here as x may be unreachable, hence not derivable from any extending or contracting LTC. The requirement that C thin w.r.t x ensures x is not critical to C so can either be derived from the current LTC or is hidden. Thinness ensures no reference to the variable m is somehow hidden under quantification over LTCs.

The [INVAR] rule is standard with the constraint that $C -$ Ext-Ind to ensure C holds in the extension where m has been assigned. The [LETFRESH] rule is commonly used and hence included for convenience, but it is entirely derivable from the other rules and axioms.

$$\frac{A \to A' \quad \{A'\} M :_m \{B'\} \quad B' \to B}{\{A\} M :_m \{B\}} \text{ [CONSEQ]} \qquad \frac{C - \text{Ext-Ind} \quad \{A\} M :_m \{B\}}{\{A \wedge C\} M :_m \{B \wedge C\}} \text{ [INVAR]}$$

$$\frac{A - \text{Ext-Ind} \quad \mathmf{\Gamma}+m : \text{Nm} \vdash \{A \wedge m\#\mathmf{\Gamma}\} M :_u \{C\}}{\mathmf{\Gamma} \vdash \{A\} \text{ let } m = \text{gensym}() \text{ in } M :_u \{C\}} \text{ [LETFRESH]}$$

Fig. 3. Key structural rules [CONSEQ] and [INVAR] and for convenience the derived [LETFRESH] rule where C thin w.r.t m is required.

Theorem 1. *All axioms and rules are sound.*

Theorem 2. *The logic for the ν-calculus is a conservative extension of the logic* [9] *for the STLC.*

All proofs can be found in the first author's forthcoming dissertation [5].

7 Reasoning Examples

Example 1. We reason about the core construct gensym() in an LTC $\mathmf{\Gamma}$. In Line 2, $(utc1)$ instantiates the postcondition to $b \bullet () = a\{a\#\mathmf{\Gamma}+b\}$ and $(f4)$ removes the b from the LTC to ensure the postcondition satisfies the thin w.r.t b requirement in [APP].

1	$I\!\!\Gamma \Vdash \{\mathsf{T}\}$ gensym $:_b \{\forall \delta.b \bullet () = a\{a\#\delta\}\}$	[GENSYM]
2	$I\!\!\Gamma \Vdash \{\mathsf{T}\}$ gensym $:_b \{b \bullet () = a\{a\#I\!\!\Gamma\}\}$	[CONSEQ], (utc1), (f4), 1
3	$I\!\!\Gamma+b \Vdash \{b \bullet () = a\{a\#I\!\!\Gamma\}\}$ () $:_c \{b \bullet c = a\{a\#I\!\!\Gamma\}\}$	[CONST]
4	$I\!\!\Gamma \Vdash \{\mathsf{T}\}$ gensym() $:_a \{a\#I\!\!\Gamma\}$	[APP], 2, 3

Example 2. We reason about the comparison of two fresh names, clearly returning false, by applying Example 1 in the relevant LTCs.

1	$I\!\!\Gamma \Vdash \{\mathsf{T}\}$ gensym() $:_a \{a\#I\!\!\Gamma\}$	*See Example 1*
2	$I\!\!\Gamma+a \Vdash \{\mathsf{T}\}$ gensym() $:_b \{b\#I\!\!\Gamma+a\}$	*See Example 1*
3	$I\!\!\Gamma+a \Vdash \{a\#I\!\!\Gamma\}$ gensym() $:_b \{a \neq b\}$	[CONSEQ], (f3), 2
4	$I\!\!\Gamma \Vdash \{\mathsf{T}\}$ gensym() = gensym() $:_u \{u = \mathsf{false}\}$	[EQ], 3

Example 3. Placing name generation inside an abstraction halts the production of fresh names until the function is applied. When y is of type Unit then this specification is identical to that of gensym.

1	$I\!\!\Gamma+\delta+y \Vdash \{\mathsf{T}\}$ gensym() $:_m \{m\#I\!\!\Gamma+\delta+y\}$	*See Example 1*
2	$I\!\!\Gamma \Vdash \{\mathsf{T}\}$ $\lambda y.$gensym() $:_u \{\forall \delta.\forall y \in (\delta).u \bullet y = m\{m\#I\!\!\Gamma+\delta+y\}\}$ [LAM], 2

Example 4. Generating a name outside an abstraction and returning that same name in the function is often compared to Example 3 [1,17]. We reason as follows: letting $A_4(p) \stackrel{def}{=} \forall \delta.\forall y \in (\delta).u \bullet y = m\{m\#I\!\!\Gamma \wedge p = m\}$.

1	$\{x\#I\!\!\Gamma\}$ $x :_m \{m\#I\!\!\Gamma \wedge x = m\}$	[VAR]
2	$\{x\#I\!\!\Gamma\}$ $\lambda y.x :_u \{A_4(x)\}$	[LAM], 1
3	$\{x\#I\!\!\Gamma\}$ $\lambda y.x :_u \{\exists x' \in (u).A_4(x')\}$	[CONSEQ], 2
4	$I\!\!\Gamma \Vdash \{\mathsf{T}\}$ let $x = $ gensym() in $\lambda y.x :_u \{\exists x' \in (u).A_4(x')\}$	[LETFRESH], 3

Proof of line 3 above, essentially proves x is derivable from u:

5	$A_4(x) \wedge \forall y \in (\emptyset).u \bullet y = m\{x = m\}$	(utc1), (u2), FOL
6	$A_4(x) \wedge \exists x' \in (u).x = x'$	(ex2), (ex3)
7	$\exists x' \in (u).(A_4(x) \wedge x = x')$	(u3), (u4)
8	$\exists x' \in (u).A_4(x')$	(eq1)

Example 5. In order to demonstrate the subtlety of hidden names, the Introduction used Program (2), which was $M \overset{def}{=}$ let $x = $ gensym() in $\lambda y.x = y$. We now use our logic to reason about M.

1	$\varGamma + x + \delta + y \Vdash \{\mathsf{T}\}\; x = y :_m \{m = (x = y)\}$	[EQ]
2	$\varGamma + x \Vdash \{\mathsf{T}\}\; \lambda y.x = y :_u \{\forall\delta.\forall y \in (\delta).u \bullet y = (x = y)\}$	[LAM], 1
3	$\varGamma + x \Vdash \{x \# \varGamma\}\; \lambda y.x = y :_u \{x \# \varGamma \wedge \forall\delta.\forall y \in (\delta).u \bullet y = (x = y)\}$	[INVAR], 2
4	$\varGamma + x \Vdash \{x \# \varGamma\}\; \lambda y.x = y :_u \{\forall y \in (\varGamma + u).u \bullet y = \mathsf{false}\}$	[CONSEQ], 3
5	$\varGamma \Vdash \{\mathsf{T}\}\; M :_u \{\forall y \in (\varGamma + u).u \bullet y = \mathsf{false}\}$	[LETFRESH]
6	$\varGamma \Vdash \{\mathsf{T}\}\; M :_u \{\forall\delta.\forall y^{\mathsf{Nm}} \in (\delta).u \bullet y = \mathsf{false}\}$	(utc2)

To prove line 4 above we apply the axioms as follows:

7	$\varGamma + x + u \Vdash x \# \varGamma \wedge \forall\delta.\forall y \in (\delta).u \bullet y = (x = y)$	
8	$x \# \varGamma \wedge \forall y \in (\varGamma + x + u).u \bullet y = (x = y)$	(utc1)
9	$x \# \varGamma + u \wedge \forall y \in (\varGamma + x + u).\; u \bullet y = (x = y)$	(f1)
10	$x \# \varGamma + u \wedge \forall y \in (\varGamma + u).\; u \bullet y = (x = y)$	(u2)
11	$\forall y \in (\varGamma + u).\; x \# \varGamma + u + y \wedge u \bullet y = (x = y)$	(f2)
12	$\forall y \in (\varGamma + u).\; x \neq y \wedge u \bullet y = (x = y)$	(f3)
13	$\forall y \in (\varGamma + u).u \bullet y = \mathsf{false}$	(e1)

Example 6. To demonstrate the release of a hidden variable using Program (3), which was $M \overset{def}{=}$ let $x = $ gensym() in $\langle x, \lambda y.x = y\rangle$, we reason as follows, with $A_6(p, q) \overset{def}{=} p \# \varGamma \wedge \forall\delta.\forall y \in (\delta).q \bullet y = (p = y)$:

1	$\{x \# \varGamma\}\; x :_b \{x = b \wedge x \# \varGamma\}$	[VAR]
2	$\{\mathsf{T}\}\; \lambda y.x = y :_c \{\forall\delta.\forall y \in (\delta).c \bullet y = (x = y)\}$	*See Example 4, lines 1-2*
3	$\{x = b \wedge x \# \varGamma\}\; \lambda y.x = y :_c \{x = \pi_1(\langle b, c\rangle) \wedge A_6(x, c)\}$	[CONSEQ], [INVAR], 2
4	$\{x = b \wedge x \# \varGamma\}\; \lambda y.x = y :_c \{A_6(\pi_1(a), \pi_2(a))[\langle b, c\rangle/a]\}$	[CONSEQ], (eq1)
5	$\{x \# \varGamma\}\; \langle x, \lambda y.x = y\rangle :_a \{A_6(\pi_1(a), \pi_2(a))\}$	[PAIR], 1, 4
6	$\varGamma \Vdash \{\mathsf{T}\}\; M :_a \{A_6(\pi_1(a), \pi_2(a))\}$	[LETFRESH], 5

8   Conclusion

We have presented the first program logic for the ν-calculus, a variant of the STLC with names as first class values. Our logic is a conservative extension with two new universal quantifiers of the logic in [9] for the STLC. We provide axioms and proof rules for the logic, prove their soundness, and show its expressive power by reasoning about well-known difficult examples from the literature.

We are currently unable to reason about this example from [16]:

$$\text{let } F = (\text{let } x, y = \text{gensym}() \text{ in } \lambda f^{\text{Nm} \to \text{Nm}}.fx = fy) \text{ in}$$
$$\text{let } G = \lambda v^{\text{Nm}}.F(\lambda u^{\text{Nm}}.v = u) \text{ in } FG$$

Is this because our logic is too inexpressive, or did we simply fail to find the right proof? Another open question is whether our logic's approach to freshness is independent of the ν-calculus's lack of integers and recursion, or not? For both questions we conjecture the former, and leave them as future work.

References

1. Benton, N., Koutavas, V.: A mechanized bisimulation for the Nu-calculus. Technical report MSR-TR-2008-129, Microsoft (2008)
2. Berger, M., Tratt, L.: Program logics for homogeneous generative run-time metaprogramming. Log. Methods Comput. Sci. (LMCS) **11**(1:5) (2015)
3. Berger, M., Tratt, L., Urban, C.: Modelling homogeneous generative metaprogramming. In: Proceedings of ECOOP, pp. 5:1–5:23 (2017)
4. Dreyer, D., Neis, G., Birkedal, L.: The impact of higher-order state and control effects on local relational reasoning. In: Proceedings of ICFP, pp. 143–156 (2010)
5. Eliott, H.P.: Program logic for fresh name generation. Ph.D. thesis, University of Sussex (expected 2021). Draft
6. Fernández, M., Gabbay, M.J., Mackie, I.: Nominal rewriting systems. In: Proceedings of PPDP, pp. 108–119 (2004)
7. Gabbay, M.J., Pitts, A.M.: A new approach to abstract syntax with variable binding. Formal Aspects Comput. **13**, 341–363 (2001)
8. Honda, K.: Elementary structures in process theory (1): sets with renaming. MSCS **10**(5), 617–663 (2000)
9. Honda, K., Yoshida, N.: A compositional logic for polymorphic higher-order functions. In: Proceedings of PPDP 2004, pp. 191–202. ACM Press (2004)
10. Mendelson, E.: Introduction to Mathematical Logic. Wadsworth Inc. (1987)
11. Milner, R., Parrow, J., Walker, D.: A calculus of mobile processes, parts I and II. Inf. Comput. **100**(1), 1–77 (1992)
12. Odersky, M.: A functional theory of local names. In: Proceedings of POPL, pp. 48–59 (1994)
13. Pierce, B.C.: Types and Programming Languages. MIT Press, Cambridge (2002)
14. Pitts, A.M.: Nominal logic, a first order theory of names and binding. Inf. Comput. **186**, 165–193 (2003)
15. Pitts, A.M.: Nominal Sets: Names and Symmetry in Computer Science. CUP (2013)
16. Pitts, A.M., Stark, I.D.B.: Observable properties of higher order functions that dynamically create local names, or: what's new? In: Borzyszkowski, A.M., Sokołowski, S. (eds.) MFCS 1993. LNCS, vol. 711, pp. 122–141. Springer, Heidelberg (1993). https://doi.org/10.1007/3-540-57182-5_8

17. Stark, I.: Names and higher-order functions. Ph.D. thesis, University of Cambridge (1994). Technical report 363, University of Cambridge Computer Laboratory
18. Urban, C., Tasson, C.: Nominal techniques in Isabelle/HOL. In: Proceedings of CADE, pp. 38–53 (2005)
19. Yoshida, N., Honda, K., Berger, M.: Logical reasoning for higher-order functions with local state. Log. Methods Comput. Sci. 4(2) (2008)

Event-Driven Temporal Logic Pattern for Control Software Requirements Specification

Vladimir Zyubin$^{(\boxtimes)}$, Igor Anureev, Natalia Garanina, Sergey Staroletov, Andrei Rozov, and Tatiana Liakh

Institute of Automation and Electrometry, Novosibirsk, Russia
{zyubin,rozov}@iae.nsk.su, {anureev,garanina}@iis.nsk.su

Abstract. This paper presents event-driven temporal logic (EDTL), a specification formalism that allows the users to describe the behavior of control software in terms of events (including timeouts) and logical operations over inputs and outputs, and therefore consider the control system as a "black box". We propose the EDTL-based pattern that provides a simple but powerful and semantically rigorous conceptual framework oriented on industrial process plant developers in order to organize their effective interaction with the software developers and provide a seamless transition to the stages of requirement consistency checking and verification.

1 Introduction

Most current proposals that are intended to improve software quality and rely on formal methods, are rejected by the mainstream practice. Fast-moving software development companies do not consider it cost-effective to apply such methods in their software development processes, because the critical issue in the field is not quality but rather the "time-to-market" [1].

The situation is different in industrial programming. This includes PLC-based control systems, embedded systems, and such present-day initiatives as cyber-physical systems, and Industrial Internet of Things, where emergent system properties such as safety, correctness, robustness, and maintainability are very important [2]. This enforces developers of such safety-critical software to use formal methods. However as the size of systems grows, expenses that are required to use formal methods, grow disproportionately. Hence, these methods can only be applied to relatively small systems [3].

Another circumstance causing formal methods to be expensive in this domain is their conceptual discrepancy with the specifics of industrial plant engineering.

This work has been funded by the state budget of the Russian Federation (IA&E project No. AAAA-A19-119120290056-0). Authors are very grateful for the charitable support they received from the JetBrains Foundation.

© IFIP International Federation for Information Processing 2021
Published by Springer Nature Switzerland AG 2021
H. Hojjat and M. Massink (Eds.): FSEN 2021, LNCS 12818, pp. 92–107, 2021.
https://doi.org/10.1007/978-3-030-89247-0_7

Modern studies show that this problem is actually very acute to this date [4]. Control software development fits well into the "client-contractor" paradigm. At the initial stages of the project (system requirements specification, program specification), the client plays a leading and irremovable role. Their input gradually decreases as the project progresses to the implementation stage. The contractor (programmer), however, plays an auxiliary and dependent role at the start. It is only at the design and implementation stages of the project that they start to gain relative independence.

The main contradictions we face here are the following: (a) the clients think in terms of events, timeouts, processes and states [5], while the contractors are limited to the programming languages they use, e.g. the IEC 61131-3 languages [6], (b) the clients do not bother seeing into the internal structure of control software, whereas the contractors neglect learning the inherent principles of processes within the plant, (c) the plant is designed by the clients and, as an artifact, it already implicitly assumes a control algorithm by design, yet the contractors need to specify this hidden algorithm in a strict form.

This explains why most bugs in critical systems are a result of incompleteness or other flaws in the software requirements, not coding errors [7]. This also means that we should focus not on requirement checking, but rather on how to formulate a complete and correct set of requirements, and further check them for consistency.

The following attempts to solve this problem are known: using a pattern-restricted natural language [8–11], using information extraction methods to get the necessary information from natural language specifications [12–14], using domain-oriented (FSM-based) languages [15], using graphic notations [16], formal requirement pattern languages [17–23], to mention a few.

Summarizing the above, we can formulate the general principles of requirements specification for control software. A requirements specification should be:

- *user-friendly*, i.e. correspondent to the process plant design and based on the concepts of events (including timeout events) and reactions;
- *independent of control software design and implementation*, that is, it should use the black box principle and operate in terms of inputs and outputs, without any knowledge of the inner structure of either the control software or the plant hardware;
- following a *unified pattern*;
- *strict*, i.e. it should have formal semantics;
- *universal*, i.e. not orientated towards any particular verification technique.

In this paper, we develop such a specification and demonstrate its use with a simple but practical case study.

The rest of the paper consists of three principal parts. In Sect. 2, we propose a conceptual schema for the requirements specification and its syntax, then in Sect. 3, we construct an informal semantics of the notation. Finally, in Sect. 4, we demonstrate the proposed notation on a hand dryer control system. In Appendix A, we present our bounded checking algorithm for the proposed specifications and discuss its implementation.

2 Syntax and Definition of EDTL-Requirements

In this section, we describe the syntax of the proposed notation for requirements.

Definition 1. *(EDTL-requirements)*
An EDTL requirement is a tuple of the following attributes:

$$R = (\textbf{trigger}, \textbf{invariant}, \textbf{final}, \textbf{delay}, \textbf{reaction}, \textbf{release}).$$

The graphical intuition for the temporal orchestration of EDTL-attributes is shown in Fig. 1. Table 1 gives the informal description of the attributes.

Table 1. The EDTL attributes

Attribute	Description
Trigger	An event after which the invariant must be true until a release event or a reaction takes place; this event is also the starting point for timeouts to produce final/release events (if any)
Invariant	A statement that must be true from the moment the trigger event occurs until the moment of a release or reaction event
Final	An event, after which a reaction must occur within the allowable delay. This event always follows the trigger event
Delay	A time limit after the final event, during which a reaction must appear
Reaction	This statement must become true within the allowable delay from the final event
Release	Upon this event, the requirement is considered satisfied

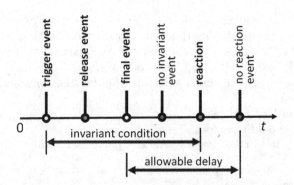

Fig. 1. Concept of a requirement specification in EDTL

The value of each attribute of EDTL-requirements is an *EDTL-formula*. This formula is a Boolean formula built from *EDTL-terms*. The EDTL-formulas are also enriched with special Boolean terms for monitoring instantaneous changes of system variables' values: *changes*, *increases*, and *decreases*. The Boolean term *passed* describes that a control system is in a state after moment specified by a term of type *time*.

Definition 2. *(EDTL-terms)*
The terms are built from typed constants, variables and functions:

- A constant of a type t is a term of the type t.
- A variable of a type t is a term of the type t.
- If $u_1, \ldots, u_n$ are terms of types $t_1, \ldots, t_n$, and f is a function of type $t_1 \times \ldots \times t_n \to t$, then $f(u_1, \ldots, u_n)$ is a term of a type t.
- If u is a term, then (u) is a term.

The set of types includes types *int* (for integers), *double* (for floating points), *bool* (for Boolean values *true* and *false*), and *time* (e.g., $1h$ and $1s$ for 1 h and 1 s). The functions include standard arithmetic operations and relations, Boolean operations and C-like bitwise operations.

EDTL-formulas are constructed from Boolean terms by standard Boolean operations and special operations for expressing instant control system changes.

Definition 3. *(EDTL-formulas)*
If ϕ and ψ are EDTL-formulas then:

- ETDL-term of type *bool* is an atomic EDTL-formula;
- $\phi \wedge \psi$ is the conjunction of ϕ and ψ;
- $\phi \vee \psi$ is the disjunction of ϕ and ψ;
- $\neg\phi$ is the negation of ϕ;
- $\backslash\phi$ is the falling edge: the value of ϕ changes from *false* to *true*;
- $/\phi$ is the rising edge: the value of ϕ changes from *true* to *false*;
- $\_\phi$ is low steady-state: the value of ϕ remains equal to *false*;
- $\sim \phi$ is high steady-state: the value of ϕ remains equal to *true*.

3 Semantics of EDTL-Requirements

3.1 Definitions for the Semantics

The syntax and informal meaning of EDTL-requirements to a control system do not depend on implementations of this control system. However, we must define an abstract model of a control system to describe the formal semantics of EDTL-requirements corresponding to their intuitive understanding. To do this we will use the cyclic scan or triggered execution model defined in the IEC 61131-3 [6].

We consider that a control system functioning consists of an infinite sequence of *scan-cycles*. Each scan cycle includes a sequence of three phases: reading input, execution, and writing output. Our model of a control system [24] abstracts from scan cycle time (the environment is considered to be slow enough to assume zero time for the input/output and execution phases of a scan cycle) [25]. Hence, we give the semantics to EDTL-requirements in discrete time paradigm: values

of input and output variables of a control system are observable in states at
the beginning of a scan cycle. Due to the black-box principle [26], we consider
that EDTL-formulas include input and output variables only. In definitions of
formal semantics, we take into account that input variables are evaluated at the
beginning of a scan cycle and not changed during the scan cycle, and, in contrast,
output variables are changed during a scan cycle and finally evaluated at the end
of the scan cycle. We consider a control system as a standard transition system:

Definition 4. *(Control systems)*
A control system is a transition system $CS = (S, I, R)$, where

- S is a set of states, and
- $I \subset S$ is a finite set of initial states, and
- $R \subseteq S \times S$ is a total transition relation.

A *path* $\pi = s_0, s_1, \ldots$ is an infinite sequence of states $s_i \in S$ such that $\forall j > 0$:
$(s_j, s_{j+1}) \in R$. In state s_i on path π, i is a number of a scan cycle (*called a time
point*), and $\pi(i) = s_i$. An *initial path* π^0 is a path starting from initial state, i.e.
$\pi^0(0) \in S_0$.

In EDTL-requirements, a special attention is paid to time (or event) constraints. Hence, we introduce *a timer point* which is the time point on a path
to define the moment of starting a timer. Timers are used to specify timeout
events. We define the value of terms on path π in the current time point i w.r.t.
timer point j. The fact that a term u has the value v in a state s_i means that
v is the value of u at the time moment i. For variables, the value is defined by
the function acc: $acc(x, s)$ returns the value of the variable x in the state s. For
time terms, the value is defined by the function $time$: $time(u, \pi(i))$ returns the
number of scan cycles which will be passed during u time with the time point i
for path π. For a function f, let $intr(f)$ be a value of f.

The function $value$ defines semantics (value) of EDTL-terms at time point i
on path π with timer point j:

Definition 5. *(Semantics of EDTL-terms)*

- if c is a constant, then $value(c, \pi, i, j) = c$;
- if x is a variable, then $value(x, \pi, i, j) = acc(x, \pi(i))$;
- if u is a time term, then $value(u, \pi, i, j) = time(u, \pi(i))$;
- $value(f(u_1, \ldots, u_n), \pi, i, j) = intr(f)(value(u_1, \pi, i, j), \ldots, value(u_n, \pi, i, j))$;
- $value((u), \pi, i, j) = value(u, \pi, i, j)$.
  Let u be not a term of type *time* and $i > 0$:
- $value(changes(u), \pi, i, j) = true$ iff $value(u, \pi, i-1, j) \neq value(u, \pi, i, j)$;
- $value(increases(u), \pi, i, j) = true$ iff $value(u, \pi, i-1, j) < value(u, \pi, i, j)$;
- $value(decreases(u), \pi, i, j) = true$ iff $value(u, \pi, i-1, j) > value(u, \pi, i, j)$;
  Let u be a term of type *time* and $i > 0$:
- $value(passed(u), \pi, i, j) = true$ iff $i \geq j + value(u, \pi, i, j)$, i.e. $value(u, \pi, i, j)$
  time steps have passed after the timer point j.

Semantics of EDTL-formulas is defined in terms of satisfiability relation between the time point with its timer point on the path of the control system: $CS, \pi, i, j \models \phi$ iff ϕ is true at time point i w.r.t. timer point j on the path π of control system CS. In this definition, we omit the name of a control system:

Definition 6. *(Semantics of EDTL-formulas)*

- $\pi, i, j \models u$ iff u is a Boolean EDTL-term and $value(u, \pi, i, j) = true$;
- $\pi, i, j \models \phi \wedge \psi$ iff $i, j \models \phi$ and $\pi, i, j \models \psi$;
- $\pi, i, j \models \phi \wedge \psi$ iff $\pi, i, j \models \phi$ or $i, j \models \psi$;
- $\pi, i, j \models \neg\phi$ iff $\pi, i, j \not\models \phi$;
- $\pi, i, j \models /\phi$ iff $i > 0$, $\pi, i\text{-}1, j \not\models \phi$ and $\pi, i, j \models \phi$;
- $\pi, i, j \models \backslash\phi$ iff $i > 0$, $\pi, i\text{-}1, j \models \phi$ and $\pi, i, j \not\models \phi$;
- $\pi, i, j \models \sim \phi$ iff $i > 0$, $\pi, i\text{-}1, j \models \phi$ and $\pi, i, j \models \phi$;
- $\pi, i, j \models \_\phi$ iff $i > 0$, $\pi, i\text{-}1, j \not\models \phi$ and $\pi, i, j \not\models \phi$.

For every EDTL-formula ϕ, $value(\phi, \pi, i, j) = true$ iff $\pi, i, j \models \phi$.

The following natural language description of EDTL-requirement semantics corresponds to the informal description of attributes in Table 1:

Following each trigger event, the invariant must hold true until either a release event or a final event. The invariant must also hold true after final event till either the release event or a reaction, and besides the reaction must take place within the specified allowable delay from the final event.

We define two kind of formal semantics for EDTL-requirements. The proof of equivalence of this two semantics is out of the scope of this paper. For EDTL-requirement tp, let $trigger$, $invariant$, $final$, $delay$, $reaction$, and $release$ be EDTL-formulas which are the values of the corresponding tp attributes.

3.2   The First Order Logic Semantics

EDTL-requirement tp is satisfied in a control system CS iff the following FOL-formula F_{tp} is true for every initial path π^0:

$$
\begin{aligned}
F_{tp} = &\forall \pi^0 \in CS \; \forall \, t \in [1, +\infty)(\\
&value(trigger, \pi^0, t, 0) \wedge \neg value(release, \pi^0, t, t) \Rightarrow \\
&\forall f \in [t, +\infty)(\forall i \in [t, f](\neg value(release, \pi^0, m, t)) \Rightarrow \\
&(\forall i \in [t, f](\neg value(final, \pi^0, i, t)) \Rightarrow \\
&\forall i \in [t, f](value(invariant, \pi^0, i, t))) \wedge \\
&(\forall i \in [t, f) \; \neg value(final, \pi^0, i, t) \wedge value(final, \pi^0, f, t) \Rightarrow \\
&\forall d \in [f, +\infty)(\forall i \in [f, d] \; \neg value(release, \pi^0, i, t) \Rightarrow \\
&(\forall i \in [f, d](\neg value(delay, \pi^0, i, f) \wedge \neg value(reaction, \pi^0, i, f) \Rightarrow \\
&\forall i \in [f, d](value(invariant, \pi^0, i, f))) \wedge \\
&(((f \neq d \Rightarrow \forall i \in [f, d)(\neg value(delay, \pi^0, i, f) \wedge \\
&\neg value(reaction, \pi^0, i, j)) \wedge value(delay, \pi^0, d, f))) \Rightarrow \\
&value(reaction, \pi^0, d+1, f)))).
\end{aligned}
$$

In this formula, t stands for the time point of the trigger event, f stands for the time point of the final event, and d stands for the time point when the delay is over. This semantics can be used in deductive verification of control systems w.r.t. EDTL-requirements. For this, the control system should be also represented as FOL-formula F_{CS} and the implication $F_{CS} \Rightarrow F_{tp}$ should be verified. For EDTL-requirement tp, the formula F_{tp} gives the constructive way to check tp on the given finite set of finite initial paths of control system CS. This bounded checking algorithm is described in Appendix A.

3.3 The Linear Temporal Logic Semantics

EDTL-requirement tp is satisfied in a control system CS iff the following LTL [27] formula Φ_{tp} is satisfied for every initial path π^0:

$$\Phi_{tp} = \mathbf{G}(trigger \rightarrow ((invariant \wedge \neg final\mathbf{W}release)\vee$$
$$(invariant\mathbf{U}(final \wedge (invariant \wedge delay\mathbf{U}(release \vee reaction)))))).$$

We use this semantics in model checking control systems w.r.t. the EDTL-requirements.

4   Case Study

The Hand dryer is a simple control system which uses a hands sensor as an input and a dryer switching device as an output. Despite the apparent simplicity, the control of the object is nontrivial due to the instability of the sensor readings caused by the movement of the hands—during the drying of hands, the sensor may indicate a short-term absence of the hands. A more detailed description of the system and the implementation of the control software can be found in [5].

Due to the blackbox principle, we abstract from the control logic and observe only the input and output values.

We formulate the following requirements:

1. If the dryer is on, then it turns off after no hands are present for 1 s.
2. If the dryer was not turned on and hands appeared, it will turn on after no more than 1 cycle.
3. If the hands are present and the dryer is on, it will not turn off.
4. If there is no hands and the dryer is not turned on, the dryer will not turn on until the hands appear.
5. The time of continuous work is no more than an hour.

The tabular form for these requirements is presented in Table 2.

To demonstrate the simplicity of using the proposed notation, we illustrate the transformation of requirements into the tabular form and back with the example of requirement R1 "If the dryer is on, then it turns off after no hands are present for 1 s" (Fig. 2).

Table 2. Tabular properties for hand dryer

Req ID	Trigger event	Release event	Final event	Allowable delay	Invariant	Reaction
R1	\H && D	H	passed(1s)	passed(0.01s)	D	!D
R2	/H && !D	false	true	true	!D	D
R3	H && D	false	!H	true	D	true
R4	!H && !D	H	false	true	!D	true
R5	/D	\D	passed(1h)	true	true	\D

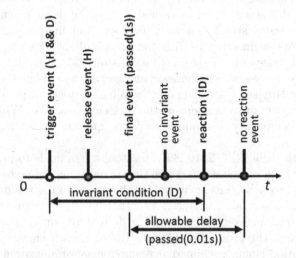

Fig. 2. Graphical representation of the requirement R1

Converting a natural-language requirement into an EDTL-record (direct transformation). The trigger event is "if the dryer is on and hand input is on falling edge", i.e. D && \H. The condition "after no hands are present" means that the appearance of hands cancels the requirement checking until the next trigger event, i.e. the release event is H. If the new state "dryer is on and no hands" is continued, the final event "within 1 s" occurs, i.e. the final event is passed(1s). The reaction to the final event is turning off the dryer (the reaction is !D). Since the original statement assumes that the dryer remains on until it is turned off, the invariant is D.

Converting an EDTL-record into a natural-language requirement (reverse transformation). The trigger event D && \H means the hand disappearing event when the dryer is on. The event starts checking the truth of the invariant D (dryer is on), until the release event H (the hand appearance). If the release event (H, or hands appear) does not occur until the final event (passed(1s), during 1 s), then the control system should react (generate reaction) to this by !D, that is by switching off the dryer. Invariant D means the dryer should be on till the dryer is switched off after 1 s.

As to the allowable delay value, it can be interpreted independently from the other attributes and serves to provide the ability to specify time delays associated with execution overheads. According to the allowable delay value, the reaction should occur within 10 ms interval of time after the final event.

5   Related Work

While various models are increasingly used in the development and verification of cyber-physical systems (see our review in [2]), the development of requirements for them today stands out as a separate discipline. According to Zave [28], requirements engineering (RE) is the branch of software engineering concerned with the real-world goals for, functions of, and constraints on software systems. In its early years, requirements engineering was about the importance of specifying requirements, focusing on the 'What' instead of the 'How'. It then moved to systematic processes and methods, focusing on the 'Why' [29]. With the increasing complexity of requirements, the question on their organization arises.

Starting with IEFC RFC 2119 [30], an attempt was made to prioritize them in baseline text form claims, at the same time, English modal verbs like *"Must"*, *"Should"*, *"May"* were used as keywords for the degree of desirability of requirements. In [31] Mavin et al. introduced a textual syntax for requirements, based on a precondition, an event trigger and a desired response. The syntax was intended for use in the production of Rolls-Royce aircraft engines. A review of formal specification languages aimed at requirements formalization was given in [32]. In particular, Ljungkrantz et al. [33] proposed an extended linear temporal logic ST-LTL to formally specify control logics of IEC 61131-3 programmable logic controllers in structured text. Their main improvement is in using previous variable values instead of next state operator as well as in introducing an operator for working with values of control variables at Nth step. This is the opposite of our presented approach and leads to more complicated specifications and proofs.

According to the approach presented by Kuzmin et al. [34], the value of each variable should be changed once and in only one place in the program during one iteration of the PLC cycle. Therefore, the change in value of each program variable is represented by two explicit LTL formulas:

$$\mathbf{GX}(V > \_V \implies OldValCond \lor FiringCond \lor V = NewValExpr);$$

$$\mathbf{GX}(V < \_V \implies OldValCond' \lor FiringCond' \lor V = NewValExpr'),$$

where _ is a pseudo-operator, allowing to refer to the previous state value of the variable V. This can be considered as part of our concept (see Definition 3).

Xiaohong Chen et al. [35] proposed a dynamic safety specification pattern with *Trigger* and *Postcondition* attributes that are similar to the components *trigger* and *reaction* in our pattern. However, their pattern has no direct analogs for the *final event*, *invariant condition* and *allowable delay* components. There is also a difference in time models. Time in their model is measured either in abstract real numbers (physical time) or in moments when an event occurs (logical time), while time in our model is measured either in values of the type *time* (in hours, minutes, seconds, etc.) or in the number of scan cycles.

The classic pattern system from [36] includes the most popular qualitative requirements for concurrent systems. Each pattern is described in a natural language, together with its formalization by formulas of temporal logics CTL and LTL [27], quantified regular expressions and graphical representation with GIL. In [9,37], these patterns are extended to the case of probabilistic systems and real-time systems, respectively. Some composite event patterns are suggested in [19,23]. In [38], the authors introduce patterns for quantitative characteristics of event occurrences, as well as a data pattern [39]. All mentioned approaches operate only patterns with semantics expressible in LTL and its real-time and probabilistic extensions. However, [40] shows the necessity in some cases to use the branching time logic CTL with the corresponding extensions. Recent work [17] combines descriptions of classical patterns with probabilistic and real-time patterns and provides their description in limited English. In [22], classification of patterns is presented in the form of an ontology, however the set of patterns is very limited, and they have no formal semantics. In [18], we proposed an ontology of specification patterns that combines patterns from existing requirement classifications with new patterns. This ontology can be used to express combinations of requirements of the following types: qualitative, real and branching time, with combined events, quantitative characteristics of events, and simple statements about data. Summarizing, the state-of-the-art formal systems of specification patterns seem too rich and sophisticated to express the simple needs of control software requirement engineers.

We can state that the use of requirements in the form of pure LTL formulas can lead to problems of their formalization when developing a system, therefore, our work has a novelty in the creation of an intermediate descriptive logical language that would unite all the considered approaches, and also allow describing control systems close to discussed features of control software development, with the purpose of further automatic verification.

6   Conclusion and Future Work

In this paper we have presented the Event-Driven Temporal Logic (EDTL) as the base of unambiguous and at the same time engineer-friendly specification of control software requirements. In contrast to known general-purpose specification languages, our approach offers a domain-oriented specification of discrete control software with scan cycles. Although EDTL does not use continuous time, it allows users to specify requirements for a wide class of control software.

We have proposed the EDTL-based six-component pattern to specify requirements that are independent of the internal structure of control software or the plant. We have developed two formal semantics of EDTL formulas using LTL and FOL. The constructiveness of the semantics is shown by implementing a bounded checking algorithm.

The EDTL makes description of requirements simple through the use of concepts such as inputs/outputs, falling/rising edges, events, and timeouts which are natural to the process and plant engineers. A requirements specification based on EDTL is independent of any particular verification technique.

In continuing this work, we intend to add support for pattern composition to the notation, develop consistency-checking methods for EDTL including events prioritization, formally prove the equivalence of the two proposed semantics as well as the soundness of the presented bounded-checking algorithm. We also plan to develop and implement EDTL-based verification methods for dynamic verification, model checking and deductive verification approaches and their combination.

A   Bounded Checking of EDTL-requirements

In this appendix, we describe an algorithm which checks if an EDTL-requirement is satisfied for every finite initial path of a control system in some finite set of such paths. To check the EDTL-requirement tp, the algorithm follows the FOL-formula F_{tp} given in Sect. 3. For control system CS, we consider finite initial paths of length $len > 0$. The algorithm (implemented in [41]) is defined by the C-like functions take and check. The EDTL-requirements tp is represented by a structure with the corresponding fields trigger, final and other, the path is represented by an array p storing the finite history of system states, and an array pp stands for a set of such paths. In contrast to the bounded model checking method, this algorithm does not explore *every* initial path of a verified system.

```
bool take (struct tp, array pp) {
    for (i = 0, i < n, i++)
        if !check (tp, pp[i]) return false;
    return true;
}
bool check (struct tp, array p) {
  trig = 1;
  while (trig < len) {
   if (value(tp.trigger, p, trig, 0) {
    if (value(tp.release, p, trig, trig)) goto checked;
    fin = trig;
    while (!value(tp.final, p, fin, trig)) {
     if (value(tp.release, p, fin, trig)) goto checked;
     if (!value(tp.invariant, p, fin, trig)) return false;
     fin++;
     if (fin == len) goto checked;
    }
    del = fin;
    while (!value(tp.delay, p, del, fin) &&
           !value(tp.reaction, p, del + 1, fin)) {
     if (value(tp.release, p, del, trig)) goto checked;
     if (!value(tp.invariant, p, del, fin)) return false;
     del++;
     if (del == len) goto checked;
    }
    if (!value(tp.release, p, del, trig) &&
        value(tp.delay, p, del, fin) &&
        !value(tp.invariant, p, del, fin)) return false;
   }
   checked: trig++;
  }
  return true;
}
```

In Figure 3, we depict a class diagram based on our implementation [41] of the bounded checking algorithm for given EDTL-requirements. We implemented the EDTL-formulas as classes based on the EDTL terms. Then we encoded the R1..R5 requirements for our case study using information from Table 2. So the user can use provided classes by implementing their own system consisted of cases inherited from *CheckableReq* and overriding six methods that specify the requirements in terms of our logic. This integrates the requirements checking process into the unit testing process.

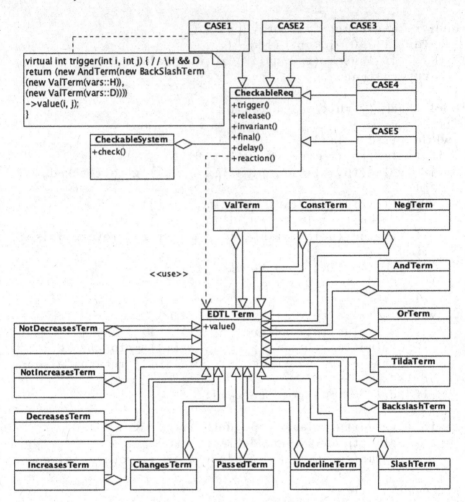

Fig. 3. Object-oriented implementation of the bounded checking algorithm for EDTL-requirements

References

1. Darvas, D., Majzik, I., Blanco Viñuela, E.: Formal verification of safety PLC based control software. In: Ábrahám, E., Huisman, M. (eds.) IFM 2016. LNCS, vol. 9681, pp. 508–522. Springer, Cham (2016). https://doi.org/10.1007/978-3-319-33693-0_32
2. Staroletov, S., et al.: Model-driven methods to design of reliable multiagent cyber-physical systems. In: Proceedings of the Conference on Modeling and Analysis of Complex Systems and Processes (MACSPro 2019), vol. 2478, pp. 74–91. CEUR Workshop Proceedings (2019)
3. Sommerville, I.: Software Engineering. Pearson Education, Harlow (2016)
4. Feng, L., et al.: Quality control scheme selection with a case of aviation equipment development. Eng. Manag. J. **32**(1), 14–25 (2020)

5. Anureev, I., Garanina, N., Liakh, T., Rozov, A., Zyubin, V., Gorlatch, S.: Two-step deductive verification of control software using reflex. In: Bjørner, N., Virbitskaite, I., Voronkov, A. (eds.) PSI 2019. LNCS, vol. 11964, pp. 50–63. Springer, Cham (2019). https://doi.org/10.1007/978-3-030-37487-7_5

6. IEC: 61131–3 Ed. 3.0 en:2013: Programmable Controllers—Part 3: Programming Languages. International Electrotechnical Commission (2013)

7. Leveson, N., Heimdahl, M., Reese, J.: Designing specification languages for process control systems: lessons learned and steps to the future. ACM Sigsoft Softw. Eng. Notes. **24**(6), 127–145 (1999). https://doi.org/10.1145/318774.318937

8. Schneider, F., Berenbach, B.: A literature survey on international standards for systems requirements engineering. In: Proceedings of the Conference on Systems Engineering Research, vol. 16, pp. 796–805, January 2013

9. Konrad, S., Cheng, B.H.: Real-time specification patterns. In: Proceedings of the 27th International Conference on Software Engineering, pp. 372–381. ACM (2005)

10. Filipovikj, P., Nyberg, M., Rodriguez-Navas, G.: Reassessing the pattern-based approach for formalizing requirements in the automotive domain. In: IEEE 22nd International Requirements Engineering Conference, pp. 444–450. IEEE (2014)

11. Jue, W., Song, Y., Wu, X. Dai, W.: A semi-formal requirement modeling pattern for designing industrial cyber-physical systems. In: Proceedings of IECON 2019–45th Annual Conference of the IEEE Industrial Electronics Society, Lisbon, Portugal, 2019. pp. 2883–2888 (2019)

12. Garanina, N., Anureev, I., Sidorova, E., Koznov, D., Zyubin, V., Gorlatch, S.: An ontology-based approach to support formal verification of concurrent systems. In: Sekerinski, E., et al. (eds.) FM 2019. LNCS, vol. 12232, pp. 114–130. Springer, Cham (2020). https://doi.org/10.1007/978-3-030-54994-7_9

13. Ghosh, S., Elenius, D., Li, W., Lincoln, P., Shankar, N., Steiner, W.: ARSE-NAL: automatic requirements specification extraction from natural language. In: Rayadurgam, S., Tkachuk, O. (eds.) NFM 2016. LNCS, vol. 9690, pp. 41–46. Springer, Cham (2016). https://doi.org/10.1007/978-3-319-40648-0_4

14. Sarmiento, E., do Prado Leite, J.C.S., Almentero, E.: C&L: generating model based test cases from natural language requirements descriptions. In: 2014 IEEE 1st International Workshop on Requirements Engineering and Testing (RET), pp. 32–38. IEEE (2014)

15. Leveson, N.G., Heimdahl, M.P.E., Hildreth, H., Reese, J.D.: Requirements specification for process-control systems. IEEE Trans. Softw. Eng. **20**(9), 684–707 (1994). https://doi.org/10.1109/32.317428

16. Pang, C., Pakonen, A., Buzhinsky, I., Vyatkin, V.: A study on user-friendly formal specification languages for requirements formalization. In: IEEE 14th International Conference on Industrial Informatics (INDIN), pp. 676–682. IEEE (2016)

17. Autili, M., Grunske, L., Lumpe, M., Pelliccione, P., Tang, A.: Aligning qualitative, real-time, and probabilistic property specification patterns using a structured English grammar. IEEE Trans. Softw. Eng. **41**(7), 620–638 (2015)

18. Garanina, N., Zubin, V., Lyakh, T., Gorlatch, S.: An ontology of specification patterns for verification of concurrent systems. In: Proceedings of the 17th International Conference on Intelligent Software Methodology Tools, and Techniques (SoMeT_18), pp. 515–528. IOS Press, Amsterdam (2018)

19. Salamah, S., Gates, A.Q., Kreinovich, V.: Validated patterns for specification of complex LTL formulas. J. Syst. Softw. **85**(8), 1915–1929 (2012)

20. Smith, M.H., Holzmann, G.J., Etessami, K.: Events and constraints: a graphical editor for capturing logic requirements of programs. In: Proceedings of Fifth IEEE

International Symposium on Requirements Engineering, 27–31 August 2001, pp. 14–22. IEEE (2001)

21. Wong, P.Y.H., Gibbons, J.: Property specifications for workflow modelling. In: Leuschel, M., Wehrheim, H. (eds.) IFM 2009. LNCS, vol. 5423, pp. 56–71. Springer, Heidelberg (2009). https://doi.org/10.1007/978-3-642-00255-7_5

22. Yu, J., Manh, T.P., Han, J., Jin, Y., Han, Y., Wang, J.: Pattern based property specification and verification for service composition. In: Aberer, K., Peng, Z., Rundensteiner, E.A., Zhang, Y., Li, X. (eds.) WISE 2006. LNCS, vol. 4255, pp. 156–168. Springer, Heidelberg (2006). https://doi.org/10.1007/11912873_18

23. Mondragon, O., Gates, A. Q., Roach, S.: Prospec: support for elicitation and formal specification of software properties. In: Proceedings of Runtime Verification Workshop. Electronic Notes in Theoretical Computer Science, vol. 89, pp. 67–88. Elsevier (2004)

24. Garanina, N., Anureev, I., Zyubin, V., Rozov, A., Liakh, T., Gorlatch, S.: Reasoning about programmable logic controllers. Syst. Inform. **17**, 33–42 (2020)

25. Mader, A.: A classification of plc models and applications. In: Boel, R., Stremersch, G. (eds.) Discrete Event Systems. SECS, vol. 569, pp. 239–246. Springer, Boston, MA (2000). https://doi.org/10.1007/978-1-4615-4493-7_24

26. Estrada-Vargas, A.P., López-Mellado, E., Lesage, J.J.: A black-box identification method for automated discrete-event systems. IEEE Trans. Autom. Sci. Eng. **14**(3), 1321–1336 (2015)

27. Clarke, E.M., Henzinger, Th.A., Veith, H., Bloem, R. (eds.): Handbook of Model Checking. Springer International Publishing, New York (2018)

28. Zave, P.: Classification of research efforts in requirements engineering. ACM Comput. Surv. (CSUR) **29**(4), 315–321 (1997)

29. Bennaceur, A., et al.: Requirements Engineering. Handbook of Software Engineering. pp. 51–92. Springer, Cham (2019)

30. Bradner, S.: Key words for use in RFCs to indicate requirement levels (1997). http://www.ietf.org/rfc/rfc2119.txt. Accessed 17 Jan 2021

31. Mavin, A., et al.: Easy approach to requirements syntax (EARS). In: 2009 17th IEEE International Requirements Engineering Conference. IEEE (2009)

32. Pang, C., Pakonen, A., Buzhinsky, I., Vyatkin, V.: A study on user-friendly formal specification languages for requirements formalization. In: 2016 IEEE 14th International Conference on Industrial Informatics (INDIN), pp. 676–682. IEEE (2016)

33. Ljungkrantz, O., Åkesson, K., Fabian, M., Yuan, C.: A formal specification language for PLC-based control logic. In: 8th IEEE International Conference on Industrial Informatics, pp. 1067–1072. IEEE (2010)

34. Kuzmin, E.V., Ryabukhin, D.A., Sokolov, V.A.: On the expressiveness of the approach to constructing PLC-programs by LTL-specification. Autom. Control. Comput. Sci. **50**(7), 510–519 (2016). https://doi.org/10.3103/S0146411616070130

35. Chen, X., Han, L., Liu, J. Sun, H.: Using safety requirement patterns to elicit requirements for railway interlocking systems. In: 2016 IEEE 24th International Requirements Engineering Conference Workshops (REW), Beijing, 2016, pp. 296–303. IEEE (2016)

36. Dwyer, M.B., Avrunin, G.S., Corbett, J.C.: Patterns in property specifications for finite-state verification. In: Proceedings of the 21st International Conference on Software Engineering, pp. 411–420. IEEE Computer Society Press (1999)

37. Grunske, L.: Specification patterns for probabilistic quality properties. In: Proceedings of the 30th International Conference on Software Engineering (ICSE 2008), pp. 31–40. ACM, New York, NY (2008)

38. Bianculli, D., Ghezzi, C., Pautasso, C., Senti, P.: Specification patterns from research to industry: a case study in service-based applications. In: Proceedings of 34th International Conference on Software Engineering (ICSE), pp. 968–976. IEEE (2012)

39. Halle, S., Villemaire, R., Cherkaoui, O.: Specifying and validating data-aware temporal web service properties. IEEE Trans. Softw. Eng. **35**(5), 669–683 (2009)

40. Post, A., Menzel, I., Podelski, A.: Applying restricted English grammar on automotive requirements—does it work? A case study. In: Berry, D., Franch, X. (eds.) REFSQ 2011. LNCS, vol. 6606, pp. 166–180. Springer, Heidelberg (2011). https://doi.org/10.1007/978-3-642-19858-8_17

41. Staroletov, S.: EDTL: Object-oriented implementation of the bounded checking algorithm for EDTL-requirements (2020). https://doi.org/10.5281/zenodo.4445663. Accessed 17 Jan 2021

Extending OCL with Map and Function Types

Kevin Lano[1(✉)] and Shekoufeh Kolahdouz-Rahimi[2]

[1] Department of Informatics, King's College London, London, UK
kevin.lano@kcl.ac.uk
[2] Department of Software Engineering, University of Isfahan, Isfahan, Iran
sh.rahimi@eng.ui.ac.ir

Abstract. Map and function types are of high utility in software specification and design, for example, maps can be used to represent configurations or caches, whilst function values can be used to enable genericity and reuse in a specification, and to support mechanisms such as callbacks or closures in an implementation. Map and function types have been incorporated into the leading programming languages, including Java, C++, Swift and Python.

The Object Constraint Language (OCL) specification notation lacks such types, and in this paper we make a proposal for a consistent extension of OCL with map and function types, and we identify modifications to OCL semantics to include these types. We also describe how map and function types are implemented using the Eclipse AgileUML toolset.

Keywords: Object Constraint Language (OCL) · Code generation · OCL semantics

1 Introduction

The Object Constraint Language (OCL) is the textual specification notation for class diagrams, metamodels and other UML models, including QVT transformations [18,19]. The OCL originated in the work of Cook and others in the 1990's on semi-formal specification languages which could be used by general software practitioners [11]. Many of the concepts of OCL originated in the Z specification language [22], but with restrictions imposed in order to align the language more closely to computational systems. For example, only a finite powerset constructor $Set(X)$ is available in OCL, compared to the general powerset operator $\mathbb{P}(X)$ of Z. Z in turn is founded in Zermelo-Fraenkel set theory (ZFC) [4], which ensures the existence of the sets required by application of the type construction operators of Z.

Figure 1 shows the type system of the current OCL 2.4 standard. When OCL is used with a particular underlying model such as a class diagram or metamodel, the class types of the model are also available in OCL (as subtypes of *Class*), as are enumerated types (subtypes of *Enumeration*). This type system is based

© IFIP International Federation for Information Processing 2021
Published by Springer Nature Switzerland AG 2021
H. Hojjat and M. Massink (Eds.): FSEN 2021, LNCS 12818, pp. 108–123, 2021.
https://doi.org/10.1007/978-3-030-89247-0_8

on the definitions of Annex A of [18], except that the Annex restricts *OclAny* to not be a supertype of collection or tuple types (Section A.2.7 of [18]); this restriction is removed in the main part of the OCL standard.

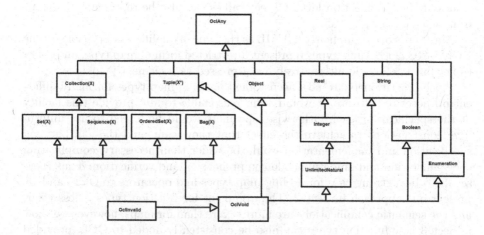

Fig. 1. Type system of OCL 2.4 standard [18]

Map and function types are now widely available in modern programming languages, and are part of the essential toolkit of software developers. They are also of high utility in software specifications, enabling concise and declarative specifications to be used for situations where associative data collections are needed, or functional genericity. Specification languages such as the EOL of Epsilon [9] and the expression languages of model transformation languages such as ATL [6] are related to OCL, and already include map types and operators. Map types were also present in Z and in the Z-based B language [13], and function types were available in Z.

Including map and function types in a specification language has advantages for code-generation from the language, enabling mechanisms such as operation caching and object indexing to be defined at a language-independent level, avoiding the need to define (in code-generators) language-specific schemes for these constructs in each target programming language. This potentially reduces the size and complexity of the code generators.

In the AgileUML toolset for UML [7], applications can be defined at a high level of abstraction using class diagrams, OCL and use cases. Consequently we divide code generation into two steps: (i) specification to design; (ii) design to code. The design is also expressed in UML, and is platform-independent, but explicit behaviour definitions are given for operations and use cases, using a pseudocode activity representation [16]. This common intermediate design stage helps to ensure semantic consistency of generated code in different target languages. Maps and function types are particularly useful at the design level, to define explicit semantics for specification-level concepts such as ≪*cached*≫

operations and ≪*identity*≫ (object identifier) attributes. They can be used to implement symbol tables for formally-specified software tools, and to store application preferences or other configuration property assignments. They can also be used to abstractly represent data structures such as CSV tables and JSON values at the specification level. Object values can also be represented as maps from feature names to values.

Map types occur implicitly in UML as the type of qualified associations (Issue OCL25-202 [20]). Tuple types represent a restricted form of map type, and n-ary tuples for $n > 2$ could alternatively be expressed as n-element maps.

Since practitioners are now accustomed to using map types for many different purposes in software, it would seem reasonable to also provide this facility at the specification level. Otherwise, specifiers would be forced to use unintuitive constructions to achieve the effect that they want, and the gap between specification and implementation would be wider than necessary, complicating code generation and hindering code comprehension and verification. Thus there seems to be a strong case for adding map types and operators to OCL, and we present one approach in Sect. 2. The argument for function types is less clear, and the semantic complications are more severe than for maps, however we show in Sect. 3 how function types can also be consistently added to OCL, provided that the status of the 'universal type' *OclAny* is modified. In Sect. 4 we discuss related work, and in the Appendix we specify further map type operators, following the format of Chapter 11 of the OCL standard [18].

2   Map Types

We propose to add a new type constructor *Map*(,) of finite maps to OCL, such that $Map(K, T)$ denotes the type of finite maps from a domain K to a range T. K and T can be any OCL types from the type system of Fig. 1, extended with *Map* types. The type $Map(K, T)$ could be regarded as a subtype of $Set(Tuple(key : K, value : T))$, however we will treat *Map* as an independent type constructor, as in EOL [9] and ATL [6].

A map is a (finite) aggregate data structure where the elements are indexed by key values. Elements may be members of the range of the map more than once, but key values must be unique. As with collections, the *invalid* value cannot be a member of a map, either as a key or range element. A Map m of type $Map(K, T)$ can be considered to have an underlying set $m \rightarrow asSet()$ of elements (pairs) of the type $Tuple(key : K, value : T)$. We use the simplified maplet notation $key \mapsto value$ for such pairs, which is the mathematical notation for map elements used in Z and B.

Following the same approach as adopted by the OCL standard for collections, we could write literal map values as $Map\{k1 \mapsto v1, ..., kn \mapsto vn\}$. An alternative notation[1] for this is $Map\{(k1, v1), ..., (kn, vn)\}$.

---

[1] Used in the ATL extension of OCL.

As discussed in the introduction, one useful application of map types is to define the semantics of caching of operation results. In particular, if a query operation

```
operation op(x : X) : Y
pre: P
post: Q
```

of class C has the stereotype $\ll$*cached*$\gg$, then in the specification-to-design step of code generation we can introduce a map-typed attribute

```
op_cache : Map(X,Y) := Map{}
```

of C, and define a platform-independent design of *op* as:

```
operation op(x : X) : Y
pre: P
activity:
  var result : Y ;
  if op_cache->includesKey(x)
  then
    return op_cache->at(x)
  else
  ( result := op_uncached(x) ;
    op_cache := op_cache->including(x,result) ;
    return result
  )
```

The operation *op_uncached* has the activity derived from Q, this is the version of the operation without caching. The above caching algorithm for *op* can then be translated into specific languages by design-to-code translators for the languages.

Similarly, if a class E has an $\ll$*identity*$\gg$ attribute $att : K$, then the design defines indexing maps

```
E_att_index : Map(K,E)
```

which enable efficient retrieval of E elements by key: $E\_att\_index \rightarrow at(k)$. This corresponds to the notation $E[k]$ in the specification. In implementations, map data structures can be used which have sub-linear time complexity for map application. This is therefore potentially more efficient than using a specification construct such as $E \rightarrow select(att = k) \rightarrow first()$ [3].

2.1   Map Type Semantics

The map type $Map(K, T)$ can be semantically represented by the mathematical type $K' \nrightarrow T'$ of finite partial/total maps from the semantic representation K' of K to the representation T' of T [15,22].

If T_1 is a subtype of T_2, then $Map(K, T_1)$ can be regarded as a subtype of $Map(K, T_2)$, because $T_1' \subseteq T_2'$, so that $m \in K' \nrightarrow T_1'$ implies that $m \in K' \nrightarrow T_2'$.

Similarly, if K_1 is a subtype of K_2, then $Map(K_1, T)$ can be regarded as a subtype of $Map(K_2, T)$.

Annex A.2 of [18] can also be extended in a direct manner to include map types. For example, following the approach of the annex, the interpretation function for map types is:

$$I(Map(s, t)) = (I(s) \nrightarrow I(t)) \cup \{\bot\}$$

where $\bot$ is the semantic interpretation of *invalid*. In the same manner, constructor and other operations for maps can be formally defined.

The role of *OclAny* needs to be examined with regard to the *Map(,)* constructor. Because the constructor is finitary, the cardinality $card(Map(K, T))$ of a map type cannot be greater than that of K or T. The situation is therefore the same as with the existing collection types, e.g., $card(Set(Real)) = card(Real)$. This holds because finite sets of real numbers can be themselves represented in a 1-1 manner as real numbers, and likewise for finite maps from *Real* to *Real*. Thus, in principle $Map(K, T)$ can be considered a subtype of *OclAny* for any K, T. However the 1-1 embeddings of $Map(K, T)$ or $Set(T)$ into *OclAny* are non-trivial (and not unique) when K or T themselves involve *OclAny*, so that subtyping in this sense cannot be simply regarded as subsetting.

There is inconsistency in [18] regarding the relation of *OclAny* to other OCL types. Sections 8.2 and 11 of [18] state that it is a supertype of all other OCL types, including collection and tuple types, as in Fig. 1, but Annex A excludes collection/tuple types from inclusion in *OclAny* (Section A.2.6). In the absence of function types it is semantically consistent for *OclAny* to generalise collection, map and tuple types. If *OclAny* can itself be used as a type argument of any parameterised type, then $Map(OclAny, OclAny)$ is embeddable in *OclAny*, and the above issue of the choice of embedding arises. This extended type system for OCL is adopted by EOL and ATL. However, in the UML-RSDS notation of AgileUML there is no universal *OclAny* type [16]. Likewise, in Z and B there is no universal type [22]. If this approach was adopted the type system would appear as Fig. 1 without the *OclAny* type.

The underlying mathematical theory of ZFC asserts that if sets a, b exist, then so does the Cartesian product $a \times b$ (axiom of pairing), powerset $\mathbb{P}(a)$, and distributed union $\bigcup(a)$. Moreover, $\mathbb{Z}$ exists (the axiom of infinity asserts the existence of $\mathbb{N}$), and sets can be formed using $\rightarrow select$ (by the axiom schema of separation), and $\rightarrow collect$ (by the axiom schema of replacement). The axioms also imply the existence of $\mathbb{R}$ (based on $\mathbb{P}(\mathbb{N})$). Countable sets isomorphic to $\mathbb{N}$ could be used as the semantic denotations of object types, with class extents (for $C.allInstances()$) being finite subsets of these. OCL maps from K to T can be based on finite sets of tuples in ZFC, i.e., on elements of $\mathbb{F}(K \times T)$. We could also weaken ZFC to ZFC^F by using $\mathbb{F}(a)$ in the powerset axiom instead of $\mathbb{P}(a)$. In this case the existence of $\mathbb{R}$ would need to be additionally asserted.

2.2   Operations on Maps

Some of the main operations on maps are given in the following and in the Appendix.

keys() : Set(K) The set of keys in the map, i.e., its domain:

```
post:
  result = self->asSet()->collect( p | p.key )->asSet()
```

Notice that $\rightarrow$*collect* returns a Bag in general, hence the second $\rightarrow$*asSet*.
   The unique key constraint of maps is expressed by:

$$m \rightarrow asSet() \rightarrow size() = m \rightarrow keys() \rightarrow size()$$

values() : Bag(T) The bag of values in the map, i.e., its range:

```
post:
  result = self->asSet()->collect( p | p.value )
```

=(c : Map(K,T)) : Boolean c and *self* are equal when both are maps of the same key and range types, and $c \rightarrow asSet() = self \rightarrow asSet()$.

<>(c : Map(K,T)) : Boolean The negation of =.

at(k : K) : T The value to which *self* maps k, *invalid* if k is not in $self \rightarrow keys()$:

```
post:
  (self->keys()->excludes(k) implies result = invalid) and
  (self->keys()->includes(k) implies
    result = self->restrict(Set{k})->values()->any())
```

2.3   Implementation

Implementations of the map type and map operators can be given in Java, Swift, C#, C++, Python and C. We have defined translations in the code generators for AgileUML [7], which can be accessed from [1] or viewed in the OCL libraries at http://www.nms.kcl.ac.uk/kevin.lano/libraries. Eg., in ocl.py for Python. Tables 1, 2 give some examples of the map type and operation mappings in different languages. X denotes the interpretation in each language of X in OCL. In C we define a custom data structure *ocltnode* based on binary search trees to represent maps. Other languages already have map types inbuilt or in standard libraries. The application of a map to a key is usually a constant-time or log-time operation in terms of the map size.

   In the directory *oclmapexamples.zip* on [1] we give examples of specifications using maps, together with the corresponding generated code in Java, C, Swift and Python.

Table 1. Mappings from extended OCL to Java, Swift, C#, C++

UML/OCL	Java 4/5/6	Swift 5	C#	C++
$Map(S, T)$	Map	Dictionary<S,T>	Dictionary	map<S,T> *
$m \rightarrow at(x)$	((T) m.get(x))	m[x]	m[x]	(*m)[x]
$m[x] = y$	m.put(x,y);	m[x] = y	m.Add(x,y);	(*m)[x] = y;

Table 2. Mappings from extended OCL to Java 7+, C and Python

UML/OCL	Java 7/8	Python	C
$Map(S, T)$	HashMap<S,T>	dict	struct ocltnode*
$m \rightarrow at(x)$	m.get(x)	m[x]	(T) lookupInMap(m, x)
$m[x] = y$	m.put(x,y);	m[x] = y	insertIntoMap(m,x,y);

3   Function Types

Being able to use functions as values was a key innovation of functional programming languages such as LISP and ML, and this facility was also provided in some procedural programming languages such as C, where a function name could be used as a pointer to the address of the function code in memory, and passed as an argument to other functions. Function types were definable in Z [22] and at the abstract specification level of B.

The two key operations on functions are *function abstraction* and *function application*. A mechanism to define function values by abstraction is now present in most modern programming languages, with different terminologies (lambda expressions in Python or Java, closures in Swift, delegates in C#, etc.). These enable a function value to be defined by specifying the values of its applications, via expressions within different contexts. Both Z and B provide a function abstraction operator, written using the λ symbol.

Function types are used implicitly in the OCL 2.4 specification, for example in the definition of the *iterate* operator [23,24]. We propose an extension of OCL with explicitly defined function types $S \rightarrow T$ (also denoted $Function(S, T)$) for types S and T, and function abstraction *lambda* $x : S$ *in* e. However, because this construction introduces the possibility of types of unbounded cardinality (Sect. 3.1), the *OclAny* type cannot be used in S, otherwise semantic contradictions appear [5]. Moreover, since equality of functions is generally undecidable, collections of functions will have undecidable membership relations.

An important use of function types is to simplify the code generation of expressions such as $E \rightarrow select(x \mid P)$, $E \rightarrow reject(x \mid P)$, $E \rightarrow collect(x \mid e)$, which depend upon other expressions P, e of arbitrary complexity. If function types are available, then the above constructs can be given uniform designs as higher-order functions independent of the specific P, e expressions. For example, *select* on E-sets could be defined by a single higher-order operation:

```
operation selectE(col : Set(E), f : E -> Boolean) : Set(E)
activity:
  var res: Set(E) := Set{} ;
  for x in col
  do
    if f(x)
    then res := res->including(x)
    else skip ;
  return res
```

An occurrence $col \rightarrow select(x \mid P)$ for set $col : Set(E)$ can then be interpreted as $selectE(col, lambda\ x : E\ in\ P)$. This avoids the need to define $select$ operations for each specific P. In the same manner, the OCL $s \rightarrow sortedBy(e)$ operator can be expressed at the design stage in terms of a function parameter $lessThan$: $T \rightarrow (T \rightarrow Integer)$ on the type T of e, and a sorting algorithm such as merge sort.

Within specifications, function types are useful to provide genericity in cases where a uniform algorithm should be applied to a wide range of different functions. For example, an optimisation procedure such as bisection or secant can be applied to any total continuous function $f : Real \rightarrow Real$:

```
operation secant(rn : Real, rprev : Real, fprev : Real, tol : Real,
    f : Real -> Real) : Real
pre: tol > 0
post:
  let fn : Real = f(rn) in
    if abs(fn) < tol
    then result = rn
    else
      result = secant(rn - fn*((rn-rprev)/(fn-fprev)),rn,fn,tol,f)
    endif
```

A similar situation arises with genetic and other evolutionary algorithms which can be parameterised by different fitness functions.

The introduction of function types would also enable a functional programming language style of specification in OCL, in terms of functions and higher-order functions. This specification style is particularly useful for application areas such as finance and machine learning.

3.1   Function Type Semantics

The OCL function type $S \rightarrow T$ can be given a semantics as the set of partial functions $S' \nrightarrow T'$ in [14, 15]. In the case that f of type $S \rightarrow T$ in OCL maps $s : S$ to $invalid$, s is considered to be outside the domain of the semantic representation f' of f: $s' \notin \mathrm{dom}(f')$. If S_1 conforms to S_2 and T_1 conforms to T_2, then $S_1 \rightarrow T_1$ conforms to $S_2 \rightarrow T_2$: every function from S_1 to T_1 can also be treated as a (partial) function from S_2 to T_2, with $invalid$ value on elements of S_2 not in S_1.

The semantics of function types can also be expressed within the framework of Annex A of [18]:

$$I(s \rightarrow t) = (I(s) \nrightarrow I(t)) \cup \{\bot\}$$

In contrast to maps, functions are immutable. They can also be non-finite and have non-finite domains and ranges. Thus the domains and ranges cannot be expressed as OCL collections in general, nor can $\rightarrow asSet()$ be computed for functions. The $S \rightarrow T$ type constructor can produce types with non-countable sets of elements, for example $Integer \rightarrow Integer$. Moreover, $S \rightarrow Boolean$ always has higher cardinality than S:

$$card(S \rightarrow Boolean) > card(S)$$

This has the implication that if $OclAny$ is regarded as a universal type extending all OCL types, then it cannot occur as the first argument of a function type, otherwise the contradiction

$$card(OclAny) \geq card(OclAny \rightarrow Boolean) > card(OclAny)$$

would arise.

Even with this restriction, the construction of a universal type $OclAny$ including all other forms of function type would require the application of powerful transfinite axioms of ZFC, i.e., to construct a set containing all elements of $\mathbb{N}$, $\mathbb{P}(\mathbb{N})$, $\mathbb{P}(\mathbb{P}(\mathbb{N}))$, ... For this reason we consider that it is preferable to either remove the concept of a universal type from the OCL type system, as in [14–16], and languages such as Z and B, or to exclude function and other parameterised types from being subtypes of the universal type.

Adopting the 'no $OclAny$' approach, the revised OCL type system incorporating map and function types would be as shown in Fig. 2.

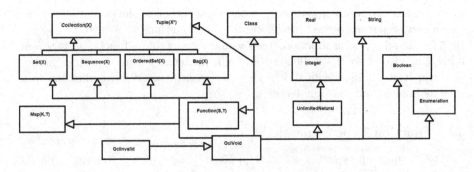

Fig. 2. Revised OCL type system

The semantics of function application is described in Section A.3.1.2 of [18].

3.2 Operations on Functions

Some of the key operations on functions are given in the following. While theoretical definitions of equality, inequality and definedness of functions can be given, these cannot be effectively computed in all cases, and hence should not be used in specifications. Only abstraction and application are valid operators for all functions.

Function Application. Denoted $f(x)$ for $f : S \to T$ and $x : S$, this is an element of T, or is *invalid*, if x is not in the domain of f.

Function Abstraction. *lambda $x : S$ in E* The function of type $S \to T$ defined by evaluating $E : T$ on elements of S.

$S ::$
$$(lambda\ x : S\ in\ E)(self)\ =\ E[self/x]$$

where $P[e/v]$ denotes the substitution of e for v in P. E should be side-effect free, and x should not occur bound in E.

An alternative notation for abstraction could be *let $x : S$ in E*, however this may introduce confusion with the existing OCL *let* operator. Indeed, *let* and *lambda* are related by *(let $x : S = v$ in E)* = *(lambda $x : S$ in E)(v)* for side-effect free E. The notation could be used with multiple arguments: *lambda $x1 : S1, ..., xn : Sn$ in E* to form anonymous functions with multiple parameters. The Currying transformation of this to *lambda $x1 : S1$ in (lambda $x2 : S2, ..., xn : Sn$ in E)* is also naturally expressed in this notation.

By definition the property of β-reduction holds for the *lambda* operator; α-conversion also holds in the sense that functions *lambda $x : S$ in E* and *lambda $y : S$ in $E[y/x]$* are equivalent if neither y or x occur as bound variables in E. The expression E may involve data identifiers other than x, and the formed lambda function is then implicitly a function of these additional variables, and can only be evaluated in contexts where they are defined. This property is termed *scope capture*.

3.3 Implementation

Table 3 gives some examples of the implementation of function types and function application and abstraction in different programming languages. Function abstraction is not supported in C or in earlier versions of Java. Instead, in C, we introduce new global operations `T op_i(S x) { return e; }` for each occurrence *lambda $x : S$ in e* of a lambda expression, and translate the expression as `op_i`. This approach does not support scope capture: e must depend only on x.

In the directory *oclfunctionexamples.zip* on [1] we give an example specification using function types, together with the corresponding generated code in Java, Swift, C and Python. Currently in AgileUML version 2.0, lambda expressions may only occur in the arguments of operation calls.

Table 3. Mappings from extended OCL to Java, Swift, Python, C++

UML/OCL	C++	Swift 5	Java 8	Python
$S \to T$	T (*)(S)	(S) -> T	Evaluation<S,T>	–
$f(x)$	(*f)(x)	f(x)	f.evaluate(x) f(x)	f(x)
lambda $x : S$ in E	[](S x) -> T { return E; }	{ (x : S) -> T in E }	(x) -> { return E; }	lambda x : E

4   Related Work

There are two main semantic approaches for OCL: (i) via translation to a classical or extended logic and set theory based on ZFC (e.g., [14,15] or Annex A of [18]), or (ii) metamodelling semantics [12], whereby OCL syntax and value domains are defined via metamodels, and expression evaluation defined in terms of instances of these models. Either approach could be used to provide a semantics for the extensions which we propose, and we have indicated above the necessary modifications for the translational semantic approach. While the semantic revisions required for function types are more severe than for map types, these can also be consistently defined, provided that the concept of a universal type (*OclAny*) is modified.

In summary, map types can be added to OCL, retaining the existing type hierarchy (Fig. 1), and with $Map(K, T)$ a subtype of *OclAny* for any K, T, including parameter types that involve *OclAny*. However, as with the subtyping of $Set(OclAny)$ with respect to *OclAny*, such subtype relations cannot be expressed as subset relationships. It would also be possible to have a type system without *OclAny* (Fig. 2).

In contrast, for function types there are three main choices:

1. Retain *OclAny* as the supertype of all types, and forbid the use of *OclAny* in the domain argument of $Function(D, R)$.
   This suffers from the flaw that subtyping of collection, tuple map and function types wrt *OclAny* will not correspond to subsetting, as above. In addition *OclAny* would need to have a high transfinite cardinality.
2. Retain *OclAny* only as a supertype of non-parameterised types (*Class, Real, String, Enumeration, Boolean*). In this case, subtyping wrt to *OclAny* could be represented as subsetting. The cardinality of *OclAny* would be *card*(*Real*).
3. Remove *OclAny* from the type system, as in Fig. 2. This prevents the formation of heterogeneous collections such as sets including a mix of strings, numbers, objects, maps, etc.

In AgileUML we adopt the third option.

OCL was the subject of intensive research in the initial years of the UML standard and MDE [5,10,11,21], however subsequently there was slow progress on the development of the language, due mainly to language engineering factors and interdependence between the standard and other OMG standards [2,23,24]. The projected revision to OCL 2.5 was abandoned, however a long-term revision and rationalisation of the language to Version 3.0 is proposed in [24]. Function types are one possible extension suggested by [24], together with OCL libraries.

A map type and operators were added to ATL from Version 0.7 onwards [6], and these are defined in a style consistent with OCL collection operators. The Map type and operators in EOL [9] are however closely aligned with the implementation of maps in Java. We initially raised the suggestion of a map type and operators for OCL in [17]. The present paper develops this proposal based on feedback, and on experience of implementing the map type and operators in a range of programming languages. A related proposal is in [25].

The Eclipse OCL version [8] provides a map type with a similar set of operators to those proposed here. Table 4 compares the AgileUML and Eclipse OCL Map operators.

Table 4. Comparison of Eclipse OCL and AgileUML map operators

Eclipse OCL	AgileUML OCL
$=, <>, \rightarrow at$	$=, <>, \rightarrow at$
$m \rightarrow excludes(k)$	$m \rightarrow excludesKey(k)$
$m \rightarrow excludes(k, v)$	$m \rightarrow excludesAll(Map\{k \mapsto v\})$
$m \rightarrow excludesAll(ks)$	$m \rightarrow keys() \rightarrow intersection(ks) \rightarrow isEmpty()$
$m \rightarrow excludesMap(m1)$	$m \rightarrow excludesAll(m1)$
$m \rightarrow excludesValue(v)$	$m \rightarrow excludesValue(v)$
$m \rightarrow excluding(k)$	$m \rightarrow restrict(m \rightarrow keys() \rightarrow excluding(k))$
$m \rightarrow excluding(k, v)$	$m - Map\{k \mapsto v\}$
$m \rightarrow excludingAll(ks)$	$m \rightarrow restrict(m \rightarrow keys() - ks)$
$m \rightarrow excludingMap(m1)$	$m - m1$
$m \rightarrow includes(k)$	$m \rightarrow includesKey(k)$
$m \rightarrow includes(k, v)$	$m \rightarrow includesAll(Map\{k \mapsto v\})$
$m \rightarrow includesAll(ks)$	$m \rightarrow keys() \rightarrow includesAll(ks)$
$m \rightarrow includesMap(m1)$	$m \rightarrow includesAll(m1)$
$m \rightarrow includesValue(v)$	$m \rightarrow includesValue(v)$
$m \rightarrow including(k, v)$	$m \rightarrow including(k, v)$
$m \rightarrow includingMap(m1)$	$m \rightarrow union(m1)$
$\rightarrow isEmpty, \rightarrow notEmpty, \rightarrow size$	$\rightarrow isEmpty, \rightarrow notEmpty, \rightarrow size$
$\rightarrow keys, \rightarrow values$	$\rightarrow keys, \rightarrow values$

The main difference is that [8] uses the terminology *excludes/includes* for operators relating a map and key, whilst we use the more explicit *excludesKey/ includesKey*. We use the collection/collection operator names *includesAll*, *excludesAll* for the analogous map/map operators, instead of for map/key set operators. Additionally, we provide a literal map notation, and further map operators such as *count*, *select*, etc. by analogy with corresponding collection operators. Our objective in this respect is to align the map operators closely with collection operators, in order to enhance the usability of the extended OCL notation.

Conclusions

We have described possible extensions of OCL with map and function types, and associated operators. A semantics has been given for these extensions, and a rationale provided, in terms of benefits for specification and code generation.

A   Additional Map Type Operators

The following map operators can also be formalised in our proposed extension of OCL.

size() : Integer

```
post: result = self->asSet()->size()
```

This is equal to $self \rightarrow keys() \rightarrow size()$.

includesValue(object : T) : Boolean True if the *object* is an element of the map range, false otherwise:

```
post:
  result = self->values()->includes(object)
```

Similarly for $\rightarrow includesKey()$, $\rightarrow excludesValue()$, $\rightarrow excludesKey()$.

count(object : T) : Integer The number of times the *object* occurs as an element of the map range (a bag):

```
post:
  result = self->values()->count(object)
```

includesAll(c2 : Map(K,T)) : Boolean True if *c2* is a map, and the set of pairs of *self* contains all those of *c2*, false otherwise:

```
post:
  result = self->asSet()->includesAll(c2->asSet())
```

Similarly for $\rightarrow excludesAll()$.

isEmpty() : Boolean, notEmpty() : Boolean Defined based on $self \rightarrow asSet()$.

max() : T, min() : T, sum() : T Defined as the corresponding operations on $self \rightarrow values()$.

asSet() : Set(Tuple(key : K, value : T)) The set of pairs of elements in the map. Since duplicate keys are not permitted, this has the same size as $self{\rightarrow}keys()$.

restrict(ks : Set(K)) : Map(K,T) Domain restriction $ks \lhd self$. The map restricted to the keys in ks. Its elements are the pairs of $self$ whose key is in ks:

```
post:
  result->asSet() =
    self->asSet()->select(ks->includes(key))
```

Range restriction is provided via the $\rightarrow select$ operator.

-(m: Map(K,T)) : Map(K,T) Map subtraction: the elements of $self$ that are not in m.

```
post:
  result->asSet() =
      self->asSet() - m->asSet()
```

union(m : Map(K,T)) : Map(K,T) Map override, the operation $self \oplus m$ or $self <+ m$ in mathematical notation. This consists of the pairs of $self$ which do not conflict with pairs of m, together with all pairs of m:

```
post:
  result->asSet() =
  m->asSet()->union(
    self->asSet()->select(p | m->keys()->excludes(p.key)))
```

This is the same as *putAll* in EOL [9]. Unlike set union, it is not commutative.

intersection(m : Map(K,T)) : Map(K,T) The pairs of $self$ which are also in m:

```
post:
  result->asSet() =
    m->asSet()->intersection(self->asSet())
```

This is associative and commutative.

including(k : K, v : T) : Map(K,T) The pairs of $self$, with the additional/overriding mapping of k to v:

$$self{\rightarrow}including(k, v) \; \hat{=} \\ self{\rightarrow}union(Map\{k \mapsto v\})$$

We also use the abbreviated notation $m[k] = v$ for $m = m@pre{\rightarrow}including(k, v)$.

excluding(k : K, v : T) : Map(K,T) The pairs of $self$, with any mapping of k to v removed:

$$self{\rightarrow}excluding(k, v) \; \hat{=} \\ self - Map\{k \mapsto v\}$$

any Defined as

$$m \rightarrow any(x \mid P) \;\hat{=}\; m \rightarrow values() \rightarrow any(x \mid P)$$

Likewise for *forAll, exists, one*.

select The map formed by restricting to range elements which satisfy the *select* condition:

$$m \rightarrow select(x \mid P(x)) \;\hat{=}\;$$
$$m \rightarrow restrict(m \rightarrow keys() \rightarrow select(k \mid P(m \rightarrow at(k))))$$

Similarly for *reject*.

References

1. AgileUML repository (2020). https://github.com/eclipse/agileuml/
2. Belaunde, M.: Evolution of the OCL OMG specification, OCL (2010)
3. Sánchez Cuadrado, J., Jouault, F., García Molina, J., Bézivin, J.: Optimization patterns for OCL-based model transformations. In: Chaudron, M.R.V. (ed.) MODELS 2008. LNCS, vol. 5421, pp. 273–284. Springer, Heidelberg (2009). https://doi.org/10.1007/978-3-642-01648-6_29
4. Ciesielski, K.: Set Theory for the Working Mathematician. Cambridge University Press, Cambridge (1997)
5. Cook, S., Kleppe, A., Mitchell, R., Rumpe, B., Warmer, J., Wills, A.: The Amsterdam manifesto on OCL. In: Clark, T., Warmer, J. (eds.) Object Modeling with the OCL. LNCS, vol. 2263, pp. 115–149. Springer, Heidelberg (2002). https://doi.org/10.1007/3-540-45669-4_7
6. Eclipse, ATL user guide, eclipse.org (2019)
7. Eclipse AgileUML project (2020). https://projects.eclipse.org/projects/modeling.agileuml
8. Eclipse OCL Version 6.4.0 (2021). https://projects.eclipse.org/projects/modeling.mdt.ocl
9. The Epsilon Object Language (2020). https://www.eclipse.org/epsilon/doc/eol
10. Hennicker, R., Hussmann, H., Bidoit, M.: On the precise meaning of OCL constraints. In: Clark, T., Warmer, J. (eds.) Object Modeling with the OCL. LNCS, vol. 2263, pp. 69–84. Springer, Heidelberg (2002). https://doi.org/10.1007/3-540-45669-4_5
11. Kleppe, A., Warmer, J., Cook, S.: Informal formality? The object constraint language and its application in the UML metamodel. In: Bézivin, J., Muller, P.-A. (eds.) UML 1998. LNCS, vol. 1618, pp. 148–161. Springer, Heidelberg (1999). https://doi.org/10.1007/978-3-540-48480-6_12
12. Kleppe, A.: Object constraint language: metamodelling semantics (Chap. 7). In: UML 2 Semantics and Applications. Wiley (2009)
13. Lano, K.: The B Language and Method. Springer, Heidelberg (1996). https://doi.org/10.1007/978-1-4471-1494-9
14. Lano, K.: A compositional semantics of UML-RSDS. Softw. Syst. Model. **8**(1), 85–116 (2009). https://doi.org/10.1007/s10270-007-0064-x
15. Lano, K., Clark, T., Kolahdouz-Rahimi, S.: A framework for model transformation verification. Form. Asp. Comput. **27**(1), 193–235 (2014). https://doi.org/10.1007/s00165-014-0313-z

16. Lano, K.: Agile Model-Based Development Using UML-RSDS. CRC Press, Boca Raton (2016)
17. Lano, K.: Map type support in OCL?, November 2018. https://www.eclipse.org/forums/index.php/t/1096077/
18. OMG, Object Constraint Language 2.4 Specification (2014)
19. OMG, MOF2 Query/View/Transformation v1.3 (2016)
20. OMG (2020). https://issues.omg.org/issues/spec/OCL/2.4
21. Richters, M., Gogolla, M.: On formalizing the UML object constraint language OCL. In: Ling, T.-W., Ram, S., Li Lee, M. (eds.) ER 1998. LNCS, vol. 1507, pp. 449–464. Springer, Heidelberg (1998). https://doi.org/10.1007/978-3-540-49524-6_35
22. Spivey, J.: The Z Notation. Prentice Hall, Hoboken (1989)
23. Willink, E.: OCL omissions and contradictions, OMG ADTF (2012)
24. Willink, E.: Reflections on OCL 2. J. Object Technol. **19**(3), 1–16 (2020)
25. Willink, E.: An OCL map type. In: OCL 2019 (2019)

Networks

Deadlock in Packet Switching Networks

Anna Stramaglia$^{(\boxtimes)}$, Jeroen J. A. Keiren, and Hans Zantema

Eindhoven University of Technology, Eindhoven, The Netherlands
{a.stramaglia,j.j.a.keiren,h.zantema}@tue.nl

Abstract. A deadlock in a packet switching network is a state in which one or more messages have not yet reached their target, yet cannot progress any further. We formalize three different notions of deadlock in the context of packet switching networks, to which we refer as global, local and weak deadlock. We establish the precise relations between these notions, and prove they characterize different sets of deadlocks. Moreover, we implement checking of deadlock freedom of packet switching networks using the symbolic model checker nuXmv. We show experimentally that the implementation is effective at finding subtle deadlock situations in packet switching networks.

Keywords: Packet switching network · Deadlock · Model checking

1 Introduction

Deadlock is a historically well known bug pattern in computer systems where, in the most general sense, a system reaches a state in which no operation can progress any further. Deadlocks can occur in many different contexts, such as operating systems [6], databases [17], computer networks, and many others [18], provided one interprets the processes and resources involved appropriately. Regardless of the context, deadlock is a situation that we generally want to avoid.

A packet switching network consists of nodes, connected by (directed) channels. Packets are exchanged in a store-and-forward manner. This means that a node in the network first receives a packet in its entirety, and then decides along which output channel to forward the packet based on a routing function. The possible steps in the network are: sending a packet to some other node, processing the packet by first receiving and then forwarding it, and finally, receiving a packet when it reaches its destination node.

Packet switching networks have been around for decades, and the problem of deadlock in such networks was already described early on [10]. Basically a deadlock arises if packets compete for available channels. There are different ways to deal with deadlocks. First, in deadlock avoidance, extra information in the network is used to dynamically ensure deadlock freedom. Second, in deadlock prevention, deadlock freedom is ensured statically, e.g. based on the network topology and the routing function. Finally, networks with deadlock detection

© IFIP International Federation for Information Processing 2021
Published by Springer Nature Switzerland AG 2021
H. Hojjat and M. Massink (Eds.): FSEN 2021, LNCS 12818, pp. 127–141, 2021.
https://doi.org/10.1007/978-3-030-89247-0_9

are less restrictive in their routing. Deadlocks that result from these relaxed routing schemes are detected and resolved using an online algorithm [4,9].

Many packet switching networks have a dynamic topology, and therefore use deadlock avoidance or deadlock detection. However, from the early 2000s, Networks on Chip (NoCs) brought packet switching and deadlock prevention to the level of interconnect networks in integrated circuits [1,7]. Since such NoCs have a static topology, they are amenable to deadlock prevention.

Deadlock prevention was studied, e.g., by Chen in 1974 [4], who referred to prevention as *"system designs with built-in constraints which guarantee freedom from deadlocks without imposing any constraints on real-time resource allocation"*. Later, in the 1980s, Toueg and Ullman addressed deadlock prevention using local controllers [13]. Duato [8] was the first one to propose necessary and sufficient conditions for deadlock-free routing in packet switching. In the context of NoCs, Verbeek [14] and Verbeek and Schmaltz [15,16] formulated a necessary and sufficient condition for deadlock-free routing that is equivalent to that of Duato. In this paper, like [15], we consider networks with deterministic routing functions. However, [15] formalizes sufficient conditions on the network that guarantee deadlock freedom; whereas, even if those conditions are not satisfied, our approach is able to prove or disprove deadlock freedom of the network. The notion of *local deadlock* we introduce in Sect. 3.2 is equivalent to those of Duato and Verbeek. This paper is based on preliminary results in [12].

Contributions. In this paper, we focus on *deadlock prevention* in packet switching networks, with a particular interest in NoCs. With this we mean the static-checking for deadlock-freedom prior to the development of the packet switching network. We restrict ourselves to networks with deterministic, incremental and node-based routing functions. We formalize three different notions of deadlock, namely global, local and weak deadlock. The definition of global deadlock is the standard definition in which no message can make progress in the entire network. A weak deadlock is a state in which no steps other than send steps are possible. A state is a local deadlock if some filled channels are blocked, i.e., they contain a message that can never be forwarded by the target of the channel. We show that every global deadlock is a weak deadlock, and every weak deadlock is a local deadlock. Furthermore, not every local deadlock is a weak deadlock. However, from a weak deadlock a local deadlock in the same network can be constructed.

Finally, we show how a packet switching network and the deadlock properties can be formalized using nuXmv [2] and CTL [5]. Our experiments indicate that different types of deadlock are found, or their absence is proven, effectively in packet switching networks. However, verification times out due to the state space explosion when numbers of nodes and channels increase.

Structure of the Paper. In Sect. 2 we define packet switching networks and their semantics. Subsequently, in Sect. 3 we introduce three notions of deadlock, that are compared in detail in Sect. 4. In Sect. 5 we describe a translation of packet switching networks and deadlocks into nuXmv and CTL, and describe an experiment with this setup. Conclusions are presented in Sect. 6. The paper includes proof sketches of the results. For full proofs, the reader is referred to [11].

2   Preliminaries

2.1   Packet Switching Network

A packet switching network consists of a set of nodes connected by (unidirectional) channels. A subset of the nodes is considered to be terminal. Any node in the network can receive a message from an incoming channel and forward it to an outgoing channel. Terminal nodes can, furthermore, send messages into the network and receive messages from the network. When forwarding a message or sending a message, this is always done in accordance with the routing function. In this paper we consider networks with a static, deterministic routing function. The framework we present could be generalized to a non-deterministic setting. Formally, a packet switching network is defined as follows [7].

Definition 1. *A packet switching network is a tuple $\mathcal{N} = (N, M, C, rout)$ where:*

- *N is a finite set of nodes,*
- *$M \subseteq N$ is the set of terminals, nodes that are able to send and receive messages, with $|M| \geq 2$,*
- *$C \subseteq N \times N$ is a finite set of channels, and*
- *$rout\colon N \times M \to C$ is a (deterministic) routing function.*

For channel $(n, m) \in C$ we write $source((n, m)) = n$ and $target((n, m)) = m$. We require $source(rout(n, m)) = n$ for every $n \in N$, $m \in M$, with $m \neq n$. We write $c = m$ to denote that channel c contains a message with destination m, and write $c = \bot$ to denote channel c is empty. We write $M_\bot$ to denote $M \cup \{\bot\}$.

Routing function *rout* decides the outgoing channel of node n to which messages with destination m should be forwarded.

For $m \in M$, $n \in N$ (with $m \neq n$), the next hop $next_m\colon N \to N$ is defined as $next_m(n) = target(rout(n, m))$.

A packet switching network is *correct* if, whenever a message is in a channel, the routing function is such that the message can reach its destination in a bounded number of steps. In essence, this means the routing function does not cause any messages to cycle in the network.

Definition 2. *Let $\mathcal{N} = (N, M, C, rout)$ be a packet switching network. The network is* correct *if for every $m \in M$, and $n \in N$ there exists $k \geq 0$ such that*

$$next_m^k(n) = m,$$

where $next_n^0(n) = n$ and $next_m^{k+1}(n) = next_m^k(next_m(n))$.

In our examples, we typically choose the routing function such that k is minimal, i.e., the routing function always follows the shortest path to the destination. In any given state of the network a channel may be free, or it may be occupied by a message. In the latter case it blocks access to that channel for other messages. Processing in the network is *asynchronous*, which means that at any moment a step can be done without central control by a clock. The content of a channel is identified by the destination $m \in M$ of the corresponding message. More precisely, the following steps can be performed in a packet switching network:

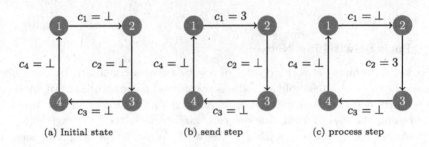

Fig. 1. A packet switching network with send, process and receive steps

Send Terminal $m \in M$ can send a message to terminal $m' \in M$ by inserting a message in channel $rout(m, m')$, provided this channel is currently empty. After sending, this channel is occupied by m'.

Receive If channel $c \in C$ with $target(c) = m$ contains a message with destination m, the message can be received by terminal m and c becomes free.

Process If channel $c \in C$ contains a message with destination $m \in M$, and $target(c) = n \neq m$ for $n \in N$, then the message can be processed by node n by forwarding it to channel $c' = rout(n, m)$. This step can only be taken if channel c' is free. As a result, the message is removed from channel c (which now becomes free) and moved to channel c'.

We illustrate these steps in a packet switching network in Example 1.

Example 1. Consider the packet switching network in Fig. 1. The network consists of four nodes, i.e., $N = \{1, 2, 3, 4\}$, all of which are terminals, so $M = N$, and four channels, $C = \{c_1, c_2, c_3, c_4\}$, shown as arrows from source to target. The routing function is $rout(n, m) = c_n$ for all $n \in N$ and $m \in M$. Initially, all channels are empty, this is shown in Fig. 1a. From the initial state it is possible to perform a *send* step from any of the nodes. For example, since channel $c_1 = \bot$, a message can be sent from node 1 to node 3. The message is routed to c_1. The resulting state is shown in Fig. 1b. Now, $c_1 = 3$ and $c_2 = \bot$, hence node 2 can perform a *process* step, and forward the message to c_2. The resulting situation is shown in Fig. 1c. Finally, since $c_2 = 3$, and $target(c_2) = 3$, node 3 can execute a *receive* step, and consume the message from channel c_2. Consequently, all channels are empty and the system is back to the initial state shown in Fig. 1a.

2.2   Semantics of Packet Switching Networks

We formalize the semantics of packet switching networks using Kripke structures.

Definition 3. *Let AP be a set of atomic propositions. A Kripke structure over AP is a four-tuple $K = (S, I, \rightarrow, L)$, where:*

- *S is a (finite) set of states,*
- *$I \subseteq S$ is the set of initial states,*

- $\to\; \subseteq S \times S$ is the transition relation, which is total, i.e., for all $s \in S$ there exists $t \in S$ such that $s \to t$, and
- $L\colon S \to 2^{AP}$ is a labelling function that assigns a set of atomic propositions to each state.

In general, the set of states in a Kripke structure may be an overapproximation of the states that can be reached from an initial state. In this paper we sometimes only consider the *reachable* states of the system.

Definition 4. Let $K = (S, I, \to, L)$ be a Kripke structure. The set of reachable states of K is defined as follows:

$$R(K) = \{s' \in S \mid \exists s \in I\colon s \to^* s'\}$$

where $\to^*$ denotes the reflexive transitive closure of $\to$.

We now formalize the semantics of a packet switching network. This captures the intuitions described in Sect. 2.1.

Definition 5. Given packet switching network $\mathcal{N} = (N, M, C, rout)$, its semantics is defined as the Kripke structure $K_{\mathcal{N}} = (S, I, \to, L)$ over $AP = \{c = m \mid c \in C \wedge m \in M_\perp\}$, defined as follows:

- $S = M_\perp^{|C|}$, i.e., the state of the network is the content of its channels. If $C = \{c_1, \ldots, c_{|C|}\}$ we write $\pi_{c_i}(s) = v_i$ if $s = (v_1, \ldots, v_{|C|}) \in S$,
- $I = \{s \in S \mid \forall c \in C\colon \pi_c(s) = \perp\}$, i.e., initially all channels are empty,
- transition relation $\to\; \subseteq S \times S$ is $\to_s \cup \to_p \cup \to_r$, where
  - $\to_s$ is the least relation satisfying

$$\frac{m, m' \in M \quad m \neq m' \quad c = rout(m, m') \quad v_c = \perp}{(v_1, \ldots, v_c, \ldots, v_{|C|}) \to_s (v_1, \ldots, m', \ldots, v_{|C|})}$$

  characterising that terminal m sends a message to terminal m',
  - $\to_p$ is the least relation satisfying

$$\frac{m \in M \quad v_c = m \quad target(c) = n \quad rout(n, m) = c' \quad v_{c'} = \perp}{(v_1, \ldots, v_c, \ldots, v_{c'}, \ldots, v_{|C|}) \to_p (v_1, \ldots, \perp, \ldots, m, \ldots, v_{|C|})}$$

  characterising that node n forwards a message with destination m that comes in on channel c to channel c', and
  - $\to_r$ is the least relation satisfying

$$\frac{m \in M \quad v_c = m \quad target(c) = m}{(v_1, \ldots, v_c, \ldots, v_{|C|}) \to_r (v_1, \ldots, \perp, \ldots, v_{|C|})}$$

  characterising that terminal m receives a message along its incoming channel c.
- $L(s) = \bigcup_{c \in C}\{c = m \mid \pi_c(s) = m\}$, for every $s \in S$.

Note that it is straightforward to show that $\to_s$, $\to_p$ and $\to_r$ are pairwise disjoint. We sometimes write, e.g., $\to_{pr}$ instead of $\to_p \cup \to_r$. We write $\nrightarrow_X$ if there is no $s' \in S$ such that $s \to_X s'$ for $x \subseteq \{s, p, r\}$. To ensure that the transition relation is total, we extend $\to$ with transitions $s \to s$ whenever $s \nrightarrow_{spr}$.

3   Deadlocks

The key question about packet switching we are interested in is whether a network is deadlock free. Intuitively, a network contains a deadlock if a message is stuck in a channel, and it will never be processed or received by the target of the channel. In practice, we can distinguish different notions of deadlock, each of which has a different interpretation of this informal requirement. We introduce three such notions, and study the relation between them.

3.1   Global Deadlock

Typically a global deadlock is a state that has no outgoing transitions. However, since we are dealing with Kripke structures, which have a total transition relation, every state has an outgoing transition. A *global deadlock* is, therefore, a state that has no outgoing transitions to a state other than itself.

Definition 6. *Let $K = (S, I, \rightarrow, L)$ be a Kripke structure. The set of global deadlock states in K is defined as:*

$$G(K) = \{s \in S \mid \nexists s' \in S\colon s \neq s' \wedge s \rightarrow s'\}$$

When $s \in G(K)$, we say that s is a global deadlock.

Example 2. Recall the packet-switching network from Example 1. The situation in which all nodes have sent a message two hops away is shown on the right.

All channels contain a value $m \in M$, but none of them can make progress because the next hop is blocked by another message. For instance, message 3 in c_1 has to reach node 3, but $rout(2,3) = c_2$ is blocked by message 4. There is a cycle of blocked channels, where all of them are filled, hence the network is in a global deadlock.

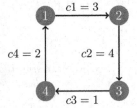

The semantics of packet switching networks guarantees that there is no global deadlock among the initial states.

Lemma 1. *Let $\mathcal{N} = (N, M, C, rout)$ be a packet switching network with $K_{\mathcal{N}} = (S, I, \rightarrow, L)$ its semantics. Then $I \cap G(K_{\mathcal{N}}) = \emptyset$*

Proof. Since $|M| \geq 2$, and all channels are initially empty, there is a terminal node that can send a message into the network.   □

3.2   Local Deadlock

Even if not all of the channels in a packet switching network are blocked, it can happen that a subset of the channels is deadlocked. Such a situation is not covered by the global deadlock. We therefore introduce the *local deadlock*. Intuitively, a state is a local deadlock if it has a channel that indefinitely contains the same message.

Definition 7. Let $\mathcal{N} = (N, M, C, rout)$ be a packet switching network, and $K_{\mathcal{N}} = (S, I, \rightarrow, L)$ its semantics. The set of local deadlock states in $K_{\mathcal{N}}$ in which channel $c \in C$ is deadlocked is defined as:

$$L_c(K_{\mathcal{N}}) = \{s \in S \mid \forall s' \in S : s \rightarrow^* s' \implies \pi_c(s) \neq \perp \wedge \pi_c(s') = \pi_c(s)\}$$

The set of local deadlock states is defined as:

$$L(K_{\mathcal{N}}) = \bigcup_{c \in C} L_c(K_{\mathcal{N}})$$

We illustrate the local deadlock in the following example.

Example 3. Consider the packet switching network with $N = M = \{1, 2, 3, 4\}$ and $C = \{c_1, c_2, c_3, c_4, c_5\}$ shown on the right. The routing function $rout(n, m) = c_5$ if $n = 3$ and $m = 2$, and c_n otherwise. None of the messages in channels c_1, c_2, c_3 and c_4 can make another step because the next hop is blocked. For instance, message 4 in c_2 has to reach node 4, but $rout(3, 4) = c_3$ is blocked by message 1.

Channel c_5, by definition of the routing function, is only used in case node 3 sends a message to node 2, $rout(3, 2) = c5$. Therefore, node 3 can still send such a message (which can be received by node 2 immediately afterwards). Thus, these two steps will always be possible, even if all of the other channels are deadlocked.

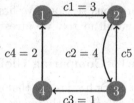

3.3 Weak Deadlock

Local deadlock does not distinguish between sending a new message—which is always possible if the target channel is empty—, and processing or receiving a message. In this section, we introduce the notion of *weak deadlock*. A state is a weak deadlock if no *receive* or *process* step is possible in that state.

Before defining weak deadlock, we first observe that in the initial states of a Kripke structure representing a packet-switching network, trivially no *process* or *receive* step is possible.

Lemma 2. Let $\mathcal{N} = (N, M, C, rout)$ be a packet switching network, and $K_{\mathcal{N}} = (S, I, \rightarrow, L)$ its semantics. Then $\forall s \in I : s \not\rightarrow_{pr}$

Proof. Initially all channels are empty. The result then follows immediately from the definitions of $\rightarrow_r$ and $\rightarrow_p$. □

Because of this observation, we explicitly exclude the initial states. The definition of weak deadlocks is as follows.

Definition 8. Let $\mathcal{N} = (N, M, C, rout)$ be a packet switching network, and $K_{\mathcal{N}} = (S, I, \rightarrow, L)$ its semantics. The set of weak deadlocks is defined as:

$$W(K_{\mathcal{N}}) = \{s \in S \setminus I \mid s \not\rightarrow_{pr}\}$$

Example 4. Consider the packet switching network with $N = M = \{1, 2, 3, 4\}$ and $C = \{c_1, c_2, c_3, c_4, c_5\}$ shown on the right. The routing function $rout(n, m) = c_5$ if $n = 2$ and $m = 1$, and c_n otherwise. None of the messages in c_1, c_2, c_3, c_4 can reach its destination because the next hop is blocked. For instance, message 2 in c_4 has to reach node 2, but $rout(1, 2) = c_1$ is blocked by message 3.

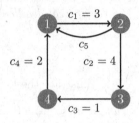

Channel c_5, by definition of the routing function, is used only when node 2 sends a message to node 1, $rout(2, 1) = c_5$. This means c_5 can be filled with value 1, after which it can be received immediately by node 1. Thus, node 2, through channel c_5, will always be able to send messages to node 1, but in this particular configuration no *process* or *receive* step is possible. Hence, this situation is a weak deadlock.

4   Expressivity of Different Notions of Deadlock

In this section we compare the different notions of deadlock introduced in the previous section. We first relate global deadlocks to local and weak deadlocks, and ultimately we investigate the relation between local and weak deadlocks.

4.1   Comparing Global Deadlocks to Local and Weak Deadlocks

It is not hard to see that every global deadlock is both a local deadlock and a weak deadlock. Furthermore, neither local nor weak deadlocks necessarily constitute a global deadlock.

We first formalize this for local deadlocks in the following lemma.

Lemma 3. *Let $\mathcal{N} = (N, M, C, rout)$ be a packet switching network, and $K_{\mathcal{N}} = (S, I, \rightarrow, L)$ its semantics. Then we have:*

$$G(K_{\mathcal{N}}) \subseteq L(K_{\mathcal{N}})$$

Proof. From the Definitions 6 and 7 it follows immediately that for all $c \in C$, $G(K_{\mathcal{N}}) \subseteq L_c(K_{\mathcal{N}})$, hence $G(K_{\mathcal{N}}) \subseteq \bigcup_{c \in C} L_c(K_{\mathcal{N}}) = L(K_{\mathcal{N}})$. $\square$

It is not generally the case that $L(K_{\mathcal{N}}) \subseteq G(K_{\mathcal{N}})$. This follows immediately from Example 3, which shows a packet-switching network with a local deadlock that is not a global deadlock. For weak deadlocks, similar results hold as formalized by the following lemma.

Lemma 4. *Let $\mathcal{N} = (N, M, C, rout)$ be a packet switching network, and $K_{\mathcal{N}} = (S, I, \rightarrow, L)$ its semantics. Then we have*

$$G(K_{\mathcal{N}}) \subseteq W(K_{\mathcal{N}})$$

Proof. Fix $s \in G(K_{\mathcal{N}})$. Note that $\nexists s' \in S : s \neq s' \wedge s \rightarrow s'$ according to Definition 6. Towards a contradiction, suppose $s \rightarrow_{pr} s'$ for some s'. It follows from the definition of $\rightarrow_{pr}$ that $s \neq s'$, and since $\rightarrow_{pr} \subseteq \rightarrow$, this is a contradiction. So, $s \nrightarrow_{pr}$. Hence according to Definition 8, $s \in W(K_{\mathcal{N}})$. So, $G(K_{\mathcal{N}}) \subseteq W(K_{\mathcal{N}})$. $\square$

Again, the converse does not necessarily hold. This follows immediately from Example 4, which shows a packet switching network with a weak deadlock that is not a global deadlock.

4.2   Comparing Local Deadlocks to Weak Deadlocks

Now that we have shown that local and weak deadlocks are not necessarily global deadlocks, the obvious question is how local and weak deadlocks are related. In particular, what we show in this section is that there is a local deadlock in a packet switching network if, and only if, there is a weak deadlock in the network.

Before we prove this main result, we first present several lemmata supporting the proof. First, in subsequent results we have to reason about the number of *process* and *receive* transitions that can be taken from a particular state, provided that no *send* transitions are taken. To this end, we first formalize the number of steps required to reach the destination for message m in channel c.

Definition 9. *Let $c \in C$ be a channel, and $m \in M_\perp$ the destination of the message carried by the channel.*

$$N(c,m) = \begin{cases} 0 & \text{if } m = \perp \\ 1 & \text{if } m = target(c) \\ 1 + N(rout(target(c),m),m) & \text{otherwise} \end{cases}$$

For correct packet switching networks, since the routing function is cycle free, we know that N is well-defined.

Lemma 5. *Let $\mathcal{N} = (N,M,C,rout)$ be a correct packet switching network, then for all channels $c \in C$ and messages $m \in M_\perp$, there exists $l \in \mathbb{N}$ such that $N(c,m) = l$.*

Proof. Fix $c \in C$ and $m \in M_\perp$. Note that if $m = \perp$, then $N(c,m) = 0$, so the result follows immediately. Now, assume that $m \neq \perp$. Since the network is correct, there must be some $k \in \mathbb{N}$ such that $next_m^k(target(c)) = m$. Pick the smallest such k. It follows using an inductive argument that $N(c,m) = k+1$. $\square$

We use this property to show that, from a given state in a packet switching network, if we only execute *process* or *receive* steps, the number of steps that can be taken is finite.

Lemma 6. *Let $\mathcal{N} = (N,M,C,rout)$ be a correct packet switching network with $K_\mathcal{N} = (S,I,\rightarrow,L)$ its semantics, then*

$$\forall s \in S \colon \exists s' \in S \colon s \rightarrow_{pr}^* s' \wedge s' \not\rightarrow_{pr}$$

i.e., the number of possible steps of type $\rightarrow_{pr}$, from state s, is bounded.

Proof. First, we define the weight of a state $s \in S$ as $wt(s) = \sum_{c \in C} N(c, \pi_c(s))$. The weight captures the total number of steps required such that all the messages currently in the network can reach their destination. Note that N is well-defined according to Lemma 5, hence wt is well-defined.

We can show that for all $s, s' \in S$ that if $s \to_{pr} s'$, then $wt(s') < wt(s)$. So, the weight of the state decreases on every transition taken in $\to_{pr}$. It follows immediately from the definition of N that, if there is a $\to_{pr}$ transition from state s, then for some channel c and message $\pi_c(s)$, $N(c, \pi_c(s)) > 0$. Therefore, the number of $\to_{pr}$ steps is finite. Hence, for all states s in K, there is a state s' such that $s \to_{pr}^* s'$ such that $s' \not\to_{pr}$. $\qquad\square$

At this point, we can finally formalize the correspondence between weak and local deadlocks. We first prove that a weak deadlock is also a local deadlock.

Theorem 1. *Let* $\mathcal{N} = (N, M, C, rout)$ *be a correct packet switching network and* $K_\mathcal{N} = (S, I, \to, L)$ *its semantics. Then we have*

$$W(K_\mathcal{N}) \subseteq L(K_\mathcal{N})$$

Proof. Fix arbitrary $s \in W(K_\mathcal{N})$. From the definition of $W(K_\mathcal{N})$, we observe that $s \notin I$ and $s' \not\to_{pr}$. Let $C' = \{c \in C \mid \pi_c(s) \neq \bot\}$ be the set of non-empty channels in state s. Since $s \notin I$, $C' \neq \emptyset$.

Observe that for all $c \in C'$, $\pi_c(s) \neq target(c)$, and $rout(target(c), \pi_c(s)) \in C'$ from the definitions of $\to_p$ and $\to_r$, since $s \not\to_{pr}$.

Next we show that for all $s' \in S$ such that $s \to^* s'$, for all $c \in C'$, $\pi_c(s') = \pi_c(s)$. We proceed by induction. If $s \to^0 s'$, then $s = s'$ and the result follows immediately. Now, assume there exists s'' such that $s \to^n s'' \to s'$. According to the induction hypothesis, for all $c \in C'$, $\pi_c(s'') = \pi_c(s)$. Fix arbitrary $c \in C'$. It follows from our observations that $\pi_c(s'') \neq target(c)$ and $rout(target(c), \pi_c(s'')) \in C'$, hence $rout(target(c), \pi_c(s'')) \neq \bot$. Therefore, the only possible transitions are a self-loop in which $s'' \to s'$ with $s'' = s'$, or a transition $\to_r$, in which case $\pi_c(s') = \pi_c(s'')$ according to the definition of $\to_r$.

Hence, it follows that $s \in L_c(K_\mathcal{N})$ for all $c \in C'$, and since c' is non-empty, $s \in L(K_\mathcal{N})$. So $W(K_\mathcal{N}) \subseteq L(K_\mathcal{N})$. $\qquad\square$

The following example shows that generally not $L(K_\mathcal{N}) \subseteq W(K_\mathcal{N})$.

Example 5. Consider the packet switching network with $N = M = \{1, 2, 3, 4\}$ and $C = \{c_1, c_2, c_3, c_4, c_5\}$ shown on the right.[1] Note that this configuration is reachable by applying the following *send* steps in any order:

from node 1 to node 3, from node 2 to node 4, from node 2 to node 1, from node 3 to node 1, and from node 4 to node 2. This results in the configuration we show. This is a local deadlock for channels c_1 through c_4. Note, however, that node 1 can receive the message from channel c_5, so this is not a weak deadlock.

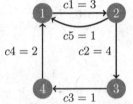

---

[1] This is the same network as in Example 4, but with $c_5 = 1$ instead of $c_5 = \bot$.

The essence of a local deadlock is a cycle of nodes, each of which is waiting for an outgoing channel to become free. This suggests that from a local deadlock, we can construct a weak deadlock by removing all messages that do not play a role in such a cycle. This is what we prove in the following theorem.

Theorem 2. *Let $\mathcal{N} = (N, M, C, rout)$ be a correct packet switching network and $K_{\mathcal{N}} = (S, I, \rightarrow, L)$ its semantics. Then we have*

$$L(K_{\mathcal{N}}) \neq \emptyset \implies W(K_{\mathcal{N}}) \neq \emptyset$$

Proof. Fix arbitrary $s \in L(K_{\mathcal{N}})$. We show that from s we can reach a state s' such that $s' \in W(K_{\mathcal{N}})$. Since $s \in L(K_{\mathcal{N}})$, there exists a channel $c \in C$ such that $s \in L_c(K_{\mathcal{N}})$, hence $\pi_c(s) \neq \perp$ and for all $s' \in S$ such that $s \rightarrow^* s'$, we have $\pi_c(s') = \pi_c(s)$. According to Lemma 6, there exists s' such that $s \rightarrow^*_{pr} s'$ and $s' \not\rightarrow_{pr}$. Pick such s'. Since $s \rightarrow^* s'$, we have $\pi_c(s') = \pi_c(s)$ and $\pi_c(s') \neq \perp$. Note that since $\pi_c(s') \neq \perp$, $s' \notin I$. Hence $s' \in W(K_{\mathcal{N}})$, so $W(K_{\mathcal{N}}) \neq \emptyset$. $\qquad\square$

5 Proof of Concept Implementation

In this section we present a proof-of-concept implementation of the theory formalized in this paper and evaluate its results. We translate packet switching networks into SMV, and the notions of deadlock to CTL. We use nuXmv [2,3] to find deadlocks in the models or show their absence.

In the rest of this section, fix packet switching network $\mathcal{N} = (N, M, C, rout)$, with Kripke structure $K_{\mathcal{N}} = (S, I, \rightarrow, L)$. For channels $c \in C$ and nodes $m \in M$, $nextC_m(c) = rout(target(c), m)$ denotes the next channel for message m when it is currently in c.

5.1 An SMV Model for Packet Switching Networks

We sketch the translation of packet switching network $\mathcal{N}$ to the SMV format used by nuXmv. The SMV model consists of the following parts:

- DECLARATIONS: $c_i \colon 1 \ldots |N|$. That is, the model has a variable c_i for every channel $c_i \in C$, whose value is in the range $0 \ldots |N|$; $c_i = 0$ encodes $c_i = \perp$.
- INITIALIZATION: $\bigwedge_{i=1}^{|C|} c_i = 0$. That is, initially all channels are empty.
- TRANSITION RELATION: The transition relation is the disjunction over all send, process and receive transitions that are specified as follows. For each $c_i \in C$ such that $source(c_i) \in M$ (i.e. its source is terminal), and message $m \neq source(c_i)$ that c_i can insert into the network, we have a SEND transition:

$$\textbf{case } c_i = 0 : \textbf{next}(c_i) = m \wedge \bigwedge_{j \neq i} \textbf{next}(c_j) = c_j;$$
$$\textbf{TRUE} \quad : \bigwedge_{i=1}^{|C|} \textbf{next}(c_i) = c_i; \qquad\qquad \textbf{esac}$$

For all channels $c_i, c_j \in C$ and messages m, such that $nextC_m(c_i) = c_j$, we have the following PROCESS transition:

```
case
    c_i = m ∧ c_j = 0 : next(c_i) = 0 ∧ next(c_j) = m ∧ ⋀_{k∉{i,j}} next(c_k) = c_k;
    TRUE              : ⋀_{i=1}^{|C|} next(c_i) = c_i;
esac
```

For all channels $c_i \in C$ and messages m such that $target(c_i) = m$, we have the following RECEIVE transition:

```
case c_i = m : next(c_i) = 0 ∧ ⋀_{j≠i} next(c_j) = c_j;
     TRUE    : ⋀_{i=1}^{|C|} next(c_i) = c_i;                          esac
```

In this encoding $\mathbf{next}$ returns the value of its argument in the next state.

5.2   Deadlock Formulas in CTL

To find deadlocks using nuXmv, we translate the properties to CTL. For the sake of readability, we give the CTL formulas as defined for the Kripke structures. These formulas are easily translated into the explicit syntax of nuXmv.

Definition 10. *The CTL formula for global deadlock is the following:*

$$\mathsf{EF}(\neg(\bigvee_{c\in C} v_c = \bot \vee \bigvee_{c\in C}\bigvee_{m\in M}(target(c) \neq m \wedge v_c = m \wedge v_{nextC_m(c)} = \bot)\vee$$

$$\bigvee_{c\in C}\bigvee_{m\in M}(target(c) = m \wedge v_c = m))).$$

This formula expresses that a state can be reached, in which non of the conditions required to take a transition holds. The disjuncts are the conditions for send, process and receive transitions, respectively.

Definition 11. *Local deadlock is defined in CTL as follows:*

$$\bigvee_{c\in C}\bigvee_{m\in M}(\mathsf{EF}(\mathsf{AG}(v_c = m))).$$

This formula checks whether, a state can be reached in which, for some channel c and message m, c contains m, and m can never be removed from c.

Definition 12. *Weak deadlock is defined in CTL as follows:*

$$\mathsf{EF}(\bigvee_{c\in C}(v_c \neq \bot) \wedge \neg(\bigvee_{c\in C}\bigvee_{m\in M}(target(c) \neq m \wedge v_c = m \wedge v_{nextC_m(c)} = \bot)\vee$$

$$\bigvee_{c\in C}\bigvee_{m\in M}(target(c) = m \wedge v_c = m))).$$

This formula expresses a non-initial state can be reached in which no *process* or *receive* transition is enabled. The conditions are the same as in Definition 10.

5.3   Experiments

We evaluate our proof-of-concept implementation on a network that consists of 17 nodes and 27 channels. The network is shown in Fig. 2a. Nodes are numbered consecutively from 1 to 17. Double-ended arrows represent pairs of channels; one channel per direction. The routing function used is the shortest path, which is unique for every pair of nodes n and n'. We vary the set of terminals in this network, and determine for each of the notions of deadlock whether a deadlock exists. A timeout is set at 2 h and 30 min.

The experiments were done using nuXmv 1.1.1, on a system running Windows 10 Home, 64 bit Intel(R) Core(TM) i7-7500U CPU @ 2.70 GHz and 8 GB of RAM.

Results. Table 1 lists the results. For each set of terminals and notion of deadlock, we report whether a deadlock is found in column 'dl' ('d' means a deadlock was found) and the execution time (s) in column 'time'; 'n/a' indicates a timeout.

For the given network, finding global deadlocks is often fast, yet for larger instances it times out. Global deadlocks are often found faster than local deadlocks, which are generally found faster than weak deadlocks.

Discussion. Table 1 shows there are sets of terminals M that are deadlock free for all types of deadlock; contain all different types of deadlock; and in which there is no global deadlock, but weak and local deadlocks are found. The results are consistent with theory: for all instances with a local deadlock, also a weak deadlock is reported (see Lemma 2). Also, there are examples with a local deadlock that do not contain a global deadlock. This is consistent with Lemma 3. Figure 2b shows the local deadlock found for $M = \{1, 5, 8, 11, 12, 13, 15\}$.

Note that execution times increase in particular for sets of terminals that require many channels in routing. This is consistent with our expectation: if more channels and more terminals are involved, the size of the reachable state space increases, which is also likely to increase the model checking time.

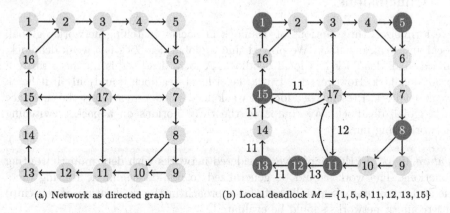

(a) Network as directed graph   (b) Local deadlock $M = \{1, 5, 8, 11, 12, 13, 15\}$

Fig. 2. 17 nodes and 27 channels packet switching network

Table 1. Deadlock results (column 'dl' contains 'd' iff a deadlock was found) and execution times (s, 'n/a' indicates timeout) using nuXmv for the network in Fig. 2a.

Set of terminals M	Global		Local		Weak	
	dl	Time	dl	Time	dl	Time
{2, 4, 6}	d	0.74	d	0.71	d	0.71
{1, 8, 10}	d	0.95	d	0.83	d	0.96
{5, 12, 14}	d	0.92	d	1.04	d	0.93
{5, 11, 14}		0.39		0.42		0.42
{11, 13, 15}		0.32		0.40		0.42
{1, 5, 9, 13}		0.69		0.74		0.70
{1, 3, 5, 15}		0.48		0.50		0.58
{3, 7, 11, 15}		0.51		0.46		0.50
{1, 2, 3, 4, 5}		0.61		0.67		0.66
{11, 12, 13, 15}		0.50	d	0.76	d	1.10
{1, 5, 9, 13, 17}		0.57		0.74		0.61
{2, 4, 6, 10, 12}	d	37.55	d	21.20	d	124.40
{3, 7, 11, 15, 17}		0.56		0.57		0.61
{2, 4, 7, 10, 12, 15, 17}		0.83		1.50		1.10
{1, 5, 8, 11, 12, 13, 15}		0.97	d	32.58	d	7204.98
{1, 5, 9, 11, 12, 13, 15}		0.82	d	62.50	d	6132.20
{1, 3, 5, 7, 9, 11, 13, 15, 17}		1.13		2.10		1.32
{2, 3, 4, 7, 10, 11, 12, 15, 17}		1.04		1.89		1.21
{2, 4, 6, 10, 12, 14}		n/a		n/a		n/a
{6, 8, 10, 12, 14, 16}		n/a		n/a		n/a
{2, 4, 6, 8, 10, 12, 14, 16}		n/a		n/a		n/a

6   Conclusions

We formalized three notions of deadlock in packet switching networks: global, local and weak deadlock. We proved that a global deadlock is a weak deadlock, and a weak deadlock is a local deadlock. A local deadlock is not necessarily a weak deadlock. However, a network has a local deadlock if and only if it has a weak deadlock. Presence of a local or weak deadlock does not imply the existence of a global deadlock. We compared the three notions on a packet switching network using nuXmv.

Future Work. In this paper we considered networks with deterministic routing functions. The work should be generalized to non-deterministic routing functions. Furthermore, scalability of the approach in the verification of (on-chip) interconnect networks should be evaluated.

References

1. Benini, L., Micheli, G.D.: Networks on chips: a new SoC paradigm. Computer **35**(1), 70–78 (2002). https://doi.org/10.1109/2.976921
2. Cavada, R., et al.: The nuXmv symbolic model checker. In: Biere, A., Bloem, R. (eds.) CAV 2014. LNCS, vol. 8559, pp. 334–342. Springer, Cham (2014). https://doi.org/10.1007/978-3-319-08867-9_22
3. Cavada, R., et al.: nuXmv 1.1.1 user manual. Technical report (2016)
4. Chen, R.C.: Deadlock prevention in message switched networks. In: Proceedings of the 1974 Annual Conference, vol. 1, p. 306–310. ACM, New York (1974). https://doi.org/10.1145/800182.810417
5. Clarke, E.M., Emerson, E.A.: Design and synthesis of synchronization skeletons using branching time temporal logic. In: Kozen, D. (ed.) Logic of Programs 1981. LNCS, vol. 131, pp. 52–71. Springer, Heidelberg (1982). https://doi.org/10.1007/BFb0025774
6. Coffman, E.G., Elphick, M.J., Shoshani, A.: Deadlock problems in computer system. In: Händler, W., Spies, P.P. (eds.) Rechnerstrukturen und Betriebsprogrammierung. LNCS, vol. 13, pp. 311–325. Springer, Heidelberg (1974). https://doi.org/10.1007/3-540-06815-5_147
7. Dally, W.J., Towles, B.P.: Principles and Practices of Interconnection Networks. Morgan Kaufmann Publishers Inc., San Francisco (2004)
8. Duato, J.: A necessary and sufficient condition for deadlock-free routing in cut-through and store-and-forward networks. IEEE Trans. Parallel Distrib. Syst. **7**(8), 841–854 (1996). https://doi.org/10.1109/71.532115
9. López, P.: Routing (Including Deadlock Avoidance). Springer, Boston (2011). https://doi.org/10.1007/978-0-387-09766-4_314
10. Merlin, P., Schweitzer, P.: Deadlock avoidance in store-and-forward networks - I: store-and-forward deadlock. IEEE Trans. Commun. **28**(3), 345–354 (1980). https://doi.org/10.1109/TCOM.1980.1094666
11. Stramaglia, A., Keiren, J., Zantema, H.: Deadlocks in packet switching networks arXiv:2101.06015 [cs.NI] (2021). https://arxiv.org/abs/2101.06015
12. Stramaglia, A.: Deadlock in packet switching networks. Master's thesis, Università degli Studi di Trieste, Dipartimento di Ingegneria e Architettura, Trieste, Italy (2020)
13. Toueg, S., Ullman, J.D.: Deadlock-free packet switching networks. SIAM J. Comput. **10**(3), 594–611 (1981). https://doi.org/10.1137/0210044
14. Verbeek, F.: Formal verification of on-chip communication fabrics. Ph.D. thesis, Radboud Universiteit Nijmegen (2013). https://hdl.handle.net/2066/103932
15. Verbeek, F., Schmaltz, J.: Formal specification of networks-on-chips: deadlock and evacuation. In: 2010 Design, Automation Test in Europe Conference Exhibition (DATE 2010), pp. 1701–1706, March 2010. https://doi.org/10.1109/DATE.2010.5457089
16. Verbeek, F., Schmaltz, J.: Formal validation of deadlock prevention in networks-on-chips. In: Proceedings of the Eighth International Workshop on the ACL2 Theorem Prover and Its Applications, ACL2 2009, pp. 128–138. ACM, New York, May 2009. https://doi.org/10.1145/1637837.1637858
17. Wolfson, O.: A new characterization of distributed deadlock in databases. In: Ausiello, G., Atzeni, P. (eds.) ICDT 1986. LNCS, vol. 243, pp. 436–444. Springer, Heidelberg (1986). https://doi.org/10.1007/3-540-17187-8_52
18. Zöbel, D.: The deadlock problem: a classifying bibliography. ACM SIGOPS Oper. Syst. Rev. **17**(4), 6–15 (1983). https://doi.org/10.1145/850752.850753

Runtime Monitoring Processes Across Blockchains

Shaun Azzopardi[1]([⊠])(iD), Joshua Ellul[2](iD), and Gordon J. Pace[2](iD)

[1] University of Gothenburg, Gothenburg, Sweden
shaun.azzopardi@gu.se
[2] University of Malta, Msida, Malta
{joshua.ellul,gordon.pace}@um.edu.mt

Abstract. Business processes have been long researched, with many tools, languages, and diagrammatic notations having been developed for automation. Recently, distributed ledger technology (of which Blockchain is one type) has been proposed for use in the monitoring of business process compliance. Such a set-up is attractive since it allows for immutability and thus a perfect record of the history of the business process regulated.

As blockchain platforms mature and their applications increase, one can observe that instead of having one blockchain as a 'one world computer' multiple blockchains will co-exist while possibly interacting. Existing work for business processes within the blockchain domain have focused on single isolated blockchain implementations. In this paper, we do away with this severely limiting assumption and propose a method to monitor business processes spanning different blockchains and other off-chain servers. We apply this work to business processes expressed in BPMN along with annotations proposed for a blockchain context. We further describe how we handle blockchain interoperability by synthesizing automatically off-chain monitors, acting as *notaries*, that handle message passing between blockchain systems, and how we employ hash-locking for cryptographically secure token swapping.

Keywords: Blockchain · Business processes · BPMN · Monitoring · Runtime verification

1 Introduction

The challenge of documenting, managing and regulating business processes has long been studied. Business processes, by their very nature typically involve the interaction between different parties, for which different techniques to monitor and regulate such business processes have been proposed and adopted—by providing a centralised service which processes relevant events from involved parties, monitors the state of the business processes and enforces or otherwise regulates such interaction. Formal correctness of the monitoring service is an appropriate correctness criterion when these parties belong to a single entity, or all trust a particular service provider.

A challenge arises with decentralisation, when business processes span different entities which may not agree on a centralised party regulating their interaction. The

© IFIP International Federation for Information Processing 2021
Published by Springer Nature Switzerland AG 2021
H. Hojjat and M. Massink (Eds.): FSEN 2021, LNCS 12818, pp. 142–156, 2021.
https://doi.org/10.1007/978-3-030-89247-0_10

1. *This procurement process will regulate the purchasing and supplying process of items between a buyer and supplier, with some required minimum amount and of some maximum amount of items purchased and supplied.*
2. *A procurement process is initiated by the buyer upon placement of a deposit in escrow, amounting to the value of the pre-agreed minimum amount of items to be ordered.*
3. *The supplier similarly must then also put a performance guarantee in escrow, amounting to the pre-agreed maximum amount of items to be ordered.*
4. *The buyer and supplier then engage in an order-deliver loop.*
5. *The buyer orders items from the supplier, which uses a courier for delivery. The courier acquires a proof of delivery from the buyer and passes this on to the supplier for payment.*
6. *After at least one order-deliver iteration, the buyer can request termination of the contract. After which the buyer and the supplier can request their respective money held in escrow.*
7. *If the buyer's orders do not amount to at least the pre-agreed minimum then the difference will be taken from their deposit and given to the supplier.*
8. *If the supplier is not able to satisfy the orders (up to the pre-agreed maximum) then the value of the missed orders are transferred from the supplier's performance guarantee to the buyer.*
9. *After the money in escrow has been refunded the procurement process terminates.*

Fig. 1. A procurement business process

maritime logistics industry, for instance, faces this challenge due to the fact that their business processes range across a wide range of sectors, but also an international range of participating parties, implying different jurisdictions and legal frameworks, despite working within international regulations [24]. The result is a fragmented system, still dependent on physical sub-processes such as the use of *bills of lading*—legal documents providing evidence of contract of carriage, confirming receipt of goods, and resolving issues related to title of goods. This challenge of decentralised processes has been addressed in literature through the use of blockchain technology and smart contracts [9, 18, 26, 27], which enable automated enforcement or monitoring of party interaction in a decentralised manner. In particular, work such as [27] showed how from a business process documented using a standard notation—Business Process Model and Notation (BPMN) [22]—smart contracts can be created to regulate the process.

Smart contracts address concerns of power and control of the computation in such a multiparty system by ensuring a decentralised computation engine on which the smart contract executes. However, over these past years multiple blockchains have been adopted by different groups of players working in parallel with centralised systems. Consider a procurement process described in Fig. 1 (and graphically in Fig. 3), in which some of the parties may already be using smart contracts to decentralise their processes. For instance, the courier process may be using a blockchain system, whilst the buyer and supplier may be using a different blockchain to manage the escrow agreement, possibly also performing payment using a cryptocurrency on yet a different blockchain. The problem is that whilst adoption of decentralisation solutions between parties with direct common interests may be logistically possible, decentralising further may not be so. For instance, couriers with no link to the supplier's market do not stand to gain by integrating with the respective solution. No matter how theoretically attractive *'one blockchain to rule them all'* may sound, it is unlikely to be achievable in practice.

Theoretically, monitoring systems distributed across different locations is not a new idea [14], however one which still has many challenges [23]. The issues we wish to tackle in the blockchain case is how a business process can be decomposed across different locations, and how the decomposed sub-process monitors can communicate together across blockchains. This interaction certainly requires blockchain-to-blockchain communication techniques, which have been explored generally in [6].

The main contributions proposed herein include: (i) the proposal of macro business process modelling annotations that allow for the specification of location of parts of a process that spans across different systems (identifying a specific blockchain or off-chain server); and (ii) an approach that makes use of this information to synthesize automatically monitoring and regulatory smart contracts residing across different on-chain and off-chain locations, along with an appropriate inter-chain communication infrastructure. We will use the procurement use case as a motivating example.

The paper is organised as follows. In Sect. 2 we layout the theoretical and practical challenges to cross-chain interopability for business processes. In Sect. 3 we describe our solution. In Sect. 5 we compare this approach to related work and in Sect. 6 we describe remaining challenges, while we conclude in Sect. 7.

2   Challenges of Full Decentralisation for Monitoring Business Processes

Business process diagrams have long been recognised as useful tools that enable for the analysis and automation of business logic. Their execution has also been explored for the purpose of monitoring and automating parts of processes (e.g. [10,15,27]).

Work in business process management has by and large relied on central authorities that manage, monitor, and enforce business processes. Centralisation however can be problematic—parties would not want the data to reside (centralised) under the control of another party, and may even find it difficult to agree on a third party, a central authority, to take this role. To address this issue of centralised trust, *blockchains* have been proposed to act as immutable, tamperproof and transparent records of both the business process (through appropriate smart contracts) and its history [9,16–18,21,26,27].

Blockchains provide an append-only transaction database along with computational logic which is stored and executed across all the different nodes whilst at the same time provides tamperproof guarantees. This is in contrast to the traditional centralised databases and programs, where there is only one trusted central copy of the database and software (which may be distributed across a single entity's infrastructure). Blockchains instead use *consensus algorithms* to ensure that any proposed transaction is agreed upon between the nodes before it is accepted. An attractive feature of blockchains is the immutability of its transaction history ensured through cryptography. Some blockchains also allow for the deployment of programs, commonly referred to as *smart contracts*, which provide guarantees with respect to the logic executed.

Blockchains typically also use a native cryptocurrency or token.[1] For example, Ethereum natively supports the *Ether* cryptocurrency, which functions similar to

---

[1] The terms are used in different ways in literature. We will use the two terms loosely here.

traditional real-world monetary value through exchanges. Such cryptocurrencies are essential to the sustainable operation of many types of blockchain systems, e.g., Ethereum version 1.0 depends on *miners* who do computationally heavy work to secure and operate the blockchain who get rewarded with Ether, while transactions cost some amount of Ether (referred to as *gas*). Ether can be transferred to different account holders (or rather accounts) on the same blockchain, e.g. for payments, which may not only belong to a human owner but could be directly owned by a smart contract. Given the flexibility of the programming infrastructure which Ethereum provides, other specific-purpose tokens can be created by coding their logic using smart contracts.

In the verification of business processes through blockchain, one typically implements and encodes processes as one or more monitoring smart contracts, allowing the progress of participants to be recorded on-chain [27]. Such a decentralised model works well for many use cases, and is of high utility when the parties are mutually untrusting.

One often overlooked issue is that **a business process may be fragmented over different organisations**, each of which may have adopted different blockchain standards and platforms and may be unwilling to undertake modifications to support integration with other parties. A group of organisations may agree to regulate their processes on one blockchain system. However there may still be pre-existing services on which the processes depend which may not be on that blockchain. The result is that of **business process islands** with no direct communication channel between them, since existing blockchain systems do not allow for external communication calls to be initiated.

Another significant issue is that (Ethereum) **transactions can be expensive**, and their mining can be **untimely** (which can adversely affect process execution). To remedy this parties may agree to only model sensitive parts of the business process on a public blockchain (e.g. payments and exchange of proofs), potentially leaving other parts for cheaper (and faster) private blockchains. Some questions that then arise are: (i) how do we model that different participants to a process are on different blockchains; and (ii) how to handle interaction between participants on different blockchains?

Consider the use case presented in Fig. 1, the business process may require the parties to put some money in escrow (Clause 2). This would ideally be done publicly where the escrow manager's logic is known, such that the parties do not need to trust yet another party to hold their escrowed amounts. Ethereum provides a perfect solution to this. However, doing other parts of a business process publicly does not add any value, e.g. how the buyer decides if to order or terminate the contract is irrelevant to the collaborative context. More so, there likely are aspects of the processes that are confidential which the parties would not want to reveal to prying eyes. Therefore different parties may be then agree to only execute the escrow logic publicly, while recording their own sub-processes internally in a private blockchain.

It is important to highlight that the escrow manager cannot act independently of the other parties, but instead reacts to the events they trigger (e.g. upon the buyer triggering termination, Clause 6, the logic in Clauses 6–9 must be enacted). Since the parties' processes may not be on the same blockchain as the escrow manager (or as each other), to fully automate the process there is a need to bridge the gap between blockchains.

Cross-chain messaging can be challenging. Sending a message directly from one blockchain to another is not generally possible, since blockchains act as closed systems. Instead cross-chain messages need to be delivered by a messenger, usually called a *notary* [6]. This, however, adds a layer of centralisation, requiring trust by both parties that the notary is acting as expected. Finding ways to mitigate the required trust in this notary is essential to prevent conflict in cross-chain collaborative process execution.

Interaction between blockchains can be more complex than simple message sending. In the context of blockchains, two parties may want to transfer or swap tokens, e.g. the ownership of a token corresponding to the delivered good may be swapped by the supplier to the buyer in exchange for a token proving delivery. The use of a notary for this kind of logic may not be suitable for this sensitive behaviour (tokens can have monetary value). Instead a provably secure method would be ideal, for example employing notions from cryptography to identify uniquely the send and intended recipient.

3   Monitoring Business Processes Across Blockchains

Our proposed approach allows the description of a decentralised business process, that may be scattered across different blockchains or servers. From this, we can automatically generate monitors as smart contracts corresponding to different participants and their subprocesses, and appropriate off-chain monitors (*notaries*) that handle cross-chain interaction between monitors on different blockchains.

In particular, we will focus on business processes specified in BPMN [22], augmented with location annotations. We shall then generate smart contracts for each on-chain sub-process, and assumed to be based on Ethereum instances, written in the Solidity smart contract language. A system overview is presented in Fig. 2[2].

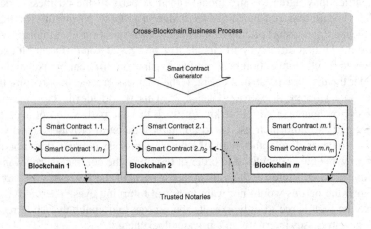

Fig. 2. System overview.

3.1   Business Process Monitoring Through Smart Contracts

Modelling and execution of business processes on blockchains is not new, with multiple approaches and tools being developed for this purpose [9, 18, 26, 27]. Such approaches

---

[2] Find a prototype here: https://github.com/shaunazzopardi/bpmn-to-solidity.

Table 1. Informal description of correspondence between BPMN symbols and their translation to Solidity code.

BPMN Symbols	As Solidity Code
Start events	A function callable by the process owner
Throwing message events	Emits a message in the form of a Solidity event, and/or calls any corresponding catching events functions
Catching message events	A function only callable by the message owner
End events	Finalises the monitoring, with no function being callable after
Pools	Correspond to one whole smart contract
Activities	Functions that owners use to signal the activity has succeeded, or that may include some Solidity logic according to its annotations in the diagram
Sequence flow	Handled implicitly by the smart contract. The smart contract can be queried for the next possible elements
Message flow	Implemented through function calls when target and source of flow are on same blockchain, or through emitting events and notary listening otherwise
Exclusive Gateway	Conditions on outgoing flows are parameters to corresponding function, with if-then-else logic used to continue the flow
Event-based Gateway	Activated automatically depending on the received events
Parallel Gateway	Execution forks in parallel directions, through keeping an array of the next elements in sequence

focused on processes that are bound to execute within a single blockchain. We build on such previous work and extend the state-of-the-art by proposing cross-blockchain and system BPMN. We assume basic knowledge of BPMN (see Fig. 3 as an example), for the standard specification see [22], and of Solidity, for its documentation see [12]. We discuss how salient BPMN aspects are facilitated through Solidity smart contracts.

In our context a BPMN diagram will be a set of pools with message flows between them, with each pool belonging to a different party to the process. We distinguish two aspects of a BPMN diagram: (i) the behaviour within the pool; and (ii) the collaborative behaviour between pools. For each pool, we generate smart contracts that monitor for the flow of the enclosed process. This is done by keeping track of the business flow through the process' elements, from a start element to an end one. Since there may be parallel flows we allow for multiple possible 'next' elements. This could be problematic with conditional gateways, but we provide for their immediate triggering. This is reflected in the below code snippet, where Elements is the type of elements in the process, and next at each point in time marks set of next elements:

```
1   enum Elements {Start, SendDeposit, Order, ..., End}
2
3   mapping(Elements => bool) next;
```

Appropriate activation functions for each element are synthesized, which can only be called successfully when the corresponding element is next in the flow. These functions have appropriate access control that allows them to only be triggered by the respective participant. The following code snippet illustrates a function that is called by the buyer party to activate the start event (with the only flow being to *SendDeposit*):

```
1   function trigger_Start() {
2       require(msg.sender == buyer);
3
4       if (nextBusinessFlowPoint[Elements.Start]) {
5           nextBusinessFlowPoint[Elements.Start] = false;
6           nextBusinessFlowPoint[Elements.SendDeposit] = true;
7       }
8   }
```

This access control also takes care of points in the process that depend on triggering by another participant (either from a different smart contract or a different blockchain). Table 1 summarises the translation for a select number of BPMN symbols. We discuss in some detail how cross-chain communication works next.

3.2 Communication Across Blockchains

Different participant pools can communicate with each other in the context of a larger business process. Existing solutions assume that this communication happens on the same blockchain, but we do not make that assumption here. For example, a group of participants may not be interested in every detail of each other's business process, but only that the synchronising behaviour between them is correct. Another motivation is that public blockchains can be expensive, thus it is more efficient to carry out only the critical part of the business process on a public blockchain while leaving the rest for each party's private blockchains. To show which blockchain a pool is targeted for we use a text annotation that includes an identifier for a blockchain. For example, a pool annotated with Ethereum is aimed for the Ethereum blockchain.

We allow for different types of interaction: (i) message flows; and (ii) token transfers and swaps. Flows between participants are appropriately tagged when they are of the latter type. When the participants use one blockchain this interaction is not problematic. Participants being on different blockchains requires specialised approaches trusted by each participant. Here we present our proposal for this interoperability.

Message Passing. In our approach cross-chain message flows are facilitated through a trusted notary. A notary in this context is an off-chain monitor that acts as an intermediary between on-chain monitors. We implement a notary as a Python service.

Essentially the notary establishes a connection to each smart contract on the respective blockchains. Through this connection it subscribes for events intended for cross-chain communication. Upon event triggering it calls the appropriate function in the intended recipient's smart contract passing the message payload.

The involved parties can inspect this code to ensure it will behave as expected. However, once deployed to a traditional server the trustless environment is lost and each party must inherently trust that the web service corresponds to the code they agreed to. To tackle this issue of trust the parties may agree to place the notary code on a trusted server owned and operated by both of them. However, ideally the processes are designed in such a way that off-chain logic need not be trusted. Another approach is for each party to monitor separately each other's smart contract to ensure each message is received unmodified (when using a blockchain visible to both parties).

Token Transfers and Atomic Swapping. One may want to encode some blockchain-specific logic such as token transfers for payments, allowing them to be directly synthesized from a BPMN diagram. We allow this by tagging inter-pool message flows not just by a message name but also by annotations describing token transfers or swaps.

For transfers we simply specify the type of the token to be sent, e.g. when sending ether we simply insert: *[Send: ETH]*, in a message flow label. When instead we wish to swap tokens we also specify the type of token to be received, e.g. if we want to swap some ether with some bitcoin we would write: *[Send: ETH, Receive: BTC]*. Here we use the annotations solely to be able to create the necessary monitoring infrastructure for the swapping and transfer, leaving the parties to agree on amounts and other case-specific validation code. In the future we envision these to also be encoded in the diagram.

For message passing our solution was simply to use a trusted notary that passes messages from one blockchain to another. Logic surrounding token transfers and swaps can however be more critical, since these may have real-world value.

Implementation-wise we simply assume that the source party will transfer the tokens to an address belonging to the target party, and that the target party will perform appropriate validation. The alternative here is simply to have a notary act as a middleman, but this does not add any utility but only creates a possible point of failure. The following code snippet illustrates the function in the target escrow smart contract that a buyer calls to deposit ether. The code is only slightly different for custom tokens.

```
1   uint depositAmount;
2   function receive_deposit() public{
3       require(msg.sender == buyer);
4       require(msg.value == depositAmount);
5
6       if(next[Elements.SendDeposit]){
7           next[Elements.SendDeposit] = false;
8           next[Elements.Order] = true;
9       }
10  }
```

To handle cross-chain swaps instead we use a cryptographically secure trustless protocol—*hash-locking* [6]. Consider two parties, each owning tokens on different blockchains, and that wish to swap them. Party A initiates the atomic swap by locking their tokens in a smart contract with a certain hash, corresponding to a secret only they know. The tokens can be withdrawn only upon presenting the secret. Party B then ensures the tokens have been locked, and then lock their counterpart tokens on their blockchain with the same hash. Party A then uses their exclusive knowledge of the secret to unlock Party B's token, upon which Party B is informed of the secret and unlocks the tokens Party A locked initially. To ensure Party A cannot just withdraw both tokens a time lock is enforced, see [6] for more detail. The smart contracts we produce have this ability to hash lock tokens, while a notary is used to monitor at which stage the swap is at, and to notify parties about locks and unlocks.

The code snippet below illustrates functions related to swapping, for example the event swap_initiated_Pay is used by the buyer to initiate a swap where they lock an amount of ether with a certain hash. Appropriate events are emitted both for the notary to pass on the message to the other party (line 6) and by the notary to notify the buyer that the swap has been reciprocated (lines 10–13).

```
1  event SwapInitiatedPay(bytes32 indexed contractId, bytes32 indexed hash);
2  function swap_initiated_Pay(bytes32 _hash, uint _amount) payable public{
3      require(msg.sender == buyer);
4      require(msg.value >= _amount);
5      bytes32 contractId = hashlock(_amount, _hash);
6      emit SwapInitiatedPay(contractId, _hash);
7  }
8
9  event SwapReciprocatedPay(bytes32 indexed _contractId);
10 function swap_reciprocated_Pay(bytes32 _contractId) public{
11     require(msg.sender == notary);
12     emit SwapReciprocatedPay(_contractId);
13 }
```

Off-Chain Processes. We also allow for processes to be deployed off-chain (as NodeJS servers). This may be beneficial when the required logic is too expensive to be performed on a public blockchain. The code of these servers follows closely that of the smart contracts, with the only exception being that these servers can communicate with and listen to the blockchain without the need of the notary.

4   Case Study

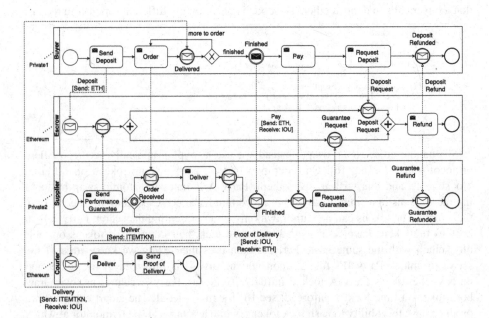

Fig. 3. Business process diagram for procurement contract (Fig. 1).

Table 2. Total gas costs of running the business process when all sub-processes are: (i) on the same blockchain; and (ii) different blockchains.

Configuration	Process	Transaction Costs (in gas)	Execution Costs (in gas)	Total
Same blockchain	Buyer	1244352	3316585	4560937
	Escrow	959764	2778631	3738395
	Supplier	1192312	3448979	4641291
	Courier	923832	2606714	3530546
	Total #1	**4427980**	**12311111**	**16739091**
All different blockchains	Buyer	1415148	3674380	5089528
	Escrow	964568	2794075	3758643
	Supplier	1476248	3878837	5355085
	Courier	1009084	3015735	4024819
	Total #2	**4865048**	**13363027**	**18228075**
	Cost of Distribution (Total #2 - Total #1)	437068	1051916	1488984

To illustrate our approach, Fig. 3 shows a BPMN business process designed for the procurement contract illustrated in Fig. 1. For brevity we only model a process that is compliant with the contract, and ignore possible misbehaviour. The parties to the process are: (i) a buyer; (ii) an escrow handler; (iii) a supplier; and (iv) a courier.

The escrow handler receives a deposit from the buyer and supplier, and refunds them when both parties have requested their respective deposit. This participant is annotated by the *Ethereum* tag, signalling that it is to be deployed on the Ethereum public blockchain. Since this will handle tokens of both parties they are both interested in it being carried out in a fully public and transparent manner, to ensure auditability.

The buyer repeatedly orders items from the supplier, and waiting for their delivery. The supplier, in turn, reacts to the buyer's orders by engaging the courier to deliver the ordered items and waiting to receive proof-of-delivery. When the buyer no longer wishes to order any further items they effect payment and request their deposit.

The courier process is started upon receiving from the supplier an amount of tokens representing the number items to be delivered. Upon delivery these are swapped with IOU tokens backed by the buyer, which they guarantee they can be swapped with ether. The courier swaps these IOUs as proof of delivery and for delivery payment with the supplier. In turn the supplier can swap these IOUs with the buyer for payment of the items. In the maritime context the proof of delivery required by the supplier corresponds to bills of lading (a delivered items receipt). In this context the supplier would be able to present all the collected bills of lading and demand payment from the buyer. Note how both the buyer and supplier are on different private blockchains, and thus the message flow from the buyer's *Order* activity must flow between these blockchains. Here, implicitly a notary is passing on this message between the blockchains.

The ease with which we can reconfigure the placement of different parts of the business process model indicates that our framework is also useful at the design and configuration level, whenever the location where the monitoring is to be deployed can be determined by the parties setting it up.

To determine the viability of our approach in this case we measured the gas costs associated with executing the process on Ethereum. In Table 2 we present the results in terms of the costs associated with the full execution of each sub-process, in terms of execution and transaction costs, for different chain placements of the sub-processes. Transaction costs relate to the cost of initiating a transaction, while execution costs are directly correlated with the computational intensity of the logic executed. We consider that all the sub-processes are deployed on the same blockchain (the theoretically lowest cost option), and that each is on a different blockchain (the theoretically highest cost option). Here we are assuming every smart contract is deployed to a public blockchain, however a party may use a private permissioned blockchain or simply an off-chain server, resulting in no need for gas payments (except for party communication).

From our experiments, the costs associated with our approach for a full business process is substantial. Consider that if we take the USD value of the total gas costs of the theoretically lowest cost (that all the processes are on the same blockchain) is around 120 USD[3]. Implementing the process across different blockchains increases this value by around 10 USD, we term this the *cost of distribution*.

From this we can conclude that performing the monitoring of a whole business process on a blockchain is not insignificant, and its attractiveness depends on the profit margin of the industry. However, our tests show that moving parts of the business process across blockchains does not cause inordinate substantial increases in costs. This can justify moving non-sensitive parts of the business process onto costless private blockchains, thus off-setting any monetary costs due to the distribution. This supports the utility of our approach to allow a BPMN model to be spread across different blockchains and/or off-chain servers. For example, if the supplier process is not on a public blockchain, then more than 30 USD can be shaved off the total cost. The decision of how to distribute a business process depends on many variables, including the level of trust between parties, the availability of private blockchains.

5   Related Work

This work is not the first to propose a blockchain-based solution to business process management. [21] proposes the use of a shared distributed ledger to log the delivery of sensor-equipped parcels, enabling service agreements to be monitored for and evaluated in a trustless manner. [1] proposes the use of a private permissioned blockchain between different parties using Hyperledger Fabric.

There are also a number of tools that facilitate the use of blockchain for similar purposes as our work. Weber et al. [27] employ the blockchain in two ways to support business process management: (i) to monitor message exchanges between processes and ensure conformance while also facilitating payments and escrow; and (ii) to coordinate the whole collaborative process execution. There are other tools available that perform similar functions, e.g. Caterpillar [18], ChorChain [9], and Lorikeet [26]. [17] extend

---

[3] When taking a conservative (at the time of writing) average, as of November 2020, gas cost of 16 Gwei per gas unit.

BPMN 2.0 choreography diagrams to utilise the power of smart contracts to enable a shared data model between processes and also the execution of some logic. Since we use process diagrams the notion of data models is already compatible with our approach, while we also allow the diagram to reference certain scripts. These works are very similar to what we offer with our approach. However we take a step further by dealing with a cross-chain distributed business processes and automatically generate off-chain code that facilitates cross-chain communication securely.

Ladleif et al. [16] is the only work we found that deals with multi-chain business processes. This work allows multi-chain choreographies, employing off-chain adapters as channels between smart contracts in different blockchains. Our approach on the other hand handles BPMN collaborations (as opposed to choreographies, i.e. the message flow between different participants). As opposed to simple cross-chain message flows our approach also adds richer interaction, including token transfers and atomic swaps.

Recent related work [13,25] considers the decomposition of global process compliance rules into rules that can be securely verified in a distributed way without requiring parties to disclose sensitive details. In our case decomposition of the business process is done simply according to the location annotations for pools.

In other work we took more formal approaches to general monitoring and analysis of smart contracts, using deontic logic [5] and automata-based behavioural specifications [2,3,11]. In that line of work we deal simply with the monitoring of one single smart contract. In this paper we do not simply monitor for compliance of the business logic, but also provide ways to carry it out across blockchains.

For a more detailed discussion and overview of general challenges for blockchain-based business process management see [10,19].

6   Remaining Challenges

From a security and trust point of view a weak point in our approach is the use of off-chain notaries to handle cross-chain communication. These act as oracles, i.e. trusted off-chain services that workaround the closed-world assumption of blockchains to keep them up to date with off-chain data sources—see [20] for a discussion and characterization of oracle patterns and costs. Since these notaries are off-chain we lose the guarantees ensured by a blockchain environment. For example, if the notary is deployed to a traditional server then there is no assurance of immutability of the code, and the owner of the server could potentially change the notary's code unilaterally. A challenge here is how to remove the need for trust, at least partially. One could explore set-ups involving the use of a common server, or cryptographic signatures of the application binary.

Our case study in Fig. 3 models the expected behaviour in a business process. However things can go wrong, for example one of the parties may not allow a swap to be carried out. One would want to include ways to recover from such misbehaviour, e.g. by allowing the swap to be re-attempted. In previous work we have explored this kind of recovery in the form of reparations [4] or compensations [8]. We have already explored this [5,7] in the context of other formal specifications for verification on the blockchain. Applying this work in the context of our annotations however remains an open problem.

Assessing the suitability of our tool requires appropriate testing of the produced artifacts. These artifacts however are not meant to be deployed in a single environment, but across different environments, which can be on-chain or off-chain. On the blockchain side, one can make use of testnets or private blockchains. While for off-chain artifacts one can simply deploy them to local servers. We are currently working on an approach to automatically generate code that performs a test runs of business processes.

We intend to apply this business process management approach in the maritime context. For this we will need to extend our prototype for a larger fragment of BPMN, including also allowing multiple participants of certain type. This is required for example to allow dynamic onboarding of courier services, rather than simply assuming one static courier service. Another possible extension is to consider that different couriers may be used in different contexts or for different goods.

Implementation wise we are limited in that we only consider Solidity smart contracts. In a future iteration it would be ideal to be able to produce code tailored for different blockchains. Moreover, our text annotations could be enriched by identifying when message flows are carried out by the same notary or not. Different pairs of participants may trust to deploy notaries on different servers. We are also investigating code optimisations, e.g., we use loops which can be costly in Ethereum.

7   Conclusions

Blockchains have been successfully proposed and used as vehicles for business process monitoring and execution. Multiple approaches and tools already exist. In this paper we extend this work in a novel direction, where we do not assume all participants are located on the same blockchain. We further consider annotations to BPMN diagrams that express blockchain related notions, e.g. transfer or swapping of tokens, and annotations of participants with the blockchain they will be located on. Our approach, with an associated prototype, generates from BPMN a set of smart contracts (currently limited Solidity). To handle cross-chain interaction we also generate notaries to securely pass on messages between participants, while we employ the notion of hash-locking to handle cryptographically safe cross-chain swaps of tokens.

References

1. Alves, P.H., et al.: Exploring blockchain technology to improve multi-party relationship in business process management systems. In: Proceedings of the 22nd International Conference on Enterprise Information Systems - Volume 2: ICEIS, pp. 817–825. INSTICC, SciTePress (2020). https://doi.org/10.5220/0009565108170825
2. Azzopardi, S., Colombo, C., Pace, G.: A technique for automata-based verification with residual reasoning. In: Proceedings of the 8th International Conference on Model-Driven Engineering and Software Development, 25–27 February 2020, MODELSWARD 2020, Valletta, Malta (2020)
3. Azzopardi, S., Ellul, J., Pace, G.J.: Monitoring smart contracts: contractlarva and open challenges beyond. In: Colombo, C., Leucker, M. (eds.) RV 2018. LNCS, vol. 11237, pp. 113–137. Springer, Cham (2018). https://doi.org/10.1007/978-3-030-03769-7_8
4. Azzopardi, S., Pace, G.J., Schapachnik, F.: Contract automata with reparations. In: Hoekstra, R. (ed.) Legal Knowledge and Information Systems - JURIX 2014: The Twenty-Seventh

Annual Conference, Jagiellonian University, Krakow, Poland, 10–12 December 2014. Frontiers in Artificial Intelligence and Applications, vol. 271, pp. 49–54. IOS Press (2014). https://doi.org/10.3233/978-1-61499-468-8-49

5. Azzopardi, S., Pace, G.J., Schapachnik, F.: On observing contracts: deontic contracts meet smart contracts. In: Palmirani, M. (ed.) Legal Knowledge and Information Systems - JURIX 2018: The Thirty-first Annual Conference, Groningen, The Netherlands, 12–14 December 2018. Frontiers in Artificial Intelligence and Applications, vol. 313, pp. 21–30. IOS Press (2018). https://doi.org/10.3233/978-1-61499-935-5-21

6. Buterin, V.: Chain interoperability. In: R3 Reports. R3 (September 2016)

7. Colombo, C., Ellul, J., Pace, G.J.: Contracts over smart contracts: recovering from violations dynamically. In: Margaria, T., Steffen, B. (eds.) ISoLA 2018. LNCS, vol. 11247, pp. 300–315. Springer, Cham (2018). https://doi.org/10.1007/978-3-030-03427-6_23

8. Colombo, C., Pace, G.J.: Comprehensive monitor-oriented compensation programming. In: Buhnova, B., Happe, L., Kofron, J. (eds.) Proceedings 11th International Workshop on Formal Engineering approaches to Software Components and Architectures, FESCA 2014, Grenoble, France, 12th April 2014. EPTCS, vol. 147, pp. 47–61 (2014). https://doi.org/10.4204/EPTCS.147.4

9. Corradini, F., Marcelletti, A., Morichetta, A., Polini, A., Re, B., Tiezzi, F.: Engineering trustable choreography-based systems using blockchain. In: Proceedings of the 35th Annual ACM Symposium on Applied Computing, pp. 1470–1479. SAC 2020, ACM, New York, NY, USA (2020). https://doi.org/10.1145/3341105.3373988

10. Di Ciccio, C., Meroni, G., Plebani, P.: Business process monitoring on blockchains: potentials and challenges. In: Nurcan, S., Reinhartz-Berger, I., Soffer, P., Zdravkovic, J. (eds.) BPMDS/EMMSAD -2020. LNBIP, vol. 387, pp. 36–51. Springer, Cham (2020). https://doi.org/10.1007/978-3-030-49418-6_3

11. Ellul, J., Pace, G.J.: Runtime verification of ethereum smart contracts. In: 2018 14th European Dependable Computing Conference (EDCC), pp. 158–163 (2018). https://doi.org/10.1109/EDCC.2018.00036

12. Ethereum: Solidity (2016). https://docs.soliditylang.org/. Accessed 10 Jan 2010

13. Fdhila, W., Rinderle-Ma, S., Knuplesch, D., Reichert, M.: Decomposition-based verification of global compliance in process choreographies. In: 2020 IEEE 24th International Enterprise Distributed Object Computing Conference (EDOC), pp. 77–86 (2020). https://doi.org/10.1109/EDOC49727.2020.00019

14. Francalanza, A., Pérez, J.A., Sánchez, C.: Runtime verification for decentralised and distributed systems. In: Bartocci, E., Falcone, Y. (eds.) Lectures on Runtime Verification. LNCS, vol. 10457, pp. 176–210. Springer, Cham (2018). https://doi.org/10.1007/978-3-319-75632-5_6

15. Hotz, L., von Riegen, S., Pokahr, A., Braubach, L., Schwinghammer, T.: Monitoring bpmn-processes with rules in a distributed environment. In: Aït-Kaci, H., Hu, Y., Nalepa, G.J., Palmirani, M., Roman, D. (eds.) Proceedings of the RuleML2012@ECAI Challenge, at the 6th International Symposium on Rules, Montpellier, France, 27th–29th August 2012. CEUR Workshop Proceedings, vol. 874. CEUR-WS.org (2012). http://ceur-ws.org/Vol-874/paper12.pdf

16. Ladleif, J., Friedow, C., Weske, M.: An architecture for multi-chain business process choreographies. In: Abramowicz, W., Klein, G. (eds.) BIS 2020. LNBIP, vol. 389, pp. 184–196. Springer, Cham (2020). https://doi.org/10.1007/978-3-030-53337-3_14

17. Ladleif, J., Weske, M., Weber, I.: Modeling and enforcing blockchain-based choreographies. In: Hildebrandt, T., van Dongen, B.F., Röglinger, M., Mendling, J. (eds.) BPM 2019. LNCS, vol. 11675, pp. 69–85. Springer, Cham (2019). https://doi.org/10.1007/978-3-030-26619-6_7

18. López-Pintado, O., García-Bañuelos, L., Dumas, M., Weber, I., Ponomarev, A.: CATER-PILLAR: A business process execution engine on the ethereum blockchain. CoRR abs/1808.03517 (2018). http://arxiv.org/abs/1808.03517

19. Mendling, J., et al.: Blockchains for business process management - challenges and opportunities. ACM Trans. Manag. Inf. Syst. **9**(1), 1–16 (2018). https://doi.org/10.1145/3183367

20. Mühlberger, R., et al.: Foundational oracle patterns: connecting blockchain to the off-chain world. In: Asatiani, A., et al. (eds.) BPM 2020. LNBIP, vol. 393, pp. 35–51. Springer, Cham (2020). https://doi.org/10.1007/978-3-030-58779-6_3

21. Müller, M., Garzon, S.R.: Blockchain-based trusted cross-organizational deliveries of sensor-equipped parcels. In: Schwardmann, U., et al. (eds.) Euro-Par 2019. LNCS, vol. 11997, pp. 191–202. Springer, Cham (2020). https://doi.org/10.1007/978-3-030-48340-1_15

22. (OMG), O.M.G.: Business process model and notation (bpmn) version 2.0 (January 2011). https://www.omg.org/spec/BPMN/2.0/PDF. Accessed 10 Jan 2010

23. Sánchez, C., et al.: A survey of challenges for runtime verification from advanced application domains (beyond software). Form. Methods Syst. Des. **54**(3), 279–335 (2019). https://doi.org/10.1007/s10703-019-00337-w

24. Song, D.W., Lee, P.T.: Maritime logistics in the global supply chain (2009)

25. Tosatto, S., Governatori, G., Beest, N.: Verifying compliance of process compositions through certification of its components. In: 2020 IEEE 24th International Enterprise Distributed Object Computing Conference (EDOC), pp. 87–96. IEEE Computer Society, Los Alamitos, CA, USA (October 2020). https://doi.ieeecomputersociety.org/10.1109/EDOC49727.2020.00020

26. Tran, A.B., Lu, Q., Weber, I.: Lorikeet: a model-driven engineering tool for blockchain-based business process execution and asset management. In: van der Aalst, W.M.P., et al. (eds.) Proceedings of the Dissertation Award, Demonstration, and Industrial Track at BPM 2018 co-located with 16th International Conference on Business Process Management (BPM 2018), Sydney, Australia, 9–14 September 2018. CEUR Workshop Proceedings, vol. 2196, pp. 56–60. CEUR-WS.org (2018). http://ceur-ws.org/Vol-2196/BPM_2018_paper_12.pdf

27. Weber, I., Xu, X., Riveret, R., Governatori, G., Ponomarev, A., Mendling, J.: Untrusted business process monitoring and execution using blockchain. In: La Rosa, M., Loos, P., Pastor, O. (eds.) BPM 2016. LNCS, vol. 9850, pp. 329–347. Springer, Cham (2016). https://doi.org/10.1007/978-3-319-45348-4_19

Solving Systems of Bilinear Equations for Transition Rate Reconstruction

Amin Soltanieh$^{(\boxtimes)}$ and Markus Siegle$^{(\boxtimes)}$

Universität der Bundeswehr München, 85579 Neubiberg, Germany
{amin.soltanieh,markus.siegle}@unibw.de

Abstract. Compositional models, specified with the help of a Markovian Stochastic Process Algebra (SPA), are widely used in performance and dependability modelling. The paper considers the problem of transition rate reconstruction: Given two SPA components with unknown rates, and given their combined flat model with fixed rates, the task is to reconstruct the rates in the components. This problem occurs frequently during so-called model repair, if a certain subset of transition rates of the flat model needs to be changed in order to satisfy some given requirement. It is important to have a structured approach to decide whether or not the rate reconstruction, satisfying the desired low-level model changes, is possible or not. In order to realize such a reconstruction, every combined model transition is transformed into an equation, resulting – for each action type – in a system of bilinear equations. If the system of equations meets a consistency condition, rate reconstruction is indeed possible. We identify a class of SPA systems for which solving the system of equations is not necessary, since by checking a set of simple conditions we can check the consistency of the system of equations. Furthermore, for general models outside this class, an iterative algorithm for solving the system of equations efficiently is proposed.

Keywords: Stochastic Process Algebra · Bilinear system of equations · Model reconstruction

1 Introduction

Stochastic Process Algebras (SPA) such as PEPA [10], EMPA [3] and CASPA [13] are often used in performance and dependability modeling, since they allow users to define complex systems in a modular and hierarchical way as interacting components. For checking system requirements in a model, probabilistic model checking, implemented in tools like PRISM [14], MRMC [12], iscasMC [7] and STORM [5], is used. Model checking usually takes place at the level of the combined model, where states are labelled with atomic propositions, and transitions are labelled with action names and rates.

In this paper, an interesting question is addressed: Given a compositional SPA model, albeit with unknown transition rates, and given the transition rates

© IFIP International Federation for Information Processing 2021
Published by Springer Nature Switzerland AG 2021
H. Hojjat and M. Massink (Eds.): FSEN 2021, LNCS 12818, pp. 157–172, 2021.
https://doi.org/10.1007/978-3-030-89247-0_11

of the associated low-level flat Markov chain, how and under which conditions can we reconstruct the transition rates of the high-level model, i.e. of the SPA components? In other words, how can we lift the combined model rate information to the high-level model? This is an important question, since users usually prefer not to work with the (large) flat model of the system, but instead work with the much smaller CTMCs of the components.

This question arises frequently in the field of model repair [2]. That is, if a property is not satisfied in a model, we may apply some modifications to the model such that the modified (repaired) model satisfies the property [2,4]. Earlier works on model repair, based on transition rate modification, has been published in [19] and [18] for different time-bounded and time-unbounded reachability properties expressed in the logic CSL [1]. However, all these researches address model repair solution at the level of the flat, combined model of the system. Whenever, for the sake of a property fulfillment, some transition rates in the combined model of the system are supposed to change, we need to know if reconstructing the components accordingly is feasible or not. Recently, in [16], a lifting algorithm has been introduced which receives the combined model rate modifications and lifts this information to the compositional high-level model, if such a lifting is possible at all. At the core of this algorithm is the construction and solution of a system of bilinear equations.

With a simple example, inspired by [17] and developed in [16], the rate reconstruction problem is explained: In Fig. 1, two components, A and B, are synchronised over action a and the resultant combined model is shown. Every transition is labelled by the tuple (act, r), where act is the action name and r is the transition rate. Assume that the combined model transition rate values $\{f_1, \ldots, f_5\}$ are given and all transition rates of the components are unknown variables $(x_{12}^{(a)}, x_{21}^{(b)}, y_{12}^{(a)}, y_{21}^{(c)})$. The transition rates in the combined model are functions of the transition rates in the components, where for action synchronisation in SPA, different semantics have been discussed and compared in the past concerning the rate of the combined transition rate [9]. In this paper, we assume that the rate of a combined transition is calculated as the product of the rates of the transitions to be synchronised, similar to the synchronisation of CTMC modules in PRISM.

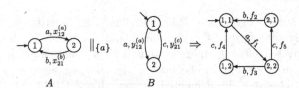

Fig. 1. Processes A and B and the resultant combined model

For reconstructing the rates of the components, every action type should be considered independently:

Action a: Action a is a synchronising action and there is only one a-transition in the combined model. So, the only equation is $x_{12}^{(a)} \cdot y_{12}^{(a)} = f_1$, and obviously, for any arbitrary value of f_1, it is always possible to choose $x_{12}^{(a)}$ freely and then set $y_{12}^{(a)}$ accordingly.

Action b: Assume $f_2 = f_3 = f$, then *local lifting* is possible, i.e. lifting the combined model transition rates to the high-level model. In this case, the only equation is $x_{21}^{(b)} = f$. In general, local lifting means that reconstruction of combined model transition rates is possible by assigning some transition rates in only one of the components.

Action c: If $f_4 = f_5$, then we have the same case as for action type b above. But let us now consider the case $f_4 \neq f_5$. The two c-transitions in the combined model stem from the only c-transition in component B, and if this transition rate is changed, both c-transitions in the combined model are equally affected. The system of equations includes two contradicting equations: $y_{21}^{(c)} = f_4$ and $y_{21}^{(c)} = f_5$. So, in this example, we cannot reconstruct the rates in the high-level components in a straight-forward manner, because there exists a context dependency for the transition rates f_4 and f_5.

However, as a solution for this problem, it has been observed in [16] that we can implement this context dependency by adding action c to the synchronisation set and inserting c-selfloops at the states of component A with unknown transition rates $x_{11}^{(c)}$ and $x_{22}^{(c)}$, as shown in Fig. 2. The modified components are denoted A' and B'. In order to find the unknown rates $x_{11}^{(c)}$, $x_{22}^{(c)}$ and $y_{21}^{(c)}$, we can transform the combined model c-transitions into the mathematical equations $x_{11}^{(c)} \cdot y_{21}^{(c)} = f_4$ and $x_{22}^{(c)} \cdot y_{21}^{(c)} = f_5$. For any pair of values f_4 and f_5, this system of equations has a solution, so reconstructing the high-level models is now possible! One possible solution is $x_{11}^{(c)} = f_4$, $x_{22}^{(c)} = f_5$ and $y_{21}^{(c)} = 1$. Note, however, that in general, the system of equations may or may not have a solution.

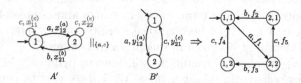

Fig. 2. Processes A' and B' with added selfloops and modified synchronising set

It is always possible to form a system of equations, representing the combined model transitions with regard to a specific action type, if the rates of the flat Markov chain are given. This system of equations, for a combined system of two interacting components, always has a specific bilinear form. Solving this system of equations efficiently can be challenging, especially for systems with very large state space. In this report, we identify a class of systems where without solving the system of equations and only by checking some simple conditions, the consistency of the system of equations can be checked and a possible solution can be obtained. For general systems outside this class, an iterative algorithm is introduced which can solve the system of equations efficiently.

2   Background

A bilinear equation is one in which the variables may be partitioned into two disjoint subsets such that the left hand side is linear in each set separately and the right hand side is a given scalar. The system of l bilinear equations can be shown in the following matrix form:

$$x^T A_i y = d_i, \qquad i = 1, 2, \dots, l \tag{1}$$

where x and y are two disjoint variable vectors of length n and m, respectively, and $A_i \in \mathbb{R}^{n \times m}$.

In [11], the solution theory is provided for *complete* bilinear systems of equations for the case that all A_i matrices are linearly independent. A bilinear system of equations is complete if the number of equations is the product of the number of x and y variables ($l = n \cdot m$). It is proved that the consistency and the solution of the complete bilinear system of equations can be obtained using matrix $G \in \mathbb{R}^{n \times m}$ from the following equation:

$$\mathrm{vec}(G) = (A^{-1})^T d \tag{2}$$

where vec is the vectorization operator which transforms a matrix into a column vector by stacking the columns of the matrix on top of one another, and A is a matrix with columns $\mathrm{vec}(A_i)$. If the rank of matrix G is one, then the system of equations is consistent and has a solution.

In the general form of a bilinear system of equations (1), every equation may include the sum of several bilinear terms. But in our situation, which is the system of two interacting components, we have a simpler case where every equation has only one bilinear term. In this case, it is always possible to sort the equations such that matrix A becomes the identity matrix. Then $\mathrm{vec}(G) = d$, which leads to the result obtained in this paper in Lemma 1.

In Sect. 3, we derive some conditions which occur frequently in models with synchronising or non-synchronising actions. We will see that by checking such a set of simple conditions, we can decide whether a solution exists or not, and if a solution exists we can obtain one. If these conditions are not satisfied, we need to solve the system of equations using other methods.

3   Special Cases Leading to Complete System

In this section, we will see that under some conditions, we can verify the consistency of the system of equations by checking a simple condition and find a possible solution. We divide this section into two parts, synchronising and non-synchronising actions, i.e. whether the system of equations corresponds to a synchronising action or a non-synchronising one. At first, we define the framework and notation for the system and then in two lemmas the *complete* systems wrt a synchronising or non-synchronising action are defined. In the rest of this report, the action type is omitted from the variable notation, since it is implicit in the context.

Definition 1 (System Definition).

Let $Sys = M_1 \parallel_{\Sigma_s} M_2$, where M_1 and M_2 are two Markovian transition systems with state spaces S_1 and S_2, and $\Sigma_s \subseteq Act$ is the set of synchronising actions. $S \subseteq S_1 \times S_2$ denotes the reachable state space of the combined model Sys (reachable from the specified initial states in M_1 and M_2).

For action $c \in Act$, $en_1 = \{a_1, \dots, a_p\} \subseteq S_1$ and $en_2 = \{b_1, \dots, b_r\} \subseteq S_2$ are the states in M_1 and M_2 where action c is enabled. Let $ne_1 = S_1 \setminus en_1 = \{a_{p+1}, \dots, a_{p+q}\}$ and $ne_2 = S_2 \setminus en_2 = \{b_{r+1}, \dots, b_{r+s}\}$ be the sets of states where action c is not enabled, so $|S_1| = p + q$ and $|S_2| = r + s$.

k_i and l_j are the number of outgoing c-transitions in states a_i and b_j, where $1 \le i \le p$ and $1 \le j \le r$. Let $m = k_1 + \dots + k_p$ and $n = l_1 + \dots + l_r$ be the total number of c-transitions in M_1 and M_2 respectively.

$a_i^{(j)}$ and $b_i^{(j)}$ are target states of c-transitions in S_1 and S_2 respectively, where $a_i^{(j)} \in S_1, 1 \le i \le p, 1 \le j \le k_i$ and $b_i^{(j)} \in S_2, 1 \le i \le r, 1 \le j \le l_i$.

$$
k_1 \begin{cases} a_1 \xrightarrow{x_{a_1 a_1^{(1)}}} a_1^{(1)} \\ \vdots \\ a_1 \xrightarrow{x_{a_1 a_1^{(k_1)}}} a_1^{(k_1)} \end{cases}
\qquad
l_1 \begin{cases} b_1 \xrightarrow{y_{b_1 b_1^{(1)}}} b_1^{(1)} \\ \vdots \\ b_1 \xrightarrow{y_{b_1 b_1^{(l_1)}}} b_1^{(l_1)} \end{cases}
$$

$$
\vdots \qquad\qquad \vdots
$$

$$
k_p \begin{cases} a_p \xrightarrow{x_{a_p a_p^{(1)}}} a_p^{(1)} \\ \vdots \\ a_p \xrightarrow{x_{a_p a_p^{(k_p)}}} a_p^{(k_p)} \end{cases}
\qquad
l_r \begin{cases} b_r \xrightarrow{y_{b_r b_r^{(1)}}} b_r^{(1)} \\ \vdots \\ b_r \xrightarrow{y_{b_r b_r^{(l_r)}}} b_r^{(l_r)} \end{cases}
$$

$$
a_{p+1} \xrightarrow{\not c} \qquad\qquad b_{r+1} \xrightarrow{\not c}
$$

$$
\vdots \qquad\qquad \vdots
$$

$$
a_{p+q} \xrightarrow{\not c} \qquad\qquad b_{r+s} \xrightarrow{\not c}
$$

$x = \{x_{a_i a_i^{(j)}} \in \mathbb{R}^+ | 1 \le i \le p, 1 \le j \le k_i\}$ and $y = \{y_{b_i b_i^{(j)}} \in \mathbb{R}^+ | 1 \le i \le r, 1 \le j \le l_i\}$ are the sought rates of the c-transitions in M_1 and M_2 respectively[1].

---

[1] x_{ab} is the transition rate from state a to b in M_1, and as a special case, x_{aa} is the rate of the selfloop at state a, used in particular in Sect. 3.2. Similarly y_{ab} for M_2.

3.1 Synchronising Action

Lemma 1 (Complete System for Synchronising Action). *For the system Sys described in Definition 1 where $c \in \Sigma_s$, if all c-transitions in M_1 can move simultaneously with all c-transitions in M_2, i.e. $en_1 \times en_2 \subseteq S$, then the resultant system of equations with regards to action c is always complete. The system of equations (3) represents all c-transitions in the combined model.*

$$
\left\{
\begin{array}{ll}
(a_1, b_1) \xrightarrow{d_1} (a_1^{(1)}, b_1^{(1)}) & x_{a_1 a_1^{(1)}} y_{b_1 b_1^{(1)}} = d_1 \\
\quad\vdots & \quad\vdots \\
(a_1, b_r) \xrightarrow{d_n} (a_1^{(1)}, b_r^{(l_r)}) & x_{a_1 a_1^{(1)}} y_{b_r b_r^{(l_r)}} = d_n \\
\hline
\quad\vdots & \quad\vdots \\
\hline
(a_p, b_1) \xrightarrow{d_{(m-1)\cdot n+1}} (a_p^{(k_p)}, b_1^{(1)}) & x_{a_p a_p^{(k_p)}} y_{b_1 b_1^{(1)}} = d_{(m-1)\cdot n+1} \\
\quad\vdots & \quad\vdots \\
(a_p, b_r) \xrightarrow{d_{m\cdot n}} (a_p^{(k_p)}, b_r^{(l_r)}) & x_{a_p a_p^{(k_p)}} y_{b_r b_r^{(l_r)}} = d_{m\cdot n}
\end{array}
\right.
\tag{3}
$$

$d = (d_1, \ldots, d_{mn})$ *is the vector of the given rates of the c-transitions in the combined model. The consistency of the system of equations can be checked using conditions (4) and a possible solution can be obtained by (5).*

Proof. If $en_1 \times en_2 \subseteq S$, then all the combined model states in (3) are reachable and there are $m \cdot n$ c-transitions in the combined model. Every combined model c-transition represents a bilinear equation. The total number of bilinear equations is the product of the number of x and y variables. So, the system of bilinear equations is complete.

The necessary and sufficient conditions for the system of equations (3) to have a solution is:

$$
\left\{
\begin{array}{l}
\dfrac{d_1}{d_2} = \dfrac{d_{n+1}}{d_{n+2}} = \ldots = \dfrac{d_{(m-1)n+1}}{d_{(m-1)n+2}} \\[2mm]
\dfrac{d_1}{d_3} = \dfrac{d_{n+1}}{d_{n+3}} = \ldots = \dfrac{d_{(m-1)n+1}}{d_{(m-1)n+3}} \\[2mm]
\quad\vdots \\[2mm]
\dfrac{d_1}{d_n} = \dfrac{d_{n+1}}{d_{2n}} = \ldots = \dfrac{d_{(m-1)n+1}}{d_{mn}}
\end{array}
\right.
\tag{4}
$$

If these conditions are satisfied, a solution can be obtained using the following equations (5). We can choose one variable freely, say $y_{b_1 b_1^{(1)}} = h$, and obtain the other variables.

$$
\left\{
\begin{array}{l}
\dfrac{y_{b_1 b_1^{(1)}}}{y_{b_1 b_1^{(2)}}} = \dfrac{d_1}{d_2} \\[2mm]
\quad\vdots \\[2mm]
\dfrac{y_{b_1 b_1^{(1)}}}{y_{b_r b_r^{(l_r)}}} = \dfrac{d_1}{d_n}
\end{array}
\right.
\Rightarrow
\left\{
\begin{array}{l}
y_{b_1 b_1^{(2)}} = h\dfrac{d_2}{d_1} \\[2mm]
\quad\vdots \\[2mm]
y_{b_r b_r^{(l_r)}} = h\dfrac{d_n}{d_1}
\end{array}
\right.
\Rightarrow
\left\{
\begin{array}{l}
x_{a_1 a_1^{(1)}} = \dfrac{d_1}{h} \\[2mm]
\quad\vdots \\[2mm]
x_{a_p a_p^{(k_p)}} = \dfrac{d_{(m-1)n+1}}{h}
\end{array}
\right.
\tag{5}
$$

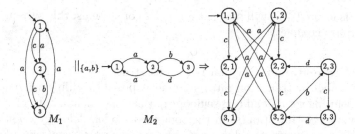

Fig. 3. Processes M_1 and M_2 and the resultant combined model

Example. In Fig. 3 there are two processes M_1 and M_2 synchronised over actions $\Sigma_s = \{a, b\}$ and the resultant combined model. We need to reconstruct the rates of a-transitions. For every a-transition in the combined model, an equation is created and the system of bilinear equations is formed.

Table 1 shows the a-transitions and the system of equations for the rates $d = (d_1, \ldots, d_6) = (3, 2, 1.5, 1, 10.5, 7)$. Figure 4 shows M_1 and M_2 with only a-transitions. Applying Definition 1 for M_1, we would have $a_1 = 1$, $k_1 = 2$ and $a_2 = 3$, $k_2 = 1$ and similar for M_2.

Table 1. a-transitions and the system of nonlinear equations.

$(1, 1) \xrightarrow{a, d_1} (2, 2) \Longrightarrow x_{12} \cdot y_{12} = d_1$	
$(1, 2) \xrightarrow{a, d_2} (2, 1) \Longrightarrow x_{12} \cdot y_{21} = d_2$	
$(1, 1) \xrightarrow{a, d_3} (3, 2) \Longrightarrow x_{13} \cdot y_{12} = d_3$	
$(1, 2) \xrightarrow{a, d_4} (3, 1) \Longrightarrow x_{13} \cdot y_{21} = d_4$	
$(3, 1) \xrightarrow{a, d_5} (1, 2) \Longrightarrow x_{31} \cdot y_{12} = d_5$	
$(3, 2) \xrightarrow{a, d_6} (1, 1) \Longrightarrow x_{31} \cdot y_{21} = d_6$	

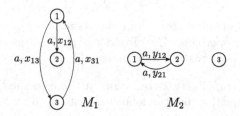

Fig. 4. Processes M_1 and M_2 with a-transitions only.

The necessary condition in Lemma (1) is satisfied, since the number of a-transitions in the combined model is equal to $m \cdot n = 6$ where $m = 3$ is the number of a-transitions in M_1 and $n = 2$ is the number of a-transitions in M_2. According to condition (4), the necessary condition for the system of equations in Table 1 to have a solution is: $\frac{d_1}{d_2} = \frac{d_3}{d_4} = \frac{d_5}{d_6}$ and vector d satisfies this condition. Therefore, this system of equations has a solution, y_{12} can be chosen freely, e.g. $y_{12} = h = 1$, and the other unknowns are determined: $y_{21} = d_2/d_1 = 2/3$, $x_{13} = d_3/h = 1.5$, $x_{12} = d_1/h = 3$, $x_{31} = d_5/h = 10.5$.

3.2   Non-synchronising Action

In this section we consider the transition rate reconstruction for non-synchronising actions. If local lifting is not possible, the action is added to the synchronising set, the necessary selfloops are added and a system of bilinear equations is formed. We will see that for a class of systems, this system of equations is always complete.

Spurious Transitions: Our aim is to reconstruct the transition rates of the high-level model by transition rate assignment, possibly adding some actions to the synchronising set and adding selfloops to the components, but not by adding nor removing any transition(s) in the combined model. Adding action c to the synchronising set incurs the danger of creating some incorrect *spurious* transitions. For instance, in the system described in Definition 1, if state (a_1, b_1) in the combined model is reachable, having two transitions $(a_1, b_1) \xrightarrow{c} (a_1^{(1)}, b_1)$ and $(a_1, b_1) \xrightarrow{c} (a_1, b_1^{(1)})$, creates a spurious transition $(a_1, b_1) \xrightarrow{c} (a_1^{(1)}, b_1^{(1)})$ which should not exist in the combined model. Therefore, the set of states $SP = en_1 \times en_2$, in the combined model must be unreachable ($SP \cap S = \emptyset$) to avoid spurious transitions. The same condition is also checked by the algorithm in [16], thus guaranteeing that the behaviour of the system is not affected by the extended synchronisation set and the added selfloops.

Lemma 2 (Complete system for Non-synchronising Action). *In the system described in Definition 1, assume that $c \notin \Sigma_s$ and local lifting is not possible, so action c is added to Σ_s and c-selfloops are added to states $a_{p+1}, \ldots, a_{p+q}$ and to states $b_{r+1}, \ldots, b_{r+s}$. If $(en_1 \times ne_2) \cup (ne_1 \times en_2) \subseteq S$ and $SP \cap S = \emptyset$, then the resultant system of equations includes two independent complete bilinear systems of equations. The consistency of these systems of equations can be checked using conditions (7), and the possible solution can be derived by equations (8).*

Proof. Every c-transition in the combined model is transformed to a bilinear equation and the following systems (6) are formed.

$$
\begin{cases}
x_{a_1 a_1^{(1)}} \cdot y_{b_{r+1} b_{r+1}} = d_1 \\
\quad \vdots \\
\underline{x_{a_1 a_1^{(k_1)}} \cdot y_{b_{r+1} b_{r+1}} = d_{k_1}} \\
\quad \vdots \\
x_{a_p a_p^{(1)}} \cdot y_{b_{r+1} b_{r+1}} = d_{k_1 + \ldots + k_{p-1} + 1} \\
\quad \vdots \\
x_{a_p a_p^{(k_p)}} \cdot y_{b_{r+1} b_{r+1}} = d_m
\end{cases}
\qquad
\begin{cases}
x_{a_{p+1} a_{p+1}} \cdot y_{b_1 b_1^{(1)}} = e_1 \\
\quad \vdots \\
\underline{x_{a_{p+1} a_{p+1}} \cdot y_{b_1 b_1^{(l_1)}} = e_{l_1}} \\
\quad \vdots \\
x_{a_{p+1} a_{p+1}} \cdot y_{b_r b_r^{(1)}} = e_{l_1 + \ldots + l_{r-1} + 1} \\
\quad \vdots \\
x_{a_{p+1} a_{p+1}} \cdot y_{b_r b_r^{(l_r)}} = e_n
\end{cases}
$$

$$\vdots \qquad\qquad\qquad \vdots$$

$$\tag{6}$$

$$\vdots \qquad\qquad\qquad \vdots$$

$$
\begin{cases}
x_{a_1 a_1^{(1)}} \cdot y_{b_{r+s} b_{r+s}} = d_{(s-1)m+1} & \qquad x_{a_{p+q} a_{p+q}} \cdot y_{b_1 b_1^{(1)}} = e_{(q-1)\cdot n+1} \\
\quad\vdots & \qquad\quad\vdots \\
x_{a_1 a_1^{(k_1)}} \cdot y_{b_{r+s} b_{r+s}} = d_{(s-1)m+k_1} & \qquad x_{a_{p+q} a_{p+q}} \cdot y_{b_1 b_1^{(l_1)}} = e_{(q-1)\cdot n+l_1} \\
\\
\quad\vdots & \qquad\quad\vdots \\
\\
x_{a_p a_p^{(1)}} \cdot y_{b_{r+s} b_{r+s}} = d_{s\cdot m-k_p+1} & \qquad x_{a_{p+q} a_{p+q}} \cdot y_{b_r b_r^{(1)}} = e_{q\cdot n-l_r+1} \\
\quad\vdots & \qquad\quad\vdots \\
x_{a_p a_p^{(k_p)}} \cdot y_{b_{r+s} b_{r+s}} = d_{s\cdot m} & \qquad x_{a_{p+q} a_{p+q}} \cdot y_{b_r b_r^{(l_r)}} = e_{q\cdot n}
\end{cases}
$$

where $d = (d_1,\ldots,d_{s\cdot m})$ and $e = (e_1,\ldots,e_{q\cdot n})$ are the c-transition rates of the combined model.

The LHS system of equations of (6) is independent of the RHS since they have no common variables. The number of equations in the LHS system of equations is $m \cdot s$ which is the product of the number of x and y variables in this system of equations. Similarly, the number of equations in the RHS system of equations is $n \cdot q$ which is the product of the number of x and y variables in this system of equations. Therefore, both the RHS and LHS systems of equations are complete bilinear systems. Satisfying the condition $(en_1 \times ne_2) \cup (ne_1 \times en_2) \subseteq S$, we can make sure that all the equations in (6) exist, otherwise there would be fewer equations and the systems of bilinear equations would be incomplete.

The necessary conditions for these two independent systems of equations to be consistent are:

$$
\begin{cases}
\dfrac{d_1}{d_2} = \dfrac{d_{m+1}}{d_{m+2}} = \ldots = \dfrac{d_{(s-1)m+1}}{d_{(s-1)m+2}} \\
\dfrac{d_1}{d_3} = \dfrac{d_{m+1}}{d_{m+3}} = \ldots = \dfrac{d_{(s-1)m+1}}{d_{(s-1)m+3}} \\
\quad\vdots \\
\dfrac{d_1}{d_m} = \dfrac{d_{m+1}}{d_{2m}} = \ldots = \dfrac{d_{(s-1)m+1}}{d_{s\cdot m}}
\end{cases}
\qquad
\begin{cases}
\dfrac{e_1}{e_2} = \dfrac{e_{n+1}}{e_{n+2}} = \ldots = \dfrac{e_{(q-1)n+1}}{e_{(q-1)n+2}} \\
\dfrac{e_1}{e_3} = \dfrac{e_{n+1}}{e_{n+3}} = \ldots = \dfrac{e_{(q-1)n+1}}{e_{(q-1)n+3}} \\
\quad\vdots \\
\dfrac{e_1}{e_n} = \dfrac{e_{n+1}}{e_{2n}} = \ldots = \dfrac{e_{(q-1)n+1}}{e_{q\cdot n}}
\end{cases}
\tag{7}
$$

If vectors d and e satisfy the conditions (7) then high-level transition rate reconstruction is possible by making action c synchronising and adding the selfloops.

We can choose two variables freely, say $x_{a_1 a_1^{(1)}} = h_1$ and $y_{b_1 b_1^{(1)}} = h_2$, and obtain the other unknowns:

$$\begin{cases} x_{a_1 a_1^{(2)}} = h_1 \cdot \frac{d_2}{d_1} \\ \vdots \\ x_{a_p a_p^{(k_p)}} = h_1 \cdot \frac{d_m}{d_1} \\ y_{b_{r+1} b_{r+1}} = \frac{d_1}{h_1} \\ \vdots \\ y_{b_{r+s} b_{r+s}} = \frac{d_{(s-1)m+1}}{h_1} \end{cases} \qquad \begin{cases} y_{b_1 b_1^{(2)}} = h_2 \cdot \frac{e_2}{e_1} \\ \vdots \\ y_{b_r b_r^{(l_r)}} = h_2 \cdot \frac{e_n}{e_1} \\ x_{a_{p+1} a_{p+1}} = \frac{e_1}{h_2} \\ \vdots \\ x_{a_{p+q} a_{p+q}} = \frac{e_{(q-1)n+1}}{h_2} \end{cases} \qquad (8)$$

4   Iterative Algorithm to Solve System of Equations

So far, we have identified special cases for which we can obtain the solution, if one exists, by checking a simple condition over the given rates d. For general systems which do not fit in with this framework, we need to solve the system of equations directly, which is computationally expensive. For example, in case of a synchronising action c, if the number of c-transitions in the combined model is less than the product of the number of c-transitions in the components, then we cannot use Lemma 1. In other words, if some of the transitions in (3) do not exist (because some states in the combined model are non-reachable), then the system is *incomplete* and Lemma 1 is not applicable anymore.

We now introduce an iterative algorithm which exploits the fact that the system of equations always has a specific form. The algorithm works for synchronising actions c. But it can also be used for non-synchronising actions c, after it has become clear that no local solution exists and after adding c to the synchronising set and adding the necessary selfloops.

Iterative Algorithm. The system of equations to be solved contains the variables $x = (x_1, \ldots, x_m)$ and $y = (y_1, \ldots, y_n)$, and the equations have the specific form $x_r \cdot y_s = d_i$, where $i \in \{1, \ldots, m \cdot n\}$, $r \in \{1, \ldots, m\}$, $s \in \{1, \ldots, n\}$ and x_r and y_s are elements of x and y vectors, respectively. The unknown variable vectors x and y represent the transition rates of the components, and $(d_1, \ldots, d_k)$ are the given combined model transition rates. Although this system of equations is a nonlinear multivariate system, this form of equations enables us to develop an iterative algorithm to solve it efficiently.

1: **Algorithm** SolveBilinEqns (*Eqns*)
2:   // The algorithm solves a system of k bilinear equations
3:   // of the form $x_r y_s = d_i$, where $i \in \{1, \ldots, m \cdot n\}$.
4:   // *Eqns* points to the totally ordered list of equations.
5: **Initialisation:** *Computed* $:= \emptyset$
6:   // The set *Computed* contains variables whose value has already been computed.
7: **repeat**
8:     *curreqn* := first remaining equation from *Eqns*
9:     // throughout, *curreqn* denotes the currently processed equation
10:     delete *curreqn* from *Eqns*
11:     assign an arbitrary non-zero value to the first variable of *curreqn* and calculate the other variable

```
12:        add these two variables and their values to Computed
13:        repeat
14:            curreqn := equation which is next in order in Eqns
15:            if both of the variables of curreqn are in the Computed set then
16:                evaluate curreqn
17:                if curreqn holds then
18:                    remove curreqn from Eqns
19:                else
20:                    return Error and exit the algorithm
21:                    // the system of equations is inconsistent and has no solution
22:                end if
23:            else if exactly one of the variables of curreqn is in the Computed set then
24:                calculate the other variable of curreqn and add it to Computed
25:                remove curreqn from Eqns
26:            else
27:                // both variables are not yet in Computed
28:                skip curreqn // the algorithm will return to this equation later
29:            end if
30:        until the last equation in Eqns has been reached
31: until  Eqns = ∅ // i.e., until all equations have been processed
```

This algorithm takes a totally ordered set of equations $Eqns$ as its input (the ordering is arbitrary, but remains fixed). The currently processed equation is called $curreqn$, and after an equation has been processed, it is removed from $Eqns$. The variables that have already been assigned a value are added to a set called $Computed$, which is initially empty. The algorithm processes the (remaining) equations in order, possibly in several iterations. When the algorithm checks the next equation in $Eqns$, three possible scenarios may occur: (1) If both of the variables are already in the $Computed$ set, the equation is evaluated, and if it holds, it is removed from $Eqns$; otherwise, the algorithm terminates unsuccessfully, because the system of equations is inconsistent. (2) If exactly one of the variables in the current equation is in the $Computed$ set, then the other variable is calculated and also added to $Computed$, and the equation is removed from $Eqns$. (3) If neither of the variables is in the $Computed$ set, the equation is skipped, and will be checked again in the next iteration of the outer repeat-until loop. The reason is that the algorithm needs to avoid setting variables too early, since that might cause some of the following equations not to hold even if the system of equations is consistent. The algorithm terminates successfully once all the equations are checked, at which state the set $Eqns$ is empty.

5 Case Study: Tandem Queueing Network

In this section, we study a tandem queueing network taken from [8] as a benchmark and compare the runtimes of the different methods for solving the system of bilinear equations.

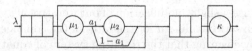

Fig. 5. M/Cox2/1-queue sequentially composed with an M/M/1-queue

5.1 System Definition

The model consists of an M/Cox2/1-queue sequentially composed with an M/M/1-queue, resulting in a finite-state CTMC[2]. Each queue has the capacity $c > 0$, where $c \in \mathbb{N}$ is an adjustable parameter. Figure 5 shows a schematic of the system. A job arrives at the system with rate λ, and the server of the first station executes service in one or two phases with rates μ_1 and μ_2. The probability that the first station executes service in both phases is a_1, and κ is the second station's service rate. We perform our experiments for different values of c and take the following values for the parameters of the queues: $\lambda = 4 \cdot c$, $a_1 = 0.1$, $\mu_1 = \mu_2 = 2$ and $\kappa = 4$.

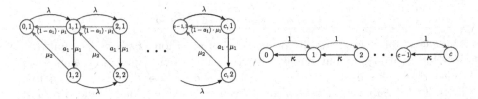

Fig. 6. CTMC models of M/Cox2/1 and M/M/1 queues (Color figure online)

CTMC models of these two queues are shown in Fig. 6, where the states of the M/Cox2/1-queue are 2-tuples, the first number showing the number of jobs, and the second number indicating the service phase. The SPA representation of the system is:

$$Sys = (M/Cox2/1) \,\|_{\{route\}}\, (M/M/1) \tag{8}$$

This model has one synchronising action, which is called *route* (highlighted in red in Fig. 6). In the first queue this action means that a job leaves the queue, and in the second queue that a job enters the queue. These two events must always occur simultaneously in both queues. Each of the $2c$ *route*-transitions of the first queue can synchronise with each of the c *route*-transitions of the second queue, so in the combined model there are $2c^2$ *route*-transitions. In other words, using the terminology of Sect. 2, the system is *complete* regarding the action *route*, so that we can use Lemma 1 to verify the system of equations' consistency and obtain a possible solution.

5.2 Runtime Comparison

In this section, we use a slight modification of our iterative algorithm from Sect. 4 to generate random sets of values d for the rates of the combined system's *route*-transitions, thereby ensuring that the resulting system of equations is consistent. This modification works as follows: Initially, we generate a fully random set of

---

[2] The PRISM source code of this model is provided at https://www. prismmodelchecker.org/casestudies/tandem.php.

values d and start running the algorithm. Once the algorithm reaches an equation which does not hold (line 20 of the algorithm), the value of the rate d_i is simply changed such that the equation becomes consistent. Similarly, we go through the remaining equations and generate the modified set d.

For such a consistent set of the combined model's *route*-transition rates $d = \{d_1, \ldots, d_{2c^2}\}$, we will now compare the runtimes needed by the different solution methods. We compare the approaches of Lemma 1, our iterative algorithm and Gurobi [6], all implemented in (resp. called from) a Matlab [15] environment. Table 2 shows the size of the system for different values of c, where the number of *route*-transitions equals the size of the system of equations, which is also the size of vector d. Table 3 shows the runtime for the three methods[3].

Table 2. Size of the system depending on parameter c

	c						
	200	250	300	350	400	450	500
Total number of states	80601	125751	180901	246051	321201	406351	501501
Total number of transitions	280599	438249	630899	858549	1121199	1418849	1751499
Number of *route*-transitions	80000	125000	180000	245000	320000	405000	500000

Table 3. Runtime in seconds

Method	c						
	200	250	300	350	400	450	500
Lemma 1	24.5	69.7	171.1	314.7	443.8	723.4	1051.8
Iterative Algorithm	29.3	86.1	196.6	350.2	477.1	801.9	1134.5
Gurobi Solver	62.2	216.2	349.6	612.3	793.3	1114.1	1492.4

As we see in Table 3, Lemma 1 is the fastest method to check the consistency of the system of equations (at least 41% faster than Gurobi), followed by our iterative algorithm. Gurobi is always the slowest method. In this comparison, one has to consider that Gurobi is a highly optimised commercial tool (one of the most powerful solvers currently available), while our own implementations consist of simple, non-optimised Matlab code. However, this result was to be expected since in Lemma 1 only some simple conditions over d are checked, and in our iterative algorithm the special structure of the bilinear system of equations is exploited, both processes being computationally much less expensive than general equation solving.

But Gurobi has the significant advantage that it allows the user to define a broad range of objectives and obtain an optimised solution. If the bilinear

---

[3] Executed on Intel Core i7-8650U CPU@ 1.90 GHz–2.11 GHz.

system of equations has a solution, it is not unique. This fact is clearly shown in Lemma 1 and Lemma 2, where an infinite number of solutions can be found by freely choosing some variables. This optimisation feature becomes especially interesting in applications of model repair, where we prefer to find the components' transition rates close to their original rates. So the following objective function, employing the Euclidean distance, can be defined and minimised by Gurobi: $\min\|x - ox\| = \min\sqrt{\sum_i (x_i - ox_i)^2}$, where ox is the set of the original transition rates wrt x as given in the PRISM specification of the system. Similarly, we can write the objective function for y variables. Such an optimisation process is computationally expensive.

We fixed the value of c at $c = 400$ and generated 50 random sets of d, always ensuring that the systems of equations is consistent. Then Gurobi was run to verify the consistency, once with optimiser and once without optimiser. The runtime comparison is shown in Table 4. As shown in the table, on average, the runtime of the Gurobi solver with optimiser is more than 80% higher than the solver's runtime. For 88% of the d vectors, Gurobi solver with optimiser returned the solution in less than 1000 s. The maximum runtime for solver with optimiser is 6082.9, which is more than twice the solver's maximum runtime.

Table 4. Runtime comparison in seconds for 50 random sets of d

$c = 400$	Gurobi solver	Gurobi solver & optimiser
Mean time value	753.6	1369.1
Min	617.2	638.3
Max	2581.7	6082.9

6   Conclusion

In this paper, we have studied the system of bilinear equations that arises during the reconstruction of transition rates in a two-component compositional model. The same type of system of equations has recently been described in the lifting algorithm from [16]. The problem is that solving such a bilinear system becomes very expensive if the number of equations is large.

In order to tackle this problem, we have identified a special class of systems where the consistency of the system of equations can be verified easily by checking some simple conditions. Once the consistency check – formulated in Lemma 1 for synchronising actions and in Lemma 2 for non-synchronising actions – holds, the solution to the system of equations is readily available. Furthermore, for general cases, where the system of equations does not possess such a special form, we have developed a simple but efficient iterative algorithm which computes a solution, if a solution exists at all.

We have compared these different solution methods to each other, but also to the popular and powerful solver Gurobi, and the comparison turned out to be very favorable for our methods. Gurobi, however, is also able to construct solutions that satisfy additional optimality conditions (such as being close to some pre-specified values), which is also demonstrated in the paper by means of an example. In the future, we plan to extend the techniques developed in this paper to systems of more than two components.

References

1. Baier, C., Haverkort, B., Hermanns, H., Katoen, J.P.: Model-checking algorithms for continuous-time Markov chains. IEEE Trans. Softw. Eng. **29**(6), 524–541 (2003)
2. Bartocci, E., Grosu, R., Katsaros, P., Ramakrishnan, C.R., Smolka, S.A.: Model repair for probabilistic systems. In: Abdulla, P.A., Leino, K.R.M. (eds.) TACAS 2011. LNCS, vol. 6605, pp. 326–340. Springer, Heidelberg (2011). https://doi.org/10.1007/978-3-642-19835-9_30
3. Bernardo, M., Gorrieri, R.: A tutorial on EMPA: a theory of concurrent processes with nondeterminism, priorities, probabilities and time. TCS **202**(1), 1–54 (1998)
4. Chatzieleftheriou, G., Katsaros, P.: Abstract model repair for probabilistic systems. Inf. Comput. **259**, 142–160 (2018)
5. Dehnert, C., Junges, S., Katoen, J.-P., Volk, M.: A STORM is coming: a modern probabilistic model checker. In: Majumdar, R., Kunčak, V. (eds.) CAV 2017. LNCS, vol. 10427, pp. 592–600. Springer, Cham (2017). https://doi.org/10.1007/978-3-319-63390-9_31
6. Gurobi Optimization, LLC: Gurobi optimizer reference manual (2020). http://www.gurobi.com
7. Hahn, E.M., Li, Y., Schewe, S., Turrini, A., Zhang, L.: ISCASMc: a web-based probabilistic model checker. In: Jones, C., Pihlajasaari, P., Sun, J. (eds.) FM 2014. LNCS, vol. 8442, pp. 312–317. Springer, Cham (2014). https://doi.org/10.1007/978-3-319-06410-9_22
8. Hermanns, H., Meyer-Kayser, J., Siegle, M.: Multi terminal binary decision diagrams to represent and analyse continuous time Markov chains. In: Proceedings of 3rd International Workshop Numerical Solution of Markov Chains (NSMC 1999), pp. 188–207. Prensas Universitarias de Zaragoza (1999)
9. Hillston, J.: The nature of synchronisation. In: Proceedings of 2nd Workshop on Process Algebras and Performance Modelling, pp. 51–70. Arbeitsberichte des IMMD 27(4), Universität Erlangen-Nürnberg (1994)
10. Hillston, J.: A Compositional Approach to Performance Modelling. Cambridge University Press, Cambridge (1996)
11. Johnson, C.R., Link, J.A.: Solution theory for complete bilinear systems of equations. Numer. Linear Algebra Appl. **16**(11–12), 929–934 (2009)
12. Katoen, J.P., Zapreev, I.S., Hahn, E.M., Hermanns, H., Jansen, D.N.: The ins and outs of the probabilistic model checker MRMC. Perform. Eval. **68**(2), 90–104 (2011)
13. Kuntz, M., Siegle, M., Werner, E.: Symbolic performance and dependability evaluation with the tool CASPA. In: Núñez, M., Maamar, Z., Pelayo, F.L., Pousttchi, K., Rubio, F. (eds.) FORTE 2004. LNCS, vol. 3236, pp. 293–307. Springer, Heidelberg (2004). https://doi.org/10.1007/978-3-540-30233-9_22
14. Kwiatkowska, M., Norman, G., Parker, D.: PRISM 4.0: verification of probabilistic real-time systems. In: Gopalakrishnan, G., Qadeer, S. (eds.) CAV 2011. LNCS, vol. 6806, pp. 585–591. Springer, Heidelberg (2011). https://doi.org/10.1007/978-3-642-22110-1_47

15. MATLAB: version 9.6.0 (R2019a). The MathWorks Inc. (2019a)
16. Soltanieh, A., Siegle, M.: It sometimes works: a lifting algorithm for repair of stochastic process algebra models. In: Hermanns, H. (ed.) MMB 2020. LNCS, vol. 12040, pp. 190–207. Springer, Cham (2020). https://doi.org/10.1007/978-3-030-43024-5_12
17. Tati, B.: Quantitative model repair of stochastic systems. Ph.D. thesis, Bundeswehr University Munich (2018)
18. Tati, B., Siegle, M.: Rate reduction for state-labelled Markov chains with upper time-bounded CSL requirements. EPTCS **220**, 77–89 (2016)
19. Tati, B.S.K., Siegle, M.: Parameter and controller synthesis for Markov chains with actions and state labels. In: 2nd International Workshop Synthesis of Complex Parameters (SynCoP 2015). OpenAccess Series in Informatics (OASIcs), vol. 44, pp. 63–76. Schloss Dagstuhl - Leibniz-Zentrum fuer Informatik (2015)

Parallel Computation

Term Rewriting on GPUs

Johri van Eerd[1], Jan Friso Groote[2(✉)] ⓘ, Pieter Hijma[2,3] ⓘ, Jan Martens[2] ⓘ,
and Anton Wijs[2] ⓘ

[1] Verum Software Tools BV, Eindhoven, The Netherlands
johri.van.eerd@verum.com
[2] Eindhoven University of Technology, Eindhoven, The Netherlands
{j.f.groote,j.j.m.martens,a.j.wijs}@tue.nl
[3] VU Amsterdam, Amsterdam, The Netherlands
pieter@cs.vu.nl

Abstract. We present a way to implement term rewriting on a GPU. We
do this by letting the GPU repeatedly perform a massively parallel evaluation of all subterms. We find that if the term rewrite systems exhibit
sufficient internal parallelism, GPU rewriting substantially outperforms
the CPU. Since we expect that our implementation can be further optimized, and because in any case GPUs will become much more powerful
in the future, this suggests that GPUs are an interesting platform for
term rewriting. As term rewriting can be viewed as a universal programming language, this also opens a route towards programming GPUs by
term rewriting, especially for irregular computations.

Keywords: Term rewriting · GPU · Programming · Parallel
computing

1 Introduction

Graphics Processing Units (GPUs) increase in computational power much faster
than the classical CPUs. GPUs are optimized for the highly parallel and regular
computations that occur in graphics processing, but they become more and
more interesting for general purpose computations (for instance, see [3,4]). It is
not without reason that modern super computers have large banks of graphical
processors installed in them [10]. GPU designers realize this and make GPUs
increasingly suitable for irregular computations. For instance, they have added
improved caches and atomic operations.

This raises the question to what extent the GPU can be used for more irregular computational tasks. The main limitation is that a highly parallel algorithm
is needed to fully utilize the power of the GPU. For irregular problems it is the
programmer's task to recognize the regularities in problems over irregular data
structures such as graphs.

The evaluation of term rewriting systems (TRSs) is an irregular problem that
is interesting for the formal methods community. For example, term rewriting
increases the expressiveness of models in the area of model checking [5] and the

© IFIP International Federation for Information Processing 2021
Published by Springer Nature Switzerland AG 2021
H. Hojjat and M. Massink (Eds.): FSEN 2021, LNCS 12818, pp. 175–189, 2021.
https://doi.org/10.1007/978-3-030-89247-0_12

performance of term rewriting is a long-standing and important objective [8]. We recall that a term rewriting system that enjoys the Church-Rosser property is parallel in nature, in the sense that rewriting can take place at any point in the system and the order in which it takes place does not influence the outcome. This suggests a very simple model for parallel evaluation. Every processor can independently work on its own section of the system and do its evaluation there. In this paper, we investigate whether and under which conditions term rewriting systems can be evaluated effectively on GPUs. We experimented with different compilation schemes from rewrite systems to GPU code and present here one where all processors evaluate all subterms in parallel. This has as drawback that terms that cannot be evaluated still require processing time. Terms can become discarded when being evaluated, and therefore garbage collection is required. All processors are also involved in this.

An earlier approach to inherently evaluate a program in parallel was done in the eighties. The Church-Rosser property for pure functional programs sparked interest from researchers, and the availability of cheap microprocessors made it possible to assemble multiple processors to work on the evaluation of one single functional program. Jones et al. proposed GRIP, a parallel reduction machine design to execute functional programs on multiple microprocessors that communicate using an on-chip bus [19]. At the same time Barendregt et al. proposed the Dutch Parallel Reduction Machine project, that follows a largely similar architecture of many microprocessors communicating over a shared memory bus [2]. Although technically feasible, the impact of these projects was limited, as the number of available processors was too small and the communication overhead too severe to become a serious contender of sequential programming. GPUs offer a different infrastructure, with in the order of a thousand fold more processors and highly integrated on chip communication. Therefore, GPUs are a new and possibly better candidate for parallel evaluation of TRSs.

Besides their use in the formal methods community, a term rewriting system is also a simple, yet universal mechanism for computation [20]. A question that follows is whether this model for computation can be used to express programs for GPUs more easily.

Current approaches for GPU programming are to design a program at a highly abstract level first and transform it in a stepwise fashion to an optimal GPU program [13]. Other approaches are to extend languages with notation for array processing tasks that can be sparked off to the GPU. Examples in the functional programming world are Accelerate [16], an embedded array processing language for Haskell, and Futhark [12], a data parallel language which generates code for NVIDIA's Compute Unified Device Architecture (CUDA) interface. While Futhark and Accelerate make it easier to use the power of the GPU, both approaches are tailored to highly regular problems. Implementing irregular problems over more complicated data structures remains challenging and requires the programmer to translate the problem to the regular structures provided in the language as seen in, for example, [11,22].

We designed experiments and compared GPU rewriting with CPU rewriting of the same terms. We find that our implementation manages to employ 80% of the bandwidth of the GPU for random accesses. For rewriting, random accesses are the performance bottleneck, and therefore our implementation uses the GPU quite well. For intrinsically parallel rewrite tasks, the GPU outperforms a CPU with up to a factor 10. The experiments also show that if the number of sub-terms that can be evaluated in parallel is reduced, rewriting slows down quite dramatically. This is due to the fact that individual GPU processors are much slower than a CPU processor and GPU cycles are spent on non-reducible terms.

This leads us to the following conclusion. Term rewriting on a GPU certainly has potential. Although our implementation performs close to the random access peak bandwidth, this does not mean that performance cannot be improved. It does mean that future optimizations need to focus on increasing regularity in the implementation, especially in memory access patterns, for example by grouping together similar terms, or techniques such as kernel unrolling in combination with organizing terms such that subterms are close to the parent terms as proposed by Nasre et al. [17]. Furthermore, we expect that GPUs quickly become faster, in particular for applications with random accesses.

However, we also observe that when the degree of parallelism in a term is reduced, it is better to let the CPU do the work. This calls for a hybrid approach where it is dynamically decided whether a term is to be evaluated on the CPU or on the GPU depending on the number of subterms that need to be rewritten. This is future work. We also see that designing inherently parallel rewriting systems is an important skill that we must learn to master.

Although much work lies ahead of us, we conclude that using GPUs to solve term rewriting processes is promising. It allows for abstract programming inde-pendent of the hardware details of GPUs, and it offers the potential of evaluating appropriate rewrite systems at least one order, and in the future orders of mag-nitude faster than a CPU.

Related to this work is the work of Nasre et al. [18] where parallel graph mutation and rewriting programs for both GPUs and CPUs are studied. In particular they study Delaunay mesh refinement (DMR) and points-to-analysis (PTA). PTA is related to term rewriting in a sense that nodes do simple rule based computations, but it is different in the sense that no new nodes are created. In DMR new nodes and edges are created but the calculations are done in a very different manner. The term rewriting in this work can be seen as a special case of graph rewriting, where symbols are seen as nodes and subterms as edges.

2   Preliminaries

We introduce term rewriting, what it means to apply rewrite rules, and an overview of the CUDA GPU computing model.

Term Rewrite Systems. A *Term Rewrite System* (*TRS*) is a set of rules. Each rule is a pair of terms, namely a left hand side and a right hand side. Given an arbitrary term t and a TRS R, rewriting means to replace occurrences in t of the left hand side of a rule in R by the corresponding right hand side, and then repeating the process on the result.

Terms are constructed from a set of variables V and a set of function symbols F. A function symbol is applied to a predefined number of arguments or sub-terms. We refer to this number as the *arity* of the function symbol, and denote the arity of a function symbol f by $ar(f)$. If $ar(f) = 0$, we say f is a *constant*. Together, the sets V and F constitute the *signature* $\Sigma = (F, V)$ of a TRS. The set of terms T_Σ over a signature Σ is inductively defined as the smallest set satisfying:

- If $t \in V$, then $t \in T_\Sigma$;
- If $f \in F$, and $t_i \in T_\Sigma$ for $1 \leq i \leq ar(f)$), then $f(t_1, \ldots, t_{ar(f)}) \in T_\Sigma$.

With $sub_i(t)$, we refer to the i-th subterm of term t. The *head symbol* of a term t is defined as $hs(f(t_1, \ldots, t_k)) = f$. If $t \in V$, $hs(t)$ is undefined. With $Var(t)$, we refer to the set of variables occurring in term t. It is defined as follows:

$$Var(t) = \begin{cases} \{t\} & \text{if } t \in V, \\ \bigcup_{1 \leq i \leq ar(t)} Var(t_i) & \text{if } t = f(t_1, \ldots, t_{ar(f)}). \end{cases}$$

Definition 1 (Term rewrite system). *A TRS R over a signature Σ is a set of pairs of terms, i.e., $R \subseteq T_\Sigma \times T_\Sigma$. Each pair $(l, r) \in R$ is called a rule, and is typically denoted by $l \to r$. Each rule $(l, r) \in R$ satisfies two properties: (1) $l \notin V$, and (2) $Var(r) \subseteq Var(l)$.*

Besides the two properties for each rule $(l, r) \in R$ stated in Definition 1, we assume that each variable $v \in V$ occurs at most once in l. A TRS with rules not satisfying this assumption can be rewritten to one that does not contain such rules. Given a rule $l \to r$, we refer to l as the left-hand-side (LHS) and to r as the right-hand-side (RHS).

Definition 2 (Substitution). *For a TRS R over a signature $\Sigma = (F, V)$, a substitution $\sigma : V \to T_\Sigma$ maps variables to terms. We write $t\sigma$ for a substitution σ applied to a term $t \in T_\Sigma$, defined as $\sigma(t)$ if $t \in V$, and $f(t_1\sigma, \ldots, t_{ar(f)}\sigma)$ if $t = f(t_1, \ldots, t_{ar(f)})$.*

Substitutions allow for a *match* between a term t and rule $l \to r$. A rule $l \to r$ is said to match t iff a substitution σ exists such that $l\sigma = t$. If such a σ exists, then we say that t *reduces* to $r\sigma$. A match $l\sigma$ of a rewrite rule $l \to r$ is also called a *redex*.

A term t is in *normal form*, denoted by $nf(t)$, iff its subterms are in normal form and there is no rule $(l, r) \in R$ and substitution σ such that $t = l\sigma$.

As an example, Listing 1.1 presents a simplified version of a merge sort rewrite system with an input tree of depth 2 consisting of empty lists (*Nil*). After the `sort` keyword, a list is given of all function symbols. After the keyword `eqn`, rewrite rules are given in the form LHS = RHS. The set of variables is given as a list after the `var` keyword. The `input` section defines the input term. In this example, all rewrite rules for functions on (Peano) numbers and Booleans are omitted, such as the less than (*Lt*) rule for natural numbers and the *Even* and

Listing 1.1. A TRS for merge sort in a binary tree of lists

```
1    sort    List = Nil() | Cons(Nat, List) | Sort(List) | ...;
2            Tree = Leaf(List) | Node(Tree, Tree);
3            Nat = Zero() | S(Nat);
4
5    var X : Nat; Y : Nat; L : List; M : List;
6
7    eqn     Merge(Nil(), M) = M;
8            Merge(L, Nil()) = L;
9            Merge(Cons(X, L), Cons(Y, M)) = Merge2(Lt(X,Y), X, L, Y, M);
10
11           Merge2(True(), X, L, Y, M) = Cons(X, Merge(L, Cons(Y, M)));
12           Merge2(False(), X, L, Y, M) = Cons(Y, Merge(Cons(X, L), M));
13
14           Sort(L) = Sort2(Gt(Len(L), S(Zero())), L);
15           Sort2(False(), L) = L;
16           Sort2(True(), L) = Merge(Sort(Even(L)), Sort(Odd(L)));
17
18   input   Node(Leaf(Sort(...)), Leaf(Sort(...)));
```

Listing 1.2. A derivation procedure, and a rewrite procedure for head symbol f

```
1    procedure derive(t, R):
2       while ¬nf(t) do
3          for i ∈ {1, ..., ar(t)} do
4             if ¬nf(sub_i(t)) then
5                derive(sub_i(t))
6          t ← rewrite_{hs(t)}(t, R)
7
8    procedure rewrite_f(t, R):
9       rewritten ← false
10      for (l → r) ∈ {(l,r) ∈ R | hs(l) = f} do
11         if ∃σ: V → T_Σ.lσ = t then
12            t ← rσ; rewritten ← true; break
13      if ¬rewritten then nf(t) ← true
14      return t
```

Odd rules for lists, which create lists consisting of all elements at even and odd positions in the given list, respectively. The potential for parallel rewriting is implicit and can be seen, for instance, in the *Sort2* rule. The two arguments of *Merge* in the RHS of *Sort2* can be evaluated in parallel. Note that *Nil()*, *Zero()* and *S(Nat)* are in normal form, but other terms may not be. The complete TRS is given in the extended version of the paper [21, Appendix A].

A TRS is *terminating* iff there are no infinite reductions possible. For instance, the rule $f(a) \rightarrow f(f(a))$ leads to an infinite reduction. In general, determining whether a given TRS is terminating is an undecidable problem [14].

The computation of a term in a terminating TRS is the repeated application of rewrite rules until the term is in normal form. Such a computation is also called a *derivation*. Note that the result of a derivation may be non-deterministically produced. Consider, for example, the rewrite rule $r = (f(f(x)) \rightarrow a)$ and the term $t = f(f(f(a)))$. Applying r on t may result in either the normal form a or $f(a)$, depending on the chosen reduction. To make rewriting deterministic, a *rewrite strategy* is needed. We focus on the *inner-most* strategy, which gives priority to selecting redexes that do not contain other redexes. In the example, this means that the LHS of r is matched on the inner $f(f(a))$ of t, leading to $f(a)$.

Algorithmically, (inner-most) rewriting is typically performed using recursion. Such an algorithm is presented in Listing 1.2. As long as a term t is not in normal form (line 2), it is first checked whether all its subterms are in normal form (lines 3–4). For each subterm not in normal form, `derive` is called recursively (line 5), by which the inner-most rewriting strategy is achieved. If the subterms are checked sequentially from left to right, we have *left-most* inner-most rewriting. A parallel rewriter may check the subterms in parallel, since inner-most redexes do not contain other redexes. Once all subterms are in normal form, the procedure `rewrite`$_{hs(t)}$ is called (line 6).

For each head symbol of the TRS, we have a dedicated rewrite procedure. The structure of these procedures is also given in Listing 1.2. The variable `rewritten` is used to keep track of whether a rewrite step has been performed (line 9). For each rewrite rule (l, r) with $hs(l) = f$, it is checked whether a match between l and t exists, and if so, $l \rightarrow r$ is applied on t (lines 10–12). If no rewrite rule was applicable, it is concluded that t is in normal form (line 13).

GPU Basics. In this paper, we focus on NVIDIA GPU architectures and CUDA. However, our algorithms can be straightforwardly applied to any GPU architecture with a high degree of hardware multithreading and the SIMT (Single Instruction Multiple Threads) model.

CUDA is NVIDIA's interface to program GPUs. It extends the C++ programming language. CUDA includes special declarations to explicitly place variables in either the main or the GPU memory, predefined keywords to refer to the IDs of individual threads and blocks of threads, synchronisation statements, a run time API for memory management, and statements to define and launch GPU functions, known as *kernels*. In this section we give a brief overview of CUDA. More details can be found in, for instance, [6].

A GPU contains a set of streaming multiprocessors (SMs), each containing a set of streaming processors (SPs). For our experiments, we used the NVIDIA TURING TITAN RTX. It has 72 SMs with 64 SPs each, i.e., in total 4608 SPs.

A CUDA program consists of a *host* program running on the CPU and a collection of CUDA kernels. Kernels describe the parallel parts of the program and are launched from the host to be executed many times in parallel by different threads on the GPU. It is required to specify the number of threads on a kernel launch and all threads execute the same kernel. Conceptually, each thread is executed by an SP. In general, GPU threads are grouped in blocks of a predefined size, usually a power of two. A block of threads is assigned to a multiprocessor.

Threads have access to different kinds of memory. Each thread has a number of on-chip registers to store thread-local data. It allow fast access. All the threads have access to the *global memory* which is large (on the TITAN RTX it is 24 GB), but slow, since it is off-chip. The host has read and write access to the global memory, which allows this memory to be used to provide the input for, and read the output of, a kernel execution.

Threads are executed using the SIMT model. This means that each thread is executed independently with its own instruction address and local state (stored in its registers), but execution is organised in groups of 32 threads, called *warps*.

The threads in a warp execute instructions in lock-step, i.e. they share a program counter. If the memory accesses of threads in a warp can be grouped together physically, i.e. if the accesses are coalesced, then the data can be obtained using a single fetch, which greatly improves the bandwidth compared to fetching physically separate data.

3   A GPU Algorithm for Term Rewriting

In this section, we address how a GPU can perform inner-most term rewriting to get the terms of a given TRS in normal form. Due to the different strengths and weaknesses of GPUs compared to CPUs, this poses two main challenges:

1. On a GPU, many threads (in the order of thousands) should be able to contribute to the computation;
2. GPUs are not very suitable for recursive algorithms. It is strongly advised to avoid recursion because each thread maintains its own stack requiring a large amount of stack space that needs to be allocated in slow global memory.

We decided to develop a so-called *topology-driven* algorithm [17], as opposed to a data-driven one. Unlike for CPUs, topology-driven algorithms are often developed for GPUs, in particular for irregular programs with complex data structures such as trees and graphs. In a topology-driven GPU algorithm, each GPU thread is assigned a particular data element, such as a graph node, and all threads repeatedly apply the same operator on their respective element. This is done until a fix-point has been reached, i.e., no thread can transform its element anymore using the operator. In many iterations of the computation, it is expected that the majority of threads will not be able to apply the operator, but on a GPU this is counterbalanced by the fact that many threads are running, making it relatively fast to check all elements in each iteration. In contrast, in a data-driven algorithm, typically used for CPUs, the elements that need processing are repeatedly collected in a queue before the operator is applied on them. Although this avoids checking all elements repeatedly, on a GPU, having thousands of threads together maintaining such a queue is typically a major source for memory contention.

In our algorithm, each thread is assigned a term, or more specifically a location where a term may be stored. As derivations are applied on a TRS, new terms may be created and some terms may be deleted. The algorithm needs to account for the number of terms dynamically changing between iterations.

First, we discuss how TRSs are represented on a GPU. Typically, GPU data structures, such as matrices and graphs, are array-based, and we also store a TRS in a collection of arrays. Each term is associated with a unique index i, and each of its attributes can be retrieved by accessing the i-th element of one of the arrays. This encourages coalesced memory access for improved bandwidth: when all threads need to retrieve the head symbol of their term, for instance, they will access consecutive elements of the array that stores head symbols. We introduce the following GPU data structures that reside in global memory:

Listing 1.3. The main loop of the rewrite algorithm, executed by the CPU

```
1    h_done = false;
2    while (!h_done) {
3        done ← h_done;
4        numBlocks = n / blockSize;
5        refcounts_read = refcounts;
6        nf_read = nf;
7        derive<<numBlocks, blockSize>>(nf, nf_read, hss, arg_0, ...);
8        h_next_fresh ← next_fresh;
9        if (h_next_fresh > 0) {
10           n = n + h_next_fresh;
11           next_fresh ← 0;
12       }
13       h_done ← done;
14       h_garbage_collecting ← garbage-collecting;
15       if (h_garbage_collecting) {
16           collect_free_indices <<numBlocks, blockSize>>(...);
17           garbage_collecting ← false;
18       }
19   }
```

- Boolean arrays nf and nf_read keep track of which terms are in normal form, the first is used for writing and the second for reading;
- Integer variable n provides the current number of terms;
- Array hss stores the head symbols of all the terms;
- Constant maxarity refers to the highest arity among the function symbols in F;
- Arrays $arg_0, \ldots, arg_{maxarity-1}$ store the indices of the subterms of each term. Index 0 is never used. If $arg_j[i] = 0$, for some $0 \leq j < maxarity - 1$, then the term stored at index i has arity $j - 1$, and all elements $arg_j[i], \ldots,$ $arg_{maxarity-1}[i]$ should be ignored.
- Boolean flag done indicates whether more rewriting iterations are needed;
- Integer arrays refcounts, refcounts_read are used to write and read the number of references to each term, respectively. When a term is not referenced, it can be deleted.

Some form of garbage collection is necessary to be able to reuse memory occupied by deleted terms. For this reason, we have the following additional data structures:

- Boolean flag garbage_collecting indicates whether garbage collecting is needed;
- Integer array free_indices stores indices that can be reused for new terms;
- Integer variables next_free_begin, next_free_end provide indices to remove elements from the front of free_indices and add elements at the end, respectively;
- Integer variable next_fresh provides a new index, greater than the largest index currently occupied by a term in the term arrays. There, a new term can be inserted.

Listing 1.3 presents the main loop of the algorithm, which is executed by the CPU. In it, two GPU kernels are repeatedly called until a fix-point has been

Listing 1.4. The derive kernel, executed by a GPU thread

```
1   derive (...) {
2     if (tid >= n) { return; }
3     refcount = refcounts_read[tid];
4     if (refcount > 0) {
5       start_rewriting = !nf_read[tid];
6       if (start_rewriting) {
7         if (all subterms are in normal form) {
8           switch (hss[tid]) {
9             case f:  rewrite_f(...);
10            ...
11            default:  nf[tid] = true;
12          }
13        }
14        done = false;
15      }
16    }
17    else {
18      garbage_collecting = true;
19    }
20  }
```

reached, indicated by **done**. To keep track of the progress, there are CPU counterparts of several variables, labeled with the '**h_**' prefix. Copying data between CPU and GPU memory is represented by ←.

While the rewriting is not finished (line 2), the GPU **done** flag is set to **false** (line 3), after which the number of thread blocks is determined. As the number of threads should be equal to the current number of terms, **n** is divided by the preset number of threads per block (**blockSize**). After that, **refcounts** is copied to **refcounts_read**, and **nf** to **nf_read**. The reading and writing of the reference counters and normal form state is separated by the use of two arrays, to avoid newly created terms already being rewritten before they have been completely stored in memory. The **derive** kernel is then launched for the selected number of blocks (line 7). This kernel, shown in Listing 1.4, is discussed later. In the kernel, the GPU threads perform one rewrite iteration. Then, at lines 8–12, **n** is updated in case the number of terms has increased. The **next_fresh** variable is used to count the number of new terms placed at fresh indices, i.e., indices larger than **n** when **derive** was launched.

Finally, with **garbage_collecting**, it is monitored whether some indices of deleted terms need to be gathered in the **free_indices** list. This gathering is done by the **collect_free_indices** kernel: if a thread detects that the reference counter of its term is 0, it decrements the counters of the subterms and the index to the term is added to the **free_indices** list. Atomic memory accesses are used to synchronise this. Notice that **free_indices** is in device memory and no unnecessary data is transferred back and forth between host and device.

In Listing 1.4, the GPU **derive** kernel is described. When the kernel is launched for **numBlocks·blockSize** threads, each of those threads executes the kernel to process its term. The global ID of each thread is **tid**. Some threads may not actually have a term to look at (if **n** is not divisible by **blockSize**), therefore they first check whether there is a corresponding term (line 2). If so, the value of the reference counter for the term is read (line 3), and if it is non-zero, a check for

Listing 1.5. An example rewrite function for the rule Plus(Zero,X)→X

```
1   rewritePlus(...) {
2       r_0 = arg0[tid];
3       r_hs_0 = hss[r_0];
4       if (r_hs_0 == Zero) {
5           r_1 = arg1[tid];
6           r_hs_1 = hss[r_1];
7           hss[tid] = r_hs_1;
8           copy_term_args(refscount, arg0, arg1, r_1, tid, r_hs_1);
9           atomicSub(&refcounts[r_0], 1);
10          atomicSub(&refcounts[r_1], 1);
11          nf[tid] = true;
12          return;
13      }
14      ...Check applicability of other Plus-rules
15  }
```

rewriting is required. Rewriting is needed if the term is not in normal form (line 5) and if all its subterms are in normal form (line 7). To avoid repetitive checking of subterms in each execution of the **derive** kernel, every thread keeps track of the last subterm it checked in the previous iteration. If rewriting is required, the suitable **rewrite**$_f$ function is called, depending on the head symbol of the term (lines 8–12). If no function is applicable, the term is in normal form (line 11). Finally, **done** is set to **false** to indicate that another rewrite iteration is required. Alternatively, if the reference counter is 0, the **garbage_collecting** flag is set. This causes the **collect_free_indices** kernel to be launched after the **derive** kernel (see Listing 1.3).

Given a TRS, the **rewrite**$_f$ functions are automatically generated by a code generator we developed, to directly encode the rewriting in CUDA code. Listing 1.5 provides example code for the rewrite rule Plus(Zero,X)→X, which expresses that adding 0 to some number X results in X. Applicability of this rule is checked by the **rewrite**$_{Plus}$ function, which may also involve other rules for terms with head symbol Plus. First, to check applicability, the index of the first subterm is retrieved, and with it, the head symbol of that term (lines 2–3). If the head symbol is Zero (line 4), the index to the second subterm is retrieved (line 5). The rewriting procedure should ensure that the term at position tid is replaced by X.

When constructing terms, sharing of subterms is applied whenever possible. For instance, if a term F(X,X) needs to be created, the index to X would be used twice in the new term, to make sure both subterm entries point to the same term in physical memory. When rewriting the term itself, however, as in the example, we have to copy the attributes of X to the location tid of the various arrays, to ensure that all terms referencing term tid are correctly updated.

This copying of terms is done by first copying the head symbol (lines 6–7), and then the indices of the subterms, which is done at line 8 by the function **copy_term_args**; it copies the number of subterms relevant for a term with the given head symbol, and increments the reference counters of those subterms. Next, the reference counters of Zero and X are atomically decremented (since

Listing 1.6. The get_new_index GPU function, executed by a GPU thread

```
1   get_new_index(...) {
2     if (tid >= n) { return; }
3     n_begin = next_free_begin; n_end = next_free_end;
4     new_id = 0;
5     if (n_begin < n_end) {
6       n_begin = atomicInc(&next_free_begin);
7       if (n_begin < n_end) {
8         new_id = free_indices[n_begin];
9       }
10    }
11    if (new_id == 0) {
12      new_id = atomicInc(&next_fresh) + n;
13    }
14    return new_id;
15  }
```

Table 1. Comparison of the CPU and GPU.

Type	Year	Name	Mem (GB)	BW aligned (GiB/s)	BW random (GiB/s)
CPU	2017	Intel Core i5-7600	32	25.7	0.607
GPU	2018	NVIDIA Titan RTX	24	555	22.8

the term Plus(Zero, X) is removed) (lines 9–10), and we know that the resulting term is in normal form, since X is in normal form (line 11).

Finally, we show how new indices are retrieved whenever a new term needs to be created. In the example of Listing 1.5, this is not needed, as the RHS of the rule has no new subterms, but for a rule such as Plus(S(0), X)→S(X), with S representing the successor function (i.e., S(0) represents 1) a new term S(X) needs to be created, with its only subterm entry pointing to the term referenced by the second subterm entry of the LHS.

Listing 1.6 shows how we retrieve a new index. Due to garbage collection, a number of indices may be available in the first n entries of the input arrays which are currently used. These are stored in the free_indices array, from index next_free_begin to index next_free_end. If this array is not empty (line 5), next_free_begin is atomically incremented to claim the next index in the free_indices array (line 6). If this increment was not performed too late (other threads have not since claimed all available indices), the index is stored in new_id (lines 7–9). Otherwise, a new index must be added at the end of the current list of terms. The variable next_fresh is used for this purpose: next_fresh + n can be used as a new index, and next_fresh needs to be incremented for use by another thread.

4   Evaluation

In this section we provide insight into the performance of the GPU rewriter. We do this in two ways: We compare our GPU rewriter with a sequential recursive left-most inner-most rewriter for the CPU (1) and (2) we analyze to what extent we make good use of the GPU resources. Because CPUs and GPUs differ widely in architecture, it is often subject of debate whether a comparison is fair [15]. We therefore include the second way of evaluating.

Table 1 shows a comparison of the used CPU and GPU. CPUs are optimized for latency: finish the program as soon as possible. In contrast, GPUs are optimized for throughput: process as many elements per time unit as possible. For GPUs, parallelism is explicit, one instruction is issued for multiple threads, and the architecture is specifically designed to hide memory latency times by scheduling new warps immediately after a memory access. The differences between architectures are highlighted by the last two columns that show that the bandwidth of the GPU for aligned access is vastly superior to that of the CPU. Even the bandwidth for random accesses on the GPU almost reaches the bandwidth for aligned accesses on the CPU.

We measure the performance of the CPU and GPU rewriter in *rewritten terms per second*. Given a TRS, both the GPU and the CPU rewriter are generated by a `Python 2.7` script. The script uses `TextX` [7] and `Jinja 2.11`[1] to parse a TRS and generate a `rewrite`$_f$ function for every rewritable head symbol f in the TRS. The code generated for the GPU rewriter is CUDA C++ with CUDA platform 10.1. For the CPU rewriter the code generated is in C++. The same `rewrite`$_f$ functions are used, and thus the rewrite rules are equal and the CPU and GPU implementations rewrite the same number of terms.

We evaluate the GPU rewriter with a TRS for sorting one or more lists of Peano numbers with merge sort (see the example in Sect. 2) and with a TRS that transforms a large number of terms.[2] These TRSs accentuate the capabilities of the GPU and the CPU. Merge sort is a divide-and-conquer algorithm amenable to parallelism, but splitting and combining lists is highly sequential.

Figure 1 shows a merge sort performed on a single list of 50 elements. The width of a red box (too small for Fig. 1a, see the zoomed in version in Fig. 1b) represents the time of a GPU rewrite step (the `derive` statement on line 7 in Listing 1.3) whereas the height represents how many terms are rewritten in parallel in this rewrite step. The figure shows that there are long tails of a low degree of parallelism before and after a brief peak of parallelism. Given Amdahl's law that states that speedup is severely limited with a low degree of parallelism [1], it is clear that merge sort on single lists is not parallel enough for GPUs.

The performance of the GPU of 74×10^3 terms/s versus the CPU 97×10^6 terms/s highlights a different issue, namely Gustafson's Law [9]: To overcome the overhead of using a highly parallel machine, we need a large problem with a high degree of parallelism to highlight the capabilities of the GPU. In order to benchmark this potential, we use the merge sort TRS applied on multiple lists: The Tree merge sort is given by a binary tree with a list of numbers at every leaf. All these lists are sorted concurrently using the same merge sort as in the previous example. The parallelism is exponential w.r.t. the depth of the tree.

Table 2 shows that the GPU outperforms the CPU more than a factor of three for a binary tree of 23 levels deep of merge sorts of lists of 5 numbers,

---

[1] https://jinja.palletsprojects.com.

[2] See [21, Appendix A] for a detailed description of the TRSs.

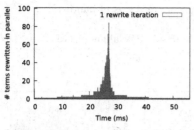

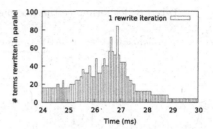

(a) Parallelism across execution time   (b) Parallelism zoomed in

Fig. 1. Merge sort of 50 elements on the GPU. (Color figure online)

Table 2. Performance of the rewrite systems.

Application	CPU rewritten terms/s	GPU rewritten terms/s	Speedup
Merge sort 50	97×10^6	74×10^3	0.76×10^{-3}
Tree merge sort 23 5	113×10^6	387×10^6	3.34
Transformation tree 22	265×10^6	3.12×10^9	11.7

which translates to sorting approximately 8 million lists. Finally, to understand the potential of the GPU, we designed the Transformation tree benchmark that expands a binary tree to 22 levels deep (4 million leaves) where each leaf is rewritten 26 times. On this benchmark, the GPU rewriter is more than a factor 10 faster than the CPU rewriter, achieving 3.12 billion rewrites per second on average over the complete run, but sustaining around 6 billion rewrites per second for half of the execution time (the rest is setting/breaking down the tree).

To understand the performance better we focus on the more realistic Tree merge sort benchmark. Figure 2 shows several graphs for the execution with which we can analyze the performance. Figure 2a shows that this rewrite system shows a high degree of parallelism for almost all of the execution time. Figure 2b shows that the rewriter shows a high throughput with peaks up to 1 billion terms rewritten per second.

Figure 2c highlights to what extent we use the capabilities of the GPU. Usually, the performance of a GPU is measured in GFLOPS, floating point operations per second, for compute intensive applications or GiB/s for data intensive applications. Since term rewriting is a symbolic manipulation that does not involve any arithmetic, it is data intensive. From Table 1 we have seen that the maximum bandwidth our GPU can achieve is 555 GiB/s for aligned accesses and 22.8 GiB/s for random accesses. Since term rewriting is an irregular problem with a high degree of random access (to subterms that can be anywhere in memory), we focus on the bandwidth for random accesses. Table 3 shows that the overall random access bandwidth of the GPU implementation reaches 18.1 GiB/s which is close to the benchmarked bandwidth. In addition, the aligned bandwidth of 95.7 GiB/s confirms that term rewriting is indeed an irregular problem and that aligned bandwidth is less of a bottleneck.

Table 3. Performance the tree merge sort in terms of bandwidth.

Application	BW random (GiB/s)	BW aligned (GiB/s)
Tree merge sort 23 5	18.1	95.7

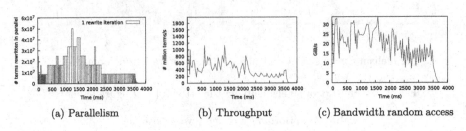

(a) Parallelism　　　　(b) Throughput　　　　(c) Bandwidth random access

Fig. 2. Merge sort of a tree of 23 deep with lists of 5 elements.

Although we are close to the random access bandwidth of the GPU, this does not mean that we have reached the limits of term rewriting on GPUs. It does mean however, that to achieve higher performance with term rewriting on GPUs, it is necessary to introduce more regularity into the implementation, reducing the random memory accesses. It also means that other often used strategies to improve graph algorithm, like reducing branch divergence will probably not yield significant performance increase. In addition, the results we present clearly show the different capabilities of GPUs and CPUs. An interesting direction for future work is to create a hybrid rewrite implementation that can empirically switch to a GPU implementation when a high degree of parallelism is available.

Acknowledgment. This work is carried out in the context of the NWO AVVA project 612.001751. We gratefully acknowledge the support of NVIDIA Corporation with the donation of the GeForce Titan RTX used for this research.

References

1. Amdahl, G.M.: Validity of the single processor approach to achieving large scale computing capabilities. In: SJCC, New York, NY, USA, pp. 483–485. ACM (1967)
2. Barendregt, H.P., van Eekelen, M.C.J.D., Plasmeijer, M.J., Hartel, P.H., Hertzberger, L.O., Vree, W.G.: The Dutch parallel reduction machine project. Future Gen. Comput. Syst. **3**(4), 261–270 (1987)
3. Bosnacki, D., Edelkamp, S., Sulewski, D., Wijs, A.: GPU-PRISM: an extension of PRISM for general purpose graphics processing units. In: PDMC-HiBi, pp. 17–19. IEEE Computer Society (2010)
4. Bošnački, D., Odenbrett, M.R., Wijs, A.J., Ligtenberg, W.P.A., Hilbers, P.A.J.: Efficient reconstruction of biological networks via transitive reduction on general purpose graphics processors. BMC Bioinform. **13**(281), 1–13 (2012)
5. Bunte, O., et al.: The mCRL2 toolset for analysing concurrent systems. In: Vojnar, T., Zhang, L. (eds.) TACAS 2019. LNCS, vol. 11428, pp. 21–39. Springer, Cham (2019). https://doi.org/10.1007/978-3-030-17465-1_2

6. Cheng, J., Grossman, M.: Professional CUDA C Programming. Wiley, New York (2014)
7. Dejanović, I., Vaderna, R., Milosavljević, G., Vuković, Ž: TextX: a Python tool for domain-specific languages implementation. Knowl.-Based Syst. **115**, 1–4 (2017)
8. Durán, F., Garavel, H.: The rewrite engines competitions: a RECtrospective. In: Beyer, D., Huisman, M., Kordon, F., Steffen, B. (eds.) TACAS 2019. LNCS, vol. 11429, pp. 93–100. Springer, Cham (2019). https://doi.org/10.1007/978-3-030-17502-3_6
9. Gustafson, J.L.: Reevaluating Amdahl's law. Commun. ACM **31**(5), 532–533 (1988)
10. Heldens, S., Hijma, P., Van Werkhoven, B., Maassen, J., Belloum, A.S.Z., Van Nieuwpoort, R.V.: The landscape of exascale research: a data-driven literature analysis. ACM Comput. Surv. **53**(2), 1–43 (2020)
11. Henriksen, T., Elsmanand, M., Oancea, C.E.: Modular acceleration: tricky cases of functional high-performance computing. In: FHPC, pp. 10–21. ACM (2018)
12. Henriksen, T., Serup, N.G.W., Elsman, M., Henglein, F., Oancea, C.E.: Futhark: purely functional GPU-programming with nested parallelism and in-place array updates. In: PLDI, pp. 556–571. ACM (2017)
13. Hijma, P., Nieuwpoort, R.V., Jacobs, C.J.H., Bal, H.E.: Stepwise-refinement for performance: a methodology for many-core programming. Concurr. Comput. Pract. Exp. **27**(17), 4515–4554 (2015)
14. Huet, G., Lankford, D.: On the uniform halting problem for term rewriting systems. Rapport de Recherche No. 283. IRIA, March 1978
15. Lee, V.W., et al.: Debunking the 100X GPU vs. CPU myth. In: ISCA. ACM Press (2010)
16. McDonell, T.L.: Optimising purely functional GPU programs. Ph.D. thesis, University of New South Wales, Sydney, Australia (2015)
17. Nasre, R., Burtscher, M., Pingali, K.: Data-driven versus topology-driven irregular computations on GPUs. In: IPDPS, 20–24 May 2013, pp. 463–474. IEEE Computer Society (2013)
18. Nasre, R., Burtscher, M., Pingali, K.: Morph algorithms on GPUs. In: PPOPP, pp. 147–156. ACM SIGPLAN (2013)
19. Jones, S.L.P., Clack, C., Salkild, J., Hardie, M.: GRIP—a high-performance architecture for parallel graph reduction. In: Kahn, G. (ed.) FPCA 1987. LNCS, vol. 274, pp. 98–112. Springer, Heidelberg (1987). https://doi.org/10.1007/3-540-18317-5_7
20. Terese. Term Rewriting Systems. Number 55 in Cambridge Tracts in Theoretical Computer Science. Cambridge University Press (2003)
21. van Eerd, J., Groote, J.F., Hijma, P., Martens, J., Wijs, A.: Term rewriting on GPUs (2020). http://arxiv.org/abs/2009.07174
22. Wijs, A., Neele, T., Bošnački, D.: GPUexplore 2.0: unleashing GPU explicit-state model checking. In: Fitzgerald, J., Heitmeyer, C., Gnesi, S., Philippou, A. (eds.) FM 2016. LNCS, vol. 9995, pp. 694–701. Springer, Cham (2016). https://doi.org/10.1007/978-3-319-48989-6_42

Promise Plus: Flexible Synchronization for Parallel Computations on Arrays

Amaury Maillé[(✉)], Ludovic Henrio, and Matthieu Moy[ⓘ]

Univ Lyon, EnsL, UCBL, CNRS, Inria, LIP, 69342 Lyon Cedex 07, France
{amaury.maille,ludovic.henrio,matthieu.moy}@ens-lyon.fr

Abstract. Parallel applications make use of parallelism where work is shared between tasks; often, tasks need to exchange data stored in arrays and synchronize depending on the availability of these data. Fine-grained synchronizations, *e.g.* one synchronization for each element in the array, may lead to too many synchronizations while coarse-grained synchronizations, *e.g.* a single synchronization for the whole array, may prevent parallelism. We propose PromisePlus, a synchronization tool allowing tasks to synchronize on chunks of arrays with a granularity configurable by the programmer.

Keywords: Promises · Programming models · Parallel programming · High-performance computing

1 Introduction

In parallel programming, a promise is a synchronization tool. Initially, a promise is *unresolved*. Then, one task produces a value that resolves the promise; another task consumes that value through a get operation on the promise. get blocks if the promise is still unresolved. When exchanging arrays between tasks, promises can be used in two ways: either as a promise of array, where a promise holds a whole array; or as an array of promises, where there are as many promises as there are elements in the array.

The contribution of this paper is *a synchronization tool "PromisePlus" that works as a trade-off between an array of promises and a promise of array.* It allows programmers to *specify the granularity of synchronization and to stream data between tasks.* Unlike usual streaming frameworks [9] which are typically implemented using FIFOs [6] with support for bulk insertion and removal, PromisePlus allows access to elements out-of-order without removing them from its internal buffer, allowing several consumer entities to access the buffer's elements. Specifying a fine-grained (resp. coarse-grained) granularity makes PromisePlus akin to an array of promises (resp. a promise of array), and yields similar results in terms of performance. Moreover, there is a guarantee that a request to an element of the PromisePlus will unblock after at most n values have been produced, where n is the granularity of the synchronization. Finally, a request to an element of the PromisePlus will never produce an undefined value.

Published by Springer Nature Switzerland AG 2021
H. Hojjat and M. Massink (Eds.): FSEN 2021, LNCS 12818, pp. 190–196, 2021.
https://doi.org/10.1007/978-3-030-89247-0_13

We begin this article with some context on HPC kernels and how they could benefit from data streaming and fine-tuned synchronizations. We subsequently present PromisePlus, benchmarks, related and future work, before concluding.

2 Context

HPC applications often perform heavy operations on huge amount of data stored in arrays. A kernel is a function applied to an array that typically produces another array as a result (*e.g. map*). Streaming data between kernels allows one kernel to start working on a partial output of another kernel; this is achieved by adding synchronization points between the two kernels. In order for the streaming to be efficient, the synchronization needs to be smart, *i.e.* synchronizations must be performed at the right points to fully exploit parallelism without wasting too much time in synchronizations.

Parallelism in HPC application usually comes from frameworks such as MPI (processes) or OpenMP (threads). These frameworks provide building blocks to perform streaming, which requires programmers to either write smart synchronization patterns on top of OpenMP/MPI or rely on third-party libraries (*e.g.* [9]) to achieve streaming. Moreover, primitives from HPC frameworks are low level, not always easy to use, and do not necessarily provide safety guarantees by construction.

As stated above, efficient streaming requires smart synchronization patterns. Ideally, these patterns should be reusable in different contexts (OpenMP threads, MPI processes) with different parameters (*e.g.* the granularity of the synchronization). Moreover, they should make the relation between data dependencies and the synchronization explicit, in order for a programmer to understand the concurrency problem solved. Finally, they should be optimized for the underlying architecture, thoroughly tested. Writing such a synchronization pattern takes time, time that programmers may not always have, forcing them to write patterns well suited for the problem at hand, but that cannot be reused as-is elsewhere and that may not always be comprehensible to outside observers.

This motivates us to propose a new synchronization tool for streaming arrays between tasks, that meets the following criteria:

- It makes the data dependency explicit: the programmer explicitly writes which data is shared between threads;
- It is configurable in a way that allows programmers to specify the granularity of the synchronization;
- It is not tied to a specific problem or a specific setup, and so is reusable;
- When the granularity is configured to the minimum (resp. maximum) value, it behaves like an array of promises (resp. a promise of array), providing the same guarantees and similar performance; moreover, every request for the i-th value of an array unblocks after an amount of values equals to the granularity has been produced;
- Contrarily to classical streaming solutions it supports the existence of several consumers for the same data, and the access to produced data in any order.

3   PromisePlus: Flexible Synchronization for Arrays

We present PromisePlus: a flexible synchronization pattern for arrays and matrices that allows data streaming between tasks.

A PromisePlus works like a standard promise, with additional support for integral indices. Both `get` and `set` work on indices; the programmer associates a value to an index through `set`, and gets access to the value associated with an index through `get`. Unlike an array of promises, performing a `get` on a given index may not immediately return once the index has received a value. PromisePlus is tied to two integral values: the *step* referred to as S that is configured at instanciation-time the PromisePlus, and *last*. *last* is the index passed to the last `set` call that triggered an unblock, initialized to -1 meaning the whole array is unresolved.

During a call to `set` with index i, if $i - last \geq S$, *last* becomes i and all calls to `get` with an index $i' \leq i$ are unblocked. This construct ensures that at most S elements have to be produced to unblock a `get`. Changing the value of S changes the granularity of synchronization.

Finally, a `set_immediate` primitive triggers an immediate synchronization, unblocking the synchronization on all previous elements of the array.

API PromisePlus exposes three functions: `set`, `get`, and `set_immediate`. Index is the type used for indices, T is the type of the values stored in the PromisePlus. A call to `set(i, v)` associates value v with index i, and if $i - last \geq S$, *last* becomes i. A call to `get(i)` blocks until $last \geq i$; then it returns the value associated with index i. A call to `set_immediate(i, v)` associates value v with index i. The value of *last* becomes i without checking the step S. This function is particularly useful to signal that the last element has been produced and no further `set` operation should be expected. Calls to `set` and/or `set_immediate` must be performed on consecutive indices.

Notes on Implementation. While blocking a consumer thread in a `get(i)`, we use busy waiting as passive waiting induces too much overhead for HPC applications. All threads must share reading access to the value of *last* while the producer thread can write it too. Enforcing that all threads see an up-to-date value when reading *last* is cost-heavy, therefore each thread has a local index that caches the value of *last*. This local index is updated with the value of *last* when it is not sufficient to unblock a call to `get(i)`. In such a case, the thread synchronizes on the shared index. Finally, the producer threads stores a local copy of *last* to avoid some cost-heavy reads. Annex A presents algorithms for `get` and `set`.

4   Benchmarks

We benchmarked two things: how PromisePlus compares to the two naive approaches "array of promises" and "promise of array", and how the average time required to solve a problem using PromisePlus changes as the step changes.

Chosen Problem. Our problem is inspired by the LU program in the NPB [5], it reproduces the same data dependencies. Given a 4D matrix, we run a function f on every element of the matrix, excluding boundary values, in parallel through several OpenMP threads. In order to update certain values, thread T_n, $n > 0$, requires values computed by thread T_{n-1}.

Matrix Shapes. We consider a work matrix of two billion values, excluding boundary values. We consider three different shapes for this matrix, leading to three different amounts of synchronization, while keeping the amount of computation constant: $101 * 161 * 62501 * 2$ (62500 synchronizations), $101 * 126 * 80001 * 2$ (80000 synchronizations) and $101 * 101 * 100001 * 2$ (100000 synchronizations).

Environment. These tests were performed on a machine equipped with four Intel(R) Xeon(R) CPU E5-4620 0 @ 2.20 GHz, with 96 threads without hyper-threading. Applications were built using GCC 8.3, C++17, and the $-O2$ flag in Release mode.

Comparison of Patterns. We compare the performance of the different patterns: array of promises, promise of array, and PromisePlus with three steps: 1, *max* that only synchronizes upon a `set_immediate`, and *opt* that is the step that achieves the best performance for a given shape. The promise of array uses home-made promises, with a `get` operation that performs a busy wait. The array of promises is tested using these same home-made promises, as well as C++ promises [8].

Figure 1 shows the results. In the legend, "P[Arr]" designates the promise of array, "Arr[P]" designates the array of promises, "Arr[SP]" designates the array of promises using C++ promises and "P+X" designates PromisePlus with a step of X. Figure 2 show the performance of PromisePlus as the step grows.

As expected, PromisePlus with a step of 1 performs similarly to the array of home-made promises with a slight overhead. Similarly, PromisePlus with a maximum step performs like the promise of array, again with a slight overhead. Both overheads are due to additional checks performed in the function `set` for PromisePlus. Also, there is an optimum step for PromisePlus that performs better than all others, with a performance gain of up to 12.63% reached in the second shape with a step of 82 compared to array of home-made promises. Finally, home-made promises are well optimized: they perform up to 45.58% better than C++ promises (Arr[P] compared to Arr[SP]).

Regarding the evolution of the average time as the step grows, an optimum step exists at which PromisePlus performs better than both the array of promise and promise of array.

5   Related Work

Streaming Futures. In [1], promises are used as a way to stream data: they can be resolved multiple times, and each `get` returns the next resolving value when available. Unlike PromisePlus, streaming futures work as FIFOs with support for multiple producers at the cost of performance, and allow theoretically infinite

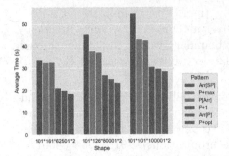

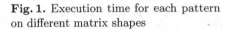

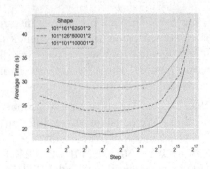

Fig. 1. Execution time for each pattern on different matrix shapes

Fig. 2. Execution time for different matrix shapes and different steps

streams. In PromisePlus, we chose to focus on performance and flexible granularity of synchronization for a better applicability to HPC. This flexibility could be ported to streaming futures, and potentially improve their performance.

Distributed Futures. Distributed futures [7] provide efficient data transfer when coupling data-parallel kernels in a task-parallel way. Spawning a task creates a distributed entity that works as a future that can be partially resolved by each process of the data-parallel computation. Once the result is computed, any process may request any chunk of the data directly from the process that holds it. Like PromisePlus, distributed futures slice the data and grants access to any computed slice, however unlike PromisePlus distributed futures require the whole computation to be over before allowing access to slices, preventing streaming. The fact that we have a less strict synchronization allows us to perform more optimizations and to find the optimal synchronization granularity.

OpenStream. OpenStream [9] is an extension of OpenMP that adds stream-like faculties to tasks. An OpenStream task may produce one or more streams, and a task may consume elements from one or more streams. A task is launched only when the elements requested on each input stream are available, this adds scheduling dependencies between tasks. A task requesting N elements from a stream before being able to be launched is akin to a PromisePlus with step N.

WeakRB. WeakRB [6] is an efficient implementation of a FIFO queue, using atomics in C, with a proof of correction.

The key differences between streams/FIFO queues and PromisePlus are the destructiveness of streams, which can be read only once and in a predefined order, and support only a single consumer in WeakRB. On the contrary, PromisePlus enforces an interaction pattern inherited from promises, where values can be read multiple times once they are ready, in any order, and by multiple consumers.

Message Sets & Join Patterns. Message sets [3] and join patterns [4] allow for a declarative way of defining synchronizations. Operations wait for messages sent by other operations before executing. This is similar to get and set in PromisePlus. The key difference is that PromisePlus was thought first and foremost for efficiency with a conditional jump and a store at worse, while join patterns and message sets typically wait passively for a message.

SkePU. SkePU [2] is a framework for algorithmic skeletons. Internally SkePU performs agressive optimizations to reduce the amount of synchronizations inside a thread, and could benefit from an optimized tool like PromisePlus to perform synchronizations between threads.

6   Future Work and Conclusion

In this paper we presented PromisePlus, an abstraction over promises that allows parallel computations to synchronize on slices of arrays with a granularity chosen by the programmer. This allows them to express different synchronization patterns through the use of a single tool. Moreover, PromisePlus is not tied to a specific framework, and as such can be used in multiple contexts. PromisePlus also features performance improvements without requiring programmers to extensively refactor their code. Finally, PromisePlus offers the same guarantee as classic promises: a call to get never produces an undefined value.

In the future we want to design static or dynamic analyses to optimize the granularity of the synchronization, allowing the programmer to focus only on where to put the synchronization points in their program.

A   Algorithms of get and set

In this annex we present algorithms for the get function of PromisePlus in Algorithm 1, and for the set function of PromisePlus in Algorithm 2.

Algorithm 1. Algorithm of get

1: **function** GET(*index*)   ▷ Get value associated with index
2:     **while** index > local_index **do**   ▷ The local index avoids a cost-heavy read of *last* if it is greater than the requested index
3:         local_index ← last
4:     **end while**
5:     **return** value associated with index
6: **end function**

Algorithm 2. Algorithm of `set`

1: **procedure** SET(*index*, *value*)   ▷ Associate value with index. If enough calls have been made, unblock calls to `get` with a lower index

Require: index is the next integer compared to the last call to `set`

2:    **if** (index - local_last) $\geq$ step **then**   ▷ Reading from a local copy of *last* in the producer thread avoids cost heavy accesses to *last*

3:        last $\leftarrow$ index   ▷ Unblock `get(i)`, i < `index`

4:        local_last $\leftarrow$ index

5:    **end if**

6:    Associate value with index

7: **end procedure**

References

1. Azadbakht, K., Boer, F., Bezirgiannis, N., Vink, E.: A formal actor-based model for streaming the future. Sci. Comput. Program. **186**, 102341 (2019). https://doi.org/10.1016/j.scico.2019.102341

2. Enmyren, J., Kessler, C.: SkePU: a multi-backend skeleton programming library for multi-GPU systems, pp. 5–14 (2010). https://doi.org/10.1145/1863482.1863487

3. Frølund, S., Agha, G.: Abstracting interactions based on message sets. In: Ciancarini, P., Nierstrasz, O., Yonezawa, A. (eds.) ECOOP 1994. LNCS, vol. 924, pp. 107–124. Springer, Heidelberg (1995). https://doi.org/10.1007/3-540-59450-7_7

4. Haller, P., Van Cutsem, T.: Implementing joins using extensible pattern matching. In: Lea, D., Zavattaro, G. (eds.) COORDINATION 2008. LNCS, vol. 5052, pp. 135–152. Springer, Heidelberg (2008). https://doi.org/10.1007/978-3-540-68265-3_9

5. Jin, H., Van der Wijngaart, R.F.: Performance characteristics of the multi-zone NAS parallel benchmarks. J. Parallel Distrib. Comput. **66**(5), 674–685 (2006). https://doi.org/10.1016/j.jpdc.2005.06.016. iPDPS 2004 Special Issue

6. Le, N., Guatto, A., Cohen, A., Pop, A.: Correct and efficient bounded FIFO queues, pp. 144–151, September 2013. https://doi.org/10.1109/SBAC-PAD.2013.8

7. Leca, P., Suijlen, W., Henrio, L., Baude, F.: Distributed futures for efficient data transfer between parallel processes, pp. 1344–1347, March 2020. https://doi.org/10.1145/3341105.3374104

8. Liskov, B., Shrira, L.: Promises: linguistic support for efficient asynchronous procedure calls in distributed systems. SIGPLAN Not. **23**(7), 260–267 (1988). https://doi.org/10.1145/960116.54016

9. Pop, A., Cohen, A.: OpenStream: expressiveness and data-flow compilation of openMP streaming programs. ACM Trans. Archit. Code Optim. **9**(4), (2013). https://doi.org/10.1145/2400682.2400712

Testing

Towards Automatic Test Case Generation for Industrial Software Systems Based on Functional Specifications

Arvin Zakeriyan, Ramtin Khosravi(✉) ⓘ, Hadi Safari, and Ehsan Khamespanah

School of Electrical and Computer Engineering, University of Tehran, Tehran, Iran
{a.zakeriyan,r.khosravi,hadi.safari,e.khamespanah}@ut.ac.ir

Abstract. High-capability software services, like transaction processing systems, need to satisfy a range of non-functional characteristics such as performance, availability, and scalability. To fulfill these needs, the core business logic is usually extended with a large amount of non-domain logic in the form of frameworks, libraries, and custom code, which sometimes cannot be cleanly separated from the domain logic. So, it is nearly impossible to generate test cases for the whole system systematically guided by structural metrics on the source code. In this paper, we propose a specification-based approach to generate test cases. In this approach, the domain logic is specified in a functional notation (based on Gallina). Test cases are generated using a search-based approach where the fitness function is defined in terms of the structural coverage of the specification (measured over an equivalent Haskell implementation). An experiment on an industrial stock exchange trading engine indicates promising results in the effectiveness of our proposed approach.

Keywords: Automatic test case generation · Formal specification based testing · Search based testing

1 Introduction

In today's computing landscape, we often encounter software services that must operate under various quality constraints such as performance and availability. This happens both in enterprise information systems, or the back-ends of Internet-based public services. Examples include stock trading matching engines that must serve the requests in an extremely short response time, airline reservation systems that must handle a large load of requests before national holidays, or highly available electronic funds transfer switches handling card-based financial transactions reliably. For this kind of software service, to which we refer as *high capability software service*[1], the processing is often broken into several short-lived requests (sometimes referred to as transactions). While they are often under critical architectural forces such as performance, scalability, and availability, other

---

[1] The term "high capability" has been borrowed from the title of [7].

© IFIP International Federation for Information Processing 2021
Published by Springer Nature Switzerland AG 2021
H. Hojjat and M. Massink (Eds.): FSEN 2021, LNCS 12818, pp. 199–214, 2021.
https://doi.org/10.1007/978-3-030-89247-0_14

non-functional requirements such as maintainability, security, etc. must be also met as other types of software systems. As such systems often play important roles, especially in financial domains, making sure they are functionally correct is as important as satisfying non-functional requirements.

The problem is that, the force to achieve the wide range of critical quality attributes brings in many non-domain elements into the system, ranging from third-party frameworks and libraries at the architecture level (e.g., in-memory object caches) down to custom optimizations in the implementation or even code hacks at the system level (e.g., bypassing TCP stack to reduce latency). While these elements affect the non-functional characteristics of the system, their combination may impact the functional correctness of the system as well. Hence, even having separately tested the domain logic during unit testing stage, it is crucial to apply a disciplined end-to-end system test to make sure that the system behaves correctly in presence of these non-domain elements.

In this paper, we report the method we developed to test a high-capability stock trading engine, with sub-millisecond response time to trading requests over hundreds of symbols and millions of shareholders. The system is mainly implemented in Java and employs many sophisticated techniques to achieve the required quality. The system already has two sets of automated tests: about 1500 unit test case in JUnit[2], and a set of about 1100 Behavior-Driven Development (BDD) tests [1], all written by the development team. Our testing approach is completely black-box and does not depend on any knowledge about the implementation of the system, hence we believe our method is applicable to many other software systems as well.

We have taken a specification-based approach to testing for two reasons. First, as said before, our goal is to make sure the system functions correctly in presence of elements embodied to meet non-functional requirements. So, we may need relatively large test cases that drive the elements to their boundaries to explore various possible scenarios. Hence, using manual oracles is not feasible while a formal specification may serve as the test oracle. Second, to attain a certain level of confidence about the functional reliability of the system, a disciplined approach must be taken to make sure the testing has met some kind of coverage criteria. Unfortunately, as the source code of the system is relatively large and the domain logic is mixed a lot with non-domain logic, defining a suitable coverage metric on the implementation code is practically infeasible. Therefore, the specification serves as a basis for disciplined test case generation too.

We have chosen Gallina (the specification language of Coq [6]), to specify the functionality of the system for three reasons. First, the functional nature of the language makes it appropriate for specifying the order matching algorithms, which are explained procedurally in the informal specifications, compared to a pre- and post-condition specification style. Second, we can use Coq to validate the specifications against some general properties. Finally, by automatically translating the specifications into Haskell programs, we make use of various tools

---

[2] http://junit.org.

such as coverage or symbolic execution tools. We will present more detail on the specification in Sect. 3.

As the system under test is not small, using symbolic execution to generate test cases systematically is infeasible. So, we take a search-based approach to test case generation. The fitness function is defined based on the specification coverage and is measured on the automatically generated Haskell code from the specification. We have used both simulated annealing and genetic algorithms to generate test cases. Our early results indicate the latter produces better results. The test case generation method is explained more in Sect. 4.

We have detected two important faults using our generated test cases. To further evaluate the method, we performed mutation analysis and coverage measurements. The early results, reported in Sect. 5, indicate that attaining the same quality as the manually written tests requires considerably less effort using our method.

In summary, the main contribution of this paper is to demonstrate the applicability of formal specification-based testing to a relatively large data-intensive software system, highly constrained to non-functional requirements. Furthermore, the use of functional notation as the formalism for specification-based testing is novel as the existing research mainly base their specification on pre- and post-conditions, algebraic specification, or automata-theoretic formalisms [12]. Finally, guiding the search-based test case generation based on a formal specification is done for the first time, to the best of our knowledge.

2 Background

The system under test in this paper is a stock market order matching engine[3] as a part of an electronic trading platform which is under development and is to be used in Tehran Stock Exchange. The matching engine supports handling orders of various types (e.g., Limit, Market to Limit, Iceberg), as well as a number of order time or volume qualifiers (e.g., 'Minimum Quantity' or 'Fill and Kill'). Also, several pre- and post-trade checks must be made (e.g., brokers' credit limit, and shareholders percentage ownership).

As other products of the same category, the matching engine is supposed to handle the incoming requests within a very low response time (sub-milliseconds). Hence, the system has a rather complicated design because of a variety of design decisions and techniques at different levels. Examples include using Disruptor framework[4] to increase performance, Project Lombok[5] to increase productivity and maintainability, and extensive use of Spring Framework as an inversion of control container to make the product configurable and testable. As using an external database increases the response time considerably, the system contains several custom data structures designed to efficiently handle a large amount of in-memory data (regarding stock symbols, shareholders, brokers, etc.). In

---

[3] https://en.wikipedia.org/wiki/Order_matching_system.
[4] http://lmax-exchange.github.io/disruptor/disruptor.html.
[5] https://projectlombok.org.

addition to architecture and design level decisions, a lot of implementation-level optimizations has been made to speed up the computations.

2.1   Running Example: Matching Limit Orders

As the reader may not be familiar with the domain of stock trading, we explain a simplified matching algorithm and use it as a running example throughout the paper. *Limit order* is one among several types of orders usually supported by matching engines. "A limit order is an order to buy or sell a stock at a specific price or better."[6] This means that a buy order can only be matched with a sell order of a price no more than its limit price, and a sell order can only be matched with a buy order of a price no less than its limit price. In its simplest form, a limit order contains an order identifier, the stock symbol, the limit price, the quantity, as well as the identifiers of the shareholder and/or broker issuing the order. A limit order may not be executed immediately, as an opposite order with a matching price may not be found. In such a case, the order enters the *order book*. The order book contains two separate priority queues of the orders in the system, one for *buy* orders and another for *sell* orders. Buy orders with the highest prices and sell orders with the lowest prices rank the highest on their respective queues. The orders with the same rank are prioritized according to their arrival times.

Order book before matching

Buy			Sell		
ID	Price	Qty	ID	Price	Qty
1	50	500	4	55	500
2	40	1000	5	60	300
3	40	800	6	70	1000

Order book after matching

Buy			Sell		
ID	Price	Qty	ID	Price	Qty
7	60	400	6	70	1000
1	50	500			
2	40	1000			
3	40	800			

Input Buy Order

ID	Price	Qty
7	60	1200

Output Trades

BID	SID	Price	Qty
7	4	55	500
7	5	60	300

Fig. 1. An example of matching limit orders: the input order (ID 7) is partially matched with the two topmost orders in the sell queue, generating the two trades (on the right). The remaining quantity is added to the buy side of the order book.

As an example, the left side of Fig. 1 shows the order book of some stock symbol in the system when a new limit order arrives. The system tries to match the new order with the orders in the opposite side queue (sell queue in this case), and tries to match as much quantity as possible. In this example, the two

---

[6] https://www.sec.gov/fast-answers/answerslimithtm.html.

topmost sell orders are matched, but the third one has a sell limit price higher than the new order's buy limit price. So, the remaining quantity of the new order is inserted into the buy priority queue. Note that a trade price is always the price of the order taken from the queue.

Another type of order is *iceberg* order type, which is similar to limit order type except that when an iceberg order enters the *order book*, only a portion of its quantity (called *disclosed quantity*) can be traded. When all of the disclosed quantity is matched, the iceberg order loses its time priority and treated as if it just entered the queue with the quantity equal to its *disclosed quantity*. This process is repeated until all of its quantity is matched. Apart from order types, an order can have a number of time or volume quantifiers. As an instance, an order with a *minimum quantity* quantifier, is executed only if a certain quantity can be traded instantaneously (i.e., before entering the queue). For example, if the new limit order in Fig. 1 has a minimum quantity attribute of value 1000, it is not executed in our case, i.e., the order is rejected and no trade is made. On the other hand, if the value of minimum quantity attribute is 500, then the result would be exactly the same as the one illustrated in the figure.

3 Functional Specification

In this section, we give an overview of the method used for specifying the system under test with the aim of test case generation. We need a specification approach that focuses on modeling computations over rich data models, provides abstraction mechanisms to enable concise specification of a large system, is supported by a mature toolset, and is acceptable by software engineers.

The first requirement ruled out automata-based notations which focus more on state-based modeling of control-intensive systems. We examined several other methods, including Event-B[7], Alloy[8], pure functional specification, and even small subsets of imperative programming languages. Based on the simple prototypes made, the functional approach seemed to best satisfy the above requirements. Features like algebraic data types, recursive computations on lists, and rich abstraction patterns based on higher-order functions enabled a readable and concise specification of the matching engine. Our first prototypes were in Haskell, and based on its success, we ported the prototypes to Gallina to enable formal analysis using Coq.

Although our basic specification pattern follows a model-based paradigm, relating the states before and after handling a request using a functional description is more understandable for the developers compared to the logical specification based on pre- and post-conditions. This is because most software engineers are familiar with functional programming, especially now, with the extensive use of the elements of functional paradigm in mainstream programming languages.

A benefit of using functional specification is that while its core concepts such as recursive functions and higher-order function are familiar to the developers,

---

[7] http://event-b.org.
[8] https://alloytools.org.

the stateless nature of the computation greatly simplifies the specification of domain logic compared to the imperative paradigm. The fact that efficiency has been a main concern in developing the system under study, made the developers prefer "update-style" over "copy style" handling of changes in the system states. At several points, the developers were surprised when they saw how simple and concise a functional specification could model a rather complicated implementation of a feature.

3.1   Basic Specification Patterns

The system specification is basically an abstract state machine. The system receives requests of various types to process. Processing a request generates a response and changes the state of the system. At an abstract level, if *Request* and *Response* represent the set of all requests and all responses respectively, and *State* represents the set of states of the system, we have handlers of type *Handler = Request × State → Response × State*. Each request type is handled by a separate handler function.

Data Parameters and States. To represent data parameters, we need to model basic entities in the system. The definitions needed to specify our running example is listed below.

```
Definition OrderID := nat.
Definition Quantity := nat.          Definition OrderQueue := list Order.
Definition Price := nat.
Inductive Side : Type := Buy | Sell.  Record OrderBook : Type := orderBook
                                      { buyQueue : OrderQueue
Record Order := order                 ; sellQueue : OrderQueue
{ oid : OrderID                       }.
; price : Price
; quantity : Quantity                 Record Trade : Type := trade
; minqty : option Quantity            { priceTraded : Price
; side : Side                         ; quantityTraded : Quantity
}.                                    }.
```

Based on these definitions, the state of the system can be defined like:

```
Record State : Type := state
{ orderbook : OrderBook
; creditinfo : CreditInfo
; ownershipinfo: OwnershipInfo
}.
```

The first field denotes the order book which is a major part of the system state. Other parts are required to enable credit limit and percentage ownership checks which we have not included in the example. The definitions of the records for modeling requests and responses are straightforward and not listed to save space.

Request Handler Functions. Each request type in the system is modeled each by a request handler function. The handler function for new order requests can be modeled conforming to the mentioned pattern for handlers. It delegates the request to the function that matches new orders.

```
Definition handleNewOrder (rq : Request) (s : State) : Response * State :=
  (* unbox and delegate the request to matchNewOrder *)

Definition matchNewOrder (o : Order) (ob : OrderBook) : OrderBook * list Trade :=
  match side o with
    | Buy ⇒
      let '(rem, sq, ts) := matchBuy o (sellQueue ob) in
        match rem with
          | None ⇒ (orderBook (buyQueue ob) sq, ts)
          | Some o' ⇒ (orderBook (enqueueBuy o' (buyQueue ob)) sq, ts)
        end
    | Sell ⇒ (* similar to Buy case, skipped in the example *)
  end.
end.
```

Finally, `matchBuy` is the function that implements the matching algorithm (here, just for limit order type). It matches a buy order $o = (i, p, q, mq, Buy)$ against the sell queue $sellq$ and returns a triple whose first component is the 'remainder of o' after possible matching which is then queued by `matchNewOrder` above. Since it is possible that o is fully executed, the type of the parameter is defined as `option Order` which may be either `None`, indicating the order is fully executed, or `Some o'` where o' is the remainder of o. The second component is the sell queue after matching and the third component is the list of trades made. As the definition is rather straightforward, we do not go into more details here.

```
Fixpoint matchBuy (o : Order) (sellq : OrderQueue) :
                   (option Order) * OrderQueue * (list Trade) :=
  match sellq with
    | [ ] ⇒ (Some o, [ ], [ ])
    | (order i1 p1 q1 mq1 s1) :: os ⇒
      match o with
        | order i p q mq s ⇒
          if p <? p1 then (Some o, sellq, [ ])
          else if q <? q1 then (None, (order i1 p1 (q1-q) mq1 s1)::os, [trade p1 q])
          else if q =? q1 then (None, os, [trade p1 q])
          else let '(o', sellq', ts') := matchBuy (order i p (q-q1) mq s) os
               in (o', sellq', (trade p1 q1)::ts')
      end
  end.
```

Decorators. As stated in Sect. 2, an order may have a number of qualifiers which may change the outcome of the matching, or act as pre- or post-checks to the requests. To model the qualifiers, we use a recursive pattern similar to Decorator design pattern in object-oriented design patterns [10]. A decorator is a higher-order function of type $Decorator = Handler \rightarrow Handler$, which encapsulates an 'inner handler' which itself may be composed of a number of decorators applied on a request handler. As an example, we define the 'Minimum Quantity' qualifier described in Sect. 2 as a decorator:

```
1   Definition minQuantityCheck (handler : Handler) : Handler :=
2     fun rq s ⇒
3       match rq with
4         | (newOrderRequest o) ⇒
5           let '(rs, s') = handler rq s in
6             match minqty o with
7               | None ⇒ (rs, s')
8               | Some mq ⇒
9                 if list_sum (List.map quantityTraded (trades rs)) <? mq then
10                  (newOrderResponse false [ ], s) (* reject the order *)
11                else
12                  (rs, s')
13              end
14        | _ ⇒ handler rq s
15      end.
```

The decorator returns a handler function that takes a request **rq** and a state **s** (line 2). The decoration is only applied on new order requests (lines 4–13), and has no effect for other request types (line 14). The request is delegated to the inner handler **handler** and the returned response and state are stored in **rs** and **s'** respectively (line 5). In case the new order has no minimum quantity qualifier, the results are returned back (line 7). Otherwise, the sum of **quantityTraded** fields of the trades made is compared to the value of the minimum quantity (line 9). If this sum is below the minimum quantity, the order is rejected (line 10). Otherwise, the results from the inner handler is returned back.

It is important to note that the implementation of this feature in the source code is much more complicated, due to the fact that the matching algorithm changes the state of the system 'in place'. This means that after the matching is completed, the trades are checked to meet the minimum quantity constraint, and if failed, all the changes to the order book must be 'rolled back'. This makes the implementation complicated, especially for more complex order types (like iceberg order type). On the other hand, the stateless nature of the functional specification makes both versions of the state available and we 'roll back' to the previous state simply by returning **s**, as in line 10.

Using the decorator pattern described here, enables us to 'compose' various qualifiers in a modular way. In the following, four decorators are applied to **handleNewOrder** (_ ∘ _ is the notation defined for function composition):

```
Definition matchingEngine : Handler :=
  creditLimitProc ∘ fillAndKillProc ∘ minQuantityCheck ∘
  (ownershipCheck 20) ∘ handleNewOrder
```

3.2   Verifying Properties on Specification

Using Gallina as the formal specification languages enables us to use Coq proof assistant to verify correctness properties on the specification. For example, the following lemma states that **matchBuy** function conserves the total quantities.

```
Lemma quantityConservation : forall o sellq,
  (queuedQuantity sellq) = totalQuantity (mb o sellq).
```

The above lemma uses two defined functions: `queuedQuantity` which calculates the sum of the quantities in an order queue, and `totalQuantity` which calculates the sum of the queued and the traded quantities. The lemma can be proved mainly using induction, case analysis, and usual rewriting tactics.

It is important to note that the informal specifications available for the matching algorithms are generally described in a procedural manner, because they are targeted for non-expert audience. So, the properties are defined by the modelers intuitively based on their understanding from the informal descriptions.

4 Test Case Generation

Following a specification-based test case generation approach, the specification may serve both as the oracle for the test inputs, and a basis for more 'smart' generation of test cases compared to plain random test case generation. To this end, we may use *specification coverage* as a measure of fitness for a generated test suite. Ideally, we may use symbolic execution to get full coverage, but it becomes impractical as the specification gets larger. Hence, we use search-based test case generation [2,11], as a middle ground between symbolic execution and plain random test case generation.

In this research, we use a local search (based on *simulated annealing*) and a global search (based on *genetic algorithm*) algorithm to generate test cases. It should be noted that our purpose is not to compare these search-based approaches but to show the possibility of using search-based test case generation from a functional specification for a complex industrial application. Before going into the details of each technique, we briefly present the fitness function used to evaluate the test suites.

4.1 Fitness Function

As mentioned before, we use the functional specification as a basis for computing the fitness of the test suites. This is done by measuring a branch coverage on the specifications. A branch in our functional specifications happens at two points: conditional ('if') expressions and pattern matching. For example, to cover the function `minQuantityCheck` listed in Sect. 3, we need to cover the matches at lines 4 and 14, the matches at lines 7 and 8, and the expressions at lines 10 and 12. We refer to each of these parts a *case*, which is an expression appearing either as a match case or an expression in an if-then-else expression.

The *fitness function* of a test suite TS (also known as its *score*) is defined as a linear combination of the covered cases and the length of the test cases: $s = 5c - l$, where c is the number of cases covered by test suite and l is the length of test suite (i.e., the number of test cases in the test suite) that is required to avoid generating long test cases. The aim is to *maximize* the score of the test suites, but as both algorithms of local and global search try to minimize an objective function, we use the additive inverse of the *score* of the test suites as the objective function.

To measure coverage in practice, we use the *program extraction* framework (a part of the Coq toolset) to convert the specification into a Haskell program and instrument the Haskell code (using a monadic construct) to collect the coverage information during execution. The search algorithms (explained below) execute the Haskell program on the inputs generated during the search, and use the coverage information generated to evaluate the inputs.

4.2   Local Search

We take advantage of *simulated annealing* as a local search algorithm which uses some heuristics to escape from local optima. Python package `simanneal`[9] is used to set up a search-based test case generation framework.

We define a *state* as an integer array representing a test suite, including at most 40 test cases. Each test case can have at most 10 orders, fed to system respectively.

Every order is represented by an integer tuple encoding its *broker, shareholder, price, quantity, side, minimum quantity, Fill and Kill (FaK) Qualifier* and *disclosed quantity* (for iceberg order types). Each part is chosen from a limited domain. Each test case is encoded by concatenation of the encoded version of 10 orders, prefixed by a boolean presence permission *grant* parameter such that a test case is included in the test suite this flag is true. This parameter is added to increase chance of removing a whole test case from test suite and generating smaller test suites with smaller test cases. Empty test cases (i.e., test cases with no order) are considered malformed and is deleted from test suite. The test case also includes the *initial credits* of 5 brokers and the *initial shares* of 10 shareholders. Finally, any state, representing a test suite, is generated of concatenation of 40 test cases.

Considering the aforementioned representation of state, a *neighboring state* can be reached by choosing a random element of the integer array representation of current state, and replacing it by a randomly selected element of domain of that field. This way, the framework can *move* from a state to a neighboring state. The initial state is generated by picking random values for each element of the integer array.

4.3   Global Search

We developed another framework based on a modified version of Python package `geneticalgorithm`[10] to find suitable test suites using an elitist genetic algorithm as an example of global search techniques. In this framework, we represent a test suite with a *chromosome* in the same way we defined a *state* for the local search algorithm. We start with a randomly generated non-seeded population as first

---

[9] https://github.com/perrygeo/simanneal.

[10] https://github.com/rmsolgi/geneticalgorithm.

generation. Each generation includes 100 chromosomes. We use mutation probability of 0.1 and cross over probability of 0.5, with uniform cross over type. We also use elites ratio (determining the number of elites in the population) of 1%, which means there is one elite in the population. We set a maximum number of generations of 1000. Using seven different runs of genetic algorithm, the objective function reduced from the value corresponding to the first randomly generation (about -120 to -130) to a lower value (even -155), over 1000 iteration.

5   Evaluation

To evaluate the effectiveness of our approach by executing the test suites, two important faults in the system were discovered. To evaluate the quality of our test suites we used two methods: comparing the coverage of our tests with the coverage of the already developed unit tests of the system, and mutation analysis. The source code of the system is about 80K lines of code, mainly written in Java. The development team has put a lot of effort in writing unit tests and BDD-style functional tests. There are more than 1500 test cases in the source code, devoting about 40% of the code base to test. It is estimated that the team has invested more than 30% of the development time on developing these tests over the course of two years development.

5.1   Test Execution

To eliminate the effects of randomness in our generated test suites, we generated 10 test suites using each test case generation algorithm and executed each on the system under test separately. To execute the generated test suites against the system, an adaptation layer was needed. This adapter is developed with the help of the development team. It takes a test case specification file including the test fixture and the sequence of orders with all their required attributes, initializes the system with respect to the specified fixture and feeds the orders to system. After sending all the orders to system, the adapter collects system outputs and compares them with the test oracles in the test case specifications.

Upon execution of tests generated using both Genetic Algorithm and Simulated Annealing, a number of test cases failed. As we discussed these cases with the development team, it became clear that there were actually two important faults in the matching engine and the results of the tests were correct. One of them was a case of missing a specific validation check on iceberg orders which lead to wrong matching. The other was a case of incomplete rollback of trades which leads to incorrect credit values for the brokers. These faults have not been detected by any of the unit or BDD tests.

5.2   Code Coverage Analysis

One way to analyze the quality of the generated test suites is to analyze the branch coverage of the source code obtained by our generated test suites compared to the branch coverage of the unit tests of the system. By branch coverage

Table 1. Branch coverage percentage of two methods compared to the development team's tests

Target Class	Dev. Tests	Simulated Annealing	Genetic Algorithm
Matching Engine	60	59.5 ± 0.5	59.8 ± 0.37
Order	85	50.7 ± 2.2	52 ± 3
Iceberg	100	83 ± 0	83 ± 0
Queue	87	70.9 ± 10.3	74.8 ± 7.2
PO Observer	70	70 ± 0	70 ± 0
Credit Observer	79	77.4 ± 2	78.5 ± 1.5

we mean the percentage of the true and false branches of the conditional constructs in the source code (e.g., 'if' statements and loop conditions) that are executed at least once. Although there are stronger coverage criteria like prime path coverage, using these methods is impractical in our case, since to the best of our knowledge there is no automatic tool to calculate these metrics on an enterprise application scale code base. To calculate the branch coverage of the test suites, we used JaCoCo[11] which is a well-known coverage analysis industrial tool.

We ran all unit and BDD tests in the system and computed the branch coverage and mutation score for them as the baseline for comparison. It must be noted that since our specification does not yet fully cover the logic of matching engine, only those classes that implement the specified part of the logic are selected for comparison.

Table 1 shows the results of the branch coverage analysis for the three test suites: the tests developed by the development team (Dev. Tests), and the ones generated by our two algorithms. The results present the average and the standard deviation of the branch coverage across the test suites for each method. In each test suite for Genetic Algorithm there are 15 test cases on average. For Simulated Annealing this number is about 19 test cases per test suite. As the table shows, in many of the classes the branch coverage of the Genetic Algorithms and Simulated Annealing is almost equal to the branch coverage of the development team's tests. The difference of the coverage in Order, Iceberg and Queue classes is due to some methods that were not yet modeled in specification. Also, the number of test cases generated for each test suite for both methods is much less than the development test suite which reduces the execution time of test suite.

5.3   Mutation Analysis

The second method used to measure the effectiveness of test cases is mutation analysis. To this aim, we used Pitest[12] tool which is widely used for mutation

---

[11] https://www.jacoco.org.
[12] https://pitest.org.

Table 2. Mutation percentage of two methods compared to the development team's tests

Target Class	Dev. Tests	Simulated Annealing	Genetic Algorithm
Matching Engine	48	55.6 ± 2.8	57.1 ± 2.1
Order	60	42.6 ± 1.7	46.2 ± 6.9
Iceberg	78	54.6 ± 4	56 ± 0
Queue	73	49.2 ± 7	56 ± 12.3
PO Observer	38	48.6 ± 8	63.8 ± 15.7
Credit Observer	75	57 ± 26.2	72.2 ± 22.9

testing in the domain of enterprise applications. It supports a wide variety of mutation operators, from which we took its default mutation operator set.

As the mutation framework cannot calculate the mutation score where there is a test failure, we had to exclude the test cases that produced the two discovered faults from the test cases to calculate the mutation score. Table 2 shows the mutation scores, i.e., the percentage of the mutants that were killed by the test suites.

As Table 2 shows, in many of the classes, more mutants were killed in test generated by both our methods compared to the development team's tests. Like in the case of branch coverage, in Order, Iceberg and Queue classes the mutation score is lower in our tests, because those classes contain logic that has not been specified yet. Also, there is a big variance in Credit and PO classes. This is because, as mentioned, some test cases had to be excluded from the test suites so that we could calculate the mutation score. These classes were the target of those tests since the bugs were related to logic in these classes. As a result, some test suites where heavily affected by the exclusion of the test cases, causing a big variance in the mutation score.

The results of both evaluation methods show that the tests generated by our method are at least as effective as the tests that were generated by domain experts and developers. This is achieved by a much smaller test suite. The effort to develop the unit and BDD tests was much more than the effort put to develop the specification and generate the required adapters to run the tests (approximately 60 man days).

6 Related Work

Formal Methods for the Analysis of Auction Theory. There is a limited number of works in the formal analysis of trading algorithms in financial market. Sarswat et al. in [16] formalized various notations for auction theory which are required for the analysis of trades in financial markets. These notations were implemented in Coq and authors defined properties like fairness, uniformity, maximality, and individual rationality using the defined notations. Lange et al. in [14] showed how theorem proving tools can be used for the analysis of the consequences of different options in auction designs. In comparison with these works, the focus of this paper is in the implementation of auction theories not in their specifications.

Formal Methods in Automatic Test Case Generation for Enterprise Applications. Asaadi et al. applied model-based testing techniques to an Electronic Funds Transfer (EFT) switch [4]. They used ISO 8583 specification to provide a formalization of the transaction flows in terms of a labeled transition system. They used input space partitioning to generate test data and the formalization for model-based testing based on input-output conformance testing. In comparison with this work, we use feedback for the better generation of test cases; however, in [4] test cases are randomly generated. In addition, they used Timed Automata [3,5] to specify ISO 8583 which cannot be used for our case, as it is data-intensive application not a control-intensive application. In contrast, Liu et al. in [15] proposed Vibration-Method for automatic generation of test cases and test oracle from model-based formal specifications, which is tailored for testing information systems in which rich data types are used. This method provides automatic test case generation based on functional scenarios, test case generation criteria, and a mechanism for deriving test oracle. The main difference between the work of [15] and this paper is in the specification language. The functional nature of the specification language of this paper makes it appropriate for specifying the order matching algorithms, which are explained procedurally in the informal specifications, compared to a pre- and post-condition specification style of [15]. In addition, by automatically translating the specifications into Haskell programs, we make use of various tools such as coverage tools. There are also some works on automatic test case generation for software components using formal method, e.g. [8,13]. These works focus on the detailed description of the behavior of components and cannot be generalized for testing an enterprise application.

7   Conclusion

In this paper, we reported our experience in applying specification-based testing to an industrial enterprise software system. The system is specified in a functional language which has a formal foundation and is not too difficult to work with for an average software engineer. We developed simple specification patterns such as the decorator which modularizes the specification and make it easier to develop and understand. Our experience showed that the size of the specification is much smaller than the functional tests developed by the development team, and could be developed by a considerably less effort. The test case generation is guided by the specification coverage with the aim of taking all corner cases into account. The overall results indicated that we can attain the same coverage and mutation score with much less effort.

In addition to the work needed to make the specification fully cover the domain logic, there is more room for improvement in several aspects. As an example, more sophisticated fitness functions may be used during test case generation, such as the ones incorporating branch distance measures [9]. Also, more patterns and abstraction mechanisms may be developed to further simplify the specification and make it more understandable.

References

1. Adzic, G.: Specification by Example: How Successful Teams Deliver the Right Software. Manning Publications, Shelter Island (2011)
2. Ali, S., Briand, L.C., Hemmati, H., Panesar-Walawege, R.K.: A systematic review of the application and empirical investigation of search-based test case generation. IEEE Trans. Software Eng. **36**(6), 742–762 (2009)
3. Alur, R., Dill, D.L.: A theory of timed automata. Theoret. Comput. Sci. **126**(2), 183–235 (1994)
4. Asaadi, H.R., Khosravi, R., Mousavi, M.R., Noroozi, N.: Towards model-based testing of electronic funds transfer systems. In: Arbab, F., Sirjani, M. (eds.) FSEN 2011. LNCS, vol. 7141, pp. 253–267. Springer, Heidelberg (2012). https://doi.org/10.1007/978-3-642-29320-7_17
5. Bengtsson, J., Larsen, K., Larsson, F., Pettersson, P., Yi, W.: UPPAAL — a tool suite for automatic verification of real-time systems. In: Alur, R., Henzinger, T.A., Sontag, E.D. (eds.) HS 1995. LNCS, vol. 1066, pp. 232–243. Springer, Heidelberg (1996). https://doi.org/10.1007/BFb0020949
6. Bertot, Y., Castéran, P.: Interactive Theorem Proving and Program Development - Coq'Art: The Calculus of Inductive Constructions. Texts in Theoretical Computer Science. An EATCS Series, Springer, Heidelberg (2004). https://doi.org/10.1007/978-3-662-07964-5
7. Dyson, P., Longshaw, A.: Architecting Enterprise Solutions: Patterns for High-Capability Internet-Based Systems. Wiley, Hoboken (2004)
8. Fang, Y., Zhu, H., Zeyda, F., Fei, Y.: Modeling and analysis of the disruptor framework in CSP. In: IEEE 8th Annual Computing and Communication Workshop and Conference, CCWC, pp. 803–809. IEEE (2018)
9. Fraser, G., Arcuri, A.: Whole test suite generation. IEEE Trans. Software Eng. **39**(2), 276–291 (2012)
10. Gamma, E., Helm, R., Johnson, R., Vlissides, J.M.: Design Patterns: Elements of Reusable Object-Oriented Software, 1st edn. Addison-Wesley Professional, Boston (1994)
11. Harman, M., McMinn, P., de Souza, J.T., Yoo, S.: Search based software engineering: techniques, taxonomy, tutorial. In: Meyer, B., Nordio, M. (eds.) LASER 2008-2010. LNCS, vol. 7007, pp. 1–59. Springer, Heidelberg (2012). https://doi.org/10.1007/978-3-642-25231-0_1
12. Hierons, R., et al.: Using formal specifications to support testing. ACM Comput. Surv. **41**(2), 1–76 (2009)
13. Kong, L., Zhu, H., Zhou, B.: Automated testing EJB components based on algebraic specifications. In: 31st Annual International Computer Software and Applications Conference, COMPSAC, vol. 2, pp. 717–722. IEEE (2007)
14. Lange, C., et al.: A qualitative comparison of the suitability of four theorem provers for basic auction theory. In: Carette, J., Aspinall, D., Lange, C., Sojka, P., Windsteiger, W. (eds.) CICM 2013. LNCS (LNAI), vol. 7961, pp. 200–215. Springer, Heidelberg (2013). https://doi.org/10.1007/978-3-642-39320-4_13

15. Liu, S., Nakajima, S.: Automatic test case and test oracle generation based on functional scenarios in formal specifications for conformance testing. IEEE Trans. Softw. Eng. (2020). https://doi.org/10.1109/TSE.2020.2999884
16. Sarswat, S., Singh, A.: Formally verified trades in financial markets. arXiv preprint arXiv:2007.10805 (2020)

Compressing Automatically Generated Unit Test Suites Through Test Parameterization

Aidin Azamnouri and Samad Paydar[✉]

Computer Engineering Department, Ferdowsi University of Mashhad, Mashhad, Iran
aidin.noori@mail.um.ac.ir, s-paydar@um.ac.ir

Abstract. Test maintenance has recently gained increasing attention from the software testing research community. When using automated unit test generation tools, the tests are typically created by random test generation or search-based algorithms. Although these tools produce a large number of tests quickly, they mostly seek to improve test coverage; overlooking other quality attributes like understandability and readability. As a result, maintaining a large and automatically generated test suite is quite challenging. In this paper, by utilizing a high level of similarity among the automatically generated tests, we propose a technique for automatically abstracting similar tests through transforming them into parameterized tests. This approach leads to the improvement of readability and understandability by reducing the size of the test suite and also by separating data and logic of the tests. We have implemented this technique as a plugin for IntelliJ IDEA and have evaluated its performance over the test suites produced by the Randoop test generation tool. The results have demonstrated that the proposed approach is able to effectively reduce the size of the test suites between 11% and 96%, with an average of 66%.

Keywords: Automated test generation · Maintainability · Readability · Unit test · Parameterized unit tests · Test suites · Randoop

1 Introduction

Unit testing is one of the test levels that has received considerable attention both from the academia and the industry practitioners. However, since each unit test targets a small scope of the software under test (SUT), it is required to generate a large number of unit tests to have the SUT appropriately tested. Furthermore, while the source code of the SUT is evolving, unit tests need to be maintained; otherwise, they may become obsolete or broken. These factors contribute to increasing the cost and complexity of unit testing, emphasizing the need for the development of automated techniques for unit test generation and maintenance.

© IFIP International Federation for Information Processing 2021
Published by Springer Nature Switzerland AG 2021
H. Hojjat and M. Massink (Eds.): FSEN 2021, LNCS 12818, pp. 215–221, 2021.
https://doi.org/10.1007/978-3-030-89247-0_15

Automated unit test generation has been an active field of research in the domain of software testing during the last decades. In this regard, different techniques and approaches have been introduced, one of the main characteristics of which is employing a predefined iterative algorithm rooted in random testing techniques, either directly or indirectly, i.e. through search-based techniques, where the main focus is on achieving a high level of test coverage. This tendency towards improving test coverage has set the stage for overlooking some other important quality attributes, one of which is maintainability of the tests. This can be attributed to the following observations: 1) automated unit test generation techniques are capable of generating a large number of tests within a short time budget. The larger the test suite, the more challenging it is to read, understand and maintain the tests, 2) these techniques use a very naive schema for naming test methods, e.g. `test01`, `test02`, and test classes, and as a result they fail to communicate the semantic of the test. Hence, reading the body of a test method is the only way to understand what it does, which increases the cost of test maintenance, and 3) the body of the test methods generated by these techniques are usually very long, causing the readability and understandability to be reduced, and the maintainability of the tests to be affected as a result.

Based on these observations, in this paper, we propose a technique that automatically factorizes the similarities in a JUnit test suite generated by an automated unit test generation technique and transforms those tests into parameterized ones. This way, a group of similar tests that only differ in terms of their test data can be replaced by a single parameterized test with a clear specification of the different test data. The parameterized test suite would be much smaller than the original test suite, and by using the constructs provided by the JUnit framework, the logic and the data of the tests can be separated from each other. This makes it possible for the human testers to more easily and effectively read and understand the tests.

The rest of the paper is organized as follows. Section 2 briefly reviews the related work. The proposed technique is introduced in Sect. 3, and evaluated in Sect. 4. Finally, Sect. 5 concludes the paper.

2   Related Work

The importance of test maintenance, and in particular, the need for readable and understandable tests is acknowledged in different works. For instance, in [6], the authors have investigated test case quality and what good test cases are. One of the conclusions many of the interviewees have arrived at, is that, for a test case to be good, it is necessary for it to be readable and understandable.

The costs and importance of test maintenance are also discussed in [9], where the authors discuss that test maintenance can be incredibly costly and time-consuming, emphasizing the need for automated techniques. In another study, [5] the authors have compared the readability of manually written tests with those of the automatically generated ones. The findings of this study include two important points: 1) readability of the tests is usually overlooked by developers, and 2) generally, automatically generated tests are less readable than the manually written ones.

Another line of research for improving test maintenance is focused on producing natural language summaries for unit tests. For instance, in [10], a technique is proposed to automatically generate natural language summaries as descriptions for JUnit tests. A similar work is presented in [7], which employs natural language processing and code summarization techniques to automatically generate accurate and readable descriptions for unit tests.

A different approach to improving test maintenance is followed by the techniques that seek to automatically generate descriptive names for test methods in unit tests. For instance, in [2], the idea of coverage goals is introduced, meaning that the statements in a test method are intended to serve different testing goals, and therefore, it is possible to generate appropriate, i.e. short and descriptive, names for the test methods by identifying their coverage goals.

Parameterizing unit tests is another approach taken into consideration for improving test understandability. For instance, [4] proposes a technique for generating parameterized unit tests by generalizing pre- and post-conditions of the test methods. Moreover, in [12], the authors introduce a semi-automatic methodology called test generalization, which helps in systematically retrofitting existing concrete unit tests (CUT) as parameterized unit tests (PUT).

Recently, a fully automated CUT-PUT retrofitting technique, called AutoPUT, was introduced in [13], which seeks to identify similar concrete unit tests as candidates to become parameterized, so that the parameterized version can be produced without any decrease in the code coverage. The findings of this study illustrated that AutoPUT can be of help in developing a reliable software by augmenting the maintainability of manually-written test suites. Compared to AutoPUT, the focus of our work is on the automatically generated test suites, which we believe are of more importance and have more potential for getting parameterized.

3   Proposed Approach

In this section, the proposed approach for generating parameterized test suites is introduced. The input of this process is a JUnit test suite and the output is the parameterized version of the input test suite. This process includes the following steps:

- **Pre-Processing:** The purpose of this step is to identify *flaky* tests in the input test suite. A flaky test is a test that its pass/fail result varies in different executions [11]. For this purpose, the input test suite is executed n times, and any test that exhibits flaky behavior is flagged to be excluded from further processing. This is because in the post-processing phase of the proposed process, a decision is made based on the execution result of each test, and since a flaky test exhibits a non-deterministic behavior, it can reduce the reliability of the decisions made. It is worth noting that in the experiments reported in Sect. 4, we have used n=5 for detecting flaky tests, which is a reasonable setting considered in the related works, for instance [1].

- **Test Clone Detection:** This step is intended to find the test methods that have identical statements, but different parameter values. For this purpose, we have developed a test clone detection component that automatically identifies, through static analysis, the *maximal test clone sets* in the input test suite. A maximal test clone set s is a set of test methods so that 1) for each pair of the test methods tm_1 and tm_2 in s, the only difference in the statements of the body of tm_1 and tm_2, would be the literal values, and 2) for every test method tm_3 that does not belong to s, and every test method tm in s, the difference between tm_3 and tm does not satisfy the above condition. The sets of test methods identified in this step are then parameterized through the next steps.
- **Literal Detection:** In this step, each maximal set of test clones S is processed and for each test method m in s, the abstract syntax tree (AST) is analyzed to identify the literal values used in m, e.g., as arguments to method calls or as the right hand side (RHS) expression in an assignment statement.
- **Test Parameterization:** The literals identified in the previous step are used to generate the @DataPoints annotation fragment for the parameterized version of the test. In addition, through replacing those literal values with place-holder variables, the logic of the test method is abstracted and used to generate the @Theory annotation fragment for the parameterized test method. This has the effect that the logic and the data of the test methods are separated, which result in improving the readability and understandability of the test.
- **Post-Processing:** Finally, the parameterized test methods generated in the previous step, are compiled and run to see if they have any errors, in which case they will be excluded. Otherwise, the coverage of the initial and parameterized versions of the test suite is evaluated to see if there is any difference. If the test coverage of the parameterized version is lower, it will be rejected, otherwise, it will be outputted as the final result of the process.

To provide an example, two test methods test01 and test02 generated by Randoop [8] for the class Primes from Apache Commons Math project are shown in Listing 1.1, and the parameterized test method generated by the proposed approach is shown in Listing 1.2, with some minor modifications for the sake of brevity.

4   Evaluation

We have implemented the proposed technique as a plugin for the IntelliJ IDEA integrated development environment and have conducted an experiment using a dataset of regression test suites generated by Randoop for 50 Java classes selected for 15 open-source Apache Commons projects. The source code and the data of the experiment are made publicly available on GitHub[1] for reproducibility purposes and further research.

---

[1] https://github.com/AidinProgrammer/CU2PT-Plugin.

In order to evaluate the performance of our proposed technique, we considered three metrics: 1) compression ratio: the percentage of the reduction in the size (physical source lines of code) of the test suite after it is parameterized by the proposed technique, 2) applicability ratio: the percentage of the tests in a test suite that are successfully converted to the parameterized format, and 3) execution time: the time budget needed for the parameterization of a test suite generated for a single class under test.

The results of the experiment demonstrated that the proposed technique is able to provide an average compression ratio of 66% over the whole dataset. Additionally, the lowest and the highest compression ratio are respectively 11% and 96%. Furthermore, in more than 56% of the classes, the compression ratio is at least 80%, meaning that the proposed technique is very likely to cause a significant decrease in the size of a given test suite. Albeit, the reason for the large differences in the compression ratios is the fact that Randoop generates different test suites based on its method sequence generation and extension algorithm. Some of the test suites include quite similar test methods and statements and some of them include more diversity in this regard.

In some of the test suites generated by Randoop, the rate of the presence of code clones is very high; the characteristic which is utilized by our proposed method, resulting in a higher compression ratio. For instance, when a class has just a few public methods, considering the speed with which Randoop generates the test sequences, there would be a large set of method sequences generated with a high level of similarity; hence, the probability of the existence of test clones among them is increased. However, if a class has too many public methods, Randoop can generate various sequences and the similarity of the method sequences is decreased, and as a result, the number of test clones would be decreased. For the test suites with a smaller test clone ratio, there would be less potential for our proposed method to compress the test suite, resulting in a smaller compression ratio.

Regarding the applicability ratio, the highest and the lowest values are respectively 100% and 15%, with an average of 75% over the whole dataset. Moreover, in more than 62% of the classes, the applicability ratio is at least 80%, evidencing the effectiveness of the proposed technique. It should be noted that during the experiment, the proposed technique converted a total of 408,000 test clones into 23,000 parameterized tests in about 7.5 h; resulting in an average execution time of 1.17 s for each parameterized test, which shows the efficiency of the proposed technique.

Listing 1.1. Example test clones generated by Randoop

```
@Test
public void test01() throws Throwable {
  if (debug) System.out.format("%n%s%n","test01");
  int i1 = Primes.nextPrime(0);
  org.junit.Assert.assertTrue(i1 == 2);
}
@Test
```

```
public void test02() throws Throwable {
  if (debug) System.out.format("%n%s%n","test02");
  int i1 = Primes.nextPrime(1);
  org.junit.Assert.assertTrue(i1 == 2);
}
```

Listing 1.2. Parameterized test for the test methods in Listing 1.1

```
@DataPoints("testData")
public static Object[][] getArguments() {
  return new Object[][]{{"test01", 0, 2}, {"test02", 1, 2}};
}
@Theory
public void test (@FromDataPoints("testData") Object[] arguments) {
  if (debug) System.out.format("%n%s%n", arguments[0]);
  int i1 = Primes.nextPrime((int) arguments[1]);
  Assert.assertTrue(i1 == (int) arguments[2]);
}
```

5 Conclusion

In this paper, an automated technique is introduced that takes as input a unit test suite generated by an automated unit test generation tool, and through static analysis and automatic code generation, compresses the given test suite by converting its constituent tests into parameterized tests. During the evaluations conducted, for more than 56% of the input classes, the proposed technique has been able to provide a compression ratio of at least 80%, providing a significant decrease in the size of the test suite while preserving the test coverage. In addition, this technique is considered efficient as it has successfully transformed over 408,000 test clones into nearly 23,000 parameterized tests in less than eight hours, which means an average execution time of 1.17 s for each parameterized test.

While the experiment discussed in this paper acknowledges the effectiveness and efficiency of the proposed technique, it is interesting to conduct more extensive experiments, including a larger dataset of test suites generated by Randoop, and also other automated unit test generation tools like EvoSuite [3]. This will be the main direction of our future work. Furthermore, we plan to investigate the performance of our technique on the test suites generated manually, as from the technical point of view, the proposed technique is not limited to test suites generated by automated tools.

References

1. Bell, J., Legunsen, O., Hilton, M., Eloussi, L., Yung, T., Marinov, D.: Deflaker: automatically detecting flaky tests. In: 2018 IEEE/ACM 40th International Conference on Software Engineering (ICSE), pp. 433–444. IEEE (2018)

2. Daka, E., Rojas, J.M., Fraser, G.: Generating unit tests with descriptive names or: would you name your children thing1 and thing2? In: Proceedings of the 26th ACM SIGSOFT International Symposium on Software Testing and Analysis, pp. 57–67 (2017)

3. Fraser, G., Arcuri, A.: EvoSuite: automatic test suite generation for object-oriented software. In: Gyimóthy, T., Zeller, A. (eds.) SIGSOFT/FSE'11 19th ACM SIG-SOFT Symposium on the Foundations of Software Engineering (FSE-19) and ESEC'11: 13th European Software Engineering Conference (ESEC-13), Szeged, Hungary, 5–9 September 2011, pp. 416–419. ACM (2011). https://doi.org/10.1145/2025113.2025179

4. Fraser, G., Zeller, A.: Generating parameterized unit tests. In: Proceedings of the 2011 International Symposium on Software Testing and Analysis, pp. 364–374 (2011)

5. Grano, G., Scalabrino, S., Gall, H.C., Oliveto, R.: An empirical investigation on the readability of manual and generated test cases. In: 2018 IEEE/ACM 26th International Conference on Program Comprehension (ICPC), pp. 348–3483. IEEE (2018)

6. Kochhar, P.S., Xia, X., Lo, D.: Practitioners' views on good software testing practices. In: 2019 IEEE/ACM 41st International Conference on Software Engineering: Software Engineering in Practice (ICSE-SEIP), pp. 61–70. IEEE (2019)

7. Li, B., Vendome, C., Linares-Vásquez, M., Poshyvanyk, D., Kraft, N.A.: Automatically documenting unit test cases. In: 2016 IEEE International Conference on Software Testing, Verification and Validation (ICST), pp. 341–352. IEEE (2016)

8. Pacheco, C., Ernst, M.D.: Randoop: feedback-directed random testing for java. In: Companion to the 22nd ACM SIGPLAN Conference on Object-Oriented Programming Systems and Applications Companion, pp. 815–816 (2007)

9. Panichella, S.: Summarization techniques for code, change, testing, and user feedback. In: 2018 IEEE Workshop on Validation, Analysis and Evolution of Software Tests (VST), pp. 1–5. IEEE (2018)

10. Panichella, S., Panichella, A., Beller, M., Zaidman, A., Gall, H.C.: The impact of test case summaries on bug fixing performance: an empirical investigation. In: Proceedings of the 38th International Conference on Software Engineering, pp. 547–558 (2016)

11. Paydar, S., Azamnouri, A.: An experimental study on flakiness and fragility of randoop regression test suites. In: Hojjat, H., Massink, M. (eds.) FSEN 2019. LNCS, vol. 11761, pp. 111–126. Springer, Cham (2019). https://doi.org/10.1007/978-3-030-31517-7_8

12. Thummalapenta, S., Marri, M.R., Xie, T., Tillmann, N., de Halleux, J.: Retrofitting unit tests for parameterized unit testing. In: Giannakopoulou, D., Orejas, F. (eds.) FASE 2011. LNCS, vol. 6603, pp. 294–309. Springer, Heidelberg (2011). https://doi.org/10.1007/978-3-642-19811-3_21

13. Tsukamoto, K., Maezawa, Y., Honiden, S.: AutoPUT: an automated technique for retrofitting closed unit tests into parameterized unit tests. In: Proceedings of the 33rd Annual ACM Symposium on Applied Computing, pp. 1944–1951 (2018)

Systematic Extraction of Tests from Object-Oriented Programs

Mohammad Ghoreshi and Hassan Haghighi[✉]

Shahid Beheshti University, Tehran, Iran
{m_ghoreshi,h_haghighi}@sbu.ac.ir

Abstract. Existing program-based automated test techniques from object-oriented programs generate only test data or test cases, which are not equipped with effective oracle to reveal the logical errors in the program. In addition, these techniques often focus on conventional code coverage criteria and intra-method testing, and are less concerned with inter-method, intra-class and inter-class testing. In this paper, we propose an automated testing approach to cover the inter-method and intra-class test levels. This approach generates tests that are equipped with effective oracles in terms of expected outcomes to reveal logical errors in the program under test. In order to demonstrate the applicability of the proposed approach, we applied it to a case study containing 14 different classes implemented in Java. Furthermore, we created artificial faulty versions of our case study, and the proposed approach was able to extract tests that reveal failures in 74% of faulty cases.

Keywords: Object-oriented testing · Automated test generation · Intra-class test level

1 Introduction

The object-oriented methodology can make finding software faults difficult because it hides the state of objects from each other and increases the complexity of relationships between program elements [1,2]. Therefore, due to considerable effort and cost in the test phase, we need to use effective automated or semi-automated testing techniques for object-oriented programs.

Various automated and semi-automated techniques, which have been proposed for object-oriented testing, fall into two categories: specification-based and program-based techniques [3]. In specification-based approaches, tests are extracted based on formal and semi-formal specifications of software systems. These methods are extract effective tests along with sufficient oracles in terms of expected outcomes that can reveal errors of the software under test [2,3]. However, in practice, they are not supported by mature automated tools. In addition, formal specifications are rarely used in industrial software development processes, except in the development of critical systems.

© IFIP International Federation for Information Processing 2021
Published by Springer Nature Switzerland AG 2021
H. Hojjat and M. Massink (Eds.): FSEN 2021, LNCS 12818, pp. 222–228, 2021.
https://doi.org/10.1007/978-3-030-89247-0_16

In program-based approaches, test cases are designed according to the program source code. Most of program-based techniques can be categorized in two groups: random-based and structure-oriented techniques. Approaches in the first group generate random method sequences for a class and evaluate each sequence to exhibit illegal behavior. The second group consists of methods which try to find a set of test inputs in order to reach high structural code coverage. Due to lack of the class and program specification, in both kinds of approaches, some method sequences are not based on the class logic; therefore, some of the designed tests have invalid method sequences. Also, lack of specification leads to tests that are not well equipped with effective oracles which reveal bugs and identify correctness or incorrectness of the test result.

One resource that can compensate for the lack of the class specification in program-based approaches is statements used in the code for purposes such as validating class fields and method parameters [4]. These statements can be in form of annotation libraries or assert statements. In this article, we present a program-based approach for testing Java programs. We use validation annotations in order to guide the test process and provide oracles in terms of some kind of assertions which reveal failures in the class under test. Unlike structure-oriented approaches, the suggested approach focuses on testing classes and extracts tests with respect to the inter-method and intra-class levels.

In the next section, we briefly review some considerable related approaches. Then, in Sect. 3, we introduce our approach. Section 4 contains the details of approach evaluation. Finally, Sect. 5 concludes the paper.

2   Related Works

Two approaches were introduced in [5] and [2] to extract tests from Object-Z formal specifications. The former only extracts intra-class level tests, but, in addition to intra-class tests, the later extracts some inter-class level tests and reuses some test artifacts through inheritance. Unlike most specification-based approaches (including approaches in [2,5]) that suffer from lack of fully automated tools, a framework was introduced in [6] for automated testing of Java programs based on JML specifications. This approach, however, only generates method level tests and does not cover inter-method and inter-class tests.

In [7], a random program-based technique, called JCrasher, was proposed to generate tests from Java programs. This technique generates random method sequences with the aim of causing runtime errors. Such random tests may not necessarily indicate errors in the program under test because they may be illegal themselves. Therefore, as the authors have suggested, this approach is more suitable for robustness testing. Another random approach using the feedback directed technique was presented in [8]. In this approach, unit tests in the format of JUnit are randomly generated for input classes. The approach has been implemented as a fully automated tool called Randoop. Because of the ease of use and scalability, this tool is known as a mature tool in the automated test case generation area, and used as a baseline for evaluating other approaches.

A structure-oriented approach, called "EvoSuite", was proposed in [9] using evolutionary algorithms in order to generate test data for programs in Java. The usability of this approach on large libraries and industrial applications has been demonstrated. It should be noted that, the focus of this approach is to generate intra-method tests that are generated in respect of structural coverage criteria (such as branch coverage), and other object-oriented test levels like intra-class and inter-class are less addressed.

In practice, usually there are no formal specifications of the classes and modules of an object-oriented software except in safety-critical software; hence, specification-based approaches are rarely used. On the other hand, in most program-based approaches, relationships between methods in the method call sequences are usually formed based on a random approach. Therefore, these sequences may not be consistent with the class and program logic and can lead to invalid tests. Moreover, due to lake of specification of the program under test, most program-based approaches are rarely equipped with effective oracles.

In the next section, we introduce an approach for testing object-oriented programs written in Java, which focuses on extracting different method call sequences consistent with the logic of a given class. This approach also covers inter-method and intra-class test levels.

3   The Proposed Approach

The proposed approach starts with a class in Java called the "class under test". First, the state variables (class fields) and related constraints and conditions are extracted from the class under test. The "Model Extractor Component" handles the extraction of class state variables as well as preconditions and postconditions of methods. Now based on this logical model and the class under test, the "Test Machine Component" extracts a test machine for that class. The test machine is a kind of state diagram whose states contain the class state space, and transitions correspond to class method calls. Finally, the "Test Case Generator Component" extracts test cases by mapping the paths of the extracted state machine to JUnit test units.

3.1   Model Extractor Component

The "Model Extractor Component" extracts a model contains the class state variables along with their constraints, as well as preconditions, and postconditions of each method, which are extracted in the form of logical Java expressions. These information can be gathered from several sources in the Java programming language. Some of these sources are annotation-based validation libraries and design by contract libraries in Java. This article uses the OVal annotation library [10], but the model component can be expanded to use other types of libraries, also in addition to the assert statement which is a built-in feature in Java. As an example, a simple stack class in Java with OVal annotations is demonstrated in the left side of the Fig. 1.

3.2 Test Machine Component

A test machine is a test artifact containing abstract information that can be used to extract test cases. Each test machine can be defined corresponding to one method, multiple methods, or a class. In the following, we first present the test machine concept, and then, we review its extraction process.

The Test Machine Concept. A test machine is a type of state diagram that consists of several states and several transitions. Each state contains a set of class variables with conditions associated with them. Test machine states make it possible to display the entire state of a class in several abstract states. For example, if x is a class variable, a state of the test machine can be represented as $(x, x \geq 10)$, which represents all states of the class where the value of the variable x is greater than 10. Transitions in a test machine connect states together. A transition in a test machine means calling one of the class methods. So by calling a method, we transfer from one state to another. In a test machine, transitions are divided into two categories: A "valid transition" which is consistent with the logical model (i.e., the postconditions of the called method); and an "Invalid transition which is not consistent with the logical model, or in other words, the postconditions of the called method does not hold in the destination state.

The Method Test Machine. In a "method test machine", states are defined on class variables (class fields) that are used in the body of the method. These variables are called effective variables. In addition, in a "method test machine", all transitions represent a call to the method for which the "method test machine" is being defined. The following steps describe how to extract a "method test machine" for a method in a class.

1. State variables partitioning: First, the input space of the effective variables are partitioned. To do this, first the type of each variable and the allowed values are queried from the logical model. Now, based on the type of the variable and its allowable values, partitions created based on "input space partitioning strategies" [3]. For example, for a numerical variable x with allowable values $x \geq 0$, three partitions x = 0, x =1 and x > 1 are created according to the "boundary values analysis" [3].

2. Constructing a pool of random objects: In this step, a pool of random objects with the type of the class under test is built. In fact, the object pool is a finite set of objects with different values. This set can be created by different techniques that generate random objects from a class. In the proposed approach, a method inspired by the Randoop approach is used to construct random objects of the class under test.

3. Extracting the test machine: We consider all extracted partitions as test machine states. Now for each state as "input state", we do as follow:
   (a) Sample objects that are placed in the input state are selected from the objects pool.

(b) For each sample object, the method for which we are extracting the test machine is performed. Now, the state of the sample object is mapped to one of the test machine states called "destination state". Therefore, we put a transition in the test machine between the "input state" and the "output partition".

Merge Test Machines. By merging two method test machines, a test machine can be obtained that produces different sequences of two method calls. Assuming two test machines A and B (corresponding to methods A and B), the following steps should be performed to combine these two test machines.

1. First, a copy of test machine A is considered as the resulting test machine.
2. For each state (called "candidate state") of the second machine (machine B), we perform the following steps:
   (a) If the candidate state is the same as one of the states in B: we ignore this state and copy its related transitions to the equivalent state in A.
   (b) If the candidate state does not have any overlap with states of machine B: we add the candidate state with its related transitions to machine A.
   (c) If the candidate state has overlap with some states of machine B: Three new states are formed based on the notion of "disjunctive normal form" and replaced the candidate state (say S1) and that state of machine B (say S2) with which the candidate state has overlap; see equation (1). Each conjunction in equation (1), like $(S1 \wedge \neg S2)$, indicates a new state in the resulting test machine. It is clear that the new states have no overlap with each other, and also, are logical equivalent to the two old states, i.e., S1 and S2.

$$S1 \vee S2 = (S1 \wedge \neg S2) \vee (S1 \wedge S2) \vee (\neg S1 \wedge S2) \tag{1}$$

The Class Test Machine. After combining two method test machines, the resulting test machine can be merged with the third method test machine in a similar way. By applying this "incremental and iterative" process to other methods, we get the whole class test machine. As an example, for mentioned stack class, by merging test machines for methods push and pop, a test machine for the class stack can be created as shown in the right side of the Fig. 1.

3.3 Test Case Generator Component

Different test cases can be extracted from an extracted test machine. In general, each path in the test machine, as a set of method calls of the class under test, can be a test case. Test cases fall into two general categories:

- Error revealing test cases: In these test cases, there must be an "invalid transition", and performing this test will reveal a logical error in the program.
- Regression test cases: In these test cases, there are no "invalid transitions" in the corresponding test machine path. Tests of this kind contain a set of correct class interactions and method interactions that lead to a (functionally) correct state. Such test cases can be used for regression testing.

```
01    public abstract class Stack
02    {
03        @Assert(expr = "_value>=0")
04        private int size;
05
06        @Post(expr = "top()!=null")
07        @Post(expr = "_this.size==_old+1",old="_this.size")
08        public void push(Object x)
09
10        @Pre(expr = "this.size>0")
11        @Post(expr = "_this.size==_old-1",old="_this.size")
12        public Object pop()
13    }
```

Fig. 1. A stack class with OVal annotations alongside with the extracted test machine.

4   Evaluation

In this section, our proposed approach is applied to a case study in order to demonstrate its applicability. The case study subject is a Java implementation of a famous puzzle game, called Tetris [11]. This implementation contains 14 classes. Using our approach, a test machine was extracted for each class. For comparison, our approach is compared to Randoop, which is a mature tool in the field of automated random test generation.

4.1   Effectiveness of Tests in Revealing Errors

To evaluate the effectiveness of tests in revealing errors, we first created 25 mutants versions of the Tetris program using the Pit tool [12]. Then, in order to generate automated tests based on each mutant (a mutant class alongside with other Tetris classes), it has been given as input to both the proposed approach and Randoop. The Randoop tool has only been able to generate error revealing test cases for 2 of 25 mutants. Our approach generated error revealing test cases for 18 mutants, i.e. 72% of the cases.

4.2   Revealing Real Error

There is a real bug in one of the source code versions of the Tetris game [11], which has been fixed in future versions. This bug is that, in certain circumstances, some blocks do not stick to the right or left wall of the game screen, and although the user wants to move the block one unit to the right or left, a gap between the block and the wall remains. Randoop could not generate error revealing tests for this version. By running our approach on this version, however, it generated different test cases that reveal failures of this type.

5   Conclusion

In this paper, we presented a new approach to generate test cases for object-oriented programs. Our approach leads the test case generation process by extracting some facts and conditions about the program under test. The approach produces effective test cases for revealing program errors. To demonstrate the approach usability, it has been applied to the Tetris game, as our case study, containing 14 different classes. The proposed approach managed to detect a significant number of errors that had been seeded into the Tetris source code.

We are currently expanding our approach to support all popular validation libraries and built-in assert statements in Java. By this, our approach can be applicable for more Java programs, and thus, we can evaluate it on more case studies including industrial and open source software. As another direction for future work, by deriving relationships between test machines of classes, inter-class test cases can be extracted that examine relationships between classes.

References

1. Alexander, R.T., Offutt, A.J.: Criteria for testing polymorphic relationships. In: Proceedings 11th International Symposium on Software Reliability Engineering, pp. 15–23. IEEE (2000)
2. Ghoreshi, M., Haghighi, H.: An incremental method for extracting tests from object-oriented specification. Inf. Softw. Technol. **78**, 1–26 (2016)
3. Ammann, P., Offutt, J.: Introduction to Software Testing. Cambridge University Press, Cambridge (2016)
4. Shamshiri, S., Just, R., Rojas, J.M., Fraser, G., McMinn, P., Arcuri, A.: Do automatically generated unit tests find real faults? An empirical study of effectiveness and challenges. In: 30th IEEE/ACM International Conference on Automated Software Engineering (ASE), pp. 201–211 (2015)
5. Carrington, D., MacColl, I., McDonald, J., Murray, L., Strooper, P.: From Object-Z specifications to ClassBench test suites. Softw. Test. Verif. Reliab. **10**(2), 111–137 (2000)
6. Milicevic, A., Misailovic, S., Marinov, D., Khurshid, S.: Korat: a tool for generating structurally complex test inputs. In: 29th International Conference on Software Engineering (ICSE'07), pp. 771–774. IEEE (2007)
7. Csallner, C., Smaragdakis, Y.: JCrasher: an automatic robustness tester for Java. Softw. Pract. Exp. **34**(11), 1025–1050 (2004)
8. Pacheco, C., Lahiri, S.K., Ernst, M.D., Ball, T.: Feedback-directed random test generation. In: 29th International Conference on Software Engineering, pp. 75–84 (2007)
9. Fraser, G., Arcuri, A.: Whole test suite generation. IEEE Trans. Softw. Eng. **39**(2), 276–291 (2012)
10. Oval: The Object Validation Framework for Java. https://sebthom.github.io/oval/. Accessed 15 Nov 2020
11. JTetris Github Repository. https://github.com/sbu-test-lab/jtetris. Accessed 15 Nov 2020
12. Coles, H., Laurent, T., Henard, C., Papadakis, M., Ventresque, A.: Pit: a practical mutation testing tool for java. In: Proceedings of the 25th International Symposium on Software Testing and Analysis, pp. 449–452 (2016)

Author Index

Printed in the United States
by Baker & Taylor Publisher Services